The Art of Protest

The Art of Protest

Culture and Activism from the Civil Rights Movement to the Streets of Seattle

T. V. Reed

University of Minnesota Press

Minneapolis · London

The companion Web site to *The Art of Protest* includes audio and visual materials, bibliographies, discographies, filmographies, and links to historical and current social movements, as well as a supplementary chapter, "Peace Symbols: Posters in Movements against the Wars in Vietnam and Iraq." Visit the book's Web site at http://www.upress.umn.edu/artofprotest.

Lines from "A Poem about My Rights," by June Jordan, are from *Naming Our Destiny: New and Selected Poems* (New York: Thunder's Mouth Press, 1989). Copyright 1989 by June Jordan. Reprinted by permission of the publisher Thunder's Mouth Press, a division of Avalon Publishing Group.

Lines from "Trying to Talk with a Man," by Adrienne Rich, are from *The Fact of a Doorframe: Selected Poems, 1950–2001* (New York: W. W. Norton & Company, Inc., 1973). Copyright 2002 by Adrienne Rich, copyright 1973 by W. W. Norton & Company, Inc. Reprinted by permission of the author and W. W. Norton & Company, Inc.

An earlier version of chapter 5 appeared in *Wicazo Sa Review* 16, no. 2 (2001): 75–96. An earlier version of chapter 6 appeared in *Cercles* 3 (2001). Portions of chapter 8 appeared as "Toward an Environmental Justice Ecocriticism," in Joni Adamson, Mei Mei Evans, and Rachel Stein, eds., *The Environmental Justice Reader* (Tucson: University of Arizona Press, 2003).

Published by the University of Minnesota Press
111 Third Avenue South, Suite 290
Minneapolis, MN 55401-2520
http://www.upress.umn.edu

Library of Congress Cataloging-in-Publication Data

Reed, T. V. (Thomas Vernon)
    The art of protest : culture and activism from the civil rights movement to the streets of Seattle / T. V. Reed.
        p.   cm.
    Includes bibliographical references and index.
    ISBN 0-8166-3770-9 (hc : alk. paper) — ISBN 0-8166-3771-7 (pb : alk. paper)
    1. Radicalism—United States.   2. Protest movements—United States.
3. Social movements in art.   4. Social movements in literature.   5. Radicalism in art.   6. Radicalism in literature.   7. Radicalism—Songs and music—History and criticism.   I. Title.
    HN90.R3R395   2005
    303.48'4—dc22   2005011442

Printed in the United States of America on acid-free paper

The University of Minnesota is an equal-opportunity educator and employer.

12 11 10 09 08 07 06 05   10 9 8 7 6 5 4 3 2 1

This book is dedicated to Ella Baker, Bernice Johnson Reagon, and the millions of political-cultural workers, past, present, and future, who march alongside them toward freedom and justice.

Beauty walks a razor's edge
—Bob Dylan

Contents

Acknowledgments   xi

Introduction   xiii

ONE
Singing Civil Rights: The Freedom Song Tradition   1

TWO
Scenarios for Revolution: The Drama of the Black Panthers   40

THREE
The Poetical Is the Political:
Feminist Poetry and the Poetics of Women's Rights   75

FOUR
Revolutionary Walls: Chicano/a Murals, Chicano/a Movements   103

FIVE
Old Cowboys, New Indians:
Hollywood Frames the American Indian Movement   129

SIX
"We Are [Not] the World":
Famine, Apartheid, and the Politics of Rock Music   156

SEVEN
ACTing UP against AIDS:
The (Very) Graphic Arts in a Moment of Crisis   179

EIGHT
Environmental Justice Ecocriticism:
Race, Class, Gender, and Literary Ecologies   218

NINE
Will the Revolution Be Cybercast?
New Media, the Battle of Seattle, and Global Justice   240

TEN
Reflections on the Cultural Study of Social Movements   286

Notes   317

Index   345

Acknowledgments

All books are collective projects, but one of this scope is more than usually indebted to a host of people who helped make it possible. The map that eventually became the territory of this book was first produced with the aid of a Mellon Fellowship at the Humanities Center of Wesleyan University. During my year there I was particularly grateful for the support of Richard Ohmann and for the friendship of Paula Rabinowitz, the other "mellow felon" that cycle. At a crucial later stage in the project, I received similar support from the Center for Cultural Studies at the University of California, Santa Cruz. Center co-directors Gail Hershatter and Chris Connolly provided a brilliantly stimulating environment, and Hayden White quite literally gave me the space to work. The Fulbright scholar program offered me the chance to work out some of the ideas in this book with a bright group of students and faculty at Freie Universität in Berlin, Germany. I am indebted to Margit Mayer and Bruce Spear for their intellectual stimulation and hospitality during my stay there at the John F. Kennedy Institut für Nordamerikastudien.

Among my many supportive colleagues in the American studies program and English department at Washington State University, I would especially like to thank Joan Burbick, Alex Hammond, Alex Kuo, Victor Villanueva, Sue Armitage, and Shawn Michelle Smith for their friendship and inspiring examples of committed scholarship and pedagogy. Among my friends in the Santa Cruz diaspora, I especially thank Katie King, Chela Sandoval, Barry Schwartz, Zoe Sofoulis, and Don Beggs. A number of graduate students at Washington State also gave support and insight as the project evolved. I note in particular the influence of Christina Castañeda, John Hausdoerffer, Sarah Hentges, Azfar Hussain, Melissa Hussain, Jennifer Mata, Lori Safin, Allyson Wolf, and Tony Zaragoza; their scholarly activism and activist scholarship gives me hope for the future.

Many of these chapters began as presentations at national meetings of the American Studies Association, my larger academic home, and I am grateful for the work of scholars Hazel Carby, Michael Cowan, Michael Denning, Paul Lauter, George Lipsitz, Lisa Lowe, Alvina Quintana, Jan-Michael Rivera, Vicki Ruiz, George Sanchez, Steve Sumida, and Robert Warrior, among many others, who make those conferences such stimulating intellectual sites. Lauter and Carlo Rotello also provided crucially important critical readings of the book in manuscript.

A less direct but more fulsome debt is owed to hundreds of cultural workers for justice (of whom for me Bernice Johnson Reagon was the paradigm and remains the paragon), who created the committed "art of change" my work attempts to reflect and reflect on. This book is a tribute to these indefatigable cultural workers, in the hope that I have done at least partial justice to their brilliant, unceasing efforts.

Closer to home, two people played an immense role in this book. Scholar-activist Noël Sturgeon, both as a model of engaged intellectual-political labor and as my most trusted consultant on the substance of this work, is owed an incalculable debt. Hart Sturgeon-Reed, who grew from infant to teenager during the production of this book, inspires me with his intellectual acuity, lightens my life with his wit, and reminds me constantly of why we must struggle to leave the next generation a better foundation from which to fight the good fight for social, economic, environmental, and cultural justice. I am deeply grateful to Noël and Hart for their love, and offer mine back to them along with the "acknowledgment" that they are the most important people in my world. The love and support of my sister Linda Ware, my mother Alice Reed, and my niece Michelle Spencer have also been a crucial part of the world out of which this writing has emerged, as has been my connection to a host of wonderful relatives in the Reed–Sturgeon network. Finally, many thanks to scholar-activist-editor Richard Morrison and all the other folks at the University of Minnesota Press who brought this book and the companion Web site out into the wider world.

Introduction

This book hopes to prove useful to three main types of readers. For students and general readers new to the subject, it presents an introduction to social movements through the rich, kaleidoscopic lens of artistic and cultural expression. For scholars of social movements, it offers intriguing observations on particular movements and useful insights into various ways to think about the relations between culture and social change. For activists, it seeks to offer inspiration and a tool kit of ideas about how art and culture can further movement goals. These three sets of readers overlap, of course, in the form of scholar activists or activist students, but to the extent that they sometimes speak different languages, or have different interests, I hope that each type of reader will be patient when encountering portions of chapters that may speak more clearly to another of these audiences. Finding a style equally appropriate to all has been my goal, but no doubt I have not always succeeded.

Social movements—the unauthorized, unofficial, anti-institutional, collective action of ordinary citizens trying to change their world—have shaped our politics, our culture, and our political culture as much as any other single force. Studying movements matters because they have played crucial roles in making national and world history. I have focused in this book on movements in the United States, but throughout I show how those movements have been connected to global changes. The United States was created through a social movement, the American Revolution, and social movements have helped make and remake our nation since. Social movements, as the term implies, have been a moving force, one of the most dynamic elements in the development of U.S. society and the culture. In particular, I believe "progressive" social movements like the ones at the heart of this book have been crucial in taking the important but vague and still unfulfilled promises of "freedom" and "democracy" announced in the revolution's best known manifesto, the Declaration of Independence, and given them more reality, more substance, and wider applicability to the majority of people—women, people of color, the poor—who were initially excluded from those promises.

More than fifty years of scholarly analysis has not generated an agreed-upon definition of social movements. But that is less of a problem than one might think, since both ordinary folks and ordinary scholars, though they may argue about borderline cases, know a movement when they see one. And seeing one may be precisely the point. One of the foremost scholars of social movements, Charles Tilly, argues convincingly that the essence of movements entails "repeated public displays" of alternative political and cultural values by a collection of people acting together outside officially sanctioned channels.[1] (It is because those official channels have failed some people that movements arise.) Movements, in contrast to their tamer, more institutionalized cousins, political parties and lobbyists, seek to bring about social change primarily through the medium of "repeated public displays," or, as I would put it, through dramatic action.

I like Tilly's definition because it plays to the prejudice of this book in focusing on some of the most dramatic movements of the past several decades. This book tells the stories of some key social movements in the second half of the twentieth century. While movements can be found across the political spectrum, I have limited myself to an interlinked set on the "progressive," left side of this spectrum. Within these limits, I have chosen movements that I think have been especially important, but there are many other equally worthy ones that I have been unable to include. I make no claim to providing a comprehensive study of progressive movements since the 1950s. But I believe this book gives a good sense of major developments in a central tradition of dramatic protest, resistance, and change. I hope my book inspires readers to delve more deeply into movements and issues I can only touch the surface of, and into movements I have been forced by constraints of time to omit or only glancingly mention.

At the same time, I have sought in other chapters to make clear that as centrally important as dramatic, public action has been to social movements, it is by no means the totality of their activity, or the sole source of their impact. I have tried to show that dramatic actions are themselves the products of usually rather undramatic, mundane daily acts of preparation, and that the impact of dramatic moments is only as great as the follow-up forms of daily organizing that accompany them. In several chapters, most obviously in those on the women's and environmental movements, I try to show that dramatic movement events happen in other, less celebrated spaces, including apartment living rooms, academic offices, and classrooms.

The particular movements I have chosen to focus on have played and continue to play a crucial role in expanding freedoms and giving greater substance to the American claim to be a democracy of, by, and for "the people." In that sense, they are the movements that have, to paraphrase poet Langston Hughes, made America America, a place that has not yet been but one day yet must be a free and just society.[2] These interlinked movements, from the 1950s through the early twenty-first century, built on ones that came before—from the revolution itself to the antislavery movement, populist farmer and labor movements, woman's suffrage, and a host of others—and they built on each other as well.

The movements chronicled in this book begin with the great African American civil rights movement of the 1950s and 1960s. That movement was not only of tremendous importance in itself, but it also created a master framework for protest that set in play key ideas, tactics, and forms of resistance for the many movements that soon followed. Indeed, many of these subsequent movements are also, among other things, "civil rights" struggles. They are struggles for the right to equal and fair treatment, and equal and fair access to the economic, political, and cultural goods of the society. The word *civil* means pertaining to the life we live in common, in community, and that is what these movements both assert the right to and attempt to practice in their own work. Many movements form strong cultures of their own, called "movement cultures," which offer alternative models of what our collective civil and civic lives might be like, as part of their argument about the ways we have continually fallen short of creating a just, egalitarian community.

This is the first book of comparative movement analysis to focus on the cultural dimension of movements.[3] In focusing mainly on the cultural elements within and the cultural impact of movements, this book seeks to fill a gap: scholars of social movements have had too little to say about culture, and cultural studies scholars have had too little to say about movements. I use the concept of "culture" in three broad, inter-related ways in the chapters that follow. First, I examine social movements as sub- or counter-cultures to dominant cultures in the country. Second, I look at the production of cultural texts (poetry, painting, music, murals, film, fiction, and so forth) in and around social movements. Third, and most broadly, I examine how the cultural texts, ideas, identities, and values generated by resistance movements have reshaped the general contours of U.S. culture (in the sense of "whole way of life").

The study of social movements has been carried out by several differ-ent kinds of investigators. Academics, including anthropologists, com-munication scholars, historians, political scientists, and especially soci-ologists, have examined movements from the perspective of their own areas of expertise. Nonacademics, especially journalists and movement activists themselves, have also contributed greatly to our understanding of movements. Overall, sociologists have certainly produced both the greatest volume of studies and the most systematic work. This book owes a great deal to the many sociologists who have studied both the particular movements I examine and the processes of social movements overall. But as sociologists themselves have noted, until fairly recently they have neglected the specifically cultural dimensions of social move-ment activity.

Social scientists have concentrated primarily on the ways in which movements have been forces of political change—changes in laws, legis-lation, voting patterns, government institutions, and so on. They have done a valuable service by subjecting movements to intensive and exten-sive study, but this work has been limited by a strong bias toward the most quantifiable elements of movements: numbers of participants, amount of money raised, laws passed in response, shaping of voting patterns, and so on. By comparison, social movements as forces of cul-tural change have been relatively neglected. One key reason for this is that culture is a messy business; it is a less easily measured object of analysis than Supreme Court rulings, congressional bills, or income pat-terns. But to ignore a whole terrain and its impact just because it is not easily quantifiable seems highly unscientific, if not downright strange.

Movements are much more than the sum of quantifiable elements. Movements, especially the kind talked about in this book, are deeply transformative experiences for those who take part in them and deeply transformative to those who are, sometimes quite indirectly or subtly but pervasively, shaped by the ideas, feelings, styles, and behaviors emerging from them. It takes nothing away from other important kinds of analysis to say that we need far more work on the cultural forms active within movements and the cultural forces movements unleash.

Cultural studies scholars, as the name suggests, have focused strongly on questions of culture. But their prime target has been trends in popular culture, and subcultures that do not take the directly political form I call "social movement cultures." Much cultural studies work has offered brilliant interpretive readings of cultural texts (movies, TV shows, pop music, or fashion), but this work has not always been well grounded in relation to the institutions and structural social forces that shape and move through culture. In my view, the best cultural studies work has attended to three interrelated levels of analysis: cultural production, the texts produced, and audience reception of those texts. I will employ all three of these at points in this book, but I am particularly interested in movements as sites for the production and reception of cultural texts. When I do use textual analysis, I am generally less interested in the formal qualities of texts or in the attempt to read their larger cultural meanings, than in their relation to each other within social movements as part of the "cultural field." French social theorist Pierre Bourdieu coined the term *cultural field* for the social space where cultural texts exist in relation to each other and in relation to texts in other social, political, and economic fields.

Though not based in extensive new empirical research, this book seeks to encourage a body of work, sometimes called "social cultural studies," that draws upon and synthesizes the best work from empirical history and social science with the interpretive tools of the cultural studies tradition.[4] While I value formal textual analysis, and have done much of it in previous work, I think it has been overvalued in cultural studies to the neglect of meaning-making contexts. In this book, I have been more interested in social movements as sites for the production and reception of cultural texts than in the formal interpretation of these texts. Or, put differently, the texts I am interested in most are the movements themselves, with their cultural productions as a means to that end.

I have tried to be precise in characterizing the relations between culture and the movements I explore here, but I am not interested in setting up a single, systematic mode of exploring the movement-culture dynamic.

Instead, I am interested in exploring a variety of ways in which culture matters to movements and movements matter to culture. Let me boldly assert here one of my key premises: that those forces labeled cultural may at times have a deeper and more widespread impact on most of our lives than political or economic forces. But my intent is not to argue for the greater importance of culture, just for its importance alongside and entangled with political, social, and economic forces that have traditionally gained more attention. These divisions—social, economic, political, cultural—are, after all, themselves cultural concepts, not real things neatly dividing the world. And giving culture a stronger footing in this list will allow us to better understand the interactions of all these interwoven forces.

Chapter Outline

This book consists of a set of interpretations of some of the key U.S. social movements from the 1950s to the beginning of the twenty-first century. Each chapter is designed to serve as an introduction to a movement for those who know little about it, but also to offer a new angle of vision to those who know the movement well. While I have been a participant in many of these movements, I make no claim to be doing the kind of work called "participant-observation." And while I have done original research on several of these movements, I make no claims to having unearthed significant amounts of new empirical information. I am acutely aware that to talk about close to a dozen movements and as many different cultural forms borders on hubris. But while my range is ambitious, my claims are modest. My main goal has been to creatively reinterpret and synthesize elements from the large body of literature available on each of these movements in light of questions of culture. Relying on a great deal of rich secondary work by scholars and activists before me, I have tried to offer fresh readings and to place them in juxtaposition in mutually illuminating ways. This has meant incurring more than the usual amount of debt to other authors, whom I hope I have adequately thanked in my notes and acknowledgments. In addition to these forms of recognition, however, I have made this book a tribute to all the movement cultural workers whose texts and insights have made it possible.

The movements I focus on are interrelated. I have emphasized a strand of movements sometimes called the "direct action" tradition. These movements have relied heavily on such direct action forms as civil dis-obedience, sit-ins, strikes, boycotts, building or land takeovers, and other dramatic confrontations. One key theme I argue throughout, however, is that the "mobilizing" engendered by dramatic actions is only ultimately effective when matched by active, in-depth, patient "organizing" of peo-ple to take control of their own lives. This distinction, which I take from the great civil rights activist/theorist Ella Baker, means that surrounding the drama of social change there takes place much undramatic day-to-day activity that alone can consolidate the work of a movement's "ritual public displays." As I trace the particular features of each movement, I also try to show how a growing set of influences diffused from move-ment to movement, building a repertoire of ideas, tactics, strategies, cultural forms, and styles.

The chapters are also intended to represent a range of examples of ways in which culture has mattered to movements. The examples both demonstrate how various art forms—music, murals, poetry, and so forth—have made particular contributions to movement cultures and social change, and raise more general questions about how culture works in and around movements. Each chapter is designed both to historicize the movement on which it focuses and to show that movement to be very much alive today. The chapters cover a range of kinds of culture, including folk culture (spirituals in the civil rights movement), high culture (poetry in the women's and fiction in the environmental move-ments), and pop culture (rock music in the anti-apartheid movement, Hollywood films and the American Indian movement), though these categories are not mutually exclusive, especially in movement culture contexts where they are often radically transformed.

Chapter 1 argues that music played a crucial role in virtually every dimension of the African American civil rights movement. It traces the rise and varied use of "freedom songs," as activists transformed deep-seated black religious and secular musical traditions into a major resource for the struggle against racial injustice. Chapter 2 focuses on the black power phase of the African American liberation struggle, demonstrating that the Black Panther Party can be seen as engaging in a deadly serious form of political drama on the national and world stage. The chapter, like most of this book, challenges easy distinctions between culture and politics, in this case between literary dramas and the "theater" of poli-tics. Chapter 3 looks at the emergence and development of a new, radical wave of women's movements beginning in the mid-1960s. Here I focus on the role of poetry as one site of feminist consciousness-raising action and as a resource in the formation of a variety of contested feminist identities rooted in differences of race, ethnicity, class, sexuality, and nationality, as they have evolved up to the present. Chapter 4 treats the Chicano/a movement, focusing on the ways in which the thousands of murals produced in and around the brown power *movimiento* embody and reflect the political and cultural changes the movement generates in its efforts to bring justice to U.S. communities of Mexican descent.

Where the first four chapters deal with cultural forms generated within movements, the next two chapters deal with relations between movements and mainstream popular culture. Chapter 5 focuses on the group that called itself the American Indian Movement (AIM), one of the key organizations in the wider Native American red power movement. This chapter examines the ways in which the movement's story has been told through the widely circulated, if inevitably distorting, medium of the Hollywood film. Chapter 6 takes a look at the role played by pop and rock music in movements of the mid-1980s, especially the student-based anti-apartheid movement. Student movements, from the 1930s through the 1960s and the 1980s and into the present, have used popular culture as an organizing tool. In focusing on one of these waves of student activism, I try to show the important potential, as well as the limits, of using pop culture as a force in the promotion of social movements.

Chapter 7 analyzes the brilliant use of graphic arts (posters, T-shirts, banners, stickers) by ACT UP (AIDS Coalition to Unleash Power), the movement group at the forefront of the fight against HIV/AIDS. I focus on how the group mobilized both the gay community and other affected populations through a direct action campaign illustrating how homophobia, racism, sexism, and class prejudice had created a deadly "epidemic of signification" that stalled progress in saving lives.

Chapter 8 directly addresses the relationship between academia and social movements, challenging the assumption that the former is all theory, the latter all practice. I complicate both sides of this image by reminding readers that academic culture is a site through which movements are practiced, and by suggesting that movements are theory-making sites just as surely as is academia. I consider the work I am doing throughout the book as support for the work of social movements, but this chapter makes this point in a more direct way by talking about an intellectual formation that has grown out of a movement context. The chapter does this by describing and arguing on behalf of an emerging trend in academic literary and cultural study that I call "environmental justice ecocriticism." I argue for the need to expand this field in the service of the grassroots environmental justice movement from which it emerges.

Chapter 9 rounds out the movement story by focusing on the broad, coalitional movement against corporate globalization. Here I analyze the ways in which the new medium of the Internet has helped foster a global culture of resistance to the poverty, environmental degradation, and human rights abuses brought about by forms of globalization that attend only to the rights of corporations and nation-states.

The story told by and about each of these movements is one of increasing interrelationship and therefore increasing complexity. Each movement has been shaped by and in turn has reshaped each of the others. By the time we get to the antiglobalization or "global justice" movement, questions of racism, gender inequality, labor and class issues, the environment, and sexuality, for example, are increasingly recognized as intimately interconnected. The dynamic that leads to this multifaceted movement is also at work within each movement as I trace its story. Chapter by chapter, I try to show how as each movement has grown and changed, it has become more and more internally aware of the need to act upon interrelations among issues, even while remaining centered on its most crucial concerns.

The first and last of the chapters on individual movements are the longest, reflecting their status as the alpha and omega of a long arc of protest. The civil rights movement begins my story because it set in place a "master frame" for much of what followed, and the movement for global justice ends the story as a consolidation and worldwide expansion of the energy of direct action movements. But the civil rights movement was already global, in terms of both its influences (anticolonial struggles in Africa, Gandhi's ideas from India, for example) and its worldwide impact. Thus, my ending point is not a claim that American movements have been globalized, but rather the opposite—a recognition that global forces have always been at work within U.S. movements and that, now more than ever, movements in the United States must see themselves as only a small part of a much larger set of transnational transformations.

Chapter 10 offers some concluding "Reflections on the Cultural Study of Social Movements." It raises more systematic questions about various relations between culture(s) and movements that are discussed and exemplified in the course of the book. Those seeking a more explicit framework of analysis through which to think about culture-movement relations may wish to read this final chapter first. It is aimed a bit more at academic movement scholars than the other chapters, but I think it can be useful to all three of my imagined communities of readers.

While my range of movements studied is incautiously broad, I make no claim to comprehensiveness. A comprehensive study, even one limited to progressive direct action movements, is not possible. There are many extremely important movements that limitations of space and time did not permit me to cover. For example, while I draw upon gay/lesbian/queer movement insights throughout, and show how their impact is interwoven with several movements I do cover (most fully in my chapter on HIV/AIDS activism), the gay/lesbian movement receives no direct treatment on its own. The new left antiwar and student movement of the 1960s and the Asian American movement are other important forces treated only indirectly here. Indeed, there are many movements I might have included had I but world enough and time (and a publisher willing to publish a book of a thousand pages). In tracing one key strand of movements, I have not covered moderate and conservative movements, though they are present here and there as background or counter-forces to the movements I do examine. I also assume it is clear that the treatments I do offer of movements here are only introductions. My hope is that this book will inspire readers to expand to the wider range of social movements and to pursue in greater depth the movements covered here.

As the author of this work I have made no pretense to be neutral with regard to the passionate political issues discussed here. I believe it is vitally important for anyone, regardless of their political ideology, to seek to be objective in the sense of trying to "get the facts straight." A clear-headed assessment of the world is far more useful than an ideological fantasy, regardless of what your ideology may be. However, as critical social theorists have been pointing out since the invention of objectivist schools like positivism and empiricism in the nineteenth century, the process of "getting the facts" is always in part "inventing what counts as the facts" and can never fully be separated from political bias. Therefore, rather than attempt to hide my views behind an unjustifiable claim of absolute objectivity, I believe it is more intellectually honest to let my biases show amid my attempt to get the (interpreted) facts straight, so that the reader can take them into consideration while evaluating my arguments.

The "arc of protest" I trace in this book is part of a much longer history, one whose outcomes are far from certain. Martin Luther King Jr. once told us that "the arc of the moral universe is long, but it bends towards justice." For Reverend Dr. King, this was in part an article of faith. But his faith in no way limited his sense that the work along this arc must be that of ordinary people often laboring in dark times. For those who would join that journey, I recommend to you, in the words of Italian theorist Antonio Gramsci, "pessimism of the intellect," combined with "optimism of the will." That is what I think you will find in the best of the many brave and thoughtful cultural workers for justice whom I honor with this book and whose deeds are directly or indirectly woven into every page.

ONE

Singing Civil Rights

The Freedom Song Tradition

Then, too, there was the music. It would be hard to overestimate the
significance of the music of the movement.
—Charles Payne, *"I've Got the Light of Freedom"*

The year is 1960. The place is the Highlander Folk School in Tennessee.
It is one of the few places in the South where black and white people
gather together to talk about the emerging civil rights movement. Police
regularly raid the school and challenge the activists. Those inside know
their lives are in constant danger from the police and the Ku Klux Klan.
On this evening some high school students are among those gathered.
The police charge in and force the activists to sit in the dark while they
harass them by searching through their things. Amid this terrifying scene,
a girl begins to sing a song that was becoming the movement's anthem,
"We Shall Overcome." Huddled in the dark, she spontaneously invents a
new lyric. She sings, "We are not afraid, we are not afraid today." Of
course, she *was* afraid in that moment. Anyone would be. But in singing
the fear is both indirectly acknowledged and directly challenged. Singing
away a bit of her fear, she asserts the rights she and countless others are
prepared to fight and die for—the right to freedom and justice in their
own land.[1]

"We Shall Overcome" belongs now to the world, sung by Germans at
the fall of the Berlin Wall and by Chinese dissidents in Tiananmen Square,
but its home will always be at the center of the movement for black freedom and justice in the United States. In a sense, the African American

civil rights movement began when the first Africans were brought as slaves to the British colonies of the "new world" in 1619. Understanding some of that long history will be necessary to our story, but when most people use the term *civil rights movement* they are referring to a powerful force for change that emerged in the mid-1950s and had its greatest impact in the 1960s. That movement is at the heart of this book not only because of its intrinsic importance as a key moment in the long struggle for black Americans to achieve equality and justice, but also because it was the "borning struggle," the movement that became the model for virtually all the progressive social movements that followed it in the latter half of the twentieth century. In terms of tactics, strategies, style, vision, ideology, and overall movement culture, the black civil rights struggle has had a profound impact on all subsequent social movements and on U.S. culture at large. It was also the first major movement covered fully by the new electronic medium of television, a medium whose power increasingly shaped the context of movements over the decades covered by this book.

The forms of culture most central to the civil rights movement were undoubtedly music and religion. The freedom songs whose story I tell in this chapter mobilized both. Music had long been a part of American movements including the antislavery movement in the nineteenth century and the labor movement in the twentieth century, among others, but the civil rights movement brought a new level of intensity of singing and left a legacy of "freedom songs" now sung all around the world. Songs were everywhere in the movement—in meetings, on the picket line, on marches, at the sit-ins, in jail, everywhere. Songs, especially as embedded in a rich church culture and later in black pop music, formed the communication network of the movement, and they also expressed the "soul" of the movement, linking its spirit to centuries of resistance to slavery and oppression.

The civil rights movement is undoubtedly the best known movement in recent American history. Unfortunately, much popular knowledge about the movement consists of half-truths and myths. Perhaps the most common and most misleading myth is the notion that the movement was started by and led by Martin Luther King Jr. The civil rights movement is often portrayed as virtually King's singlehanded effort. But as a far less well-known but equally important figure in the movement, Ella Baker, put it, King did not make the movement, the movement made

King. As we will see, Reverend King was an important figure but he was only one among thousands of activists and hundreds of leaders. While he was a great orator and a great translator of the movement's ideas to mainstream America, he was more often a follower of the movement's actions than a leader of them. His high public visibility often obscured the extent to which the movement worked from a model of collective leadership and was driven by thousands of ordinary citizens struggling without media coverage or even public recognition.[2]

Related to the exaggerated importance given to King is a tendency to emphasize national leadership and centralized organizations. Central organizations like the National Association for the Advancement of Colored People (NAACP, founded in 1909) and the Southern Christian Leadership Conference (SCLC, founded in 1957) were important forces. The NAACP was the key, if not the only, black political organization in many communities. It served as a vital network of activists the movement drew upon in the late 1950s and early 1960s. But the efforts of local people working under the guise of the NAACP were often quite different from, more innovative and more radical than, those of the national office, which had long stressed slow progress through the courts. Similarly, while SCLC became the most visible civil rights organization under Dr. King's leadership, the national office also often found itself trying to catch up with what bolder local pastors and parishioners were doing. This pattern was intensified when the most important civil rights organization of the 1960s, the Student Non-violent Coordinating Committee (SNCC, founded in 1961), emerged with its philosophy precisely based on the idea of cultivating local, group-centered leadership rather than building a central, hierarchical national organization.[3]

In a sense, there were dozens of civil rights movements in communities throughout the South (and the North), many of which were quite independent of national leaders like King. The backbone of the struggle consisted of hundreds of grassroots organizers, local people still mostly unsung, who sought not notoriety but justice, and who toiled, usually amid life-threatening danger, for many years before and after the most dramatic demonstrations, protests, marches, and speeches that are the best known manifestations of the movement. There were important local and regional variations in the movement that need also to be acknowledged, especially differences between urban and rural contexts. Indeed, in each of the hundreds of local communities where the movement emerged, particular political, social, and cultural mixes shaped the struggle to unique contours.

Another myth has the movement suddenly and spontaneously emerging out of nowhere. But the large-scale, dramatic events that captured media attention did not arise spontaneously. They were made possible by countless hours, months, and years of work by local activists from all classes and segments of the black community. Moreover, black women did much of that local work. A focus on the (mostly male) national leaders obscures the extent to which women were the majority of movement workers and often the dominant force in many parts of the decentralized movement. Too narrow a definition of national leadership also distorts the role of women like Ella Baker, Septima Clark, and Fannie Lou Hamer, all women with deep respect for local traditions and shared leadership, who nonetheless played roles that were decidedly national in scope. It is unlikely that any figure in the movement logged more traveling miles around the nation in these years than Ella Baker, a woman key to the founding and functioning of both of the most important organizations of the movement, SCLC and SNCC.[4] Similarly, homophobia has meant that the presence of gay men and women in the civil rights struggle has not been given its due. "Gay-baiting" (using someone's real or alleged homosexuality as a way to discredit or blackmail them) was sometimes used to stifle the movement, both locally and nationally. In the case of key movement strategist Bayard Rustin, both his homosexuality and charges that he was a communist (another common way of attacking folks, known as "red-baiting") were used in efforts to limit his effectiveness.[5]

Yet another key myth misrepresents the integrated nature of the movement, exaggerating the role of white people. There is certainly a partial truth in this, in terms of both the goals of the movement (which included an end to racial segregation) and the practice of the movement, in which white people sometimes played important roles and exhibited great courage in fighting for a cause that did not directly benefit them. But the civil rights movement was fundamentally a movement by black people themselves, many of whom remained highly skeptical about the possibilities of racial harmony even if the legal basis of segregation could be brought to an end. A focus on the role of white people is too often used to cover the continuing racism in U.S. society in the name of the fiction that if we just stop talking about race, we will be suddenly transported into a colorblind utopia. In one of the strangest twists of political logic, blacks and other people of color are thereby blamed for racism, as if pointing to its ugly, ongoing existence were to create it, rather than a crucial part of the effort needed to eradicate it finally from the culture.

Popular understanding of the movement also sometimes exaggerates its visionary and spiritual dimension to the detriment of its more pragmatic side. Spirituality and the black church were important forces in the movement. But even the most famous visionary moment in the history of the movement, Reverend King's "I Have a Dream" speech, was delivered at a march (whose original planning stretched back long before King was even an adult) for "jobs and freedom," with jobs getting top billing. The movement often succeeded most fully when it brought direct economic and political pressure to bear on white business people and white politicians. Its moral appeals were important, but they were always backed by such nonviolent direct actions as sit-ins, boycotts, mass marches, and strikes, not to mention the threat of having to deal with still more radical blacks tomorrow if you didn't deal with civil rights activists today. Nonviolence in the movement was directed at and formed as *power*, a power as much political and economic as moral or spiritual.[6] King himself became increasingly convinced, as the 1960s wore on, that freedom without fundamental economic change would be empty. His last major organizing campaign focused on a demand for economic justice for poor people of all races in the United States. King died believing that some form of democratic socialism would probably be needed to achieve racial justice in the United States.

So, if the civil rights movement was not quite what the mainstream media make it out to be, what was it? It was a fundamentally radical, grassroots, decentralized, mass-based, often women-led movement of thousands of black people (and some white allies) bent on forcing a deeply racist society to grant them freedom, dignity, and economic justice. The phrase "deeply racist" is meant to question another too easily presented myth of the movement—that its only real opposition was from ignorant, pot-bellied southern sheriffs with ties to the Ku Klux Klan. In fact, racism was (and is) as deeply entrenched in the North as in the South, and racist assumptions shaped the responses of well-meaning white moderates and liberals as much as those of the more overt kinds of bigot whom it is easy to parody. Moreover, the middle-class, genteel racism of the businessmen of the White Citizen's Council was as crucial as Klan terrorism in blocking black freedom, and the council frequently used the Klan to do its dirty work.

The movement, as it was simply known to its participants, had deep roots and continues to echo today, but its heyday was from the mid-1950s to the mid-1960s. The civil rights movement's most visible target was the system of racial apartheid in the South known as "segregation." Laws separating the races shaped every aspect of southern culture. Separate and much less well-funded and -maintained facilities for blacks—schools, restaurants, hospitals, public drinking fountains, even cemeteries—constantly conveyed a clear insult to a people deemed inferior by white segregators. But this legally sanctioned system of racial separation backed by white terrorism was only the visible marker of a much deeper system of racial oppression that ensured blacks a politically and economically degraded status, in the North as well as in the South.

The core public strategy of the movement was based on nonviolent direct actions (civil disobedience, sit-ins, freedom rides, boycotts, building of alternative institutions, strikes, and other actions) aimed at ending the system of racial apartheid in the American South, securing the right to vote and other basic political rights for blacks, and bringing down the wider racist system of which these injustices were but a part. In regard to the first two goals, ending segregation and securing basic political rights, the movement proved a phenomenally successful, crucially important moment in a long, unfinished struggle.

The other, equally important part of the movement was its impact on black people themselves. The ultimate terror of racism lies in its ability to make the subjects of racism believe in their own inferiority. This process, often given the overly simple label "internalized racism," manifests itself in many differing ways, some blatant, others subtle. Whether successful or not at achieving particular goals set at any stage of the struggle, the movement was always successful in challenging this vicious force. Whether it was the act of signing a voter registration form for the first time, or of appearing as a witness against a white person in court, or even the bravery it sometimes took just to talk to an organizer, the movement was made up of thousands of small and grand actions that chipped away or sometimes dramatically swept away generations of oppression as it had shaped the self-image of black people. Historians and social scientists have few tools for measuring such supposedly "subjective" changes, but they are at the core of the civil rights story.

Preconditions: Why the Civil Rights Movement Happened When It Did

Five main sets of large-scale changes provided preconditions that were seized by the black community to form the new movement: (1) population shifts and economic changes; (2) racial pride and resentment in the wake of World War II; (3) new federal policies, stemming partly from Cold War realities; (4) the example provided by anticolonial struggles in the Third World; and (5) new political strategies and tactics culled from the tradition of nonviolent civil disobedience.

First, a series of population shifts and economic changes repositioned the black community both geographically and occupationally. The Great Migration to the North that began after slavery continued well into the twentieth century, creating important centers of *relative* freedom in the North. These centers, such as New York's Harlem and Chicago's Southside, provided comparatively safe spaces in which models of black freedom were forged and from which campaigns into the segregated South could be launched to join an organizing tradition already at work there.

The declining importance and increasing mechanization of southern agriculture, paralleled by a rise in the number of industrial jobs available in the region, created larger urban black communities, which gave rise to a sense of collective power not felt as easily in rural isolation. Industrialization also brought a certain amount of unionization. While the South was and remains today a very inhospitable place for organizing labor unions, courageous and successful unions were created there, and blacks joined in significant numbers, mostly in segregated unions, occasionally in integrated ones. Labor unions became in effect training centers where future leaders of the civil rights movement picked up valuable organizing skills and learned social movement tactics and strategies. It is no coincidence that the Highlander Folk School in Tennessee, which began in the 1930s with a focus mostly on labor organizing, became a key civil rights training center in the 1950s.[7] Nor is it simply fortuitous that the most famous song of the civil rights movement, "We Shall Overcome," was first adapted as a labor song before it was transformed into the movement's anthem. Many connections existed between the labor movement and the civil rights movement.[8]

To these regional shifts in demographics and economics must be added a more national one. In its role as one of the two superpowers after World War II, the U.S. economy began the largest and most sustained period of growth in world history. Because the economic pie was widely and accurately perceived to be growing for all Americans, many white Americans became less resistant to modest gains by African Americans and other so-called racial "minorities." These economic conditions, of course, varied from state to state and county to county in the South (as well as in the North), and one can trace with some precision the degree of resistance to civil rights work based on the extent of economic stakes held by whites. It is no accident, for example, that some of the most difficult organizing took place in isolated rural counties where the new economy had not penetrated, and where whites felt they had the most to lose economically from black competitors.

A second set of precipitating factors revolves around the impact of World War II. Many African Americans fought courageously for freedom in that war. Most often they did so in racially segregated units. But under pressure from forces led by A. Philip Randolph, the great black union leader who later led the March on Washington, the federal government was forced to provide fairer labor practices for black women and men in the defense industries as the war began, and to desegregate the military during the war. These efforts provided a model for other desegregation efforts after the war, while at the same time pointing up the irony that blacks were fighting Nazi racism in the name of a freedom they did not possess at home. For many African Americans, particularly those from the South, the war provided the first glimpse of wider worlds where black oppression was not so absolute. Returning home from the war, often as decorated heroes, black soldiers expected and at times demanded respect from the white community, only to be met with renewed racist hostility. A postwar wave of lynchings of blacks in the South attests to the resistance such pride encountered from whites. Many of the key organizers of the 1940s and 1950s who built the foundation for the wider movement of the late 1950s and early 1960s were black veterans. The sentiments also found their way directly into a freedom song: "I'm an American fighting man / I'll defend this country as long as I can / And if I can defend it overseas / Why don't you set my people free!"[9]

A third set of factors involved some small but important shifts at the level of the federal government. The wartime desegregation efforts culminated in the integration of the federal government itself, a controversial act in the borderline southern city of Washington, D.C. Following World War II, the Cold War against the Soviet Union brought new pressures to bear. How would national politicians in the leading nation of what they were calling "the free world" deal with the obvious unfreedom of African American citizens? Southern apartheid became an international embarrassment to the U.S. government, and incrementally pieces of civil rights legislation began to appear during the Truman and Eisenhower administrations.

This atmosphere also contributed to the far more significant action taken by the U.S. Supreme Court. After almost a half-century of court cases and organizing efforts spearheaded by the NAACP, in 1954, in the landmark case *Brown v. Board of Education,* the nation's highest court declared certain types of school segregation illegal. While the ruling was limited and would only very slowly be enforced by the executive branch, it proved immensely psychologically important to black Americans generally and to an emerging core of civil rights activists in particular. It also provided a key legal precedent for local activists seeking to chip away at the myriad forms of segregation, not only of schools but also of public facilities and private businesses. As it turned out, the federal government had to be pulled kicking and screaming into support of the movement, even in the somewhat more liberal years of the Kennedy and Johnson administrations, but *Brown v. Board of Education* initially held out great promise that the national government might aid in the battle against segregation and other systematic forms of racism enforced at the state and local levels. In the terminology of social movement scholars, this landmark Supreme Court case indicated a shift in the "political opportunity structure" available to activists. Its suggestion of "movement" in the federal structures further fueled "movements" at the grassroots level.[10]

Fourth, the rise of anticolonial struggles in the 1950s and early 1960s in the Third World, especially in Africa, provided inspiring examples for African Americans. The example of black people rising up to throw off white European colonial governments in African countries like Chad, the Congo, Dahomey, Gabon, Ivory Coast, Mali, Nigeria, Senegal, Somalia, Upper Volta, Zaire, and others, was a potent stimulus. The contrast between these newly liberated homelands and American apartheid was stark, and many African Americans began to conceptualize their segregated communities as internal colonies within the United States. A particularly strong wave of successful independence struggles in a dozen African countries in 1960–61 coincided with and inspired the student-led sit-in movement at segregated lunch counters and other sites in those same years. Black novelist James Baldwin drew the direct connection in a single, colorful sentence: "All of Africa will be free before we can get a lousy cup of coffee."[11]

The fifth key factor was the development of a new set of political ideologies, strategies, and tactics. The anticolonial struggle in India, culminating in independence from Britain in 1948, not only provided inspiration, like the African struggles, but also, more concretely, gave the movement a successful contemporary model of nonviolent revolution. The movement adapted and adopted numerous philosophical, strategic, and tactical elements from the anticolonial movement led by Mahatma Gandhi, who himself had drawn upon a long American tradition of civil disobedience. Stretching from seventeenth-century Quakers to nineteenth-century abolitionists to early twentieth-century women's right activists, and given philosophical form by Henry David Thoreau, this rich tradition provided a wealth of ideas and examples. Civil rights activists gradually merged these ideas and tactics with traditional forms of black activism and black Christianity. The key movement group that developed these nonviolent philosophies, strategies, and tactics was the Congress of Racial Equality (CORE). Founded in 1942, CORE was the offshoot of the radical pacifist Quaker organization, the Fellowship of Reconciliation. In the 1940s and early 1950s, through boycotts and sit-ins in the slightly less daunting atmosphere of the North, CORE and like-minded groups honed the techniques that would become widespread a few years later in the South. Key activists in this tradition, such as James Lawson, Glenn Smiley, Bayard Rustin, and James Farmer, provided philosophical guidance and practical training in nonviolence to those already forging a new phase of struggle across the South. They are also the people largely responsible for educating Dr. King in the tradition he so effectively popularized.[12]

Roots of the Movement

All these factors played a role in creating ripe conditions for a new movement, but none of those opportunities would have been seized without people ready and schooled to act upon these openings. Part of the myth of the civil rights movement is that it appeared suddenly, even miraculously, and spontaneously. Perhaps that is the way it looked to some white people who had the luxury of not paying much attention to black lives. But when the structural factors discussed above made the time right for change, the movement of the 1950s and 1960s formed itself around deeply rooted, longstanding cultural and political institutions based in many generations of black struggle. Across those many generations, the most important institution of the black community was the black church. The church had its origins in slavery where, as in the civil rights movement, it served politically ambiguous purposes. On the one hand, the church had been allowed to form in part because slave owners thought it might help pacify black slaves with a message of deliverance in the afterlife. Embraced on such terms, black Christianity could have a quite conservative effect. But preachers and parishioners also fashioned a very different kind of black Protestant Christianity, one in which messages of deliverance were read not as a heavenly promise but as an earthly goal. Nat Turner was only one of many black preachers who led slave revolts. Under slavery, black Christianity developed a kind of double coding in which Bible stories became liberation stories. For example, the captivity of the Israelites in Egypt became a metaphor of slavery, and the promised land of Canaan became a very literal promise of freedom in Canada. Black ministers and black choral singers developed sermons and songs that contained elaborate coded messages about this-worldly routes to freedom, such as the ones provided by the "underground railroad" of safe houses that led escaped slaves from the South to relative freedom in the North or in the still safer territory of Canada. Even when not used in this directly political effort to achieve freedom, the songs and sermons became a kind of liberation theology that kept alive alternative visions of the world that would, under movement conditions, be turned again to more earthly, political ends.

In the aftermath of slavery, the long struggle to give emancipation a substantive meaning continued to involve the church in a central way. Especially in those places where all or most political rights and spaces for political activity continued to be denied to blacks, the church served *de facto* as their political arena. One of the ironic effects of segregation was that it contributed to the formation of tightly knit black communities, and in those communities the churches became the heart of social and political as well as religious life. Black ministers were often the political leaders of the community. Thus, when the new societal conditions opened up possibilities for a new kind of civil rights struggle, that movement often came wrapped in the language of black Christianity and was often represented publicly by ministers. Many preachers, but by no means all, became key figures in the freedom movement. Some clergymen (and they were almost exclusively men) avoided or opposed the movement, often because, as the most prestigious and sometimes also the most prosperous men in black communities, they felt they had the most to lose.

Any movement needs certain basic institutional infrastructures to function: an organizational foundation; a way to raise money; places to meet; a way to spread the word to new recruits. In many places, particularly in urban areas of the black South, the church provided all these resources. Church buildings became movement meeting places. Church social networks became movement networks. The church collection plate became the way to raise movement money. And moving from infrastructure to ideas, church sermons and church music became transformed into movement "sermons" and movement music that aided in the recruitment of thousands of participants. This process was not automatic or inevitable. Many conservative currents in black churches fought this transformation. But where it was done well, hundreds of black ministers and black congregations were rapidly transformed into components of a growing movement. The church also provided a degree of cover for movement activities. Black churches were bombed in terrorist attacks by the Klan and its sympathizers, and many black ministers died for the cause, but churches were relatively safe meeting places and ministers the most respectable ambassadors to the wider white world. In both the white world and the black community itself, church involvement often sanctified the movement, made it more legitimate and less frightening in the eyes of many people. While over time some limits to the church-based part of the movement became clear, church culture as it became transformed into movement culture was a key force for change, particularly for older segments of the community.[13]

Two other key sets of networks also proved crucial to the movement's ability to act upon new opportunities: the expanding group of black colleges and universities, and the large network of local NAACP chapters. Black colleges played a central role in the wave of sit-ins in 1960 and 1961 that eventually involved some seventy thousand students and supporters. The NAACP was crucially important not so much as a national organization but rather as a network of local people who either on their own or nudged by people from outside the community seized the opportunity to go beyond the organization's own national agenda to create bolder movement actions.

Liberation Musicology

While many black cultural forms contributed to the civil rights movement, most participants and most analysts agree that music was the key force in shaping, spreading, and sustaining the movement's culture and through culture its politics. As the three key networks of churches, colleges, and NAACP chapters were galvanized into action, no cultural force played a greater role at all levels of struggle than what became known as the "freedom songs." Alongside and entwined with the "liberation theology" of black ministers stood the great "liberation musicology" contained in the tradition of African American song. Singing proved to have wide appeal across class, regional, generational, gender, and other lines of difference. It also crossed another line of distinction in the movement, voiced most succinctly by Ella Baker. Baker often spoke of the difference between "mobilizing" people and "organizing" them. Mobilizing focused on getting lots of bodies into the street for marches and large-scale demonstrations. Such actions had great dramatic value, and they were often a way to ensure media coverage of the movement. But they also tended to be fairly passive and transient events that did not necessarily bring the deepest changes. In contrast, the organizing tradition, as Baker defined it, focused on the slower but deeper task of bringing out the leadership potential in all people, and on building group-centered, as opposed to individual, leadership in communities that would do the ongoing work of changing people and institutions.[14]

The freedom songs were used by mobilizers like Reverend King, and by organizers like Baker, Septima Clark and Miles Horton.[15] For the organizers, the value of freedom songs lay especially in their capacity to take the liberation messages latent in the black preaching tradition and make them available to ordinary people. The group-centered process of singing, with leaders emerging periodically out of the group to "line out" a new chorus, was at once an instance of and a metaphor for the general model of nonhierarchical leadership the organizers were seeking to instill. It was also the perfect tool for organizing communities that were for the most part deeply rooted in an oral cultural tradition. As the great singer-activist-ethnomusicologist Bernice Johnson Reagon argues, freedom songs are one of the best records we have of the transformation of consciousness in the ordinary people, the masses, who took part in the movement.[16]

It is extremely difficult to invent a *movement culture* from scratch. It is far more effective to adapt existing cultural structures to support the new goals, ideas, and strategies set by the movement. No movement ever did this more effectively than the civil rights movement. One of the great tasks facing the movement as it took on new energy in the mid-1950s was how to bring the strengths of tradition to bear on new conditions. Almost by definition, traditions are conservative. Their job is to conserve the past. But traditions are made, not simply given, when people choose from myriad possible cultural forms those ones they will preserve or reanimate as traditions. The legacy of American racism and resistance to it meant that black culture included broad traditions of struggle. But how could you bring that tradition of struggle into the contemporary scene with its new opportunities and new tactics? The genius of the early movement was to bring the full weight of the liberation theology of black church music into the new struggle.

Following the "river of song" as it flows through the movement will allow us to see what forces were at play at various times, what ideas were central and how they evolved, as well as to capture some sense of what the movement felt like to those who enacted it. Music was the heart and soul of the movement, but it was always also a highly practical tool in the struggle.

Music as History

Like much else about the movement, the use of freedom songs that appears to be a natural or inevitable development was the result of much conscious, deliberate organizing over many years. Music did not enter the movement spontaneously, immediately, or automatically. An amorphous "freedom song" legacy had to be uncovered, reworked, made into a useable tradition. This involved planning, skills sharing, and active dissemination, not just natural evolution. Even when new songs, or new parts of songs, did arise spontaneously, this should be understood as a process something like the "spontaneous" improvisations of jazz in which "inspiration" is built on hours and hours of careful preparation.

In reaching older black people especially, church music functioned brilliantly as a way of pouring new content into old forms. The transition to the radically new ideas particular to the civil rights struggle was made far easier when attached emotionally and intellectually to the feelings and ideas found in the old spirituals and gospel songs. Some of the traditional hymns could be carried over into the movement intact, with no changes, because the change of context gave them new meaning: "I'm on my way to freedom land, I'm on my way"; "This little light, I'm gonna let it shine, let it shine, let it shine." The limits set by segregation may not have been as total as those set by slavery, but a deep desire for freedom arose out of both conditions. Other traditional freedom hymns were remade in the movement, sometimes with practiced spontaneity, other times through studied rewriting or rearranging. Lyrics were changed to incorporate the particular meanings of the new times. Eventually, whole new topical songs were created.

In two different but reinforcing ways music gave a sense of history to the movement. First, the "traditional" gospel songs and spirituals provided a feeling of continuity over long periods of time. This was important in letting those for whom the movement seemed disturbingly new feel that it was also something quite old and familiar. It also gave a sense of depth and patience. While the theme of having waited long enough was often and rightfully voiced on many occasions, the movement frequently depended upon a slow, evolving process. Organizing cannot be rushed. Whenever the immediate stakes seemed not worth the danger, pain, and frustration of the work, songs brought up from the days of slavery offered a gentle reminder of how ancestors had faced far worse circumstances. At the same time, they also fired hearts with indignation that a hundred years after supposed emancipation, blacks still were not free.

A second, different role played by music as history making we might call "instant historicizing." This refers to the altering of old songs and the creation of new songs that told stories of the evolving movement. Where the old songs gave roots, the new songs celebrated the new accomplishments of the living generations. Writing new songs or new verses allowed each new community to claim its specific place in the long tradition of black struggle. This was especially the case when old spirituals were rewritten with lyrics about Nashville, or Hinds County, Jackson,

McComb, or wherever the latest struggle had emerged. Often the two kinds of historicizing—finding roots and naming the history being made in the present—were combined, as the songs would generally begin with the older verses for a basis, and then add the contemporary events into the narrative.[17] More extended writings of movement sites, events, and people into history occurred in the form of new, topical songs like "The Ballad of the Sit-ins." Perhaps not coincidentally, tracing the development of the role of music in the movement seems to follow closely the growth and development of the movement generally. Three clusters of events in particular are key to the rise of both the music and the movement: the Montgomery bus boycott, the student-led sit-ins, and the Albany, Georgia, movement.

Many histories place the Montgomery, Alabama, bus boycott of 1955–56 as the beginning point of the new phase of black struggle that came to be called the civil rights movement.[18] Other boycotts aimed at segregated public transportation had occurred earlier in the decade in Baton Rouge, Louisiana, Tallahassee, Florida, and elsewhere, but the Montgomery action was particularly well orchestrated and effectively publicized by movement activists. Myth has the boycott arising spontaneously when one tired woman refused to give up her seat on a city bus to a white man. But it wasn't quite as simple as that. Rosa Parks, the woman in question, had been a leading activist in her community for many years. Not long before her defiant act, she had been a guest at Highlander Folk School, that key movement center, where she learned a good many "freedom songs," and a good deal about civil disobedience tactics. Her refusal to go along with segregation law by giving up her seat was indeed a spontaneous decision that day, but it came from a life prepared for struggle through many years in the NAACP, and the quick transformation of a seemingly isolated act into a full-fledged boycott was the result of careful planning by experienced activists.

The individual who first seized upon Rosa Parks's heroic act was E. D. Nixon, a man with a long history of activism in the radical black union, the Brotherhood of Sleeping Car Porters, and in the local chapter of the NAACP. Nixon had been waiting and preparing for just such an opening as that provided by Parks. He immediately called into play the key networks in the community, beginning with the ministers. Most of the local ministers threw themselves unhesitatingly into the action. One young minister, a newcomer to the community, was a bit more reluctant but soon saw the light. His name was Martin Luther King Jr. Soon Nixon had King not only involved but filling a central role. Precisely because he was new to the community, King appeared to Nixon to be a good, neutral choice for leadership since he would not be caught up in any old personality conflicts or jealousies among the established ministers. And a fine choice it was, as King soon became a superb public relations person for the movement, and the finest orator of his generation.

While Nixon and the ministers played important roles, women were the real force behind the bus boycott. After Parks provided the impulse, Jo Ann Robinson and her Women's Political Council did the grassroots organizing and developed the logistics that gave the boycott its bite. Robinson was an English teacher at nearby Alabama State College who had often felt the sting of segregation and racist insult, despite her relatively privileged occupation. She mobilized not only the council but also dozens of students and fellow teachers. Working furiously over the weekend after Parks's arrest, the Women's Political Council and its allies distributed thirty-five thousand leaflets and by Monday had organized an extraordinarily successful boycott. Only a handful of Montgomery's thousands of black citizens rode the bus that first day, 5 December 1955, and few did in the weeks and months to come. Robinson's women organized carpools and commandeered every vehicle that could move, including a few horse-drawn ones! Many, many people walked, sometimes as much as ten or twelve miles a day, rather than continue to face the insult of segregated buses. For a year they walked and walked, withholding their business and cutting deeply into the profits of the bus line.

Thus it is no accident that several of the freedom songs that emerged in Montgomery as symbols of their efforts had a whole lot of walking in them. When five thousand of Montgomery's black citizens gathered inside and outside the Holt Street Baptist Church on the evening of the first day of the boycott, they led off the evening with an old hymn called "Onward Christian Soldiers" with the refrain "Onward Christian soldiers, marching as to war." The song, written in 1864, set the movement in the context of Christianity and American history, and was one that all parishioners, whether new to civil rights struggle or veterans, would know. What would those gathered hear in the song and feel as they sang it? They would hear and feel that theirs was a righteous cause. They would hear and feel that they would need strength and fortitude, for it would be a protracted struggle. They would hear and feel that the war that

Rosa Parks had touched off would surely need as many foot soldiers as it could muster, would need an army. The song was an appropriate one to start with because the people assembled there were about to decide whether or not to continue the boycott that had initially been scheduled for just that one day. The song gave the key for a crowd that was readying to commit to a long battle, one that lasted more than a year. The song, however, was also one largely identified with the white Christian tradition, and as such it illustrates the rather conservative, middle-class constituency that initially set the tone in Montgomery. A certain version of "racial uplift" ideology in parts of the middle- and upper-class portions of the black community viewed the old black spiritual songs as something to leave behind, as works full of excessive emotionality, as "primitive" and "unsophisticated" reminders of darker times. The freedom song movement as it emerged had to fight against this view of things, and in so doing it helped bridge class divides in black communities.

Another old spiritual that became popular in Montgomery, "Walk Together Children," even more literally seemed to fit the scene and mood, and was more rooted in black tradition: "Walk together children, don't you get weary. / Walk together children, don't get weary. / There's a great camp meeting in the Promised Land." These and similar songs were deeply familiar to the respectable church-going folks at the heart of the Montgomery movement. They needed no changing come movement time, but were given new life and urgency by the movement. Reverend King later recalled that people would sometimes come to meetings two hours before they were scheduled in order to get in some good singing sessions: "Usually the hymns preceding the meeting were unaccompanied lined hymns of low pitch and long meter. One could not help but be moved by these traditional songs, which brought to mind the long history of the Negro's suffering."[19] At the outset of this new phase of struggle that some came to call the Second American Revolution, others the Second Reconstruction, the older hymns gave a sense of gravity, depth, and continuity to the movement. They made it clear that far more than comfort on a bus was at stake, that the boycotters were all part of a long, long story of suffering and triumph. That deep sense of history was carried more fully by song than by any other medium. At a time when few works of "black history" existed (most of what came to be so labeled emerged out of the movement), and when a major segment of the community had been kept illiterate, song played an immense educational role.

In the wake of the success of the boycott, Martin Luther King Jr. was thrown into national prominence, and along with others he worked to form an organization to further spread the movement gospel. The resulting group, founded in 1957, came to be called the Southern Christian Leadership Conference. As the name suggests, SCLC began as a conference of southern black ministers interested in furthering the freedom struggle, then evolved into a permanent organization to share information, resources, tactics, and strategies, especially via the network of Baptist, AME, and other black churches. While promising leadership, most often in the years between the Montgomery boycott and a mass upsurge after 1960, SCLC primarily filled a coordinating and informational function as most activity was generated and sustained at the level of local communities. Few of the local struggles received the dramatic attention accorded to Montgomery. One exception occurred in Little Rock, Arkansas, in 1957, when federal troops had to be called in to protect black students whose efforts to integrate public schools in that city met with violent white resistance. That clash received national news coverage.

During the second half of the 1950s, most of the work was done by local people who patiently built networks, tested alliances, identified friends, measured foes, and learned organizing skills and the tactics of nonviolent civil disobedience. A significant part of that work was done at the Highlander Folk School (later Folk Center) where songs played a central role in building a network of activists. Song sessions, often led by the new music director there, Guy Carawan, proved an ideal way to build solidarity, friendship, and trust. Part of the training of organizers involved the use of music, as a repertoire of freedom songs evolved. Visitors from all parts of the South and North brought with them local songs or local variations on traditional ones. Misnamed the "fallow years" by observers looking only for dramatic action, the late 1950s were a crucial period of planting seeds that would lead to a spectacular harvest. Harvest season, as it turned out, was announced in 1960 by four black college students in Greensboro, North Carolina.

The Sit-in Revolution: Students Take Up the Song

Four black college students, inspired in part by a comic book about the Montgomery bus boycott, and armed with rudimentary knowledge of the movement tactic known as the sit-in, walked nervously up to the "whites only" food counter at the Woolworth's store in Greensboro, North Carolina, on 1 February 1960, and asked politely to be served. Like Rosa Parks, these young men (Izell Blair, Joseph McNeil, Franklin McCain, and David Richmond) were in the right place at the right time to run smack into a "history-making day." The tactic was not new, but at that moment the act struck a chord with a new generation of young people. Soon the young men were joined by other students from their college. And those students were soon joined by students in other cities. Utilizing the black college network, a wave of student protest swept across the South. Within two weeks of the Greensboro action, sit-ins had spread to fifteen cities. By the end of March more than twenty northern college campuses were also involved. Within eighteen months sit-ins had spread to over one hundred cities in twenty states and involved more than seventy thousand demonstrators, most college and high school students. There were more than thirty-five hundred arrests for civil disobedience. Much of the effort in this particular use of the sit-in tactic was directed at private businesses, rather than the public facilities that had often been the main focus earlier. Targeting national chains like Woolworth's and Kress department stores, these sit-ins pointed up corporate complicity in state-sanctioned segregation, and also helped spread the movement to the North where these large chains were picketed and boycotted in solidarity with southern antisegregation efforts.[20]

In the South itself, one of the strongest local centers of student protest was Nashville, Tennessee. From there came one of the key movement music groups, the Nashville Quartet (James Bevel, Bernard Lafayette, Joseph Carter, and Samuel Collier). Their specialty was the popular music of black youth, "rhythm and blues." The sit-ins announced that a new generation was now the cutting edge of the movement, and, fittingly, that generation added its music to the fray. Unlike the traditional songs, which often had a strong liberation component already built in, the adaptation of popular student music required more radical alterations. For example, popular singer Little Willie John had a hit song at the time called "You Better Leave My Kitten Alone." It was a typical song of lover's jealousy, warning a rival away from the singer's girlfriend. But in the Nashville Quartet's version, the "kitten" became "segregation," and the "you" became plural: "You better leave segregation alone / because they [white folks] love segregation like a hound dog loves a bone." I don't know if the "hound dog" line is a little slap at Elvis Presley whose "hound dog" sound was widely understood as ripping off black musical style, but the main message is clear: black folks had better leave segregation alone because white folks' dogged attachment to it was a sign of what they had to lose.

The most adapted singer's repertoire was no doubt that of rhythm and blues soul singer Ray Charles. His songs, blending the traditionally opposed forms of gospel (God's music) and the blues (Devil's music), appealed to young people in emotional and political transition. The Nashville Quartet, for example, celebrated the successful citywide integration of Nashville lunch counters with a new rendition of Charles's song, "Moving On." Ray had sung of moving on from a love affair gone bad. In the movement version, the bad relationship was with that embodiment of segregation, Jim Crow: "Segregation's been here from time to time / but we just ain't gonna pay it no mind // It's moving on—It's moving on—It's moving... // Old Jim Crow's moving on down the track / He's got his bags and he won't be back." The song brings news of a new day, and the notion of "moving" captured perfectly the feeling of motion the movement embodied (it also worked nicely as a marching song, in which the phrase "we're moving on" became literal). For the skeptics, the line is added: "Well I thought they was jiving about Jim Crow's gone / but I went down to his house and he sure wasn't home / He's moving on." Important here is the sense of personal witness. The movement workers had truly seen Jim Crow on the run, and they were going to continue to run him and his friends out of town.[21]

The thousands of sit-in participants clearly needed to be organized, and in stepped the organizer's organizer, Ella Baker, to help that process along, with a fair amount of musical help. Baker persuaded SCLC to fund a conference of student leaders, held on 17 April 1960. While SCLC had originally hoped to form a kind of youth auxiliary, Baker and others argued for an independent student organization. Out of that meeting came the Student Non-violent Coordinating Committee (SNCC, pronounced "snick," founded in 1961), the movement group that became the center of struggle in the years to come. The number of student participants never regained the level reached early in 1960. Instead, SNCC became a core group, never with more than a couple of hundred members, who spread throughout the South, bringing with them the message that building local, group-centered leadership, rather than a centralized organization, was the key to success.

Many SNCC veterans point to the freedom song sessions held by Highlander music director Guy Carawan as a powerful force in harmonizing the diverse group of students at the founding conference into an organization. Carawan also offered the youth movement a further gift, his "Ballad of the Sit-ins": "The time was 1960, the place the USA / February 1st became a history making day / Greensboro across the land the news spread far and wide / When silently and bravely youth took a giant stride."

It is revealing of the independent spirit that drove SNCC that this song, written by the white southerner Carawan, was quickly adapted and changed by the four young black members of the Nashville Quartet. The Nashville students both shifted it musically from ballad form to a complicated rhythm and blues arrangement, and dropped a key lyric. Carawan had written the line, "We are soldiers in the army of Martin Luther King." While the students respected King, they also distanced themselves from him, especially from the patriarchal style of leadership he and SCLC embodied. Some referred to him as "De Lawd," and they refused to sing the line about being in his army. Thus, the song embodies the dynamic by which important white contributions to the movement were always contextualized within what was at base a black liberation struggle.

Albany: The Singing Movement Comes of Age

While the sit-ins and their follow-up, the freedom rides, were dramatic actions garnering national media coverage, they were not typical of the movement's development. More typical was the slow, long-term process of community organizing. An example of this kind of work, which was also a high point in the freedom song movement, occurred in Albany, Georgia, in 1961 and 1962. Bernice Reagon offers numerous examples of freedom songs that evolved not only lyrically but musically as they moved from site to site of struggle. The high mark of this process was no doubt the Albany campaign as well. From Reagon's perspective, as well as the testimony of many others, the community of civil rights workers in Albany took over, deepened, and expanded the role of freedom songs as none had before. "The mass meetings always started with freedom songs. Most of the meeting was singing. Songs were the bed of everything."[22] Even allowing for a little local bias (Reagon is from Albany), she makes an excellent case. Albany was the place where all the components of the freedom song repertoire coalesced into a kind of musical united front.

The old spirituals had deep resonance with the older members of the community, and again played a key role in bringing people together across class lines. Of course, the students brought their pop adaptations into full play (it didn't hurt that one of their favorite pop singers to adapt, Ray Charles, was born in Albany). Another key source for the freedom song repertoire that also received important makeovers in Albany was old labor songs like "Which Side Are You On?" The adult community was the backbone of the Albany movement, and all the freedom songs went through a new baptism into a deeper spirit coming out of a rich local tradition of religious singing.

The musical alliance that was Albany culminated in the formation of the most aggressive force yet for disseminating the power of freedom songs, the Freedom Singers (originally Chuck Neblett, Ruth Harris, Bernice Johnson Reagon, Cordell Reagon, and Berth Gober). While other musical groups, such as the Montgomery Gospel Trio, the Nashville Quartet, and so forth, had played important local roles, the power of music in the Albany campaign convinced SNCC that a musical group could play an even larger movement role. The Freedom Singers eventually crossed the country many times, singing the movement story and raising funds through their concerts. They were particularly effective in bringing movement messages to the North and to young people on college campuses. The Freedom Singers also became associated with a burgeoning white folk song revival centered in Greenwich Village, New York. That connection proved a key link in recruiting northern white students to the civil rights cause. Freedom Summer of 1964, a massive SNCC campaign that brought more than a thousand northern students to Mississippi for three months of intensive movement activity, was greatly facilitated by links the Freedom Singers had made. Freedom Summer in turn proved to be of immense importance as a training ground for many of the activists who built the full range of student, antiwar, women's liberation, gay liberation, and other movements of the 1960s.[23] The Freedom Singers gave institutional form to something that had already become clear: music was a vital political force in the movement.

White Terrorism and Litanies against Fear

"When you get together at a mass meeting you sing the songs which symbolize transformation, which make that revolution of courage inside you," said Bernice Johnson Reagon.[24] And, as movement historian Charles

Payne writes, "The music operated as a kind of litany against fear."[25] Or, as put in song: "Oh freedom over me, Oh freedom / I'll be buried in my grave before I'll be a slave / No segregation over me, No segregation / I'll be buried in my grave before I'll be a slave."[26] The brutal murder of fourteen-year-old Emmett Till, a Chicago native visiting relatives in Greenwood, Mississippi, in 1955 was in many respects an ordinary act of southern white terrorism. Estimates suggest that between the end of the Civil War and the 1950s, more than four thousand lynchings of blacks by whites occurred in America (most, but not all, in the South). Well into the twentieth century, lynching was a "spectator sport" enjoyed by all classes in the white community; whole families would come out to watch. Postcards of favorite lynchings were made to send to friends and relatives.[27] Thus, while Till's case was nothing new, the context of new times brought new attention to it. Till's twin "crimes"—allegedly speaking "fresh" to a white woman and mentioning that he had a white girlfriend back home in the North—were typical of the slight pretexts used to justify these murders. Till was taken out of his home late at night, tortured, mutilated, shot, and dumped in the Tallahatchie River with a weight attached to his body. The weight was not enough to keep the crime from surfacing, and when it did, it led to a trial that received national attention. The act was common enough that one local white man could muse that he didn't see what all the fuss was about since "that river is full of niggers."[28] What was new was not the act, but the national and even international attention that it drew. The shift in attitudes suggested by the *Brown v. Board of Education* victory in 1954 was further evidenced by media attention and some protestations of outrage from parts of the white community. Still, it was not enough, and despite confessing to the murder, the two men responsible were acquitted and "southern justice" affirmed.

The Till case was one of many atrocities of whites against blacks that gained attention or, more often, remained in obscurity during the movement years. At least two other murders of blacks, both tied, unlike Till, directly to movement activity, occurred in Mississippi in 1955 alone. The new level of black resistance in the wake of the *Brown* decision was matched by renewed white terror and organization. The white Citizens' Council, for example, emerged at this time. Described as combining "the agenda of the Klan with the demeanor of the Rotary" club, it provided a seemingly more respectable face for white supremacy, but was ready to use any means necessary to maintain white power.[29] But each new act of terror and each new level of renewed white support for segregation was met with greater resolve and redoubled efforts by the antiracist forces of the movement. Many of the young women and men who formed the cadre of activists in the peak movement years of the early 1960s recalled seeing images of Till's dead, damaged body in the pages of *Jet* magazine. Some vowed then and there to avenge his death.[30] Till's story was kept alive by movement song activists, and later folk-rock singer Bob Dylan further immortalized him lyrically in his "Ballad of Emmett Till."

The unmistakable intended meaning of the Till murder and others like it is put succinctly by Charles Payne: "Black life could be snuffed out on whim, you could be killed because some ignorant white man didn't like the color of your shirt or the way you drove your wagon.... Those who wanted to work for change had to understand that they were challenging a system that could and would take their lives casually."[31] Most of the imagined acts that allegedly precipitated lynching were as flimsy as the accusation used in the Till case. If one could be killed for an innocent remark, or in another contemporaneous case, for not getting out of the way of a white man driving his car, then how much more dangerous must it have been to openly challenge the racial hierarchy that random terror was meant to uphold. Imagine what danger faced a civil rights worker under such conditions. Virtually everyone who took up the civil rights cause in the South, black or white, was essentially put under threat of death. They could expect to lose their jobs, be beaten many times, have their homes fire-bombed or fired on in drive-by shootings, have threats made against the lives of their children and other relatives. If these acts of intimidation did not work, and for most they did not, then the next level was assassination. The list of those who died for the civil rights cause is a long one.

While song was not the only means by which fear was overcome, it appears again and again in accounts of that process. The "litanies against fear" that freedom songs became were an indispensable part of a deep-seated process of personal political transformation. As Bruce Hartford remembers it, "We were singing.... Somehow, I can't explain it, through the singing and the sense of solidarity we made a kind of psychological barrier between us and the mob. Somehow we made such a wall of strength that they couldn't physically push through it to hit us with their sticks. It wasn't visual, but you could almost see our singing and our unity pushing them back."[32] Cordell Reagon's choice of words is likewise revealing in this regard: "You know you are . . . going to get . . . beaten, you know you might even get killed, but the sound, the power of the community, was watching over you and keeping you safe."[33] Note that it is "sound" that contains the power of community, the sound of the freedom songs.

The direct practical power of this singing as empowerment is illustrated by an occurrence during one of the dramatic follow-ups to the sit-in wave, the "freedom rides." The freedom riders were black and white activists attempting to ride interstate buses across the South, stopping at and integrating bus stations along the way. The rides met with brutal resistance at virtually every stop. There were so many casualties among the CORE volunteers who started the rides that SNCC had to step in to replenish the ranks. After the bombing of buses in two cities, after brutal beatings in other cities, the freedom riders crossed the border into the most vicious state in all the South, Mississippi. One of the ride organizers, CORE's James Farmer, recalls that crossing: "Our hearts jumped into our mouths. The Mississippi National Guard flanked the highway, their guns pointed toward the forest on both sides of the road. One of the riders broke out singing, and we all picked it up. I remember the words: 'I'm taking a ride on the Greyhound bus line / I'm riding the front seat to Jackson this time / Hallelujah I'm a traveling / Hallelujah ain't it fine / Hallelujah I'm a traveling / Down freedom's main line.'"[34] This spontaneous generation of new verses helped calm the fear by reminding the freedom riders that they had been there before, and they had survived. At the same time, it incorporated the new foe into the familiar terrain of the foe already met and faced down, and thereby cut the enemy down to size.

Another kind of song used against white terrorism was the parody. These songs seem aimed at demystifying whites, showing their hypocrisy and the relative poverty of their motives in the struggle. This song, for example, was sung to the tune "Jesus Loves Me, This I Know": "Jesus loves me cause I'm white / Lynch me a nigger every night. / Hate the Jews and I hate the Pope / Jes' me and my rope. / Jesus loves me, the Citizens' Council told me so." And here is a rather different verse sung to "We Shall Overcome": "Deep in my heart, I do believe / We shall keep the niggers down / They will never be free-eee-eee / They will never be registered, / We shall keep the niggers down."[35] As Charles Payne notes, much of the humor in these songs was "an attack on fear." The Klan and the Citizens' Councils that held people in thrall were made less threatening. The courage to take on the life-threatening task of organizing could be gently instilled.

The Western tradition as embodied in the English language makes a series of reductive oppositional concepts that make little sense in the context of the civil rights movement. Practical/idealistic, transcendent/immanent, sacred/secular, spiritual/political, these oppositions make little sense in a movement where transcendence, idealism, and spirituality generated great, immanent, practical, earthly power. "Over my head I see freedom in the air." There is a transcendence of self here that is also an immanent sense of personal power. It is not transcendence based necessarily in faith in a reward somewhere else. Traditional religion could offer that. It was very much a sense of power and satisfaction and personal reward felt in the moment, in the movement. Freedom songs deepened the sense of religious devotion in those whose connection to the movement was rooted in Christianity, but it also worked on the spirit of those with more secular orientations. Transcendence was immanent in the fight. Freedom was in the air freedom fighters breathed, not up in heaven. One verse that might otherwise seem strange makes perfect sense in this context: "we'll never turn back until we've all been free." Note that it is not until all "are free" but all have "been free." The movement didn't just talk about freedom, it gave it. Being free was part of the experience of the movement. But "freedom is a constant struggle," not a state achieved once and for all. At the deepest level, that sense of freedom came from overcoming the fear of death. While transcending the fear of death is often discussed as a metaphysical issue, in the movement it was very much a practical political issue. Fear, including the ultimate fear of death, had long been and was still a tool of white oppression. Without the ability to overcome that fear, there would have been no civil rights movement, no matter what political opportunities or economic structures came into place.

Music as Strategy and Tactic

The movement did not happen because black people just "woke up one morning with their minds set on freedom." "Freedom is a constant struggle." "You have to keep your eyes on the prize," not "let anybody turn you round." You have to know "which side you're on," "never turn back until we've all been free and we have equality." "We shall not be moved." "Ninety-nine and half percent" of commitment won't do. "You better leave segregation alone."

These are lines quoted or paraphrased from freedom songs, rearranged a bit and with a few prepositional phrases to provide continuity. I mean to suggest in this way that a good many ideas about movement needs, values, tactics, and ideology were conveyed and reiterated through song. In addition to the key role of fighting off paralyzing fear, songs played other strategic and tactical roles. As Charles Payne notes, "The changing fortunes of the movement and the morale of its participants could have been gauged by the intensity of the singing at the meetings. Music had always been a central part of the black religious experience. Ministers knew that a good choir was a good recruiting device. In the same fashion, many who came to meetings came just to hear the singing."[36]

This is music that bypasses the commercial interests of the music industry, and it also downplays the importance of singing expertise. Singing in the black tradition is very much a participatory event. Thus, going to a meeting, even just to listen, could quickly lead to deeper levels of involvement. Get their voices, one might say, and their politics will follow. Music becomes more deeply ingrained in memory than mere talk, and this quality made it a powerful organizing tool. It is one thing to hear a political speech and remember an idea or two. It is quite another to sing a song and have its politically charged verses become emblazoned on your memory. In singing you take on a deeper level of commitment to an idea than if you only hear it spoken of. The movement was all about "commitment," and singing was often a halfway house to commitment.

Music could be used to deepen specific kinds of engagement as well. Mississippi organizer Sam Block, for example, recalls using songs strategically to ease people into greater degrees of leadership. He recalls that freedom songs were important as "an organizing tool to bring people together—not only to bring them together but also the organizational glue to hold them together. I started to give people the responsibility of thinking about a song they would want to sing that night and of changing that song, you know, from a gospel song [to a freedom one]."[37] This deepening of commitment through song had much to do with the body as well. Civil rights workers spoke often of "putting your body on the line" for the cause. Bodies were literally the weapon of the movement, and "on the line" often meant in the line of fire, for fists, firehoses, spit, and sometimes bullets. The act of singing, as Bernice Reagon describes so well, is also a deeply physical thing. To let your voice go, to put it "out there," was also in meetings a kind of rehearsal for, and in demonstrations an act of, putting your body on the line. The sense of personal power felt in the act of singing in full resonance among a mass of fellows was translated into movement power on the front lines. Reagon recalls a voter registration meeting in 1962 in which "the Negroes began to sing. The voices that were weak at first gained strength as they moved up the scale with the old familiar words 'We are climbing Jacob's ladder.'" When the local sheriff came to disrupt the meeting, the singing grew stronger, culminating in a rousing chorus of "We Shall Overcome" as the sheriff retreated.

Beyond helping recruitment and deepening commitment, music served to convey the key values and tactics of the movement. Kerran Sanger notes that often the order of verses in a song enacted a move from abstractions (freedom, equality) to concrete acts to secure that value (sitting in, going to jail, breaking an injunction).[38] Various kinds of mass demonstrations, from marches to civil disobedience actions, were central to the movement. Initially, most demonstrations were silent, since any sign of "rowdiness" would be used as a pretext for assault. Songs were first used only in rallies and in workshops teaching nonviolence. But eventually it became clear that they could become key elements in demonstrations and civil disobedience actions. Any time large numbers of black people gathered in the South, they were viewed as a threat, as a potential mob. Singing (along with prayer) became a perfect way both to keep a mass from becoming a mob, and to convey to opponents that one was witnessing an organized event, not a mob action. Songs conveyed messages of quiet defiance, not rage, and clarified the values, stakes, and issues of the action. Singing could be both a rehearsal for collective activity and a direct part of the action. Singers are not generally imagined as threatening figures. By their very posture and activity, the singing activists conveyed their nonviolent intentions.

Songs were often the primary means to convey this difficult idea of nonviolent struggle. Nonviolence was a core value of the movement, but like much else it was interpreted differently by different civil rights workers. For some it was a deeply held, often religious principle. For others, its value was primarily tactical. In some situations, particularly in rural areas, activists were sometimes forced to carry guns in self-defense, even as they remained committed to nonviolence in their movement actions. Especially in a situation where the opponent had a near monopoly on the tools of violence, and where the use of that violence was often legitimated by public opinion, nonviolence is a powerful weapon. Many songs juxtapose acts of violence on the part of the segregationists to the nonviolence of the protesters: "We've met jail and violence too / But God's love has seen us through," or "We're gonna board that big Greyhound / Carrying love from town to town." These verses, both from "Keep Your Eyes on the Prize," refer to the movement's adaptation of Christian love for one's enemies, as interpreted through the long tradition of pacifism. Love was almost as great a theme as freedom in the movement, used effectively to contrast with the hate unleashed by white supremacy in the form of police dog attacks, beatings, and myriad other forms of violence.

When situations did threaten to get out of control of the organizers, music could also serve more proactively as a tactic to change the mood and thereby the action of the participants. Music could calm a tense situation. Or music could ignite a tired mass. Sometimes the same song could do either, depending on the tempo and spirit with which it was sung. There is no such thing as a definitive version of a freedom song, because they were constantly adapted to the needs of particular situations, conditions, and locales.

"We Shall Not Be Moved": Communicating outside the Movement

That the freedom songs played many and varied roles internally in the movement is abundantly clear. But what about songs as a means of communicating to the worlds outside the movement? Did the music have the power to transform people not involved in the movement? Outright racist defenders of white supremacy were largely immune to that power, though a few stories of such extreme conversions can be found. But among those undecided, those unsure of how to think about the movement, the effect could be quite significant. Many, many accounts exist of bystanders being deeply moved by the dignity and power of the protesters in song. As one activist put it, "The music doesn't change governments. Some bureaucrat or some politician isn't going to be changed by some music he hears. But we can change people—individual people.

The people can change governments."[39] In particular, the movement's singing power had an impact on the press, whose surprising degree of sympathy for the civil rights activists is neither typical nor predictable, given the norms of the profession. Compared to political rhetoric, with which most white reporters had the familiarity that breeds contempt, movement music was something else, a different register of ideas and feelings against which the press had fewer built-in defenses. One white southern journalist recalls that the "songs, the mass meetings, not only made common place rituals of the society I lived in, the white society, seem pale by contrast, but spoke a condemnation that made them too, unpalatable."[40] Stories are also told of jailers and police sometimes moved by the songs to lessen their brutality. Southern wardens often seemed to enjoy the singing as a change from the dull routines of prison life, little suspecting that they were witnessing not "darkies" singing but activists communicating.

The nature of the audience of movement songs is a complicated question. On the one hand, lyrical phrases like "We shall not be moved" seem like statements directed at outsiders. But more often they seem to me to be directed internally as a reminder not to "be moved." Similarly, we hear the phrase "We are not afraid," and this seems at once wishful thinking and a truth. Or, more properly, it is wishful thinking becoming truth as the act of singing itself gives the courage not initially felt. Movement songs seldom seem directly aimed at outsiders, because to do so would be to lessen the activists' sense of their own power. It was more as if they were willing to be overheard making their musical declarations.

The more important outside audience for freedom songs was no doubt the fence-sitters, sympathetic perhaps but confused, frightened, or just not yet knowledgeable enough concerning what the movement was all about. James Farmer, in jail during the freedom rides, rewrote the 1930s labor song, "Which Side Are You On?" as a freedom song with just this kind of work in mind: "I rewrote the old labor song . . . on the spur of the moment in the Hinds County jail. After the Freedom Riders who were imprisoned [with me] had been discussing and speculating about the attitude of local Negroes regarding the Freedom Rides." With this in mind, his rewrite directly challenges the fence-sitters: "They say in Hinds County, no neutrals have we met / You're either for the Freedom Ride or you 'tom' for [segregationist governor] Ross Barnett // Oh people can you stand it, tell me how you can / Will you be an Uncle Tom or will you be a man?" Challenging white-subservient "Uncle Toms" was the most aggressive form of address to those not yet in the movement. More common were songs of invitation, or songs that acknowledged levels of commitment. A good example occurs in the song "I'm on My Way to Freedom Land": "I'll ask my brother to come with me / I'm on my way, Great God, I'm on my way // If he can't come, I'm gonna go anyhow...// If you can't go, don't hinder me // ... If you can't go, let your children go, / I'm on my way, Great God, I'm on my way to freedom land."[41] This lyric allows three levels of commitment: "come with me," or at least "don't hinder me" (perhaps by being an informer), and if you can't help, at least "let your children go." This last line is especially important because as the movement became youth-driven in many places after 1960, generational conflict became a vital issue. The best young organizers were those who built upon the knowledge and organizational base of the World War II generation of activists in order to help bridge this gap. A brilliant practitioner of this was young black organizer Bob Moses, who after leaving graduate school at Harvard to join SNCC, worked closely and respectfully with the older Mississippi veteran activist Amzie Moore. As Charles Payne characterizes it, "Older activists [had] created...cooptable networks, and a younger generation found new uses for them."[42] In this process as in so many others, music proved a useful bridging tool to bring older people in or at least to let their "children go" to movement land.

Music, Collectivity, and Identity

Beyond particular strategic needs, music strengthened and transformed personal and collective identity for movement workers. One of the main dynamics in any social movement is the relationship between individual and collective identity. People enter movements as individuals, and must continue to feel a sense of individual commitment, but at the same time they must gain a sense of collective identity as part of the group effort that is the defining feature of movements. The civil rights movement handled this delicate balance of individualism and collectivity better than most movements, and once again, music played a significant role. Listen, for example, to this line from the most famous song in movement repertoire, "We Shall Overcome": "Deep in my heart I do believe, we shall overcome some day." Note how the line starts with an individualized statement of commitment "I do believe," then shifts to the collective with "we shall overcome." The song actually began its life as a black spiritual, "I'll Be Alright," and was adapted in 1945 by the mostly black, mostly female members of a tobacco union in Charlotte, North Carolina. It was they who turned the "I'll" to "We" to support their collective union struggle. The song received further refinement and adaptation to the civil rights struggle by Zilphia Horton, the first music director at Highlander. She taught it to folksinger Pete Seeger who in turn taught it in 1950 to the man who became Highlander's second music director, Guy Carawan. But it was not until 1960, when Carawan held a South-wide song workshop, that the song started to gain a central role in the movement. Three weeks after that, it was a featured song at the founding SNCC convention. In making it their own, the students further changed it musically and lyrically. Thus, the song most identified with the collective identity of the movement evolved through many *individuals* contributing to its creation.

Music, of course, was not the only force in shaping movement identities, but it clearly was among the most powerful. Bernice Reagon beautifully illustrates, for example, how a moment of musical improvisation can be a direct outgrowth of, and contributor to, collective action, even as it also brings personal transformation. In the midst of a tense moment during the struggle in Albany, Reagon recalls: "Charlie Jones looked at me and said, 'Bernice, sing a song.' And I started 'Over My Head I See Trouble in the Air.' By the time I got to where 'trouble' was supposed to be, I didn't see any trouble, so I put 'freedom' in there."[43] I suggest that in the moment, Reagon is not simply expressing a change of feeling, but enacting it as the music changes her. As she describes it: "The voice I have now I got the first time I sang in a movement meeting, after I got out of jail. I did the song, 'Over My Head I See Freedom in the Air,' but I had never heard that voice before. I had never been that me before. And once I became that me, I have never let that me go."[44] The notion of being born again in the spirit is deep in certain Christian traditions. As Reagon suggests, the movement bred such feelings too. The sense of a freedom deeper than freedom pervades the stories told by movement folks. The word *transcendence* is usually used to describe something above and beyond mere politics. But in the movement, transcendence of self was also a discovery of self. Gaining a sense of "somebodiness" that was so crucially a part of the movement's work often came paradoxically when the self was given up to a larger whole, a collective spirit.

The claiming of a positive sense of blackness is often credited to the black power phase of the African American freedom struggle in the latter part of the 1960s, but the civil rights years laid down some important elements of that identity reclamation project. And music was a key part of that project. For many southern blacks, particularly those from the middle classes, the great spirituals and gospel songs reworked by the movement were part of a heritage they sought to deny in favor of cultural forms with more cachet in the white world. For many movement participants, reclaiming freedom songs was part of claiming an identity as self-defined black people proud of their ancestry, rather than as white-defined "Negroes." The urban black power identity, discussed in the next chapter, owes more of a debt to the civil rights phase of the movement than is generally acknowledged.

Charles Payne summarizes this evolutionary process as embodied in the music and other rituals of local mass meetings: "Mixtures of the sacred and the profane, the mass meetings could be a very powerful social ritual. They attracted people and then helped them develop a sense of involvement and solidarity. By acting out new definitions of their individual and collective selves, people helped make those selves become real. Informed and challenged by the speakers, pumped up by the singing and the laughing and the sense of community, many of those who only meant to go once out of curiosity left that first meeting thinking they might come once more, just to see."[45] And that "once more" often became many more, and that performed self-singing became the real self acting for change.

Music as Captivity Narrative

Why *freedom* songs? Why not justice songs, or equality songs, or some other term? *Freedom* was the touchstone word of the movement. The songs and the movement had an elective affinity: freedom was from the beginning a major theme of the movement, but the songs played a role in making that concept even more central to movement ideology. Why was that word so important? It had both breadth and depth. First, there was the historical depth, the resonance with the major fact of black history, slavery, as we have already discussed. In addition, the term points to an open-ended present and future; it could mean many things in the imaginations of many different participants and potential participants. *Freedom* was also one of the few political words almost universally embraced by Americans, at least in theory. *Equality,* probably the only competitor for the label, is by comparison, a far more controversial concept. Perhaps most important, in the South the concept of freedom had great resonance because all black people in the region had felt deeply a sense of unfreedom, had felt fettered by having to restrain and contain themselves in order to play the roles demanded by a segregated society. While equality might have suggested a desire to be like white people, freedom suggested an open horizon to explore the many realms that had been declared out of bounds to black people. Freedom worked on many levels, from the most intimate to the most broadly public.

There is another, more specific way in which freedom resonated especially well in the movement. One of the most important sites for both the composition and singing of freedom songs was jail. Much of the movement was based on the tactic of nonviolent civil disobedience, the purposeful breaking of a law judged to be unjust. Since the whole system of segregation was unjust to blacks, occasions for going to jail were many. Beyond that, the entire civil rights movement was essentially declared illegal by the white southern power structure that harassed activists constantly, arresting them for petty or made-up offenses above and beyond acts of civil disobedience. Going to jail, therefore, was a major fact of life for movement participants, and it could be the most grueling and dangerous part of the work. It could be particularly frightening for those raised with conservative religious views. Thus, several songs have God endorsing and even demanding the experience: "Well, have you been to jail? certainly Lord, / Certainly, certainly, certainly Lord."[46]

Freedom songs also became a favorite way to pass time, maintain solidarity, keep spirits high, and communicate while in jail. Incarceration also provided long hours of time to write, rewrite, and otherwise develop the freedom song tradition. "We were in the Hinds County jail, and we were fasting and singing all the time. We were in separate cells, but we could sing to each other so it wasn't bad."[47] Another account shows how music kept solidarity alive even in solitary confinement. Bob Zellner, a white southern movement activist, was placed in solitary after being threatened with castration by other white prisoners. His movement mate Chuck McDew was placed in solitary at the same time. They were in five-by-seven-foot cells with only a five-inch-square ventilation opening and a small grate in the ceiling. Zellner heard a familiar whisper coming from the ceiling, and realized McDew was in the cell directly above him: "Then we sang. As the police pounded on the door threatening to whip us we sang 'Woke Up This Morning with My Mind Set on Freedom.' Even after they turned the heaters on and blasted us with unbearable heat for seven days, we continued to sing— 'We'll walk hand in hand.' "[48]

Freedom songs did some of their best work in jail where they made all the more palpable the feeling that freedom was in the air, air that could move freely, like the mind and the spirit, out of the confines of a prison cell or the prison house of a racist society.

Musical Pleasures

In stressing the important, even instrumental role music played in the movement, one should remember that singing could be a plain old source of pleasure and recreation. Movement work was often unimaginably arduous. In such a context, but in any movement context really, there needs to be time for pleasure and relaxation. And there too music was often the key. In addition to songs drawn into the movement for specific practical uses, there was music around just for fun. SNCC activist and later U.S. congressional representative John Lewis recalls that in addition to the freedom songs, and sometimes as a respite from them, he spent many a long drive down country roads listening to the latest pop songs on local radio stations, especially with the emergence of "soul" music in the 1960s.

"Soul" music later became, according to former Black Panther leader Elaine Brown, the "soundtrack" to the black power movement and may have, to a far lesser degree, played a political role in that phase of the black freedom struggle. But in the context of the civil rights struggle, it was more often the soundtrack used to forget the movement for a while. Some pop songs, like Ray Charles's "Hit the Road, Jack," which became "Get Your Rights, Jack," or Harry Belafonte's "Banana Boat Song," which found a freedom rider version, did become part of the freedom song repertoire. But Lewis's point is that the hard, patient, dangerous work of organizing was grueling, and any movement that does not leave room for just plain fun is likely to burn out its participants. Given the constant threat they faced, this need was particularly strong in those freedom fighters in the rural deep South, but everywhere music was in the air, sometimes even in the form of freedom from freedom songs with their powerfully disturbing reminders of the struggle.[49]

Singing as and against Ideology

"When Mrs. Hamer finishes singing a few freedom songs one is aware that he has truly heard a fine political speech, stripped of the usual rhetoric and filled with the anger and determination of the civil rights movement. And on the other hand in her speeches there is the constant thunder of and drive of music."[50] Fannie Lou Hamer was not alone in being able to turn a series of songs into political speech. Many organizers learned to do something like this. The movement's best organizers understood that success required an unusual degree of openness in terms of movement ideology and strategy. Situations varied so much from state to state, county to county, and between rural and urban black communities, not to mention the varied class, gender, sexual, and educational backgrounds that further complicated organizing. A single approach to ideology and struggle would most certainly have failed to create the solidarity necessary to succeed. Given this situation, songs were uniquely suited as organizing tools. As we saw, sometimes people would just come for the music, and then find themselves drawn into the fray before they knew it. Movement ideas could be conveyed to the illiterate and to the literate who were deeply rooted in an oral tradition.

The larger point here is that music, as the center but hardly the whole of the movement culture, functioned as an overarching site. It served not only as an active tactical force and strategic unifier but also, more fundamentally, as a baseline context in which differences could coexist. Movement cultures function best when they both express and move beyond ideology. Ideologies—elaborated key ideas and values—are crucially important to any movement. But they are also often the points of contention that pull movements apart. The very vagueness (or more positively, open-endedness) of "cultural" forms, which has kept many social scientists from examining them seriously as a movement force, is precisely one of their virtues. Sometimes open-ended expressions can do work that more precise forms cannot. The "freedom" in freedom songs was never very precisely defined. As we have seen, it could be made very concrete in particular situations, such as the freedom to be served respectfully at a lunch counter. But it could also mean many things to many different people. Freedom songs formed the core of an extraordinarily rich movement culture that harmonized diverse constituencies, values, strategies, tactics, and goals, and in doing so they became a central force in moving this nation further down that long, unfinished journey to a place beyond racism.

From Freedom Songs to Power Plays

The accomplishments of the civil rights movement between the mid-1950s and mid-1960s are quite astonishing. Two major federal civil rights acts in 1964 and 1965 greatly extended rights for all Americans, especially for people of color. By the late 1960s the vicious system of legal segregation in the South had been almost totally dismantled, and with it much of the systematic white terrorism that stood behind it. The Citizenship Schools and Freedom Schools that grew up during the movement had also by mid-decade laid the groundwork for the radical reworking of black history that was a key stage in the evolution of what we now call "multiculturalism." Indeed, it is hard to overestimate the effect of the civil rights movement in transforming American culture. Yet its limitations must also be confronted. For many participants who could not see the long-term impact of their actions, the movement seemed as much a failure as a success by the mid-1960s. More recently, the movement has borne the burden of mainstream acceptance, becoming hallowed as an American success story by the very forces of complacency that stood in the 1960s and stand now in the way of further progress toward racial justice. The movement has become a museum piece, its radical power stuck in amber, its meanings reduced to Martin Luther King Day platitudes. This process of denying or forgetting the radical dimensions of the movement began already in the late 1960s when new, allegedly more radical forces arose in challenge.

On the Meredith march, one of the last great events of the civil rights phase, SNCC leader Stokely Carmichael scripted a performance that would signal a shift to new sites and styles of black struggle. Carmichael planned his speech for the rally that night as a direct counter to and challenge of Martin Luther King's leadership of the march. Carmichael's chosen method of combat was a battle of key words. In such rallies, it was common for a speaker to shout, in call and response style, "What do we want?" to which the traditional civil rights response was "Freedom now!" But on this night Carmichael had asked his comrade Willie

Ricks to seed the audience with people armed with a different script. Timed to Carmichael's call, Ricks and others shouted back not "Freedom now!" but rather "Black power! Black power!" The phrase quickly drew media attention, and was read as signaling a split in the movement. As open-ended as the term *freedom,* the phrase *black power* came to have a dizzying array of meanings, but at that moment it did indeed signal a sea change in the movement.[51]

The civil rights movement had always been about power. It wielded its power quite successfully in all the ways discussed here, and more important, it empowered thousands of ordinary African Americans. But especially for those on the front lines of SNCC and others among the hardcore organizers, the accomplishments seemed thin compared to the sacrifice, and the emotional and physical scars ran deep. In relation to the abiding poverty and continuing racism in the South and the North, they did not feel very powerful. These people understood better than most the work still undone. They particularly understood it when they looked to the northern ghettos where a long period of freedom from legal segregation had not removed other deep economic, political, and cultural forces of racial injustice. Drawing strength from the southern struggle even as it strongly critiqued it, the black power phase of black struggle took center stage.

TWO

Scenarios for Revolution
The Drama of the Black Panthers

The scene opens in the parking lot of the California state capitol building in Sacramento. It is the spring of 1967. Thirty young black people,
twenty-four men and six women, are pulling rifles, twelve-gauge shot-
guns, and .357-magnum handguns out of their car trunks and loading
them. Dressed in uniforms of black berets, black leather jackets, and
powder blue shirts, they begin to move in loose formation up the steps
to the capitol. One of the young black men on the scene shouts, "Look
at Reagan run!" as then governor and future president Ronald Reagan
beats a hasty retreat in the face of this phalanx of armed black Americans. But the troops are not especially interested in the governor. They
are headed into the legislative chamber. Some hold their guns pointed
to the sky, others point them to the ground. As they walk around the
outer perimeter of the assembly chamber, people clear a path for them
amid many astonished looks. Photographers and TV camera operators
are ahead of them, walking backward as they move closer to the doors of
the chamber. About five or six feet from the gateway into the assembly
hall, a security officer jumps in front of the black man at the head of the
action and shouts, "Where the hell are you goin'?" The man calmly
replies, "I am going to exercise my constitutional right to see my government making laws, and my right under the second amendment to
bear arms."

Someone shouts with alarm, "There are Black Panthers with guns on
the second floor of the capitol!" And he is right. It is 2 May 1967, and the
men and women who appear to be about to raid the center of govern-

ment are members of the recently formed Black Panther Party for Self-Defense. They have driven up in a caravan of cars from their headquarters in Oakland.

Some of the armed Panthers make their way onto the assembly floor, others are in the viewing balcony above. As the cameras continue to roll, very confused-looking legislators mumble and shout. Amid much agitation, the Panthers leave the scene and return to the capitol steps, where Panther chairman Bobby Seale, leader of the action, reads Panther minister of defense Huey Newton's "Executive Mandate #1": "The Black Panther Party for Self-Defense calls upon the American people in general and the black people in particular to take careful note of the racist California Legislature which is now considering legislation aimed at keeping black people disarmed and powerless at the very same time that racist police agencies throughout the country are intensifying the terror, brutality, murder and repression of black people."[1] That night, TV news around California, the nation, and the world presented pictures of the dramatic encounter, including Seale reading the mandate, as in the background, possibly for the first time, the noun *motherfucker* makes its way onto broadcast television.

The black power movement was mostly an urban, northern movement complementing, building on, and critiquing the mostly southern, often more rural, civil rights phase of the black freedom movement. Some argue that black power is part of the civil rights struggle, others see it as a break with the movement. It was both. The peak years of black power, roughly 1965–75, brought a profound transformation in American life, inside and beyond black communities. Black power brought a sweeping change in consciousness and identity for black people, and it shaped every level of African American life. While moderate and even conservative voices continued to exist in the black community, the dominant voices of the era spoke the language of black power.

The loudest of these voices belonged to members of the Black Panther Party, who burst onto the stage of history through the "scene" I narrated above. The "real life" events on the capitol steps unfolded in the dramatic way I have told them. The guerrilla theater siege of Sacramento was one of many dramatic moments in what was a very dramatic time. The talking blues, proto-rap artist Gil Scott-Heron sang in 1968 that the "revolution will not be televised." But he was only half right. Much of the revolution going on in America at that time was televised, or at least reported via the television, and that fact shaped the history of the period in positive and negative ways. The black power phase of the civil rights/black liberation movement dominated much of the iconography and dramaturgy of the late 1960s. The phrase "the drama of the Black Panthers" in my chapter subtitle is meant to name two different things: (1) a body of theater work designed to act as part of the cultural arm of the black power movement; and (2) the fact that much of the black power movement itself, particularly the Black Panther Party, can be understood as a kind of theatrical performance. This second point is not meant to belittle the Black Panthers, but rather to take them more seriously. All politics involves a theatrical element, and a failure to understand the relation between the "poetics" and the "politics" of the Panthers is a failure to understand them at all.[2] Much of the public activity of the Black Panthers was built around highly dramatic, stylized confrontations, often involving guns and the police. These are among the main actions that earned them notoriety. This theatricality was in many ways the most important cultural contribution of the Panthers, but it was also their greatest political limitation.

Hegemony—the process of getting people to unwittingly consent to their own oppression—takes place largely by accretion, by having many, many sites reinforcing the same ideas. In the case of black Americans, many sites in white and black America were very much teaching messages of black intellectual and cultural inferiority at the moment black power arose. The cultural front of the black power movement exerted considerable influence because it managed to launch new messages of black pride and empowerment into so many different spaces on so many levels of culture. The black power movement included an intellectual formation, led by figures as diverse as Malcolm X, Huey Newton, Toni Cade Bambara, Angela Davis, Ron Karenga, and Stokely Carmichael, among many others, and it spawned an immensely influential new intellectual field, black studies. Black power also included a variety of pervasive cultural formations in the literary and performing arts centered on the notion of an independent "black aesthetic." The black arts/black aesthetic movement reshaped virtually all the arts: jazz and soul music, painting, dance, poetry, and theater. Black power also reshaped black theology, sports, even black folkways. It influenced what people ate ("soul food"), what clothes and hairstyles they wore (African-derived fashions, "natural" or "Afro" hair), what holidays they celebrated (Kwanzaa instead of Christmas), the language they spoke (a "soulful rap" expressing black pride, declaiming that "black is beautiful"), and the gestures they made (black power handshakes, the raised-fist black power salute).

Many of these attributes and styles were said to possess "soul," something like the everyday-life or folk equivalent of the black aesthetic in its celebration of the unique and positive dimensions of black style.[3] Black power cultural forms also reshaped popular culture, particularly music, drawing in previously nonpolitical performers like James Brown ("Say It Loud, I'm Black and I'm Proud"), and generating a radical revision of the talking blues in artists like Gil Scott-Heron and the Last Poets. While music was not as central a force in the black power movement as it had been in the civil rights struggle, it did provide the soundtrack for black power, and even the Black Panthers had their own soul music group, The Lumpens. In sum, virtually no corner of black life remained untouched by radical cultural revisions.

The black power movement had within it a vast array of political ideologies, and its most radical political agenda certainly was not achieved. But as historian William Van Deburg argues, if it did not achieve the political revolution many called for, it did succeed in revolutionizing black consciousness in ways that continue to echo today and have profound political importance. Van Deburg contends that "black power is best understood as a broad, adaptive, cultural term serving to connect and illuminate the differing ideological orientations of the movement's supporters. Conceptualized in this manner, the black power movement does not appear, [as] it so often has, a cacophony of voices and actions resulting in only minuscule gains for black people. Viewing the movement through the window of culture allows us to see that language, folk culture, religion, and the literary and performing arts served to spread the militants' philosophy farther than did mimeographed political broadsides."[4] Especially if one includes speeches among the "performing arts" and also, as I will argue here, certain black power movement actions as "theater," I think this is an important insight. Much of the black power movement's political impact came through cultural channels, but without the political movement that impact would have been much reduced. The changes brought by the movement varied considerably in long-term impact, and the key force accounting for these variations was the degree to which style changes were connected to specific political ideas and movement fractions.

Black Nationalisms

As we saw at the end of chapter 1, the phrase *black power* had its origin in a highly staged event during the southern struggle. Stokely Carmichael's dramatic use of the new phrase encapsulated an important rhetorical and political shift in the black movement. The move from "freedom now" to "black power" embodied a sense that overthrowing the constraints of segregation would not be enough if substantial shifts in economic and political power failed to follow. The new slogan's immediate effect was to deepen a split in the southern movement, but its larger, long-range impact was mostly in northern ghettos.

Both the flair for dramatic symbolism and the rhetorical weight of the phrase "black power!" moved rapidly to the center of the urban northern phase of the movement. By 1967 "black power" was the term most often used to name the northern struggle. The desperate, angry mood of the ghettos was apparent through a series of "riots" or "urban insurrections," depending on your ideological viewpoint, that tore up America in the 1960s. A series of "long hot summers" began with a violent riot in the African American Watts section of Los Angeles in 1965, and was followed in subsequent years by massive insurrections in Chicago, Detroit, Newark, and a hundred other cities across the country. The government commission investigating the "civil disturbances" found evidence of "two Americas, one Black, one white," moving in opposite directions. The black power movement attempted to give shape to the inchoate "black rage" that fueled the riots, and to turn it into empowerment rather than self-destruction.[5]

Stokely Carmichael's version of "black power" had been sharpened during his organizing of an alternative political party in Lowndes County, Alabama, one of the most dangerous places in the South to organize. The symbol of that party was a black panther, and some folks involved referred to it as the "black panther party." When a year later two brash young black men, Huey Newton and Bobby Seale, formed a new political organization in Oakland, California, one of the nation's toughest ghettos, they named that party the Black Panther Party for Self-Defense in homage to their Lowndes County predecessors.

The new organization formed by Newton and Seale quickly became the most visible, best known embodiment of the symbolism, rhetoric, and ideology of this black power movement. The movement drew not only on radical currents in the southern struggle, but also on a long history, going back at least to the eighteenth century, of African American ideas and organizing under the concept of "black nationalism." While present in a variety of incarnations with quite different ideological agendas, from conservative to revolutionary, the essence of black nationalism was the notion that in some sense blacks in America were a nation apart. Rather than viewing this as a liability to be overcome through integration into white America, black nationalists argued that black people should organize themselves to reflect pride in their history and culture, and to gain a significant degree of independent economic and political power. Due especially to the work of Malcolm X, black nationalism was a mass force again by the time of his assassination in 1965.

The black nationalism of the 1960s is traditionally divided into two main forms, cultural nationalism and political nationalism. Cultural nationalists stressed the development of independent artistic and cultural forms based in black tradition. Political nationalists stressed contestation with and the need to radically alter the white-dominated political and economic system. I want to complicate this useful but limiting distinction by suggesting that cultural nationalism (represented by individuals like poet-playwright Amiri Baraka) and political nationalism (represented by the Black Panther Party) overlapped and intertwined in significant ways. The distinction was and is a serious one; in at least one case it was a deadly one, when armed conflict broke out between representatives of the "political" Panthers and the "cultural" nationalists of Ron Karenga in Los Angeles. But the cultural/political distinction is also misleading, both because the cultural nationalists had political ideas and impact, and, more to the point of this chapter, because the political nationalists had cultural ideas and impact, an impact made largely through dramatic action.

A New Stage of Struggle

The early 1960s saw the rise of two entwined forces that would have a dramatic impact on the style of the Panthers: the rhetoric of Malcolm X and the theater of Leroi Jones/Amiri Baraka. I want to outline here a three-stage evolution of "black power dramatics," from the dramatic speeches of Malcolm X to the plays of Amiri Baraka to the real-life dramatic actions of the Black Panthers. Malcolm was to the northern ghetto what Reverend Martin Luther King Jr. had been to the southern struggle—the great articulator. Malcolm's views on Reverend King and the civil rights struggle changed over time from hostility to respect and qualified support, but throughout his life he argued that conditions in the urban North demanded a different kind of rhetoric and a different kind of strategy than the one used in the southern struggle. Malcolm became the master of a rhetorically violent but carefully legal wake-up call to the urban ghettos. He understood that for blacks in the North the issue was not segregation, though there was plenty of that (missing only the legal sanction given the southern form). Rather, the issue was systematic degradation through a thousand deprivations—poverty, demeaning jobs or unemployment, police brutality, everyday racist insults, inadequate schools, substandard health care—that often led to a sense of self-hatred and despair. Malcolm believed that only a kind of shock therapy addressed to "Negroes" could turn them into proud black actors on the national and world stage. Malcolm's speeches sought, through a metaphor drawn from slave days, to separate out what he called the "house Negro" (or Uncle Tom) who upheld or accepted white racism, from the "field Negroes" who had plotted slave insurrections or violent revenge on the white masters.[6]

At the same time, and under the influence of Malcolm X's rhetoric, a young black poet and playwright named Leroi Jones was turning himself into Amiri Baraka. Jones transformed himself from a Greenwich Village bohemian poet into the playwright Baraka who offered dramatic theater to match the dramatic rhetoric of Malcolm's new black nationalism. As part of a wider black arts movement that included radical poetry, fiction, art, and music, a theater of action aimed to support and/ or enact a black revolution rose rapidly in the mid-1960s. The beginnings of black power theater are usually traced to the work of Jones, who, mirroring a larger process of renaming and collective transformation in black identity in the 1960s, gave up his "slave name" to be reborn as Amiri Baraka. Most historians of black culture see the production of Baraka's play *The Dutchman*, in 1964, as the opening salvo in the black theater revolution. *The Slave* followed in that same year, and before long a whole movement emerged, with dozens of young playwrights following Baraka's lead.

In 1965, in an important symbolic gesture, Baraka moved from Greenwich Village to Harlem, where he began the Black Arts Repertory Theatre and School (BARTS). The school became a testing ground for many black actors and playwrights, as well as a place for Baraka himself to experiment. The civil rights movement had already produced one important theatrical group, the Free Southern Theater, organized by SNCC, and as black power emerged within SNCC that company's work also metamorphosed into a significant black power theatrical force in the South. As it evolved, black power theater took many forms, from full-scale plays to short vignettes meant to be enacted as street theater on corners or lots in the ghetto. The most common form was the one-act play—long enough to develop significant ideas but short enough to reach an audience not used to theater-going. This latter point was important, as the playwrights sought to reach audiences beyond the small middle-class black play-going contingent.

As theater historian Mance Williams describes it, the central task of black power theater was to use dramatic enactments to overcome internalized self-hatred in blacks "who had been brainwashed and psychologically maimed by centuries of physical and mental abuse" (a notion of therapeutic violence found in the immensely influential psychiatrist and theorist of decolonization, Frantz Fanon). For Baraka, violence (rhetorical at least) was a key component of black arts, an element necessary to break through crusted layers of internalized oppression in blacks (and less directly to break through layers of complacency in whites). At the level of style, the black theater movement sought to instill pride by celebrating existing cultural elements in the black community, and synthesizing them into elements of a distinctive "black aesthetic." This meant, according to Williams, that "it would synthesize and codify all those creative and artistic expressions peculiar to Afro-Americans," including not only such indigenous arts forms as gospel music, spirituals, jazz, the blues, and black dance forms, but also such broader cultural styles as black English (black slang, syntax, diction, and speech rhythms) and even elements of black kinesics (ways of walking, gesturing, and body language generally).[7] All these things were, often for the first time, brought into black drama during these revolutionary years. The new black theater often utilized the "call and response" pattern that was built into black religion and much black music to help create a more participatory experience. Sometimes this was accomplished by putting an actual church service on stage with a minister preaching black power or an on-stage "congregation" challenging the lack of black power rhetoric in a traditional minister. Either way, the audience was encouraged to join in. This not only got a black power message across but also undermined the authority of conservative clergy who often stood in the way of the new radical phase of the movement.

In the spirit of black nationalist independence, Baraka insisted that his Black Arts Theatre be run, produced, directed, and acted entirely by blacks, and performed to all-black audiences. In cases where white characters needed to be played, Baraka had black actors apply "whiteface," in symbolic contrast to the long racist tradition of minstrelsy, in which white artists donned blackface makeup to give stereotyped imitations of blacks. In his own plays, Baraka sometimes created self-consciously stereotyped whites as comic figures. His theater would be a "theater of assault":

> The Revolutionary Theatre, which is now peopled with victims, will soon begin to be peopled with new kinds of heroes . . . not the weak Hamlets debating whether or not they are ready to die for what's on their minds, but men and women (and minds) digging out from under a thousand years of "high art" and weakfaced dalliance. We must make an art that will function as to call down the actual wrath of world spirit. We are witchdoctors, and assassins, but we will open a place for the true scientists to expand our consciousness. This is a theatre of assault. The play that will split the heavens for us will be called THE DESTRUCTION OF AMERICA. The heroes will be Crazy Horse, Denmark Vessey, Patrice Lumumba, but not history, not memory, not sad sentimental groping for a warmth in our despair; these will be new men, new heroes, and their enemies most of you who are reading this.[8]

Baraka's assaults on white racism and black fear of freedom were very powerful, and played an important role in the creation of a "black aesthetic" throughout the arts that echoes to this day.

At the same time, Baraka's work was also often virulently misogynist, sexist, anti-Semitic, homophobic, and based on a confining notion of a biological black essence. One reason to champion Black Panther theater over Baraka's work is that the party took official positions against these hideous views, though certainly many members struggled unevenly with them at the personal level.

Where cultural nationalism often became frozen in black essences, the revolutionary political nationalism of the Panthers continued to evolve as political alliances broadened their vision. Newton expressed his distance from purely cultural nationalists in these words:

> There are two kinds of nationalism, revolutionary nationalism and reactionary nationalism. Revolutionary nationalism is first dependent upon a people's revolution with the end goal being the people in power....
>
> Cultural nationalism, or pork chop nationalism, as I sometimes call it, is basically a problem of having the wrong political perspective. It seems to be a reaction instead of responding to political oppression. The cultural nationalists are concerned with returning to the old African culture and thereby regaining their identity and freedom. In other words, they feel that the African culture will automatically bring political freedom....
>
> The Black Panther Party, which is a revolutionary group of black people, realizes that we have to have an identity. We have to realize our Black heritage in order to give us strength to move on and progress. But as far as returning to the old African culture, it's unnecessary and it's not advantageous in many respects. We believe that culture itself will not liberate us. We're going to need some stronger stuff.[9]

The Panthers' political approach to culture proved richer than Baraka's cultural approach to politics, a fact Baraka himself implicitly acknowledged when he later developed positions closer to the Marxist internationalism of the party.

Revolutionary Consciousness

While the Panthers rejected what Newton called "pork chop" cultural nationalism (as if eating soul food was inherently liberating), they still learned from it, especially from Baraka's black power drama. Baraka's theatrical ideas influenced the Panthers, both directly through encounters with his work (he lived in San Francisco in the late 1960s), and through the playwright-theorist's influence on another key figure in the new black theater movement, Ed Bullins. A young playwright who had studied with Baraka, Bullins became for a brief time minister of culture for the Panthers and was in their orbit during their and his formative years.[10] According to theater historian Williams, it was Bullins who sought to move black power dramatic ideas more out into the community as "street theater."[11] He is a key link along this line of moving theatricality ever more fully into the movement itself.

Bullins was also a founding member of Black House, a community center/theater in San Francisco that was taken over by the Panthers soon after another Black House founder, Eldridge Cleaver, became minister of information for the party. The Panthers' takeover of a community theater is neatly emblematic of my argument that the party became the leading edge of political-cultural theatrical nationalism. While the seizure of Black House, and Bullins's association with the party, offers evidence of the Panthers' direct connection to black power theater, my claim is broader. My notion is that the party took a feel for drama beyond the playhouse into Panther political actions. They took the kind of shock action theatrics practiced by the new black playwrights out of the theaters and into the streets.

Precisely where the interest in drama came from is something of a side issue, but it is a suggestive fact that Panther cofounder Bobby Seale had acted in local plays, and was by Newton's account a brilliant mimic who undermined the political positions of other, less radical white and black leaders through his right-on imitations of their voices and styles: "[Seale] could also imitate down to the last detail some of the brothers around us. I would crack my sides laughing, not only because his imitations were so good, but also because he could convey certain attitudes and characteristics so sharply. He caught all their shortcomings, the way their ideas failed to meet the needs of the people."[12] In a related claim, I suggest that Panther actions were an imitative extension and critique of cultural nationalist theater.

What theater historian Williams says about the theory and practice of black drama in the 1960s could be said equally well of the theory and practice of the Black Panther Party: "Many of the Black Revolutionary Plays were based on myth, but the myth of revolution the Black playwrights created was no less real than if it had actually taken place. Since theatre occurs in the mind, within the imagination of the spectators, the illusion of revolution can affect the audience if its members are willing to accept the possibility of the real events. In most cases these plays were rituals and rites, designed for purposes of purgation and catharsis and intended, through stylistic incantations, to will into reality an actual revolution."[13] As Williams suggests, the line between a "real" revolution and a revolution in consciousness is not absolute. It is in play along this ambiguous line that I would locate the main successes of both black power theater and black power as theater.

Much of this dramatic theory, it seems to me, describes Black Panther ideology as well as the party's manifestos and speeches. Their impact was dramatic, and their drama drove their impact. Certainly in the life consciousness of one of the most famous black revolutionaries of the era, Angela Davis, it was two dramatic events that she recalled as key moments in her political awakening. Davis remembers that it was hearing Malcolm X speak at Brandeis University that first awakened her to blackness, and it was seeing the image of the armed Panthers on the steps of the California legislature that affirmed in her a sense of the possibility of concerted black revolutionary action. Studying in Germany at the time with Marxist philosopher Theodor Adorno, Davis saw that image of the Panthers in the local Frankfurt newspaper and knew instantly that something new was abrew in her homeland.[14] It would not be long before Davis's own iconic image would have a similarly empowering effect on young black and nonblack women and men throughout the world. To lesser and greater degrees, dramatic images of the Panthers (and their allies like Davis) awakened countless numbers of Negroes into African Americanness. The mass media became enamored of the Panthers, and provided them an audience many times larger than that attending the plays of Baraka, Bullins, and the whole tribe of black playwrights.

Black Panther Power Plays

As Angela Davis confirms, for many the Black Panther Party burst onto the national and international scene through those carefully staged events at the state capitol building in Sacramento with which this chapter began. For my purposes it is a nice coincidence that at the time the governor of California was Ronald Reagan, a man who himself had been an actor, and who would later play a starring role as president in a tragicomic, partly successful attempt in the 1980s to roll back many of the gains made by the wave of social movements that peaked in the 1960s.

The director and lead actor of the Sacramento action, Newton and Seale, had been friends at Merritt Junior College and later talked politics together in the Oakland Poverty Center where Seale worked. Seeing firsthand the limits of government poverty programs deepened their sense of the troubles in the black community and confirmed their belief that liberal reform would not touch those problems. Like their idol Malcolm, they understood the need for black people to organize themselves independent of white influence, and the need to find allies in the wider (and whiter) society. In 1965 the assassination of Malcolm and the riots in Watts deepened their conviction that the black community needed new leadership. Their answer was to draft a Ten-Point Program for a group they called the Black Panther Party for Self-Defense.[15] The ten points included bold demands for decent housing, education in black history, full employment, and release of all people of color from military service (because they should not fight in a racist war in Vietnam) and from prisons (in white America their only real crime was being black). The document ended by quoting the Declaration of Independence to drive home the point that the black community was declaring independence from white supremacy.

The influences behind Black Panther ideology are summed up neatly by the allegorical naming of Chairman Bobby Seale's son, who was born during the black power era. Seale named the boy Malik Nkrumah Stagolee Seale. Malik, the Muslim name adopted by Malcolm X, represents the legacy of black nationalism in the U.S.; Nkrumah, for Kwame Nkrumah, famed leader of anticolonialism in Africa, represents the Third World internationalism of the Panthers; and Stagolee, notorious bad dude of black folklore, represents the Panthers' commitment to the ordinary street "brothas and sistas" of the black community.

This last identity is perhaps the most original contribution of the Panthers, for just as Baraka had put street dudes on the stage as characters, Black Panther theater took black street style and recoded it with a revolutionary new message. The aura of violence in the blues/folkloric image of Stagolee as the tough black dude (and to a lesser degree bluesy "nasty gals") gets transferred into a threat of black self-defense, and possibly offense, against whites. Many young black men and women, often after passing through the battle zones of riots/insurrections, began to transform the strut and stride of the street hustler into the assertive posture of the black revolutionary. Anthropologists and sociologists have long noted the deep importance of "performativity" in the black community, the premium put on highly stylized forms of behavior. In this cultural context, Panther style was substance. The black aesthetic movement popularized the expression "black is beautiful," but it was the beautiful men and women of the Panthers, standing erect, nattily dressed in black leather, arms raised in clenched-fist black power salutes, marching in tight formation, who gave body to the phrase. The Panthers were nothing if not telegenic. The television screens in late 1960s America were filled with images of Panthers looking both black and powerful. The message contained in those theatrical gestures helped awaken thousands of black people to new ways of being, especially when backed by street-level organizing, powerful community word of mouth, and concrete programs.

While the Sacramento action was the party's most famous theatrical work, I would argue that it was merely an extension of the theatrical practice at the center of their activity. The Panthers also understood early on that they needed to win over the ghetto community with more than talk. They were not above such far-from-revolutionary acts as getting a stoplight installed in a dangerous intersection when the city power structure's indifference to black life had led to the death of several children. Informing the city officials that armed Panthers would stand guard at the intersection until a light was installed proved just the leverage needed to get the job done. Eventually they evolved a whole series of "survival programs" as interim offers of the many things demanded in the Ten-Point Program—including free food, education, clothing, medical care, and legal counseling.

A better known early part of the Panthers' dramatic presence in the black community took the form of their policing of the police. Panther members, armed with rifles and law books, would follow police officers around Oakland, patrolling for police brutality and other violations of the rights of black citizens of the city. In the spirit of the civil rights movement, they were creating an alternative, parallel institution. But this one was different. In effect, this strategy was the mirror image of that key civil rights movement strategy, civil disobedience. Law books and civil codes were used to symbolize that the police were engaged in uncivil disobedience to law, and that the Panthers were there to enforce the letter of the law. The action reversed the gaze of surveillance, so that the watchers were now the ones being watched.

Carrying guns was meant to challenge symbolically the state's monopoly on the use of violence, and to give notice that guns used to enforce white supremacy would be met by black self-defense. Realizing that legal fictions covered up oppressive practices, the Panthers were not attacking the law but exposing its racist application. Where in the South segregation laws were the clear enemy, in the North a more complex situation existed in which putatively equal laws rendered invisible *de facto* segregation in housing and employment, unequal schools, and routine police harassment and brutality for the unwritten crime of being black in white America.

As an article in the party paper summarized their position: "The Black Panther Party recognizes, as do all Marxist revolutionaries, that the only response to the violence of the ruling class is the revolutionary violence of the people. The Black Panther Party recognizes this truth not as some unspecified Marxist-Leninist truism, but as the basic premise of relating to the colonial oppression of Black people in the heartland of Imperialism where the white ruling class, through its occupation police forces, agents and dope peddlers, institutionally terrorizes the Black community. Revolutionary strategy for Black people in America begins with the defensive movement of picking up the Gun, as the condition for ending the pigs' reign of terror by the Gun."[16]

The Panthers knew that their actions would be seen very differently in the "two Americas, one white, one Black" described in the U.S. government's official report on the civil disturbances rocking the ghetto. Bobby Seale's discussion of Newton's planning around the Sacramento "invasion" (as the white world reported it) shows his clear sense of this dual audience: "When brother Huey planned Sacramento he said, 'Now the papers are going to call us thugs and hoodlums.'... But the brothers on the block who the man's been calling thugs and hoodlums for 100 years, they're going to say, 'Them's some out of sight thugs and hoodlums up there.'"[17] Indeed, events like Sacramento brought the "brothers" and the "sisters" pouring into the organization. In less than two years, there were Panther chapters in cities around the country, including New York; New Haven, Connecticut; Raleigh, North Carolina; Detroit, Michigan; Chicago; and Los Angeles. The party's newspaper, *The Black Panther*, had a peak circulation of nearly 140,000 by 1970. A Harris poll done for *Time* Magazine in March 1970 found that one out of four blacks in America had a "great deal of admiration" for the Panthers. A Market Dynamics/ABC poll taken later that same year found the Panthers judged to be the organization "most likely" to increase the effectiveness of the black liberation struggle. Two-thirds of blacks polled showed admiration for the organization, despite by that time four years of vilification in the white press and constant harassment by law enforcement.

Does this mean that Black Panther revolutionary ideology was embraced by the black community? Probably not. It was far more likely that Black Panther theater was embraced by the community in the sense that images of proud black men and women in black berets facing down cops gave evidence of a new kind of black person in the world, one who would not bow to racism any more. In this sense, Black Panther theater proved far more successful than the specifics of Black Panther ideology, though the former sometimes carried with it significant elements of the latter, especially for the hundreds who were drawn by those images to join the party.

The task of playing along the line I have been sketching between "poetics" and "politics," and between two very different audiences, was a very tricky one. Some of the difficulties are clear in this interview of Panther David Hilliard with two CBS correspondents, George Herman and Ike Pappas, and *Washington Post* reporter Bernard Nossiter on 28 December 1969.

> MR. PAPPAS: . . . I was at the [anti–Vietnam War] Moratorium Day ceremonies and I heard [you say] "We will kill Richard Nixon. We will kill anyone. Any blankety-blank who stands in the way of our freedom." And it is a very simple question: Do you think Richard Nixon is standing in the way of your freedom? Number two, would you kill him?

> MR. HILLIARD: . . . I would say that Richard Nixon is the chief spokesman for the American people. He is the highest official in this land. If Richard Nixon stands in opposition to freedom guaranteed to us under the alleged constitution, then the man is designated as enemy. But I did not and I will not here designate—I will not take responsibility of saying assassinate anybody.

> MR. NOSSITER: Well, what you are suggesting, Mr. Hilliard, is that this was a metaphor, a figure of speech out in San Francisco.

> MR. HILLIARD: I am saying that it was political rhetoric. We can call it a metaphor. It is the language of the ghetto. This is the way we relate. Even the profanity, the profanity is within the idiom of the oppressed people. So in the context of that speech I said that and I am not going to take that back.

> MR. NOSSITER: Okay. Then let me ask you this: Is your revolutionary— are your revolutionary slogans, are these too metaphors? Is this also rhetoric or do Panthers literally believe that a violent overthrow of the government must take place in this country?

> MR. HILLIARD: Let's just say this: Let's say that we could have our freedom without a shot being fired, but we know that the imperialists, that the fascists on a very local level would not withdraw from the arena without violence. They have proven themselves very violent and thus

far haven't done anything to insure us our freedom. We were in the forefront of peaceful demonstrations for peace abroad, while right here at home we are being victims of attacks day and night by the criminal agencies manifested in police departments. Our slogan is that we want an abolition to war, but we do understand that in order to get rid of the gun it will be necessary to take up the gun.[18]

Hilliard is trying tortuously to add nuance to a discussion the journalists want to force into easy oppositions. He is trying to talk about the violence of racism as it affects the black community in America, and he is arguing that the possibility of radical change without violence has been rejected by the powers that be. He is also suggesting that his "political rhetoric" performed for a black audience (in "the language of the ghetto") is systematically misheard by the white world. He is even willing to grant that his violent talk is a "metaphor," but at the same time he does not want to lose its force as a "weapon" of change justified as defense against racist and "imperialist" violence. As the party did often, Hilliard is pointing to the hypocrisy of a power structure that drops tons of bombs on Vietnam and exercises police brutality daily in the ghettos and yet criticizes the violence of his mere words.

While the Leninist-Maoist rhetoric of the Panthers could at times become numbing, it was often combined with enough street-smart "jive" to serve as radical political education. Just as the cool hustler became the cool revolutionary, the fast-talking jive of the street became a machine-gun fast rhetoric uniting class and racial analysis: "The United States of America is a barbaric organization controlled and operated by avaricious, sadistic, bloodthirsty thieves. The United States of America is the Number One exploiter and oppressor of the whole world. The inhuman capitalistic system which defines the core reality of the United States is the root of the evil that has polluted the very fabric of existence."[19] As Nikhil Singh points out, the Panthers had dramatic success in their "attempts to politicize and reshape the frequently episodic and disjointed life-world of urban, Black subalterns by replacing everyday violence and temporary fulfillments of hustling and surviving with a purposive framework for political action."[20]

Most of the dramatic impact of the Panthers came not in the form of shootouts, but in day-to-day performances: speeches, marches into demonstrations and rallies, press conferences, and so forth. They were an unmistakable presence both in the black community and in the white media, especially television. As Van Deburg remarks, the "black power movement brought irrevocable changes in the Afro-Americans' attitudes both about themselves and about the legitimacy of the white world order."[21] No single force moved those changes along more than the attitudes projected in both the rhetoric and the iconographic postures of the Panthers. While to many the Panthers may have seemed to be engaging in mere posturing, to many others their revolutionary posture spoke volumes about no longer knuckling under to white power. Those people may not have believed that a revolution was at hand, but they got the message that only a new kind of black person would dare even to speak revolution to the white world.

Panther Party Organization and Ideology

The organizational pattern chosen by Newton and Seale for their new party was essentially a military one. Feeling that black people on the street needed discipline, they structured the Black Panther Party as a rigid hierarchy with a central committee made up of various ministers (of defense, information, culture, and so forth), and emphasized military-style training in arms use and marching in formation. The Marxist vanguard element was based on the idea that "the people" needed to be educated to their oppressed condition and have resistance to oppression modeled for them by a dedicated cadre of revolutionary activists. In contrast to the organizing tradition invoked in the southern struggle, the party took a position, derived indirectly from Lenin and Mao, that radical change needed to be pushed by an enlightened elite.

While the rigidity of this organizational structure would come to haunt the party, the Panthers espoused an open-ended, coalitional politics that allowed them to evolve politically over time. Newton describes the main changes he, as the party's chief theorist, did much to shape:

> In 1966 we called . . . ourselves Black Nationalists because we thought that nationhood was the answer. Shortly after that we decided that what was really needed was a revolutionary nationalism, that is a nationalism plus socialism. After analyzing conditions a little more, we found that it was impractical and even contradictory. . . . We saw that in order to be free we had to crush the ruling circle and therefore we had to unite with the peoples of the world. So we called ourselves Internationalists. . . . But

since no nation exists [in a transnational world], and since the United
States is in fact an empire, it is impossible for us to be Internationalists.
These transformations and phenomena require us to call ourselves
"intercommunalists" because nations have been transformed into
communities of the world.[22]

The Panthers were a key force in the development of a Third World/
internal colonial position that featured alliances with postcolonial and
revolutionary groups in the developing world, and alliances with other
radicals of color within the United States. The rhetorical/political trick
of identifying U.S. people of color as part of the Third World transformed an American "minority" into a global "majority." The Panthers
developed alliances with revolutionary groups in Cuba, Southeast Asia,
the Middle East, and Africa, and with U.S. radicals including the American Indian Movement (AIM), the Chicano Brown Berets, the Puerto
Rican Young Lords, and the Asian American I Wor Keun (Red Guard).
They also allied themselves with white radicals like those in the Peace
and Freedom Party and Students for a Democratic Society (SDS).

Late in the 1960s the Panthers made connections also to feminist and
gay liberationist groups. The clearest example of this is a piece Newton
published as a pamphlet in 1970, and reissued in 1972, as part of a collection of his essays and speeches, *To Die for the People,* edited by Toni
Morrison. Entitled "The Women's Liberation and Gay Liberation Movements," the essay was apparently prompted in part by his friend, the
French playwright Jean Genet, known for his radical gay views. Newton
wrote, "We haven't established a revolutionary value system; we're only
in the process of establishing it. I don't remember us ever constituting any
value that said that a revolutionary must say offensive things towards
homosexuals, or that a revolutionary should make sure that women do
not speak out about their own particular kind of injustice. . . . [We Pan-
thers] say that we recognize the women's right to be free. We haven't said
much about the homosexual at all, and we must relate to the homosexual movement because it's a real thing. And I know through reading
and through my life experience, my observations, that homosexuals are
not given freedom and liberty by anyone in society. Maybe they might
be the most oppressed people in the society."[23] These statements, and
the alliances built to put them into practice, undercut the isolation and
freezing of "blackness" that limited the effectiveness of many other black
nationalist organizations. To be sure, the Panthers did not always prac-

tice what they preached, but they left a legacy of struggle with multiple forms of oppression that has often been lost in histories of black power that deal only with race and in recent forms of neo-nationalism that claim the Panther legacy but remain sexist and homophobic, and treat blackness as a cultural or biological essence, rather than as a historically constructed and changing strategic identity.

These ideological positions are an important legacy for those who care about progressive change in black America. They can serve as an antidote to insular black separatist versions of nationalism that isolate the black community from the kind of wider alliances that alone can bring significant, structural economic and political change. It is important to realize that the Panthers' larger ideological gestures were always matched by the specific demands of the Ten-Point Program, and by their everyday actions in bringing food, medicine, education, transportation, childcare, and elder care to the communities via the survival programs.

Courtroom Dramas and Acts of Repression

The inability, or unwillingness, of the white world and its forces of law and order to appreciate the distinctions Hilliard and other Panthers labored to explain meant that the real theatricality of the Panthers' violent rhetoric led to much real violence in the form of gunfights with the police. From the police patrols onward, the Panthers had always been extremely careful to know and work within the law. When the law they were protesting in Sacramento was passed, for example, they immediately stopped the armed police patrols. Not surprisingly, Panther street theater, with its use of former real-life street "hoodlums" among the supporting cast, did not play so well to law enforcement audiences. Not only did the local Oakland police dedicate themselves to stamping out the organization, but soon FBI director J. Edgar Hoover declared the Panthers the "most dangerous extremist group in America." Eventually, so many FBI-placed "extras" (infiltrators) became part of Panther dramas that the question of who was writing the script becomes impossible to answer.

A murderous cat-and-mouse game, in which the cool-cat Panthers came more and more to look like the mice, began to unfold. It became increasingly difficult for the party to uphold its claim to be working within the letter of the law. Those Sacramento protesters had been

Black Panthers invade the California state capitol. Courtesy of the *Sacramento Bee*.

arrested, with most getting six-month sentences. This continued a pattern already set by the Oakland police, and dozens of harassing arrests followed. Most of these trumped-up arrests ended in acquittals, but even those tied up the organization's funds and personnel for years to come. In select cases, notably that of party chairman Huey Newton himself, arrested for the alleged murder of a police officer, the trials became national and international events. Though eventually acquitted of the crime after a series of trials, Newton spent three years in prison, from 1967 to 1970. Those were crucial years for the party. While Newton continued to try to direct that Panthers from inside prison walls, and a massive "Free Huey" campaign became a major rallying point and fundraising source for the group, the loss was considerable. Much of the time Panther theater was reduced to the "radical chic" drawing room dramas lampooned by conservative new journalist Tom Wolfe. These well-staged shakedowns of rich and guilty white liberals proved effective in raising funds but did little to push the revolution forward.[24]

Co-founder Seale also became involved in a major courtroom drama when he and seven white radicals became the notorious Chicago Eight, charged with fomenting the confrontations surrounding the Democratic

Party convention in Chicago in 1968. Seale's co-defendants included Abbie Hoffman and Jerry Rubin, the clown princes of the white new left and founders of the surrealist, countercultural Youth International Party, or Yippies. The theatrical Yippie organizers came to their trial dressed in the costumes of the American Revolution and did their best (and their best was very good) to turn the courtroom into a circus. Denied a change of lawyer, Seale was forced to represent himself in the trial. He soon so irritated the judge, Julius Hoffman (whom Abbie facetiously called Uncle Julie), that he was declared in contempt, and ordered bound and gagged in the courtroom. This image of Seale, the sole black defendant, receiving not blind but shackled and gagged justice in the white man's courtroom played powerfully in the court of black public opinion, confirming the Panthers' longstanding claim that they faced only kangaroo courts, not courts of justice.

With key leaders already in jail, the FBI and other agencies unleashed a sweeping, vicious program of repression against the Panthers and other radicals in the late 1960s through COINTELPRO (short for Counter Intelligence Program). Between 1967 and 1971 COINTELPRO employed more than seven thousand undercover agents and police informers to infiltrate the Panthers and other radical groups with the mission of disrupting their efforts by any means necessary. This included falsifying documents in an attempt to create power struggles within the organization and between the Panthers and other black radical groups. Most COINTELPRO efforts were focused on increasing the level of violence among the Panthers; in at least one case this meant providing dynamite to a Panther chapter.[25] The state was attempting to erase the distinction between self-defense and offense, and it successfully forced a literalization of Panther theater. Pushing the Black Panther Party across the line from symbolic to literal violence was one of the main goals of COINTELPRO.

The two most important intellectuals influencing the black power movement, Frantz Fanon and Malcolm X, both had argued that violence was one of the necessary means of awakening Negroes into the power of blackness. Fanon, writing in the context of anticolonial struggles of Third World majority populations ousting white minorities, analyzed how in revolutionary situations symbolic violence could turn into armed struggle. But the late 1960s in America was not a revolutionary situation in the military sense. The Panthers' genius was in showing that the threat of violent self-defense could be used to expose the everyday violence of police brutality and the structural violence of poverty. In March 1968, the Panther minister of information expressed it this way in the party paper: "Let us make one thing crystal clear: We do not claim the right to indiscriminate violence. We seek no bloodbath. We are not out to kill up white people. On the contrary, it is the cops who claim the right to indiscriminate violence and practice it everyday. It is the cops who have been bathing black people in blood and who seem bent on killing off black people."[26] Unfortunately, both the police and some elements within the Panthers were not so "crystal clear" on this distinction, and soon a series of not-so-revolutionary pitched gun battles began. The government's efforts to increase the level of violence in the Panthers testify tellingly to the foolishness of violence in a nonrevolutionary situation. Or, in my terms, they testify to the necessity of maintaining the distinction between theatrical violence and violent theatrics. Doing so might have extended the longevity of the Panther Party, not to say the lives of many Panther members.

Many encounters between police and the party, like the killing of Chicago Panther leaders Fred Hampton and Mark Clark, were effectively political assassinations by the alleged upholders of "law and order." Hampton and Clark were shot dead in their beds in a predawn raid in December 1969. Some eighty thousand Chicagoans paid homage to the slain Panthers and checked out for themselves the truth of the police version of the events by taking a Panther-sponsored tour of the murder scene. Other encounters were more ambiguous or implicate some Panthers in their own undoing. Where claims of self-defense and rhetorical evocations of revolutionary violence often stirred "the people," the actual gun battles that led to so many dead and imprisoned Panthers had a chilling effect on resistance. By the end of 1969, 30 Panthers faced capital punishment charges, 40 faced life imprisonment, 55 faced terms of up to thirty years, and another 155 were in jail or being pursued by the law.[27] Many of these Panthers were not as lucky in their verdicts as leader Newton had been; several are still in prison thirty years after their convictions.[28] Getting caught up in gunfights with police played into the hands of the state, both because the government's greater force showed up the weakness of the would-be revolutionary forces, and because the real battle at that moment was still the symbolic one, the battle to shift the consciousness of forces for and against radical change.

With a lot of help from agents provocateurs from the FBI and dozens of other branches of "law enforcement," the Panthers lost that delicate balance achieved by Malcolm X—knowing the difference between rhetorical violence and very real bullets. Much liberal and some radical critique has faulted the Panthers for their use of violence. But any critique needs to sort out very different kinds of violence in and around the party. I agree with the position taken by one of the Panthers' most astute recent analysts, Nikhil Pal Singh:

> Generally, the evocation of trauma and failure is depicted as a question of who was the most violent during the 1960s, a discussion that proceeds as if violence is something transparent, rather than a concept in need of careful contextualization and theorization. Indeed, many accounts confirm this by regularly sliding between condemnation of Panther gunplay and criticism of their militant or violent rhetoric, as if these are the same thing, or as if one automatically produces the other. This collapse of politics and poetics spurs obsessional efforts at adjudication, at sorting out the innocent from the guilty, the victims from the villains, and deciding where the Panthers finally fall. The irony of this is that while the Panthers' rhetoric is often dismissed as inflated, overheated and out of touch, it invariably returns as the implicit cause and/or emblem of an all-too-real body count that effectively ends the discussion. What has resulted is a flattening and even erasure of the richness and ambiguity of the Panthers' racial and political self-fashioning, along with a more careful analysis and differentiation of the manifest and symbolic forms of violence that they deployed and confronted.[29]

As I have suggested, sorting out the "manifest and symbolic forms of violence" in the world of the Panthers is a difficult task. There is no doubt that the party's performances were riddled with "ambiguities," not to say contradictions. All sides of those contradictions have lessons to teach, and no side of them should be ignored, in celebration or in condemnation.

Curtain Time: The Decline and Fall of the Panthers

The Panthers' period of greatest influence, roughly 1966–71, was cut short by external repression and internal battles. Eventually Panthers not only fought and killed other black activists, like those in Ron Karenga's Los Angeles–based United Slaves (US), but also fought and killed each other. Feeling under siege from all sides, Newton made a decision in 1972 to further centralize the organization and move into the electoral arena.

He asked all Panthers from around the country to move to Oakland to strengthen the electoral base for a run for mayor by Bobby Seale and for city council by soon-to-be Panther Party chair Elaine Brown. Though Seale finished second among a host of candidates, he lost a runoff election. Brown too failed in her bid for a spot on the city council.

The party began to implode soon after the electoral failure. Paralleling founder Newton's descent into drug addiction and physical abuse of other Panthers, the party continued largely as a shadow of itself. Sorting out the gangsterism from the revolutionism during this phase is not always easy. But it is clear that when the revolutionism was thwarted, only gangsterism remained. The decline of the party is a sad tale indeed, not just on its own terms but for the ways in which it mirrors the decline in the wider black community from activism to despair to a gangster culture that for many was all that was left when radical resistance was suppressed.[30]

Debate continues to swirl as to whether internal dissension or external repression best accounts for the decline of the organization. Certainly the latter exacerbated the former. But it is too simple to let the party off the hook by seeing it purely as a victim. The original paramilitary structure of the party became increasingly centralized and authoritarian in ways that made it easy to foster paranoia in the leaders. The Panthers' failure to appreciate the extent of their symbolic power undermined their efforts to delegitimate the state's monopoly of violence. By playing into the hands of agents provocateurs ("law enforcement" agents paid to infiltrate the group and encourage violence), they left themselves vulnerable to hundreds of arrests and countless legal battles. They fatally confused militancy and militarism. Ultimately, this led to a lot of dead and imprisoned Panthers—a loss that permanently weakened the movement and sowed seeds of paranoia in the survivors. Strong doses of vanguardist elitism and masculinist egotism often cut leaders off from the grassroots forces in the party, while their hierarchical, clandestine, paramilitary organizational form also bred paranoia that left the Panthers vulnerable to this infiltration and disruption.

In addition to the structural problems, some of the people attracted to the party, including several in key leadership positions like Eldridge Cleaver and, in his later days, Newton himself, were "crazy mothafuckas" in far too literal a sense. Their personal pathologies, leading in Cleaver's case to revolutionary fantasies and in Newton's case to drug addiction, deeply damaged the organization. If the Panthers had been a more democratic, grassroots organization, such leaders could have been held in check. Instead a star system emerged in Panther theatrics, with figures like Cleaver and Newton acting out a drama of little or no interest to the rest of the party, let alone the rest of black America.

However, the pathologies of some members should not obscure the dedication to improving the lives of millions of black (and other) Americans that motivated the several thousand, still largely unstudied "foot soldiers" of the party. One historian deeply critical of the party's self-destructive elitist and authoritarian streak notes, nevertheless, that "the Panthers contributed significantly to making America a more democratic, egalitarian, and human society. Party members led the movement to end police brutality and create civilian police-review boards. The BPP's free breakfast programs became a catalyst for today's free meals to poor school children. More than most progressive political groups, the party highlighted, connected to and protested U.S. oppression abroad and U.S injustice at home."[31] Panthers and Panther associates like Angela Davis also have been at the forefront of the prisoner rights movement. That movement continues to grow in the face of the massive expansion of the "prison-industrial complex," which has put more young black men in jail than in college.

Beyond the Theater of the Gun

The problem with stressing the most violent scenes in the Panthers' theatrical repertoire is that this obscures other important dimensions of the party's legacy—for example, Huey Newton's strong stand against homophobia in mainstream and black communities, and his alliance with the emerging gay liberation movement in the early 1970s. It also tends to obscure the central role of women in the organization, and the ways in which they and some of the men challenged "male chauvinism" and misogyny inside and outside the party. Two-thirds of the party members were women. Some women held key positions, including, in the case of Elaine Brown, the top position.[32] The theater of guns also overshadows the less dramatic, daily work of the party: the petitions, the phone calls to the press, hawking the *Black Panther* newspaper on the streets, serving food in the breakfast program. While there were numerous showboaters, especially among the men in the organization, there were also dedicated women and men who brought with them practical organizing skills. Perhaps it is telling that while all the party's media stars survived the black power era, the party's best grassroots organizer, Fred Hampton, was singled out for police assassination.

An overemphasis on violence also obscures the internationalism and the coalitional nature of the Panthers, their alliances with the external and internal Third World. Unlike many strands of black nationalism before, during, and since the black power era, Panther nationalism was not based on some unchanging notion of black identity. While mobilizing a sense of pride in blackness was important in the work of organizing their core constituency in the underclass, Panther politics was never an "identity politics." It involved coalitions with radical white groups and radicals of color in the United States and around the world. An often less remembered aspect of Panther theater is their actions on the world stage, where they enacted a foreign policy with regard to Cuba, Algeria, numerous African states, and China. Meetings of Panther leaders with heads of state in these countries dramatized a kind of secession of people of color from the United States and embodied the politics theorized by Newton as "intercommunalism." This was a community-to-community connection that bypassed the nation-state, and anticipated the kind of "globalization from below" being enacted by some on the left today.

Gun fetishism also obscures the less dramatic, but equally important pragmatic side of the party represented by the "survival programs"—the free breakfast programs, the schools, elder care, and health clinics. The party's electoral campaigns, though ultimately unsuccessful, provided another public stage for putting forth key elements of their revolutionary ideas. To romantic nationalists, these are signs of a sellout of the radical movement. In reality, they were among the strongest links to local communities and a key means through which radical ideas were disseminated. Most Panthers saw no contradiction between revolutionary rhetoric and "taking care of business" in the neighborhood through activities too easily labeled as reformist. Newton argued that hungry students are poor students, that the future of black and other poor communities, including future revolutionary possibilities, would be lost if children went hungry. The party characterized the survival programs as socialism in action, but also made it clear that these were stopgap measures, not

New York Black Panther rally for Huey Newton. Courtesy of Roz Payne.

the revolutionary change they fought for.[33] Refusing the easy dichotomy of reform versus revolution, the Panthers' survival programs were both much needed practical services and symbolic acts designed to show up the violence done by the lack of such services in white capitalist America.

Powers of Culture

As historian William Van Deburg puts it, "As a movement in and of culture, black power was itself an art form. In the words of Lerone Bennett Jr., it made 'everything political and everything cultural.'"[34] I would add, however, that while the political and the cultural can be collapsed into one by movements in moments of active struggle, they can also be driven asunder again. The message of Black Panther theater is twofold: first, that the cultural form called drama can be a vital political tool; second, that for the cultural to be truly effective politically, it must remain connected to social movement groups with a clear, explicit agenda for structural economic and political change.

The Panthers' revolutionary rhetoric was most meaningful when tied to their famous Ten-Point Program and to their survival programs, a stirring mix of concrete demands and utopian vision.[35] When they ceased to organize at the grassroots level, they not only stalled the progress of the revolution but left themselves without the protection once accorded them by the community (at one point early on, for example, community members prevented a planned police raid on party headquarters by massing outside, placing themselves between the Panthers and the police).

When the Panthers had been destroyed by COINTELPRO and their own internal difficulties, it did not prove difficult to turn revolutionary style into a mere style revolution. The Panthers' Stagolee as revolutionary was turned back into an apolitical black dude, or worse still into a cop, through a wave of "blaxploitation" films in the late 1970s, such as *Shaft*. African garb (dashiki robes for men, headdresses for women, tiki necklaces for both) and "natural" hair (mimicking the revolutionary "Afro" of Angela Davis and Panther women) soon became the commodified signs of blackness empty of political meaning. To paraphrase the words of Panther Bobby Seale, power does not grow out of the sleeve of a dashiki. But, contra Seale's pal Huey Newton's paraphrase of Mao, neither does power grow out of the barrel of a gun, at least not when the other side has an endless and more powerful supply.

The real weapon of the Panthers was a sense of how to deploy theatrically powerful imagery to evoke a sense of black power in the black underclass. The survival programs and the Ten-Point Program's call for "land, bread, housing, education, clothing, justice and peace," when combined with dramatic images of black women and men standing up to the powers of the U.S. government, helped create a new kind of black person. At their best, the Panthers dramatically melded questions of black identity to questions of economic, political, and cultural change. By contrast, theatricality without organizing severely limits the depth of change. Put in the terms of this analysis, the Panthers provided too few spaces for average black Americans to take part as actors, not spectators, in their dramatic actions for change.

As playwright Jean Genet, for a time a close confidant of Panther leaders, put it, "Wherever they went [in the world], Americans were the masters, so the Panthers would do their best to terrorize the masters by the only means available to them. Spectacle."[36] By at times confusing their spectacular revolutionary theater with a revolutionary situation, the Panthers ultimately squandered a good deal of their "black power." But as Frantz Fanon wrote in that key 1960s text, *The Wretched of the Earth*, "Decolonization never takes place unnoticed for it transforms

Angela Davis and Jean Genet. Courtesy of Robert Cohen.

individuals and modifies them fundamentally. It transforms spectators crushed with their inessentiality into privileged actors with the grandiose glare of history's floodlights upon them."[37]

For a brief but utterly transformative moment, the Black Panthers turned the glare of history's floodlights onto the Third World inside and outside the United States, and turned many colonized spectators into privileged actors on the world stage.

Panther Legacies in Hip-Hop Scenarios

A vast amount of cultural criticism, particularly from black feminist and "womanist" authors, has profoundly rethought the nature and limits of black nationalism in the years since the Panthers' heyday. As is often the case with movements, their very successes become in turn problems. In the case of black power, its successes have resulted in a certain level of black nationalism becoming "common sense" in black communities. But as Gramsci argues, "common sense" is the seat of both useful and useless ideas. And in becoming common sense, less useful ideas become deeply entrenched, taken for granted, and difficult to dislodge. The diffusion of black power movement ideas into everyday life, as Wahneema Lubiano, among others, has argued, has led to both positive values and dangerously unreflective ones.[38] In particular, the sexist, homophobic, and essentialist dimensions of black power have often carried over in the process of translation from movement ideology to common sense. I want to end this chapter by looking at one "dramatic" site where this positive and negative process is at work, the cultural formation surrounding "rap" music and "hip-hop" culture.

One key factor in the relative success of social movements seeking to better the lives of poor, marginalized people in the 1960s was the widespread perception that the great American economic pie was getting bigger and bigger. And this perception was generally right; the period between the end of World War II and the end of the Vietnam War in 1975 saw the largest, most sustained economic growth in human history. The American economy, initially free of any competition given the devastating effects of World War II on other national economies, meant tremendous financial gain reaped, unevenly to be sure, by most citizens of the country.

But by the mid-1970s President Lyndon Johnson's "war on poverty" was long gone, and soon a war on the poor was taking its place. Amid a sense that the pie had stopped growing, fear of competition from minorities fueled a white backlash that eventually segued into the "voodoo economics" of President Ronald Reagan, boldly robbing the poor to fatten the rich. Devastating new levels of poverty in inner cities arose when whites flocked in great numbers to the suburbs, leaving a tax base too small to adequately deal with even the basic need for schools and neighborhood safety for the people of color left behind.

Out of these conditions, there emerged in the late 1970s a powerful cultural force in black and Latino communities, creating art forms—especially rap/hip-hop music—that had strong links to black and brown nationalism. The rap music and hip-hop culture that arose out of the devastation of inner-city ghettos and barrios was from the beginning a highly schizophrenic phenomenon. The first two rap songs to make the move from neighborhood folk culture to the national pop culture reflect this split. One of those songs, "Rapper's Delight," by the Sugar Hill Gang, was, as the title implies, a fairly lighthearted, commercially marketable piece of fluff. The other song to emerge, "The Message," by Grandmaster Flash and the Furious Five, was, as its title implies, a song that had something to say—in this case a strong, clear message of anger about the horrendous conditions in the inner city. For the next two decades, complicated variations on rap as delight and rap as political message vied for the airwaves. The two sides of rap, of course, intermingled, for the line between message and entertainment is never absolute.[39]

Certain rap groups and artists like Public Enemy, Paris, and Dead Prez clearly took some of their messages from the Black Panthers. Their efforts display both the strengths and weaknesses of rap as a political art and the Panthers as role models. On the one hand, messages found in some rap lyrics have played a role in keeping black nationalist discourses generally, and the name Black Panthers specifically, alive during a movement doldrum period. At the same time, while paying homage to the Panthers, many rappers have displayed an ideological confusion that shows their limited understanding of the Panthers or replicates their least admirable dimensions.

The late Tupac Shakur illustrates several levels of contradiction. His stories of black pride and empowerment were important ones for many young black men and women. At the same time, his songs, and even more his videos, often played into the hands of commercial sexism and materialism. And Tupac's hip-hop homage to women like his Black Panther mother Afeni Shakur inadvertently played into a family-values scenario worthy of a conservative Republican.[40] Other black nationalist rappers have had too little to say about sexism and homophobia in other rappers, and have sometimes shown evidence of both in their own music, despite corrective jabs from feminist rappers like Queen Latifah, Salt 'n' Peppa, and Roxanne Shante.

In addition, as Angela Davis has noted, Public Enemy sometimes deified and reified the masculinist paramilitary "look" of the Panthers, rather than their political substance. Ideological confusion is also demonstrated when self-proclaimed Panther rapper Paris, among others, embraces the socially conservative Nation of Islam along with the revolutionary socialist Panthers.[41] But, as I have shown, the Panthers too were riddled with contradictions. And certain rap acts remain among the most important forces of resistance in black communities. Rappers are among the most likely voices to spark new national movements for economic, social, and political change. Many are doing just that now at the local level. From the Stop the Violence movement of the 1980s to the Speak Truth to Power Tour in 2003, "conscious hip-hop" has embraced the best legacy of the Black Panthers—those points where brilliant theatricality connect to concrete, grassroots efforts to change the world.

Appendix: Ten-Point Program of the Black Panther Party

October 1966 Black Panther Party
'   Platform and Program
What We Want
What We Believe

1. We want freedom. We want power to determine the destiny of our Black Community.

We believe that Black people will not be free until we are able to determine our destiny.

2. We want full employment for our people.

We believe that the federal government is responsible and obligated to give every man employment or a guaranteed income. We believe that if the white American businessmen will not give full employment, then the means of production should be taken from the businessmen and placed in the community so that the people of the community can organize and employ all of its people and give a high standard of living.

3. We want an end to the robbery by the white man of our Black Community.

We believe that this racist government has robbed us and now we are demanding the overdue debt of forty acres and two mules. Forty acres and two mules was promised 100 years ago as restitution for slave labor and mass murder of Black people. We will accept the payment as currency which will be distributed to our many communities. The Germans are now aiding the Jews in Israel for the genocide of the Jewish people. The Germans murdered six million Jews. The American racist has taken part in the slaughter of over twenty million Black people; therefore, we feel that this is a modest demand that we make.

4. We want decent housing, fit for shelter of human beings.

We believe that if the white landlords will not give decent housing to our Black community, then the housing and the land should be made into cooperatives so that our community, with government aid, can build and make decent housing for its people.

5. We want education for our people that exposes the true nature of this decadent American society. We want education that teaches us our true history and our role in the present-day society.

We believe in an educational system that will give to our people a knowledge of self. If a man does not have knowledge of himself and his position in society and the world, then he has little chance to relate to anything else.

6. We want all Black men to be exempt from military service.

We believe that Black people should not be forced to fight in the military service to defend a racist government that does not protect us. We will not fight and kill other people of color in the world who, like Black people, are being victimized by the white racist government of America. We will protect ourselves from the force and violence of the racist police and the racist military, by whatever means necessary.

7. We want an immediate end to police brutality and murder of Black people.

We believe we can end police brutality in our Black community by organizing Black self-defense groups that are dedicated to defending our Black community from racist police oppression and brutality. The Second Amendment to the Constitution of the United States gives a right to bear arms. We therefore believe that all Black people should arm themselves for self defense.

8. We want freedom for all Black men held in federal, state, county and city prisons and jails.

We believe that all Black people should be released from the many jails and prisons because they have not received a fair and impartial trial.

9. We want all Black people when brought to trial to be tried in court by a jury of their peer group or people from their Black communities, as defined by the Constitution of the United States.

We believe that the courts should follow the United States Constitution so that Black people will receive fair trials. The 14th Amendment of the U.S. Constitution gives a man a right to be tried by his peer group. A peer is a person from a similar economic, social, religious, geographical, environmental, historical and racial background. To do this the court will be forced to select a jury from the Black community from which the Black defendant came. We have been, and are being tried by all-white juries that have no understanding of the "average reasoning man" of the Black community.

10. *We want land, bread, housing, education, clothing, justice and peace. And as our major political objective, a United Nations–supervised plebiscite to be held throughout the Black colony in which only Black colonial subjects will be allowed to participate for the purpose of determining the will of Black people as to their national destiny.*

When in the course of human events, it becomes necessary for one people to dissolve the political bands which have connected them with another, and to assume, among the powers of the earth, the separate and equal station to which the laws of nature and nature's God entitle them, a decent respect to the opinions of mankind requires that they should declare the causes which impel them to the separation.

We hold these truths to be self evident, that all men are created equal; that they are endowed by their Creator with certain unalienable rights; that among these are life, liberty, and the pursuit of happiness. *That, to secure these rights, governments are instituted among men, deriving their just powers from the consent of the governed; that, whenever any form of government becomes destructive of these ends, it is the right of the people to alter or to abolish it, and to institute a new government, laying its foundation on such principles, and organizing its powers in such form, as to them shall seem most likely to effect their safety and happiness.* Prudence, indeed, will dictate that governments long established should not be changed for light and transient causes; and accordingly, all experience hath shown, that mankind are more disposed to suffer, while evils are sufferable, than to right themselves by abolishing the forms to which they are accustomed. *But, when a long train of abuses and usurpations, pursuing invariably the same object, evinces a design to reduce them under absolute despotism, it is their right, it is their duty, to throw off such government, and to provide new guards for their future security.*

THREE

The Poetical Is the Political

Feminist Poetry and the Poetics of Women's Rights

For women, poetry is not a luxury. It is a vital necessity of our existence. It forms the quality of the light within which we predicate our hopes and dreams toward survival and change, first made into language, then into idea, and then into more tangible action. Poetry is the way we give name to the nameless so it can be thought.

—Audre Lorde, "Poetry Is Not a Luxury," *Sister Outsider*

No social movement in the past fifty years has had a greater cultural impact than the women's movement, which reemerged in the 1960s and has grown in multifaceted ways into the present. The tremendous impact of feminism in everyday life includes, but extends far beyond, changes in laws, legislation, and political institutions. The texture of the life of every single person living in the United States was changed by the new feminism.

Here is a short list of ideas about women that were unimaginably radical for most American men and women to think, let alone endorse, up to the 1960s, which are now viewed largely as common-sense statements.

- Women as a group have a right to earn as much as men.
- Traditionally defined women's jobs (nurses, maids, elementary school teachers, childcare workers) should be paid at a rate comparable to similar work done by men.
- There are few, if any, jobs that women can't do.
- Women should have equal access to higher education, including fields traditionally reserved for men.

- Female writers, artists, and musicians should have respect, support, and opportunities equal to those given males in these cultural fields.
- Women are entitled to sexual pleasure as much as men are.
- Women should not be confined to housework but should be respected for it when they choose it.
- Women and men should share household and parenting work.
- Women don't need to be in a relationship with a man to be happy.
- Treating women as mere sex objects is wrong.
- Women should not be subject to sexual harassment in the workplace or in school.
- Girls and women should be encouraged to engage in sport.
- Women should have equal power in interpersonal relationships with men.
- Women have a role in the military.
- Women have a right to feel safe from the threat of rape.
- Battering women is a political issue, not a personal matter.
- Women have a right to be part of the decision if and when to have children.
- Women have as much of a place in the business world and the political world as men do.

Before the women's movement reemerged in the mid-1960s, not one of these ideas was widely held by men or by women; most would have considered them unacceptable. Today, while often still unrealized, these are ideas most Americans embrace. As with most social movements, however, the people who came to support these views often distance themselves from the means by which the ideas came into being—feminist activism—as something too radical to identify with.

In this chapter I will trace the social movement process by which the once radical idea that women were entitled to equality with men moved from the margins to the center, from the unimaginable to common sense. First, I'll describe the general contours of the women's movement, and then I'll use feminist poetry as a case study for how feminist ideas were formed in women's movement cultures and subsequently projected out into the wider culture. One key aspect of this process was something called "consciousness-raising." Feminist consciousness-raising in the late 1960s involved women meeting in small discussion/action groups to share their personal experiences in order to turn them into analyses of common political and structural sources of inequality for women. Consciousness-raising, while certainly not the only women's movement method, touched all realms of feminist action.

Compared to the drama of civil disobedience of sit-ins, or the shock of tragic shoot-outs with the police, the poetic "dramas of consciousness-raising" described in this chapter may at first sound quite tame. But part of my point is to suggest that they are anything but tame in their effects. Feminists did and do engage in many large, dynamic public demonstrations, and "zap actions" (small group acts of civil disobedience) were a key part of the movement, especially in the early years. These included the infamous attack on the Miss America pageant in 1968 that earned feminists the misnomer "bra burners" (no bras were burned, but many were thrown in a freedom trash can to symbolize the throwing off of the constraints of male-dominated notions of femininity and women's body image). But to argue that poems are every bit as dramatic as these demonstrations, or as confrontations with police, is to make a feminist point: what counts as dramatic has often been defined in limiting ways based on male-centered visions of heroic performance. If the goal is to change the world, there is reason to believe that publicly performed or privately read poems have been a force as powerful as any other. Before the 1960s poetry was still mainly a genteel, feminized but male-dominated form, and that aura still lingers around it. But there was nothing genteel about the raucous, often sexually frank, and always politically charged poetry that came out of the women's movement. Moving poetry from polite lecture halls and quiet living rooms out into the streets was part of many 1960s movements, but no one did it more intensely or effectively than the poets of the women's movement, and in doing so they reclaimed public space as women's space.

Consciousness-raising was especially important in that key feminist theoretical act of challenging the boundaries of what counted as "political" by rethinking the border between public and private life. One of the best known slogans to emerge out of the new women's movement was the phrase "the personal is political." The basic argument was that given the historical separation of the Western world into a male public sphere (of business, art, and government) and a female private sphere (of domestic and family issues), only shifting the definition of politics to include the "personal" private sphere could address the full range of ways in which women were oppressed. This decidedly did not mean that the movement was uninterested in public issues, but only that even those public issues needed to be rethought in terms that refused the easy separation between personal and political realms. On the one hand, the movement sought to give women the right to access all the goods of the public sphere: equal access to education, good jobs, fair wages, positions of political power, and so forth. And on the other hand, it meant redefining the "personal" private sphere, where many dimensions of gender relations were formed, as a "political" sphere of discussion and contestation.

"Poetry Is Not a Luxury": Poems and/as Consciousness-Raising

Consciousness-raising was crucial in forming feminist thought on a whole range of issues, from economics to government to education, but it was particularly useful in giving a name to the "nameless" forms of oppression felt in realms previously relegated to the nonpolitical arena of "personal" relations. The premise of this chapter comes primarily from an essay by feminist poet/activist/theorist Audre Lorde, quoted in the chapter epigraph. As a child of Jamaican immigrants, a working-class black woman, a mother, a lesbian, and a socialist, Lorde richly embodied the complex multiplicities within and around feminism. In her landmark essay "Poetry Is Not a Luxury," Lorde provides one of the strongest and clearest cases for the value of consciousness-raising without ever using the word. What she describes instead is the process of writing a poem. This is no coincidence, I will argue, but rather a convergence. For both consciousness-raising and poetry writing make the subjective objective, make the inner world of "personal" experience available for public "political" discussion. While poetry is often thought of as a pure expression of personal feelings, only very bad poetry does that. Good poetry makes personal experience available to others by giving it an outward form.

As I look at poetry in this chapter as *one* key place where women's movement ideas, attitudes, positions, and actions were formed, expressed, and circulated to wider communities, I will also be using poetry as a metaphor for the larger process of inventing feminist analysis and diffusing feminist ideas and actions throughout the culture. The modern women's movement has never fit the mold of social movement theory very well, partly because that theory still largely holds to the division between the cultural and the political that the women's movement has done so much to challenge. The women's movement can be and has been forced into that older mold, but in doing so much of the nature, power, and influence of the movement is lost. No movement shows more clearly what is left out of the social movement story when the full range of culture is not explored.[1]

Some social scientists divide social movement activity into (serious) "instrumental" social and political action, and (merely) "expressive" cultural activity. We will never find the real women's movement if we use these categories. Culture was a prime "instrument" of change for the movement, not some decorative, "expressive" addition. So-called cultural activity, or what might more accurately be called "cultural politics," created changes in consciousness that provided the basis for calls for legislative and other forms of political change. And changes in consciousness were even more important in shaping behavioral change in those "personal" realms that feminist consciousness-raising redefined as "political," such as family life; male-female interactions in the kitchen, the bedroom, and the living room; female-female solidarity; female bodily self-image; and the right to reproductive decision-making. Feminist cultural activity also brought attention to the politics of cultural sites between government and the private realm: the workplace, the medical office, the classroom, the church.

Culture can be defined both as a kind of action in itself and as all those meaning-making processes that make any kind of acting in the world possible. It is surely possible to "act thoughtlessly," but we generally denigrate such actions and claim to prefer consciously "thought out" actions. Much of our behavior is driven by social norms we do not think about. However, movements, especially movements like feminism with a strong interest in reshaping culture, are thoughtful about those actions we take for granted most of the time. They are of great importance precisely because they are one of the key sites where re-socialization, or re-education, is particularly intensive and extensive.[2]

Only the dead parts of a culture are merely "expressive." Culture is fundamentally a creative process, a ceaseless process of unmaking old meanings and making new ones, unmaking old ways of being, thinking and acting, and making newer ones. Social movement theorists Andrew Jamison and Ron Eyerman have offered the useful term *cognitive praxis* to describe the ways in which movements bring new ideas into the world that have great, dare I say instrumental, impact. In an even broader sense, movements engage in many varieties of "cultural praxis" or "cultural poetics"—the generation of new ideas and also new "structures of feeling," new ways of being and seeing, new thought-feelings

and felt-thoughts. In this sense, the phrase "poetry of women's liberation" refers to actual poems and to a larger "cultural poetics" of social
change. Culture, to paraphrase Lorde, is not a luxury for feminism; it is
a material force at the heart of the movement.

Roots and Strands of the New Feminism(s)

The new energy around the rights and power of women that came into
focus in the late 1960s is sometimes called the "Second Wave" of feminism, in recognition of earlier, "First Wave" efforts that began in the
mid-nineteenth century and culminated with women's right to vote,
established in the Nineteenth Amendment to the Constitution in 1920.[3]
While useful in linking the new movement to the past, the term *second
wave* has also been criticized for linking the movement to the limitations
of the earlier phase, especially with regard to racism and class inequality, limitations that have continued into the more recent period.[4] The
"waves" story has served to marginalize the key roles played by women
of color in feminist organizing across the centuries. But it is less than
wave metaphor than who defines the content of the metaphor that is at
stake. Those critical of the whiteness of the waves have sometimes inadvertently erased the important role played by women of color of all
classes, and working-class white women, in both "waves," *despite* racism
and class privilege, and their increasingly central role in what is sometimes called the Third Wave of feminism, currently under way. As feminist theorist Ednie Garrison has argued, the wave metaphor may need
to be reinterpreted more than abandoned—seen not as a solid wall of
(white) water but rather more like radio waves emanating from and
traveling out in many different directions.[5]

   While the systematic denigration of women that came to be known
as sexism was close to a universal female condition in the 1960s, different
women experienced sexism in very different ways. Because feminist consciousness emerges out of the specific, material conditions of particular
women, there are many different origins for the women's movement(s)
that arose during that era. Differences in class, race, region, nationality,
and sexuality led to very different ways of articulating the nature and
needs of women. Conflicts within feminism around these and a host of
other social differences have been extremely difficult and have not been
resolved to this day. But struggling with differences among women has

also led to ever broadening constituencies committed to equality for all women.

The new women's activism that sprang up in the 1960s not only came from many different social locations but also took many different forms. Some movement historians divide these forms too neatly into categories like liberal feminism, radical feminism, socialist feminism, cultural feminism, and the like. In reality there was much cross-over and overlap of people and ideas in the various kinds of organizations and approaches. Movement historians Myra Marx Ferree and Beth Hess argue convincingly that the tendencies should not be seen as "branches," since branches of a tree remain separate and distinct, but rather as "strands," since strands weave together but may also unravel at certain points.[6] Common delineators used for the general strands of the new feminist activism include "reformist" and "revolutionary," "bureaucratic" and "collectivist," "liberal" and radical," and "equal rights" and "women's liberationist." As Katie King suggests, these categories are far more easily seen in retrospect than they were in the heat of early struggles to define a new feminism.[7]

Some new feminist groups focused primarily on reforming the government in ways more favorable to women. This tendency eventually coalesced around large organizations like NOW (National Organization for Women), WPAC (Women's Political Action Caucus), and WEAL (Women's Equity Action League). At other times and for other issues, the movement activists preferred to organize themselves in smaller, less hierarchical groups, which Steven Buechler has characterized as "movement communities," as opposed to more formal "movement organizations."[8] Some of the time feminist activism has been embedded in struggles around racial and class oppression in which gender cannot be neatly isolated as a factor (a variable, in social science lingo). At times feminists have worked in separatist groups centered in ethnic identity, class, nationality, or sexual preference, while at other times they have organized in groups and coalitions that cut across these differences. Similarly, sometimes feminists have worked for specific, limited reforms, while at other times the call has been for more sweepingly radical change of whole systems of male domination and the larger race-class systems in which they are embedded. Chicana feminist theorist Chela Sandoval has argued that from the perspective of U.S. feminists of color, these various elements of feminism can be seen not as opposed schools but as a toolkit of tactics to be used in various combinations depending upon the issues and conditions at hand.[9]

One key source of the new feminist energy that arose in the 1960s was community organizing among working-class women of color. Not necessarily articulated as feminist struggle, this important strand has often been ignored or downplayed in stories of the women's movement centered in the experiences of white, middle-class women. Women struggling for economic survival in black, Native American, Chicana/Latina, Asian/Pacific American, and working-class white communities never easily accepted gendered limits on their actions, and often realized that sexism inhibited their efforts to fight against the racial and class oppression faced by their communities. They formed activist groups like the ANC Mothers Anonymous and the National Welfare Rights Organization that forged a feminist path within other movements, including the labor movement. Race-based power movements often drew the first loyalty of women of color. Women played key roles in all these struggles but also often found themselves struggling against male dominance within the racial revolution. Some asserted themselves within ethnic nationalist struggles; others formed explicitly feminist groups of color like the National Black Feminist Organization, the Combahee River Collective, Hijas de Cuauhtemoc, Asian Sisters, and Women of All Red Nations (WARN). These groups were a key force of antisexist action and codified a long history of struggling simultaneously with the intersections of gender, race, and class long before white feminist theory began to recite this mantra.[10] From the beginning, the women's movement— or more accurately, women's movements—emerged from within and were entangled with a host of other social movements. While for some white, middle-class women these other movements provided merely a model to appropriate, for working-class white women and women of color there could be no disentangling of the struggle against racial and class oppression from the struggle over gender oppression.

Black feminist Frances M. Beal referred to the condition of women of color as "double jeopardy," and a similar case of "double jeopardy" characterizes the position of white, middle-class lesbians, while working-class lesbians and lesbians of color face even greater difficulties (triple jeopardy?).[11] While stereotyped dismissal homophobically characterizes all feminists as lesbians, in fact lesbians had to fight their way into recognition in feminist organizations. In the most notorious example, the leader of NOW, Betty Friedan, referred to lesbians as a "lavender menace" whose visible presence could damage efforts by feminists to achieve legitimacy. When announcing this menace, Friedan assumed she was speaking of women outside the organization, but not long after, in a classic "zap" action, lesbians within NOW turned off the lights at a meeting, took off their coats, and had a mass "coming out" party, wearing shirts bearing the slogan "Lavender Menace" and taking over the meeting.

Lesbians of color within nationalist and straight feminist groups met similar resistance and offered similar challenges through ideas and actions pioneered by the black feminist group known as the Combahee River Collective, among others. Feminist theory written or inspired by lesbians of color came to show brilliantly that racism, sexism, and heterosexism are intimately tied together, that fighting homophobia is a key element of fighting for women's equality, and thus that struggles for gay/lesbian rights before and during the rise of what came to be narrowly defined by some as "the" women's movement played a crucial role in the wider struggle for gender equality.

A key force shaping the consciousness of some of the women who became leading feminist activists was the experience of relative freedom and empowerment on the home front during World War II. During the war, women were recruited to fill a variety of previously male-identified jobs in factories, government, and business. When the war ended, most of these women were summarily drummed out of their new jobs. Middle-class white women were told to return to the home as "housewives." Many working-class women became feminists when they heard their once highly touted contributions to the economy reduced or ridiculed, and saw their paychecks shrink as they lost men's jobs and men's wages. Many women of color who had experienced higher paying factory work during the war were forced back into domestic service as maids, or had to return to lower paid jobs as waitresses, cooks, or janitors—a different form of "redomestication" to "women's work" as food makers and cleaners.

After the war, a vast government and corporate public relations campaign was put in place to turn "Rosie the Riveter" into Dolly the Homemaker, or Maria the Maid, but the transformation was not embraced by all middle-class women, and could not be embraced by most working-class white women and women of color who survived on work outside their own homes. There had been a 50 percent increase in the number of married women in the workforce during the war, and of the women workers polled at the end of the war in 1945, more than 75 percent expressed a desire to keep their jobs. Despite the campaign to redomesticate women, a significant number remained in the labor force, and some middle-class women who did not remain regretted their decision when domesticity proved considerably less satisfying than promised. Thus many of the women who would reanimate feminism in the 1960s and beyond, including many middle-class women, were working women or had grown up with working mothers.

Redomestication also included a huge rise in the birth rate after the war, the famous "baby boom" that gave its name to the generation that came of age in the 1960s. Much of the baby boom occurred among middle-class families in the new social space of "suburbs." A deeply racist "white flight" from increasingly multiracial urban areas ensured quick growth of these new suburban spaces. Suburbs were built upon a new model of the isolated, "nuclear" family, in contrast to the centuries-old model of extended families with many aunts, uncles, cousins, grandparents, and other relatives living together or nearby. Many women experienced these new arrangements as isolating and depressing, and were unconvinced by the new ideology of "feminine mystique" that celebrated the joys of housewifery.[12] For these women, the problem was not the role of homemaking, but the claim that this was the *only* "natural" or "proper" role for women, even as actual homemaking was trivialized in the new suburban system. Many middle-class women experiencing these conditions joined the fight for equal rights, and many passed on to their daughters an even stronger will to fight for radical improvements in the conditions of women's lives.

President John F. Kennedy's Presidential Committee on the Status of Women, formed in 1961, is often cited as a precursor of the more moderate, government reform or "equal-rights" strand of the movement. Long-time feminist and former first lady, Eleanor Roosevelt chaired the committee, and her personal prestige did much to draw attention to its work. Roosevelt also provided a link with the previous wave of feminist activism that had continued, despite hitting "doldrums," from the 1920s to the 1960s. Feminist scholars have shown that many cultural links helped maintain feminist energy despite relatively low levels of public engagement during the intervening decades.[13] The equal-rights strand drew strength from, but was also profoundly limited by, this past, and it was primarily the more radical waves of activism emerging out of poor communities and newly radicalized, middle-class, young white women that transformed the meaning of feminism into something far deeper and more profound than new rights. With grassroots support from these other strands, the reform branch achieved some key legislative victories: the Equal Pay Act of 1963, the Civil Rights Act of 1964 (broadened from an initial application only to race to include "sex discrimination" as well); the Title IX ruling on women in athletics; the *Roe v. Wade* Supreme Court decision on reproductive rights (1973); and a host of other legislative and legal rulings favorable to women. Much of this activity was then funneled into the campaign to pass a comprehensive Equal Rights Amendment to the Constitution. Though ultimately unsuccessful, the campaign did much to educate women around the country about the rights they did and did not have.

The other, more radical strands of the women's movement, which emerged in the late 1960s, include the tendency most commonly known as "women's liberation." This strand had its roots in other social movements of the era, especially the civil rights movement, ethnic nationalist movements, the student movement, and the anti–Vietnam war movement.[14] Less formal "movement communities" and collectives were particularly popular among the (often) younger, more revolutionary elements of the movement, who dubbed their goal the "liberation" of women in the context of other liberation movements based in race and class. Detractors referred to them scornfully as "women's libbers." This strand included many female college students and recent college graduates, reflecting the increasing number of women in higher education during these years, a trend driven by the postwar economic boom. Deferral of marriage and a broadening of intellectual horizons during college years, along with the freedom from unwanted pregnancy provided by the new "birth control pill," contributed greatly to the ranks of independent young women attracted to the liberation movement.

Working-class, community-activist feminisms also linked up to the women's liberation strand through the involvement of young, mostly middle-class white women in the civil rights movement and the student-led new left emerging in and around college campuses. New left groups like Students for a Democratic Society (SDS) sought alliance with civil rights groups to build an interracial movement of the poor. Efforts like SDS's Economic Research and Action Projects (ERAP) brought many

young white women into contact with women of color who were community activists. While the projects were sometimes marred by conde-
scension, they were also powerful models of attempts to acknowledge and
resist the privileges that came with whiteness and affluence.[15] Women-
to-women dialogues across divides of race and class in these projects
helped shape the kind of feminisms that emerged later in the decade.[16]

The women who formed the core and the corps of this strand of the
movement drew upon a great deal of social movement experience, and
some of that experience moved them to create their own movement.
Many women in the civil rights, ethnic power, student, and antiwar
movements experienced marginalization, harassment, disrespect, and
an unequal workload. Sensitized to issues of inequality and injustice by
these other movements, they turned their analyses back upon their male
colleagues, demonstrating that they were not living up to their own egalitarian ideals when it came to the treatment of women. Two of the most
important early manifestos in this development were position papers
drafted within SNCC in 1964 and 1965, one by a young black activist,
Ruby Doris Smith Robinson, the other by two young white women in
the organization, Casey Hayden and Mary King. Both of these essays
argued, as would many others in short order, that the position of women
in SNCC had analogies to the position of blacks in white America. By
the late 1960s the concept of "sexism" emerged as the central movement
term, designed to parallel the concept of "racism." The analogy, while
immensely productive of new ideas and attitudes, was also highly problematic, since race and gender were different in many respects, and
paralleling them initially seemed to erase women of color. As a later
book title colorfully expressed it: "all the women are white, all the blacks
are men, but some of us are brave."[17]

While some men within SNCC and other radical movement groups
responded favorably to the claims made by women, many more did not,
calling their claims trivial and a distraction from the "real" struggles
around race, class, and war. Some feminists continued to work on issues
of gender equity within these movements, forming "women's caucuses"
within organizations. While some success was achieved in this way, and
while women continued to work on all these issues, increasingly feminists
felt the need to carve out an independent movement to address their
concerns. Initially this proved easier for white women; many women of

color continued to feel that racial oppression had to be their central concern, or was a parallel rather than an intersecting concern. African American activist Florynce Kennedy, for example, listed her affiliations in 1970 as the black liberation movement and the women's liberation movement. But all the radical feminist groups formed in the late 1960s and early 1970s were deeply shaped by the mood set by groups like the Black Panthers; they saw women's liberation as part of a larger revolutionary movement to overthrow a racist, capitalist, *and* patriarchal order.[18]

When these young activists started their own women's liberation groups, they drew deeply upon the antihierarchical forms that were dominant in groups like SNCC and the radical SDS. But having seen the limits to real equality within those supposedly egalitarian groups, they were even more deeply suspicious of the tendency of inequalities of power to emerge even within organizations dedicated to equality. Thus, the movement communities these women formed were even more carefully designed to fend off hierarchy. Just as blacks had come to feel that the presence of whites in their liberation movement hampered the independent development of black empowerment, many of these early efforts insisted on being women-only groups.

Consciousness-Raising

The typical social science story of the women's movement has a difficult time dealing with the fact that large-scale, mass organizations with clear hierarchies were only a small part of the movement. Indeed, they were often seen as part of the problem. The most common form was the small group or collective. These "CR groups" or "rap groups," consisting most often of from five to twenty women, gave a mass movement an unusually intimate form and forum highly appropriate to the movement's goals and ideologies.[19] While sometimes associated with white women's liberationist part of the movement, consciousness-raising, under various names, has been central to all feminist struggles. Toni Cade [Bambara], for example, wrote in 1970: "Throughout the country in recent years, black women have been forming work-study groups, discussion clubs, cooperative nurseries . . . women's workshops on the campuses, women's caucuses within existing organizations, Afro-American women's magazines."[20]

As the other common name for CR groups, "rap" groups (from the black English term for intense conversation), suggests, the roots of the form are partly in practices like the consensus-seeking meetings in SNCC (see chapter 1). The women's liberation strand of the late 1960s and early 1970s systematized what is often a more inchoate movement process. A handful of CR groups became famous because of their location in big cities or because of their widely circulated publications: for example, Bread and Roses, New York Radical Women, the Furies, Redstockings, Radicalesbians, the Combahee River Collective, WITCH. But by the late 1960s and early 1970s there were thousands of such groups in cities and small towns across America.[21]

As African American feminist Cellestine Ware characterized it in her brilliant book, *Woman Power* (1970), the role of CR groups was to express, compare, analyze, theorize, and then organize against all the ways in which women were oppressed. This meant thinking about and challenging the specific sexist structures in every "public" and "private" social space: the factory, sweatshop, kitchen, bedroom, classroom, boardroom, playing field, courtroom, or the halls of Congress. From the beginning, the new feminists realized that this largely unexplored set of analyses needed to be made from the ground up, through a process of comparing individual women's stories and turning them into a set of structural analyses. The point was to move from collected personal experiences to theorized general conditions, and then to further actions flowing from the analyses.[22]

A new language had to be invented to characterize the experiences of oppression and liberation that had no name. Sometimes this meant literally inventing new words; for instance, the newly minted concept "sexism" was used to examine the ways in which discrimination against women was built into the very structure of the language. Women challenged every generic use of *man* or *he* claiming to speak for all "humanity," and they invented or adopted words to displace the presumptive "man" at the center of all public activity: *firefighter* for *fireman, worker* for *workman, business executive* for *businessman, chair* for *chairman, police officer* for *policeman, representative* or *senator* for *congressman,* and so on across all the various social spaces and places where women were absent or underrepresented. This task also moved in the opposite direction, replacing feminized and invariably lesser female versions of terms. Thus, *flight attendant* replaced *stewardess,* or more to the point of this chapter, *poet* came to be used in place of the condescending *poetess.* But beyond neologisms, the deeper task was to find language to express oppressions and liberations that had no name.

Whether from formal CR groups, informal discussions, or shared writings, there emerged from consciousness-raising a host of new issues for the agenda of women's liberation. Shared stories moved women from the isolation of battering to a collective analysis of domestic violence, from a personal sense of sexual inadequacy to calls for equal sexual pleasure for women, from a sense of the social "double jeopardy" of being a woman and of color to women-of-color feminisms, from personal fears about pregnancy or forced sterilization to calls for reproductive rights, from poverty viewed as personal failure to analyses of welfare rights and the feminization of poverty, from personal experiences of intimidation by the boss to the concept of sexual harassment, and so on for dozens of issues that were moved from the personal to the political through collective dialogue, discussion, and debate.

The formal CR group, according to the early women's movement activist Pam Allen, proceeded through four stages: opening up (revealing personal feelings); sharing (through dialogue with other group members); analyzing (seeking general patterns by comparing to other experiences); and abstracting (creating a theory). Sometimes misunderstood as therapy, which it no doubt became on some occasions in some groups, CR was intended to strengthen the theoretical basis for revolutionary action. As feminist theorist and women's movement historian Katie King notes, the aim of "CR is not to exchange or relive experience, nor is it cathartic. Rather, its purpose is to teach women to think abstractly, and the purpose of thinking abstractly is to create theory in order to clarify and clear the ground for action."[23] Much important feminist thought and action emerged from this process, and was presented in written form in such early feminist anthologies as *Sisterhood Is Powerful* (1970), *The Black Woman* (1970), *Radical Feminism* (1973) (which collects materials from three earlier collections, *Notes from the First Year, Second Year* and *Third Year*), and, in poetic form, *No More Masks! An Anthology of Poems by Women* (1973).

As several feminist critics have argued, some kind of positing of group commonality plays a necessary heuristic role in all feminist organizing (or any other movement that includes an element of collective identity).[24] The problem arises with the rush to give that heuristic concept a specific content. Some feminists can be justly accused of this kind of "essential-ism," arguments that homogenize all women as essentially alike (in op-pression or in resistance).[25] But there has always been a way of drawing on experiences, a way of doing consciousness-raising, that suggests a path through this dilemma. Rather than simply being replaced, consciousness-raising can be, and often has been, re-placed into a more varied public space where conflicting and complementary "experiences" have pro-vided the bases for painful but productive arguments within feminism that have broadened and deepened the movement(s). This is precisely what happened in many parts of the early feminist movement, and has continued to happen ever since. As I suggested, formal consciousness-raising groups in the women's movement of the late 1960s and early 1970s were just the particular form of a larger, more general process of raising consciousness that goes on in many movements and many forms. In women's movements, one of the key forms, though hardly the only one, has the been the writing, reading, and performing of poetry.

Women's Movement Poetry and the Range of Feminist Issues

Poems about women in economic poverty and spiritual poverty; poems about battering and resistance to battering; poems about sisterly soli-darity and unsisterly betrayal; poems about factory work and maid work; poems about men as oppressors or men as lovers or men as lov-ing oppressors; poems about women loving women; poems about the power in menstruation and the beauty of vaginas; poems about bad sex and good sex; poems in Spanglish and Niuyorican, black English and white Wellesley diction; poems about the pain of abortion and the pain of childbirth; poems about sterilization of poor women and the sterile lives of upper-class women; poems about women's history and women's future; poems about reform and revolution; poems about women in barrios and Chinatowns, Indian reservations and ghettos; poems revalu-ing traditional women's work and celebrating women breaking barriers into male-dominated jobs; poems about women lumberjacks and women quilters; poems about witches and bitches, *brujas* and voodoo queens; poems about women athletes and bookish women; poems about breast-feeding and breast cancer; poems about laundry and feminist theology; poems about war and peace; poems about women in Vietnam and Span-ish Harlem; poems about Harriet Tubman and Marilyn Monroe; poems about Wall Street and Main Street; poems about changing diapers and changing lives; even poems about writing poems. Poems poured forth by the hundreds from the new wave of feminist activity crystallizing in the late 1960s.

Andrea Chessman and Polly Joan assert in their *Guide to Women's Publishing* that "poetry was the medium of the movement," and that while "every revolutionary movement has had its poets and its poetry, no other movement has been so grounded in poetry as Feminism."[26] I do not think it is necessary to call poetry "the" medium of the movement, but it has certainly played a very important role for many feminists. One reason for this is that no movement has had a more sweeping need for epistemological transformation, for transformation in the nature and scope of knowledge. In effect, the feminist movement claims that half of the world's population has largely been excluded from production of what counts as knowledge about that world. As noted above, the women's movement has transformed every field of human knowledge, from business to science to politics to art and literature to "home economics."

Feminist poetry is certainly not alone in bringing about this profound transformation, but it touches all these social and cultural realms, among others. But feminism also has brought about a more general transformation of consciousness above and beyond these particular realms. To get at these two different dimensions, I will look first at "women's movement poetry" as a general tool of social change, and then at a more narrowly defined "feminist poetry movement" as an example of a formation aimed at one particular cultural sphere, the profession of poem-making.

The movement understood that knowledge was power, and that knowledge/power was vested in language. At the center of this was the notion that dimensions of women's voices had been silenced, distorted, or trivialized for centuries. Thus poetry, as one of the richest tools for exploring the dynamic meaning-making processes of language, was bound to become an important movement resource. Poetry is particularly well equipped to challenge two crucial dichotomies: the separation of private and public spheres, and the split between "emotion" and "intellect." Poems had practical advantages as well. They could be produced in the interstices of the busy multitasking lives most women lead. They took far less time to write than books, and they were far easier to reproduce and circulate. They could be nailed to trees and telephone poles, taped to windows, and slid under doors. They lent themselves to performance in public, during a highly dramatic, performative era. They could also be set to music, turned into song.

The whole panoply of feminist issues that emerged from formal CR groups and from dozens of other sites of consciousness-raising activity can be found in poetry produced in and around the movement. In addition to anthologies of feminist poetry, most of the general anthologies of feminist thought from the new movement included poetry. The widely circulated collection, *Sisterhood Is Powerful: An Anthology of Writings from the Women's Liberation Movement* (1970), for example, was edited by a poet, Robin Morgan, and included a section entitled "The Hand That Cradles the Rock: Poetry as Protest." And one of the first major collections of feminist writings to center on women of color, *The Black Woman*, was edited by fiction writer/poet Toni Cade [Bambara], and privileged poems as the first set of readings. This is not because poetry "reflected" feminist issues, but because poetry was one of the main tools used to identify, name, formulate, and disseminate those issues. Poetry was consciousness-raising. Poetry was theory. Poetry was feminist practice.

When the radical women's liberation phase, with its emphasis on interconnections between race, class, and gender, was being displaced in the mid-1970s by a more mainstream brand of feminism, poetry became a key site for the articulation and contestation of feminisms. Poets like Adrienne Rich, Audre Lorde, Janice Mirikitani, Sonia Sanchez, Susan Griffin, Nikki Giovanni, Alice Walker, Wendy Rose, Judy Grahn, Pat Parker, Irena Klepfitz, Robin Morgan, Nellie Wong, Chrystos, June Jordan, Marge Piercy, Lorna Dee Cervantes, Joy Harjo, and Cherríe Moraga used poetry as part of an ongoing dialogue about the nature(s) and purpose(s) of feminism(s). In this context poems become mediators between a collective "woman" and particular communities of "women." Poetry plays an important role in diffusing these subject positions out into the wider culture where their impact is often independent of knowledge of their movement origins.

For some people who might be recruited to a movement and for some people already in it, poems (and other forms of art) are more effective in conveying movement ideology than are manifestos and other directly political forms. Katie King has argued that what she calls "art theoretical" discourses, including poetry, were central to the production of feminist cultures that were in turn "the primary location of feminist identity politics in the 70s and 80s."[27] These "art theoretical" "writing technolo-gies" (King includes "song" and "story" alongside "poetry") were espe-cially important in the struggles of various women-of-color feminists to dislodge white, middle-class women from the center of feminist thought. In this sense, poetry as theory and consciousness-raising did much to challenge the limits of theory emerging from the often fairly segregated movement groups.

Two poets edited one of the most influential books in the history of feminist thought, *This Bridge Called My Back: Radical Writing by Women of Color,* and much of its content takes the form of poetry. *This Bridge* not only featured poetry alongside more conventional forms of analysis, but also insisted that poetry was a form of feminist theory. Poems in that anthology (and others like it) drew upon personal experience mediated through race and ethnicity as well as gender, to show up the limiting "whiteness" of the identity proffered as normative in much women's movement culture. While poetry was by no means the only medium through which this critique was offered, it was a particularly powerful one.

Many other forms and forums of writing—manifestos, academic books and articles, novels and short stories, speeches, debates, and that close cousin to poetry, the song lyric—also contributed greatly to this process. King notes that mixed genres were particularly effective as their challenging of generic boundaries embodied their efforts to challenge the borders of what counted as feminism and feminist theory. This category would include, for example, Audre Lorde's mixing of autobiog-raphy, poetry, fiction, legend, and essay in her "biomythography" *Zami* (1982), or the mixing of *poemas, cuentos,* and *essais* in Gloria Anzaldúa's *Borderlands/La Frontera* (1987) and Cherríe Moraga's *Loving in the War Years* (1983).[28] The writing of poems, however, preceded even these longer works. Lorde suggests why this might be so: she notes that poetry is economical not only in terms of expression but also in terms of the material support needed to produce it: "poetry can be done between shifts, in the hospital pantry, on the subway, on scraps of surplus paper. Over the last few years writing a novel on tight finances, I came to appreciate the enormous differences in the material demands between poetry and prose. As we reclaim our literature, poetry has been the major voice of poor, working class [women], and [women of color]."[29]

This Bridge uses poetry to articulate both a collective "women-of-color position" and various ethnic-specific positionings. Other collections of writings, again invariably mixing poetry with prose fiction and nonfiction, focused on specific ethno-racialized communities of women. These texts identify points of solidarity and difference within such groups as Chicanas/Latinas *(Making Face, Making Soul: Hacienda Caras)*, African American women *(The Black Woman,* and *Home Girls: A Black Feminist Anthology)*, native women *(Reinventing the Enemy's Language: Contemporary Native American Women's Writings of North America)*, and Asian/Pacific American women *(Making Waves: An Anthology of Writings by and about Asian American Women)*. Lesbians of color played significant roles in all of these volumes, and each deals seriously with issues of sexuality as interwoven with class and other differences within communities of color. Similar volumes like *Nice Jewish Girls: A Lesbian Anthology* did much the same for a variety of self-defined feminist movement subcultures.[30] In these volumes poetry does much of the work of "auto-ethnography," of showing the experience of the self to be part of and in tension with the experience of the collective, the social group. The poems also become what Young calls "auto-theoretical" works in which self-exploration, as in all good consciousness-raising, is the beginning, not the end, of a process leading to theory and action. Again, the point is that poetry does not simply "reflect" ideas already in the air, but rather in giving "form" brings the ideas into public existence, and helps to invent identities, not merely to express them. Movements in general are highly productive places, sites of a great deal of "cultural poetics" — the bringing into visibility and audibility of new thoughts and feelings. In this case, the cultural poetics occurs through actual poetry. But the lines across genres in this respect are constantly transgressed; Rich, Lorde, and Anzaldúa are as well known for their essays as for their poems, and each reinforces and adds nuance to the other.

The process of feminist consciousness-raising continues. As it does so, poetry plays a role in each new site or phase of activity, helping to form new issues and new feminist identities. The rise of antimilitarist, environmentalist feminisms in the 1980s and early 1990s, for example, was inspired in part by poet Susan Griffin's lyrical study *Women and Nature* (1978), and various "ecofeminist" anthologies used poetry to present new ways of thinking about relations between the devaluing of women and the denigration of nature.[31] And the critically important challenges to the ethnocentric dimension of U.S. feminisms, emerging under the impact of feminist movements in the Southern Hemisphere

and of postcolonial theory in the universities, have also used poetry as
one key mode of contestation. Figures like Chandra Mohanty, Gayatri
Spivak, Trinh T. Minh-ha, Lata Mani, Caren Kaplan, Inderpal Grewal,
and Rey Chow gained prominence in the early 1990s by analyzing and
countering homogenizing, racist conceptions of "women in the Third
World" found in much U.S. feminism. This process gained support from
poets whose defamiliarizing verses challenged dominant Anglo-American
feminist paradigms. Trinh's poetic, auto-ethnographic *Woman/Native/
Other* offers one example, while Spivak's literary critical essays on Ben-
gali women poets and storytellers present another.[32] Over time, virtually
every constituency or position within the wide terrain of feminisms has
been constructed in part through poetry, from the most essentialist
statements of universal womanhood to the most deconstructive celebrations of postmodern fragmented subjectivities.

The Feminist Poetry Movement as a Cultural Formation

Let us turn now from "women's movement poetry" to the "feminist
poetry movement." The distinction is partly artificial, since the two forms
of activity overlap and intertwine, but it is useful to separate them in
order to understand the full cultural impact of feminism(s). The distinction can be put this way: in "women's movement poetry" the movement
comes first and is the central focus, with poetry as one of many means
of serving the movement, while in the "feminist poetry movement"
poetry comes first and the central concern is to establish a new kind of
poetry.[33] The feminist poetry movement is a cultural formation by and
aimed at professional poets and the cultural institutions (publishing
houses, literature departments, bookstores) surrounding them. The feminist poetry movement is both inside and beyond the women's movement. It is what British cultural theorist Raymond Williams calls a "formation," an intellectual or cultural school of thought, like impressionism
in painting or naturalism in fiction writing, that can have "significant
and sometimes decisive influence on the active development of a culture, and which [has] a variable and often oblique relation to formal
institutions."[34]

As historian of the feminist poetry movement Kim Whitehead puts
it, "feminist poetry began in a hundred places at once, in writing workshops and at open readings, on the kitchen tables of self-publishing poet/
activists, and in the work of already established poets who began slowly

to transform their ideas about formal strategies and thematic possibilities."[35] The grassroots troops of the new feminist poetry movement grew out of the hundreds of consciousness-raising groups and collectives. As these radical new feminist poets began to emerge, they caught the attention of some powerful, already-established women poets whose own poetry began to change under the influence of the movement. Poets like Adrienne Rich, June Jordan, and Gwendolyn Brooks were in varying degrees part of the poetry establishment when the women's movement emerged. The movement helped them understand ways in which they felt marginalized, stifled, or distorted by the male-dominated institutions and formations of the poetry world. At the same time, some of these poets had anticipated feminist themes in their work and with increasing self-consciousness brought that work to bear in the context of creating the women's movement. This led not only to a reworking by these poets of their own work, but also to a rethinking and researching of the role of women in the history of poetry.

Among living links to a longer legacy, no poet was more important to the movement than Muriel Rukeyser. A winner of the prestigious Yale Younger Poets prize in 1935, Rukeyser had given up a career of safe verse-making to immerse herself in the social and political struggles of the Depression years, a commitment she brought with her into the movements she associated with in the 1960s. Rukeyser, along with younger but established poets like Rich (who also had won the Yale prize for her first, premovement volume) became indefatigable teachers of poetry and poetics to the emerging generation of women's movement poets. Over time this process moved the category "woman poet" from a dismissive term to one charged with possibility.

As it emerged, the feminist poetry movement drew upon several other compatible developments in the field of poetry. Three strands from existing schools of poetry were particularly influential as rewritten into the terms of an emerging feminist poetic consciousness. First, the beat poets had begun in the 1950s a return of poetry to public performance. Poetry had become a rather genteel affair, more often read in libraries or living rooms. Beat poets like Allen Ginsburg were infamous for their raucous public poetry rituals. This process was then taken up by many protest poets in the 1960s, particularly antiwar poets (including Ginsburg himself) and poets in the black arts and other cultural nationalist movements. No group developed this return to poetry as performance, rather than silent reading, more powerfully than feminist poets who fostered hundreds of public readings in feminist bookstores, music festivals, and demonstrations. Second, the confessional school of poets, founded by figures like Robert Lowell in the 1950s and including some proto-feminist poets like Sylvia Plath and Anne Sexton, had opened up possibilities for personal psychological exploration that played well into the intimate psychological dynamics of emerging feminist experience. And third, the Black Mountain poets, among others, had begun moving poetry away from rigid formal lines to more open, free-verse forms. These forms were both better suited to the open explorations of self-in-society of feminist poets, and less daunting than rigid metrical poetry for women excluded from formal literary training.

Just as the early feminist movement scoured all history for examples of women struggling to liberate themselves from male-defined institutions and social roles, when the feminist poetry movement emerged, it naturally set out to find its poetic precursors. This task entailed both uncovering women poets buried under male-centered poetic histories, and rereading and reinterpreting female poets who had managed to find some hold in the mostly male-defined pantheon of important poets. In the United States it was nineteenth-century poet Emily Dickinson who served most often as a distant American foremother to the feminist poetry formation. The full range of Dickinson's poetry had only recently become available in the 1950s, and as her reputation grew as one of the two great poets of the latter half of the nineteenth century (alongside Walt Whitman), feminists struggled to rescue her from those who would ignore the powerful things she had to say about the minds and spirits of women.

Several poetry anthologies appearing in the early years of the new women's movement played a key role in solidifying the formation. The most successful of these was *No More Masks! An Anthology of Poems by Women* (1973), edited by Florence Howe (co-founder of Feminist Press) and Ellen Bass.[36] The collection starts with poems by Amy Lowell, Gertrude Stein, and other members of the modernist poetry movement of the early twentieth century, then presents an array of contemporary poets "shaped in the women's liberation movement." The collection includes 220 pieces from 86 poets, about 20 of them women of color. The title comes, not surprisingly, from a feminist poem by Rukeyser telling women to take off the false faces put upon them by patriarchy, and the subtitle indicates that the search for "poems by women" did not necessarily restrict the collection to a political definition of "feminist poet."

Howe reports in the preface to a later edition of the anthology that the book began as something of a "lark, a game" of collecting women poets that she engaged in with her then student Bass. As she puts it, "in the early seventies it was still possible to use a card catalog under the word 'women' and find 'poets,' though we could not have known then that many poets had slipped away, out of that net into invisibility." This process of scouring library card catalogs netted about fifty established women poets for the collection, and then, Howe notes, the "younger poets found us: Word spread quickly in the early seventies through women's liberation newspapers and newsletters. We received three hundred submissions through the mail."[37] From this Howe and Bass culled the collection, with only their "inchoate" feminism and an insistence that the "poem please us aesthetically" to guide them. This second criterion, the aesthetic one, is the mark of the formation on their efforts. The larger task, which might define the formation, is expressed by Howe as a set of questions in the preface to the original edition: "A nagging doubt: are women victims of prejudiced editors or are women poets out of the mainstream of modern poetry? What is the mainstream? And what do women write about?"[38]

No More Masks! was one of several anthologies that took on the task of answering these questions by making available for the first time a wide range of historical and contemporary poems by women. Other, similar volumes emerged in this same time period. It was clearly the moment when the formation was strong enough to begin shaping its own tradition. One such work was *Rising Tides: Twentieth-Century American Women Poets* (1973), whose goals were stated baldly in a prefatory paragraph: "Because representation in most poetry anthologies of the past has not gone beyond tokenism, most women writers have remained minor figures in the male-dominated literary world. This book is an attempt to make both men and women aware of the vital force women poets today represent." As the back cover put it, "Rising out of the same growing consciousness that spawned the women's liberation movement, this book is a feminist statement in the largest sense."[39] A year later came *The World Split Open: Four Centuries of Women Poets in England and America, 1552–1950* (1974), a collection whose title, again from a Rukeyser poem ("What would happen if one woman told the truth about her life? / The world would split open"), shows its connection to the movement, and whose subtitle indicates that it is aimed at helping to establish a still longer tradition.

By the end of the twentieth century, this literary formation had contributed mightily to a rewriting of the entire history of poetry. It is now possible to go to any literary bookstore in America and find dozens of anthologies dedicated to one or another of numerous strands and schools of feminist and/or women's poetry. Under the onslaught of this formation, and interrelated formations in ethnic and gay writing, literary history has been rewritten. It now not only includes but has been radically changed by the presence of a panoply of female (and often feminist) poets. And the future of poetry by women has been forever shaped by this remaking of the universe of poetry into an available *tradition* for women to build upon, just as surely as the wider culture was radically rewritten from top to bottom by feminist challenges to dominant paradigms of thought and action.

As impressive as the success of the "feminist poetry formation" was, it was only one among many similar feminist intellectual and cultural formations. Parallel efforts in academe, for example, gave birth to the closely connected formation of feminist literary studies, and also to feminist sociology, feminist political science, feminist anthropology, feminist science, and so on. Few, if any, realms of the arts or sciences remain unaffected by the kind of feminist formation represented by the feminist poetry movement. Each of these formations has had both a local impact on the particular area, and a mutually reinforcing impact across these realms of thought, such that they form a broader feminist intellectual/ cultural formation of great power.

Building Feminist Cultural Institutions

Both women's movement poetry and the feminist poetry movement depended upon the creation and development of parallel, feminist institutions. I have argued that, given the centrality of experience, emotion, language reformation, and intimate spheres of action to the feminist process of consciousness-raising, poetry with its linguistic and affective precision was well suited to play a major role in diffusing feminist ideas out into the world. But a very concrete process of institution building underwrote this predisposition. Drawing on the tradition found in

the civil rights, new left, and ethnic nationalist movements of creating
"parallel institutions" to challenge inadequate or corrupt ones in the
dominant society, all strands of women's movements built formal alternative cultural structures. Many CR groups, the first level of institutionalization, for example, became writing groups. Feminist CR/writing
groups in turn produced at first feminist broadsides, and then underground journals run by feminist publishing collectives. Feminist publishing collectives sponsored poetry readings and poetry festivals that
widened the audience, encouraging small feminist presses to move into
bigger projects. These processes produced and rediscovered enough writing to justify the creation of small feminist bookstores, and small feminist bookstores encouraged the creation of larger feminist presses. Larger
feminist presses proved the existence of a market for women's writing
that mainstream publishing houses could not ignore. They began then
to broker deals with mainstream publishing houses that guaranteed a
wider audience for feminist writers, and netted the feminist presses
profits that allowed them to bring more radical writers into print.[40] By
1978 a phenomenal seventy-three feminist periodicals and sixty-six feminist presses had sprung up, along with dozens of women's bookstores.[41]

While institutionalization certainly involved some watering down
upon entry into the "mainstream," many feminist writers resisted and
continue to resist that process and the individualizing, divide-and-
conquer strategy it often entails. When, for example, white feminist poet
Adrienne Rich won the National Book Award in 1974, she indicated, as
part of a joint statement written with two African American feminist
poets, fellow nominees Alice Walker and Audre Lorde, that she accepted
the award "not as an individual but in the name of all women whose
voices have gone and still go unheard in a patriarchal world." More generally, poets and editors negotiate between movement and nonmove-
ment sites, making individual and collective decisions about when to
support feminist presses and when to send their work out as incursions
into the wider world.

The process of feminist institution building also includes an academic
institution, women's studies departments, with a strong literary component that assisted the feminist poetry movement and used literature
as one means of classroom consciousness-raising. This led to efforts to
rewrite the canon of literature to include far more women's literature
and a significant amount of feminist literature. This process moved from

movement anthologies to women's studies textbooks to such major revisionist works as the *Heath Anthology of American Literature*, which in turn forced a reworking of such mainstream collections as the *Norton Anthology of American Literature*. This process has taken several decades, but from these small group beginnings there has emerged a vast body of feminist writing that has touched every level, layer, and corner of American society. There is now a great body of feminist thought enmeshed in virtually every literary anthology available for use in the classroom or by the casual reader.

Ultimately, Toni Morrison's Nobel Prize for literature, and the vast women-of-color literary movement she embodies, grows out of movement contexts through these layers of mediation. As usual, by the time that point is reached, the originating movement contexts have been lost in the mists of time (and hegemony), but their diffusion is nevertheless movement work. One might note by way of materially tracing this process that Morrison edited and wrote introductions for both the first collection of Huey Newton's Black Panther writings, *To Die for the People,* and one of the most important early collections of black feminist thought, *The Black Woman,* compiled by Toni Cade [Bambara]. Again, this can stand as but one example of a massive *diffusing* of feminist and other radical movement ideas into the mainstream. That this process also involves some *defusing,* some lessoning of the explosive impact found when texts are produced and received within a movement culture, is no doubt true. But that just suggests the need for ongoing movement struggle, struggle that should include taking far more credit for the powerful impact already achieved by the incorporation of feminist ideas into common-sense, mainstream thought and action.

Third Wave Poetics?

The debates within feminism in the 1980s and 1990s are interpreted differently. To some liberal white women committed to maintaining a status quo, the debates were seen as divisive, particularly in the context of a "backlash" against feminism in the years of Reaganism and Christian conservatism.[42] To women in the Third World, U.S. women of color, and their white allies who believe feminism should not be dominated by one set of privileged voices, the turmoil, however painful, has been healthy and transformative. Similar ferment surrounds the language and concept of a "third wave" of feminism. Some suggest that the critique of "hegemonic feminism" by lesbians and women of color in the United States and the Third World itself constituted a third-wave movement. Others see this as a process that has cleared the way, making it possible for a younger generation to take the movement in new directions. For others still, the wave metaphor is always falsely homogenizing, untrue to the variety of sites of feminist movement activity.[43] But however one characterizes it, feminist activity is alive and well in the twenty-first century, both in the form of ongoing women's movements and in the impact of feminism within other progressive movements.

It is also clear that as these movements continue, poetry will continue to be a powerful feminist tool. The feminist music movement, which has always been closely linked to feminist poetry, was given renewed energy in the 1990s by new feminist music, most notably the independent folk/rock of Ani DiFranco, the post-punk energy of Riot Grrrls, and feminist rap by performers like Queen Latifah. The feminist poetry movement is also one of the forces behind the renewed energy in performed, or "spoken word," poetry. Growing as well out of the powerful hip-hop culture pioneered by black and Latino/a youth (which in turn owes much to black power and Latino/a nationalist poetics), spoken word performance is an important site of feminist consciousness-raising for younger women (and men), and a sign that poetry will continue to be one key site of feminist action for years to come.

FOUR

Revolutionary Walls

Chicano/a Murals, Chicano/a Movements

The people we now call Mexican Americans, or Chicanos, came into existence through resistance to two wars of conquest. The first was that of Spanish conquistadors, who in the sixteenth century invaded and decimated the native peoples of the territories now known as Mexico and the southwestern United States. Rape, concubinage, and intermarriage between the Spaniards, various indigenous peoples, African slaves, and others eventually created *la raza cósmica,* the multihued mix of peoples that is Mexico. The second war of conquest was that of the United States against Mexico. The U.S. states of Texas, New Mexico, Arizona, Utah, Nevada, and California, as well as parts of Wyoming and Colorado, were part of Mexico before they were forcibly brought under U.S. dominion through the Texas and Mexican-American wars of the mid-nineteenth century. Begun on a dubious pretense and resisted by many in the United States as a war of imperial conquest, the Mexican-American War ended in 1848 with the Treaty of Guadalupe Hidalgo. Forced on a defeated Mexico, the treaty extended the U.S. empire into the Southwest and California. Overnight, thousands of Mexicans found themselves strangers in their own land, putatively "American" now but generally treated as second-class citizens.

Mexican Americans can rightfully claim deeper roots in these regions of the United States than most other citizens, yet they are often confused with and portrayed as "illegal aliens." Maintaining their cultural heritage while becoming citizens of the United States was a complicated process involving sporadic open conflict (like the Mexican American outlaws who fought ranchers and Rangers in Texas), as well as subtle daily acts of resistance during many generations. The process of "becoming Mexican American," as George Sánchez named it, was long, complex, and multifaceted.[1] It produced identities riddled with contradictions resulting from decades of racism, externally imposed and internalized.

Before the 1960s, many Mexican Americans, especially those in a small but influential middle class, believed that the best way to be accepted as Americans was to deny much of the Mexican and Indian side of their heritage and to assimilate into the white or "Anglo" world. But that world was most often hostile and exploitative rather than welcoming. Despite legal gains made by Mexican American civil rights groups like LULAC (the League of United Latin American Citizens, a group similar to the NAACP), the veterans' group GI Forum, and others, Mexican Americans entered the 1960s segregated in *barrios* (Spanish for "neighborhoods"), with inferior schools and services, high unemployment, and a staggering rate of poverty. They were routinely subject to racist insults to their culture, as well as brutality from the police and discrimination from employers. The once open border between the United States and Mexico had become a zone of harassment separating families and loved ones, and subjecting both Mexican visitors and Mexican American citizens to constant threats of deportation or refusal of reentry.

But resistance was also present amid assimilation and acquiescence. The popular front social movement of the 1930s and 1940s, driven by labor union struggles, shaped many future leaders of what would become the Chicano movement.[2] Mexican American labor leaders like Josephina Fierro de Bright and the "cannery women" strikers in California, and Bert Corona of the Los Angeles branch of the longshoremen's union, set models for later activism and in some cases directly involved themselves in the new struggles of the 1960s and 1970s. Many Mexican American activists in the 1930s were also part of El Congreso de Pueblo de Habla Español, an important progressive political coalition of "Spanish-speaking people." Despite significant racism among the white working class, the workplace in the 1930s and 1940s also included multiracial coalitions, reflecting the sense that class unity was needed to overcome the racist "divide and conquer" strategies of employers.[3]

When the new "Chicano generation" rose to prominence in the 1960s, it had to negotiate the complications of these multiple identities, challenging assimilation, building on activist models laid by predecessors, improvising new elements, and exorcising elements of internalized racism that hindered the creation of a newly politicized sense of self and community. Despite these difficulties, the efforts made by people of Mexican descent living in the United States to claim the right to their own dignity, identity, language, and culture broadened in the 1960s to become *el movimiento*, the Chicano movement.

Various social factors help account for the rise of new activism: the urbanization of Mexican Americans, an increase in the Mexican American population (which doubled after World War II in some areas like Los Angeles), a larger proportion of youth as part of the "baby boom," more Mexican American students in college thanks to financial aid for students of color in the wake of the black civil rights movement, and a new group of Mexican American activists who learned organizing skills in student-centered protest groups like SNCC, SDS, and the Berkeley Free Speech Movement. Women like Maria Varela and Elizabeth "Betita" Martinez, both SNCC veterans and the former a cofounder of SDS, brought a new kind of movement know-how into the community. Veteran labor movement activists like Corona and César Chávez added to the storehouse of community organizing skills.[4]

As the 1960s rolled on, a new generation, led by students but including many from earlier generations as well, began to call themselves "Chicano," a term taken from street slang that announced the emergence of a new political identity. Chicanos reversed the policies and ideologies of assimilation and sought instead to recover, understand, and celebrate the cultural heritage that made them unique, while insisting on their economic and political rights as citizens of the United States.[5] Many identified with the Mexican revolutionaries of the early twentieth century and sought sweeping, radical change to wipe out racism and class inequality.

Murals in Movement, Movement in Murals

While Chicano movement artists worked and continue to work in many media, and while artists from many other racial and ethnic backgrounds work with murals, most historians and critics note a special affinity between the Chicano movement and the community mural movement.[6] Some sense of this affinity can be conveyed by noting that in the Los Angeles area alone (from which I will draw most of my examples) more than a thousand Chicano murals have been created since 1965. Chicano murals can also be found in great numbers throughout Texas, the Southwest, and some Midwest cities like Chicago, where large numbers of Mexican Americans live.

The most common reason given for the attractiveness of the mural form for Chicano (male) and Chicana (female) artist-activists is the inspiration of the great Mexican muralists of the 1920s and 1930s: Diego Rivera, José Clemente Orozco, and David Alfaro Siquieros. These men were important to the cultural politics of Mexico, and during the 1930s they were significant figures on the cultural side of the popular front labor movement in the United States. To a large extent the modern mural art form is the invention of these Mexican artists. "Los tres grandes" ("the three greats"), as they are known, were important models not only as major modern artists but also as political activists who rooted their muralism in support for the struggles of the poorest, most exploited members of their communities. The work of the Mexican muralists was extended into the United States during the 1930s through government-sponsored mural programs that eventually covered the walls of hundreds of post offices and other public buildings. Knowledge of this legacy inspired many of the creators of Chicano murals and played a role in the general public appeal of murals.

But there was another key element in that popularity—the prior existence in the barrio of a model of popular painted public art. This was *pulquería* art, the painting of landscapes and other scenes on the exterior walls of taverns, restaurants, shops, and other public buildings in Mexico and in U.S. barrios. The tradition of *pulquería* art lent a sense of familiarity to the murals that began to appear in the community with the rise of the Chicano movement. Just as the adaptation of black church music for the purposes of the civil rights movement allowed a radical new content to enter through a familiar, nonthreatening mode, the existence of *pulquería* art probably lessened the shock of the radical new messages being conveyed by community murals.

Other features of early Chicano murals drew from an image-system familiar to many in the barrios. These include the use of images drawn from Mexicano/Chicano religious observations, particularly *altares* (the small religious shrines found in many Chicano homes), as well as *estampas* and *almanaques* (chrome-lithographed religious prints and calendars). On the more secular side, muralists drew upon the style of customized *ranflas* (low-rider cars), on *tatuajes* (home-made india ink tatoos), and *placas* (spray-painted graffiti logos). Initially less familiar but soon ubiquitous images drawn from indigenous art, especially Aztec, Olmec, Mayan, and Toltec sources, round out those elements that contributed to a specifically Chicano aesthetic. Add to these sources images drawn from American pop culture that had, by the 1960s, become part of a national youth culture shared by young Chicanos, and you have the main image repertoire used for movement murals. In various combinations these images became the aesthetic base for the articulation of complex, painted political messages that played a key role in reinventing Mexican Americans as Chicanos.

Painting History on the Wall

As I explore the interwoven histories of Chicano/a movement(s) and Chicana/o murals, I'll view the murals as expressions of key aspects of and issues in *el movimiento,* while periodically addressing the political possibilities and limits of the community mural as a form. I'll discuss a series of murals created by Chicano and Chicana artists from the late 1960s to the present, emphasizing that, like other movements, the Chicano movement continues, despite setbacks and changes, to this day.

The intertwined nature of the Chicano movement and the mural movement is apparent already in one of the first Chicano murals executed in California. Painted by Antonio Bernal on the wall of the offices of United Farm Workers/El Teatro Campesino cultural center in Del Rey in 1968, this mural can be read as a kind of origin story of the Chicano movement.[7]

To begin with, the location of the mural immediately points to one of the political struggles that gave birth to the Chicano movement and underscores that murals were not the only important Chicano movement art form. El Teatro Campesino (The Farmworkers' Theater) was a vital theater group that grew up on the front lines of the farmworkers' union movement led by César Chávez and Dolores Huerta. El Teatro Campesino originated in the fields in *actos* (one-act skits) performed by farmworkers themselves that urged their *compañeros* and *compañeras* to support the union. Under the guidance of Luis Valdez, El Teatro later expanded its repertoire to take up issues facing urban Chicanos and acted to bridge rural farmworker families and their city counterparts. El Teatro inspired many other Chicano theater troupes that formed throughout California, Texas, and the Southwest.

Turning to the mural itself, and "reading" it from left to right, we get a clear, strong portrait of the forces feeding into and inspiring the Chicano movement. On the far left we see La Adelita, mythical heroine of the Mexican Revolution of 1910. La Adelita is a kind of composite figure for all the *soldaderas* (women warriors) who fought in the revolution, one whose spirit has often been celebrated in *corridos* (political ballads, which have a long history in Mexican and Mexican American culture). That revolution sought to return control of Mexico to ordinary peasants and workers, particularly to those of Indian ancestry who had never fully accepted Spanish domination. This celebration of *indigenismo* (the native *indio* component of Mexican identity) was part of a similar celebration of the Indian part of Chicano identity and a downplaying of the European side (seen as too close to the dominant U.S. Anglo identity).

Alongside La Adelita are two heroes of the revolution, Emiliano Zapata and Pancho Villa. These two peasant leaders became folk heroes to young Chicanos who saw themselves as involved in a similar guerrilla struggle of poor farm laborers and industrial workers against Anglo domination in the United States. To the right of Villa is the legendary Joaquín Murieta, the Mexican/Californian Robin Hood of the gold rush era. Murieta is said to have fought bravely against European American gold miners who stole the claims of Mexican Californians. The gold rush era was the time when the transition of California from a Mexican to an Anglo state was largely completed, primarily through the illegal seizure not only of mine holdings but of many of the landholdings of Mexican Californians under the newly imposed, Anglo-dominated state government. Murieta symbolizes resistance within the confines of the once Mexican parts of the United States, just as Zapata and Villa represent resistance by ordinary people to class and racial hierarchy within Mexico proper. Like La Adelita, Murieta has been and continues to be the subject of numerous *corridos*.

These four figures from history served to evoke a heritage of struggle by the peoples inhabiting the space where Mexico and the United States have permeable boundaries. They express that *el movimiento*, though often led by young people, quickly developed a strong sense of history and drew strength from a long line of figures that had struggled in greater Mexico (including the U.S. Southwest) for justice against oppression. Retelling the history of Mexico and of Americans of Mexican descent was a key part of the movement. This desire to create a new history free of stereotyped docile Mexicans with an inferior culture led to struggles to form Chicano studies programs that could assure these new stories a place in the curriculum. A militant generation of Chicano historians and social scientists gave rise to new scholarship that saw the United States as an imperial power that, having conquered part of Mexico, tried to force its people to conform to Anglo values, language, and culture. They emphasized the ways in which attempts to impose European American culture were defeated by strong familial and communal resistance from Americans of Mexican descent. Neighborhood murals in which historical figures like these were portrayed as quite literally larger than life became important "textbooks" that spurred an interest in history. This interest could then be nourished by the writings of insurgent historians whose academic work carried the movement to high schools and colleges, where hundreds of students walked out of classes or went on strike for an education that respected their heritage and identity. These "blowouts," as they were known, started in high schools in southern California and were immensely inspirational. They challenged older people to catch up with the younger ones.

Moving into more recent times, the next two figures in the mural represent struggles that fueled Chicano pride and activism more directly in the mid-1960s: César Chávez of the farm workers movement, and Reies López Tijerina of the Hispano land grant struggle in the Southwest. Chávez was a community organizer who became a union organizer and therefore understood that workers are always part of larger communities. While the United Farm Workers (UFW) union had members of many ethnic groups, the majority were Chicanos, and Chávez and union cofounder Dolores Huerta placed symbols of Mexican and Mexican American culture at the heart of their nonviolent organizing efforts. The UFW flag (which Chávez holds in the mural) proudly bore a black Aztec eagle against a red background, a symbol soon to become identified with the Chicano/a movement generally. The union began its first *huelga* (strike) on 16 September 1965, the day commemorated as the beginning of the Mexican Revolution. And when they marched, the UFW members carried a statue of the Virgen de Guadeloupe, patron saint of the Mexican poor, thus linking the Catholic faith of the majority of union members to the struggle, as black Christianity helped form a base for the civil rights movement. In this way Chávez sought to reclaim the spirit of Christianity from a conservative church hierarchy, much as Reverend

King and other black ministers had reclaimed the protesting spirit of black Protestantism. While Chávez, deeply influenced by the multiracial labor coalitions of the popular front era, never saw himself as leading a Chicano union or as part of an exclusively Chicano movement, the union and its members became powerful symbols whose strikes, marches, boycotts, and other protests inspired pride and resistance among the new Chicano generation.

Next to Chávez stands another figure of great importance to an emerging Chicano movement. Reies López Tijerina led the Hispano land grant movement during the mid- and late 1960s in the Southwest. Tijerina and his followers claimed descent from the original, pre-Anglo Spanish settlers *(hispanos)* of the Southwest whose land had been stolen by the invading Yankees. After repeated attempts to press their claims in court, Tijerina's Alianza took up armed rebellion on 5 June 1967, surrounding and then occupying a courthouse symbolic of their land claims. Word of Tijerina's guerrilla action spread quickly among the Chicano community, offering a contemporary exemplar of the kind of resistance practiced by Zapata and Villa. Though hardly a revolution, the courthouse raid seemed to link the legendary bandits and revolutionaries of the past to the current moment and to reinforce a sense among many militant young Chicanos that perhaps only armed resistance could overthrow Anglo colonization of the U.S. peoples of Mexican descent.

More broadly, Tijerina's focus on land fed into the developing notion of Aztlán, quasi-mythical ancient homeland of the Aztecs, said to cover most of those areas of the United States that now have large Chicano populations. A desire to reclaim Aztlán was a deeply symbolic expression of the right to feel at home within the confines of the United States, and an attempt to found a newly awakened Chicano *raza* (people, nation) on the resurrected memory of a homeland that predated by hundreds of years the coming of Europeans. Evocations of Aztlán became common in the political rhetoric, poetry, music, and murals of the movement.

Finally, the mural depicts to the right of Tijerina two African Americans, a composite Black Panther/Malcolm X figure, and Martin Luther King Jr. These figures express Chicano solidarity with the struggles of African Americans and also presumably acknowledge the debt of the Chicano movement to the model of struggle provided by the civil rights and black power movements. César Chávez frequently acknowledged his debt to King's concept of nonviolent resistance, and it is not hard to draw a parallel between Tijerina's tactics and those of the Black Panthers and other militant African Americans with whom he made alliances. The inclusion of these figures suggests that el movimiento was allied to a larger movement for justice for all peoples oppressed within a United States dominated by rich white men and an all-white notion of "American" culture.

If I were to give the image of community conveyed in Bernal's mural a name, it would be something like "community as militant or revolutionary solidarity." To achieve this image of solidarity, the mural collages together, or some would say paints over, several ideological differences. The nonviolent strategies of King and Chávez, for example, exist unproblematically alongside the armed struggle represented by the Mexican revolutionaries, the Black Panthers, and Tijerina. And while the overall image was surely intended to evoke an emerging chicanismo, a Chicano nationalism similar to the black nationalism discussed in chapter 2, none of the pictured individuals, including the contemporary ones, were full supporters of a nationalist position. But this expresses both a truth of the movement and one of the strengths of muralism. The truth is that a spirit of common struggle did unite a great many Chicanos at this time, despite ideological, tactical, regional, gender, class, and other differences. No medium was better equipped to express this solidarity-in-difference than the wordless form of the mural where the complexities of verbal political positionings are muted in a visual language of pure juxtaposition—all the figures forming a single, united front of resistance. This sense of united effort was given historical depth not only by the historical figures in the scene but also in the style of the mural, which draws from the Mexican muralists who had drawn from the style of ancient Indian friezes (which, like Bernal's mural, typically depict people in three-quarter profile).

Out of this ethos, inspired by Chávez, Tijerina, and the Mexican revolutionaries, with models of action, culture, and rhetoric drawn from these figures and from the black liberation struggle, and out of an increasing dissatisfaction with liberal assimilation, a vibrant, widespread Chicano movement had arrived by 1968. El movimiento was expressed largely through regional power bases rather than a single national organization. In Texas and parts of the Southwest the Mexican American Youth Organization (MAYO) and its offspring La Raza Unida Party played the central organizing role. La Raza Unida challenged Anglo dominance through city, county, state, and national electoral campaigns that were at the same time movements of community and Chicano cultural pride. In Denver the Crusade for Justice, led by Rudolfo "Corky" Gonzales, was a powerful grassroots movement with a strong separatist bent that celebrated Chicano culture and the most militant heroes of the Mexican and Cuban revolutions. Significantly, Gonzales was also the product of an urban barrio; a bit younger than Chávez and Tijerina, he was better able to express the spirit of an increasingly young and urban Mexican American generation. Gonzales's epic poem, *Yo Soy Joaquín* ("I Am Joaquín"), later made into a short film by Luis Valdez of El Teatro Campesino, was a powerful compilation of Chicano history from the Aztecs to the United Farm Workers, which drew together and popularized many of the key themes and aesthetic motifs of Chicano cultural nationalism.[8]

California was the center not only of the United Farm Workers but also of the struggle for Chicano studies in the universities, a struggle won usually through student protests and strikes. In Santa Barbara, California, the creation of El Movimiento Estudiantil Chicano de Aztlán (MEChA) in 1968 united several existing student groups into the single most important student group of the Chicano movement, one that became a force on and off campus, in high schools as well as community colleges and universities. California was also home to one of the most radical, paramilitary groups in the movement, the Brown Berets, a group with many similarities to the Black Panthers that protested police brutality in the barrios and often provided security for marches and rallies. These various groups had differing ideas and agendas, some reflecting regional variations in the lives of Chicanos, some representing differences in political ideology, but all were imbued with a sense that Chicanos would never accept being second-class citizens ashamed of their culture. Some of the energy of MEChA emerged from the great student "blowouts" of March 1968. Begun as a student strike at Abraham Lincoln School in East Los Angeles, the blowouts eventually involved more than ten thousand students and effectively shut down the city school system. The thirty-six demands of the strike committee included hiring Mexican American and Spanish-speaking teachers and administrators, offering classes in the history of Mexican and Mexican American culture, and ending other racist practices in the schools. On the picket lines outside the schools and school board headquarters, signs proclaiming "Chicano Power!" and "¡Viva La Raza!" drew media atten-tion. As the first major mass protest specifically against racism by Mexi-can Americans, the events had a stunning impact on an emerging gen-eration of young activists.

Another famous Chicano mural that embodies this ethos and extends the scope of solidarity even beyond Aztlán is based on a widely circu-lated poster with a close-up image of Latino revolutionary guerrilla Che Guevara next to the declaration "We Are Not a Minority." Both the poster and the mural versions parody the "Uncle Sam Wants You" recruitment posters of World War I. They became in effect a kind of "Uncle Che Wants You" recruitment device for the Chicano movement. The mural version of the image shows the ability of murals to be at once powerfully direct and yet usefully ambiguous in their rhetoric (even when assisted by some words). For example, to some viewers this piece offers a clear revolutionary message, either a cultural nationalist one about internal colonialism oppressing Chicanos, or a revolutionary internationalist one suggesting worldwide solidarity by peoples of color. These two related but different brands of revolutionism were both prominent in the 1960s and early 1970s. The notion of "internal colonialism," developed power-fully in one of the books that shaped the Chicano movement, Rudolfo Acuña's *Occupied America,* argues that the position of Chicanos within the southwestern United States is parallel to the status of a nation under European colonialism: the dominant culture attempts to impose its forms on a subject people, extracts a wealth of resources from those occupied territories, and gives back little other than paternalistic claims to be helping backward peoples. The "internal colony" notion was a powerful one, especially when tied to the idea of Aztlán as Chicano "homeland."

While this first interpretation stresses the situation within the United States, a second interpretation of the Che mural places it within a wider claim about an *international* movement of resistance. Che Guevara was an Argentinean by birth who played a decisive role in the Cuban Revo-lution against a corrupt U.S.–backed regime, and later died fighting for a similar cause in Bolivia. Just as the black movement drew strength from the image of anticolonial struggles in Africa, Chicanos drew special in-spiration from the struggles in Spanish-speaking countries of South America against European and U.S. colonialism. In the black power move-ment some groups, like the Panthers, stressed alliance with any groups, including white radicals, furthering revolutionary change, while others held a separatist all-black position. Similarly, Chicano groups divided over this strategic question. This division is usefully invisible in the mural.

Probably the majority of people in the community would read the Che mural more modestly and generally as a reminder that in the wider world, people of color are the majority, not the minority, and that within the United States no one should accept the second-class status that the term *minority* conveys. There is also an attempt to give historical depth to the community through an infusion of *indigenismo* in the form of the letter *A* done in the shape of a Mayan pyramid. These various political positions do not easily coexist, and they became the source of bitter ideological struggle, especially in the early 1970s. But the mural shows that the phrase "We Are Not a Minority" is meaningful to a very large segment of the Chicano community, a community that the visual rhetoric of such murals helped to form.

The Del Rey and Che murals dramatically convey the political bravado of the early years of the movement, roughly 1968 to the early 1970s, when certain cracks and contradictions just beneath the surface could still be plastered over. Eventually, failure to come to terms with ideological contradictions between reformism and revolutionism, as well as others regarding gender and class, would be part of the undoing of the most radical phase of the movement. I want to suggest here that these murals were expressing a strategic ambiguity or openness that is a key ingredient in moments of movement formation. Such images of community speak a connection caught in *el movimiento*'s terms by *carnalismo*, a "blood" connection deeper than ideology and carried not biologically, as the term misleadingly suggests, but through a shared cultural history of exploitation, oppression, and resistance. Such a notion is part of an "essentialist" moment that is probably an inescapable phase in any emerging movement. "Essentialist" notions (suggesting a natural, biological, essential connectedness) must always be weighed strategically against the costs of suppressing necessary debate about political and cultural differences. These moments embody a confusion between the idea that the movement *expresses* the community, and the truer sense that it is part of an attempt to *invent* such a community, one that existed previously as at best a potentiality.

If these first two murals capture well the radical, even revolutionary, fervor of the early Chicano movement, we turn now to some murals that express the equally important and equally pervasive, pragmatic side of *el movimiento*. I want to examine some murals that were used more as survival strategies within the everyday life of the barrio than as revolutionary signs. The pragmatic messages of this type of mural were generally of two types: those designed to instill pride by fighting racist stereotypes, and those designed to lessen intracommunity violence. The former concern, for example, is embodied in a mural by members of East Los Streetscapers (Wayne Alaniz-Healy and David Rivas Botello), *La Familia*. At one level it is a piece so conservative it might easily be titled "family values." Its male-led familial utopia is intended in part as a reply to stereotyped representations of Mexican Americans as shiftless street kids and gang members, or as parents who let their children run wild in the streets. The mural is a vivid indication of the deep value placed by Chicanos on family life, both inside and outside the movement culture proper.

This mural is more than an image of the family in a narrow sense because the image of *la familia* is superimposed over a series of scenes from rural and urban Chicano lives, which appear to be linked by the radiating power of the family (represented by rays of sunlight). The family is thus not simply an image of home life but of community and Chicano national life—community as a kind of meta-family headed by a meta-patriarch whose authority is superimposed on the diverse scenes of community activity. The male figure in the mural dominates the scene, his female partner tucked under his arm: it is his power, not hers, that holds together "the" community. This image is paralleled quite explicitly at times in the political rhetoric of the late 1960s and early 1970s when talk of "the family of Chicanos" served to unify forces. But it also served as one focal point for Chicana feminist critiques of patriarchal relations in the movement as they elaborated parallels between male dominance of families and male dominance of *el movimiento*.

A more complex and striking image of family life was painted in what became known in the mid-1970s as Chicano Park in San Diego. This mural is not only a fascinating composition in its own right but also has a story that raises some important issues about the politics of public space entailed in mural making. In the image, a male farmworker appears at once to be crucified on this freeway pylon "canvas" and to be spreading his strong arms/wings like the Aztec eagle on the UFW flag. He is both a powerful patriarch protecting his brood and a victim of labor exploitation, at once pre-Christian *indio* and a Catholic martyr. Again, these elements might evoke complicated political and cultural contradictions if put into words, but here they are held together effortlessly by the powerful nonverbal language of muralism.

The park in which this and almost two dozen other murals appear was created through a struggle over public space—one that most community mural work entails to some degree but that is dramatically illustrated by the history of this particular project. A struggle for public land erupted when a longstanding request for a park in the Barrio Logan section of San Diego was answered instead with a city plan to shove an eight-lane interstate freeway through the heart of the barrio, displacing more than five thousand people. This struggle over land could be linked to the history of Chicano resistance to Anglo landgrabbing going back to the mid-nineteenth century, while also remaining very much a pragmatic current issue. More broadly, it can stand for the attempt in barrios across the country to create Aztlán, for what the park makers were doing was reclaiming local space as their own. Aztlán was both a mythical homeland and a very real way to rename the land where Chicanos lived. As one of the participants in the park struggle put it: "In English *barrio* means 'ghetto.' In Spanish it means 'neighborhood.'" Aztlán was not just a mythical place in the past but a symbol of the way in which the Chicano *movimiento* was returning the barrios to the people who lived there, making them places that celebrated and defended the interrelated cultures created by Mexicans and U.S. citizens of Mexican descent. Nothing stated that reclamation more visibly than the proliferation of thousands of murals produced in and around the Chicano movement culture.

While the freeway could not be stopped, an attempt to set up a Highway Patrol parking lot beneath the freeway was met by an occupying army of Chicanos who claimed the site as their own. Surrounding and then appropriating the bulldozers sent to lay out the parking lot, the community members began instead to build a "Chicano Park." After a long, intense struggle, the community won their battle and the park was built, complete with a Centro Cultural de la Raza that is still a community rallying point today. This Chicano cultural center was one of dozens of similar spaces throughout California, Texas, the Southwest, Colorado, and anywhere else Chicano communities existed. These cultural centers acted as educational institutions, organizing points, and artists' studios, where dance, music, art, theater, and other cultural forms were taught in the context of Chicano history. In turn, students in these centers became teachers of that history as part of the struggle for Chicano dignity and rights.

That struggle included a large-scale "muralization" of San Diego's Chicano Park over a period of many years, including a "muralthon" in 1977–78 involving artists and mural collectives from all over the state. The crucified farmworker mural was done earlier by José Montoya and the Rebel Chicano Art Front (a legendary Chicano art collective centered in Sacramento, California) and inspired other muralists to use the park's unique "canvases." What is perhaps most ingenious in that work is the incorporation of the particularities of the setting into the composition, especially the freeway pylon itself, which becomes the mural's cross. But it is only the most striking of many imaginative efforts to incorporate the far from ideal site into the overall composition. This effort at site-specific composition is an unusually vivid and effective extension of the normal process of community mural making. (Here I use *community* in its more local, neighborhood sense.) Many muralists spend days and weeks seeking the right site in a given community, and weeks more learning about the community's particular needs and values, before attempting a mural. Both the space and the mural content are thus often complexly negotiated texts, texts that raise issues in the community to new levels of debate. At the same time community murals, placed on the outside of buildings rather than inside museums, challenge dominant notions of the art object as fetishized individual production with no real connection to any audience.

A second major arena of pragmatic community concern articulated through murals is a kind of flip side of concern to portray the Chicano community as strong in family values—an effort to acknowledge and examine the issue of gang violence. While such violence has frequently been the focus of racist moral panics directed from outside the community by the dominant society, these murals offer a perspective from the inside where these events can be seen correctly as being most often intracommunity violence conditioned by oppression. A piece known informally as *Homeboy*, for example, painted in 1974 by Manuel Cruz in the Romana Gardens Housing Project in East Los Angeles, joins issues of gang violence with a key theme of much early Chicano mural work, the articulation of the Indian dimensions of Chicano identity. In the mural,

Aztec human sacrifice is recoded as community suicide in the form of a gang of homeboys killing another homeboy. While *indigenismo* was later criticized by some people as an uncritical celebration of the Aztec and other Indian empires that failed to acknowledge their oppressive elements, there is here already an ironic suggestion that the much mythologized Aztec religious practice of human sacrifice is preferable to the meaningless street sacrifice of homeboy life. But there is also an inspiring suggestion that a historically deep warrior spirit has been misdirected to rub out fellow members of *la raza* rather than to uphold and build cultural traditions.

An extraordinary piece entitled *The Wall That Cracked Open,* on a related theme, richly documents the power of a mural as public art to intervene directly at a specific site of social struggle. Executed by Willie Herrón in City Terrace, East Los Angeles, in 1972, this mural was done on a cracked wall in an alley where the artist's brother was beaten nearly to death by gang members, and it ingeniously incorporates the already present gang graffiti into the composition. The multiply layered message here includes the idea that the graffiti is itself part of an aesthetic impulse that could be further developed and redirected, just as gang violence could be redirected in more politically charged directions. Mural projects were sometimes used to accomplish precisely that form of redirection.

One of the most artistically unusual Chicano murals brings together several issues, from the local to the national to the international, suggesting their linkage as part of the continuum of Chicano experience. The piece is *Black and White Moratorium Mural,* by Willie Herrón and Gronk, done in 1973 at the Estrada Courts housing project in East Los Angeles (undoubtedly the most muralized housing project in the world, with more than ninety murals). As the name suggests, the mural is unusual first for being done in black and white rather than the far more common rainbow of bright colors, but the subdued colors are appropriate to the subject matter. The subject is war, war abroad and at home, and the black, white, and gray tones echo one of the great antiwar paintings of the twentieth century, Pablo Picasso's *Guernica.* The wall commemorates an event known as the Chicano moratorium, a march and rally in August 1970 involving more than thirty thousand people who opposed the war in Vietnam and linked that war to war at home against Chicanos. While often misrepresented as a white student movement, the antiwar movement had many dimensions, many constituencies, and

Black and White Moratorium Wall, by Willie Herrón and Gronk, 1973. Courtesy of Social and Public Art Resource Center.

many links to other issues. This march organized by *el movimiento* was part of the national moratorium, a tactic that declared an escalating series of strike days against the war (a new day was added for each month the war continued). The Chicano march was protesting that people of color in general, and Chicanos in particular, were dying in the war at a rate far above their percentage of the population. The war was being fought disproportionately by people whose experiences of racism and poverty made them far more vulnerable to being drafted and to enlisting out of economic need. The mural vividly depicts the police riot unleashed against the demonstrators at the end of the rally, capturing the screams of victims and linking this police brutality to similar acts visited routinely on barrio residents. In that riot, the Los Angeles police, in what they claimed was an accident but what others believed to be an assassination, killed Chicano journalist Rubén Salazar.

Salazar had worked for the *Los Angeles Times* and was one of the very few journalists who were acting to transmit *el movimiento*'s ideas fairly to a mainstream public. His death was a major blow and has been commemorated in other murals and artworks in addition to this one. The rally and the mural that memorializes it also pointed to the ways in which President Lyndon Johnson's "Great Society" economic reforms were being decimated by the costs of the war. As a consequence, more

Chicanos were dying in the streets of the United States from the economic violence that leads to gangs and drug abuse. In these ways the
mural brilliantly encapsulates the arguments of the Chicano movement
as they moved from the barrio to the national government to international politics and back again.

ChicanismA

Most participants in and observers of the Chicano movement agree that
the first phase of the movement had come to an end by the mid-1970s.
That period accomplished a great deal. *El movimiento* had succeeded in
creating a new sense of identity that all people of Mexican descent
benefited from and were affected by, even those more conservative folks
who rejected the term *Chicano*. A new sense of the dignity and depth of
Mexican and Mexican American character and culture had been achieved
through the work of countless organizers, including the cultural workers
who made poems, paintings, dramas, movies, dances, and, most visibly
and tangibly, murals, to represent the key components of this new identity. But this insurgent phase of the movement was also riddled with
problems and had reached certain political limits. Many factors contributed to these problems, not the least of which was a great deal of
political repression of the kind we saw enacted against the Black Panthers and other radical groups. Internal factors also limited this phase of
the movement, most centered on limited definitions of *chicanismo* and
ethnic nationalism.

For one thing, La Adelita notwithstanding, we can note a heavily male
cast to the murals I have analyzed thus far in this chapter. This emphasis accurately reflects early domination of both *el movimiento* and the
mural movement by men. But Chicanas, who had been deeply involved
in both movements all along, were by the mid-1970s asserting an increasingly powerful presence as activists and artists. Their presence was the
single most important element in expanding and reopening the story
being told about the Chicano community through *el movimiento*. The
double oppression experienced by Chicanas positioned them to articulate a richer movement vision that supported much of the cultural
nationalist stance but also recognized that there were other issues both
within and beyond the Chicano community that needed to be addressed.
Chicana feminist reinterpretations of community became the key force
in moving toward a more fully inclusive politics. These issues are theo-

La Ofrenda ("The Offering") for Dolores Huerta. Courtesy of Social and Public Art Resource Center.

rized explicitly in the crucial works of Norma Alarcón, Gloria Anzaldúa, Cherríe Moraga, Alvina Quintana, and Chela Sandoval, among others, but they are also articulated through the Chicana murals of Judy Baca, Yreina Cervantes, and many others.

The piece *La Ofrenda* ("The Offering") by Yreina Cervantes, for example, helps to retell the history of the Chicana/o movement. It places Dolores Huerta, UFW cofounder along with Chávez, in her rightful place at the center of the movement. This is important not just for doing greater justice to Huerta as an individual but for symbolizing all the work done in the 1960s, 1970s, and earlier by Chicana activists and cultural workers—work that had been downplayed, ignored, or over-shadowed by the dramatic self-importance often claimed by men in the movement. Women did much of the most effective, day-to-day, grass-roots organizing, the work that truly sustains a movement, while men too often occupied themselves with strategizing sessions quite removed from the concrete realities of ordinary Chicano lives. Obviously, not all men behaved this way, and some women did manage against great odds to achieve leadership positions, but too often the pattern was one of male generals and female foot soldiers. Indeed, La Adelita is only further evi-dence of this, since she is not a real individual like "General" Zapata, but a composite figure of all the anonymous women who followed him and Villa into battle. And this very image of battle was part of the problem: for too many in the movement, the rhetoric of armed struggle became the only language to express Chicano manhood, and a fetishizing of the gun, as with the Black Panthers, often got in the way of the real struggle for the hearts and minds of everyday Chicanos.

Thus, Cervantes's mural also represents work done by Chicanas to incorporate the quieter heroism of everyday community life into the movement story—in this case, the world of religious life as represented by an allusion to the home altar. *La Ofrenda* is also indicative of the feminist articulation of solidarity among women that helped to cross certain rigid community borders. Thus, for example, Huerta's Chicana heroism in the United States is connected to the struggle of Salvadoran women being victimized by U.S. policy and military repression in El Salvador. Giving Huerta her rightful place in the movement is paralleled by a feminist rearticulation of the continuing struggle of farmworkers in the United States in such murals as *Las Lechugueras* ("The Lettuce Pickers") by Juana Alicia. This piece offers an "x-ray vision" of a child in the womb of a lettuce picker in the field to dramatically depict how the environmental and personal dangers of pesticides present a still greater potential for harm to pregnant farmworkers and their unborn children. The mural powerfully supports efforts by the farmworkers' union to limit the use of pesticides and other agricultural chemicals that harm farmworkers.

An emerging sense of a Latina solidarity that cuts across national community borders was also articulated by Chicana feminist mural collectives like the San Francisco Bay area's Mujeres Muralistas. Originally formed in 1974 by three Chicanas (Patricia Rodríguez, Irene Pérez, and Graciela Carrillo) and one Venezuelan (Consuelo Méndez), the evolving collective included other Latinas and Chicanas in subsequent incarnations and became an emblem of cross-national communication for the diverse Spanish-speaking populations of the Mission district. Their piece *Latinoamérica,* for example, develops this theme by using a common feminist focus on everyday women's activities and common threads of color to blend designs executed by different Latina artists drawing upon their differing national styles and traditions.

At the level of aesthetic inspiration, the rediscovery of the work of Frida Kahlo played an important consciousness-raising role for many

Chicana and some Chicano artists. Long before her rediscovery by the New York art crowd, an exhibit of Kahlo's work at Galería de La Raza in San Francisco's Latino Mission district contributed to the feminist rewriting of art history. A piece entitled *Homenaje a Frida Kahlo* ("Homage to Frida Kahlo"), painted by Mike Ríos to announce the exhibit, not only helps to mark Kahlo's emergence from the very large shadow of her husband, the muralist Diego Rivera, but also points to another dimension of the reappropriation of public space by the mural form.

Ríos's mural is actually painted on a commercial billboard near the gallery where Kahlo's show was appearing. Over a period of two years the muralists and other community supporters engaged in a battle with the owners of the billboard, painting over its commercial messages with their artistic/political ones, until eventually the owners gave up and donated the billboard to Galería de la Raza. This kind of reappropriation of billboards and other public walls has been a significant part of the mural movement—an important assertion of community rights over property rights and an argument about the very public nature of public buildings. In the context of the Chicano *movimiento* this retaking of public space was part of a rebuilding of Aztlán not as mythic land in the mists of time but here and now as a liberated zone.

Mural/Movement

I end this chapter with a discussion of the collective work guided by Chicana feminist muralist Judith Francisca Baca, both because she is among the most prolific and visionary muralists in the world and because her work brings together and extends many of the themes regarding the relation between murals and movement cultures that I have sketched thus far. Baca painted her murals in the spirit of what Charles Payne calls the "organizing tradition" pioneered in the civil rights movement. Her extraordinary career also offers further evidence that the dual identity of Chicana and feminist helped to expand the vision of the Chicano and mural movements toward connection with a wider multicultural resistance force. But in using Baca as my exemplar, I want to make clear that she herself works collectively and that she is only one among many other cultural workers who are equally deserving of attention.

Baca's work extends to something near its logical extreme a theme of communal production that has long been at the heart of mural work. Most of the work I have discussed so far has been the work of mural collectives, often involving numerous nonartists from the community in which the mural is to appear and usually based on input from the community. Baca has moved this process to a new level of complexity and political power. For example, she was director of the Citywide Murals project in Los Angeles in the mid-1970s that produced over two hundred fifty murals, many done under her direct supervision. That project entailed major input from Baca and other Chicano/as, but was also a multiracial effort throughout the diverse neighborhoods of the city. Funded in part by the city, this project also illustrates the deep tensions community murals generate, and the complicated political negotiations they involve. This project and others like it become struggles between those hegemonic forces of the dominant culture seeking to turn murals into barrio and ghetto "beautification" projects, designed literally to paint over signs of deprivation and exploitation, and those forces seeking to turn murals into critical sites of communal resistance that precisely point out exploitation, while also celebrating cultures drowned out in the so-called mainstream. The continued power of muralism will lie in resisting the former force and defending the latter.

The Great Wall of Los Angeles and Radical Multiculturalism

The kind of large-scale vision that informed the Citywide Murals project is taken in a different, even more spectacular direction in Baca's supervision of the largest mural ever undertaken—the half-mile-long "Great Wall of Los Angeles." This work is a radically multicultural retelling of the history of Los Angeles and California from prehistoric times to the present. Begun appropriately in the bicentennial year 1976 and continued through five subsequent summers (with projections for extensions in the future), the work was accomplished through Baca's direction of teams of Asian American, Native American, African American, Anglo, and Chicano youth. Many of these young people came to her project out of the criminal justice system, with mural work offered as an alternative to further jail time. Far from being a captive labor force, the young people working on the mural were encouraged to become involved in the complex invention, design, and execution of the work. Baca and her team thus sought to create a liberated force for community change.

As in her other projects, Baca facilitated the creation of the "Great Wall" by bringing together professional historians, community storytellers, and a variety of people from all the communities who were to be

Judy Baca and crew at the Great Wall of Los Angeles. Courtesy of Social and Public
Art Resource Center.

represented on the mural. The young people took part in intensive revisionist history classes that included lively exchanges about their past
and even livelier arguments about their futures. In these classes, in the
streets, and on the "Great Wall" itself, the revisionist history now appearing in textbooks was anticipated and incorporated in story forms that
linked the past to the vitally contested political terrain of the present. In
fact, the wall came to be used by local teachers as a kind of painted text-
book that lets their students walk through time.

The "Great Wall" that emerged from this collective process presents a
powerful set of images, linked by narrative bridges. The mural links
diverse communities, weaving a history of interracial conflict into a wider
history of shared oppression and resistance. Here the multiculturalism
inherent in the Chicano identity, combined with a feminist vision of
everyday personal political linkages, has facilitated the creation of a
complex vision of the separate but interacting histories of Los Angeles,
California, and America's diverse populations. Mural panels laid out in
chronological order depict a range of peoples and events, often in very
telling juxtaposition. The section on the 1940s, for example, includes
panels on the internment during World War II of Japanese Americans,
the flight to Los Angeles of Jewish refugees from Nazi Germany, and the
"zoot suit riots" unleashed by attacks made by white sailors on Chicano

street kid *pachucos*. The mural stories richly interweave race, class, sexuality, and gender, often with great humor. One panel, for example, centers on an image of Rosie the Riveter, symbol of the independent working woman, who is being sucked by a vacuum cleaner into a television set. It wittily makes the connection between a redomestication of women in these "father knows best" years of the 1950s, and the racial phenomenon known as "white flight"—the flight of many whites to the suburbs as cities became more and more racially integrated.

What emerges from Baca's method of composition and from the mural itself is a sense of the integrity of the different ethnic enclaves and cultures of the city, and their inextricable interconnection. The rich story of Chicano/as in "Califas" (California) is maintained, but written also in terms of gender, class, and sexuality, and linked to other racialized groups. This entire story of multiple intersections, and the power system at its core, must be addressed if a radically democratic, truly multicultural society is to become more than a glittering promise.

Connecting these issues has become a matter of central concern to all resistance movements in recent years. They bring along with them difficult questions. How, for example, can movements balance the danger of an almost infinitely fragmentable politics of identity against the dangers of a prematurely homogenizing emphasis on common interest that erases important cultural as well as ideological differences? How can ethnic identities be created that honor the diversity of gender, class, and sexuality within the community, while maintaining a united front against intersecting dominations? The Chicano community mural movement and projects like the "Great Wall" and the Citywide Murals program offer at least some glimmerings of a how a movement-inspired public art can move us closer to answers to these questions.

From Representation to Articulation: Reimagining Community

The interlinked Chicano and community mural movements allow us to see that community is a powerful concept, a powerfully enabling *fiction*, yet with real points of reference in the world. However, the struggle to suppress differences (of gender, class, sexuality, nationality, and ideology, among others), particularly at the height of the nationalist phase, reminds us of how often the term *community* is used to close debate rather than open up possibilities. There are, no doubt, necessary moments when communal racial, class, or gender identity must be articulated univocally. But can we find ways to speak that acknowledge unity as the provisional product of multivocal debate and as a negotiable contribution to a necessarily multicultural alliance? If a community must at times speak as one voice in order to generate the utmost power, is it possible still in that voicing to recognize dissent, internal otherness, or difference? Can an identity-based movement progress from a *politics of representation*, which presumes to speak for an already known community, to a *politics of articulation* that freely portrays community as an always contested process, not a set thing?[9]

Can community be conceived as an ongoing, strategic, and negotiated reality, and still be community? Or is every gain in self-consciousness necessarily a loss in solidarity? Is there some quality of community that can be recognized as preceding or exceeding ideology without resort to exclusionary and mystifying claims to blood consciousness? Is there a view of interconnectedness that is not so easily assimilated to an empty, homogenizing kind of humanism long allied to oppression? Can community be reconceived in something like concentric circles, communities layered one upon another, but also with loose ends, openings of the circle?

The Chicano/a community mural movement, with its development into a "critical multiculturalism," offers a model through which to think about some of these questions.[10] As the twenty-first century began, Chicano/a nationalisms were again gaining ground. Some versions seem doomed to repeat mistakes of the past. Others seem more open to multiple identities amid solidarity. A younger generation of Chicana/o muralists emerged in the 1990s to take up the movement/mural connection. Artists like Alma López combine fierce racial pride with open treatment of once forbidden topics like straight and lesbian sexuality. Like her subject matter, López's style, alternating between the traditional mural form and the newer digital mural format, reflects both continuity and change.

Moving On

The wider Chicano movement evolved through the 1980s and 1990s and into the twenty-first century in directions often paralleling those of the mural movement as represented by Baca. New scholarship and new "movements within the movement" brought the concerns of Chicanas, gays and lesbians, and other previously marginalized groups to the center of concern. New immigration from Latin America reinforced a need to think multiethnically within the Spanish-speaking U.S. community, even as still wider multicultural coalitions seemed necessary to progress further. Chicana/o studies evolved more complex, absolutely vital positions, though sometimes these seemed to move further away from contexts of movement contestation. The strengths and limits of Chicano nationalism have been carefully examined, and both the theory and practice of new models of organizing are richly visible. *El movimiento* continues to grow and change, to face the challenges of a conservative backlash (represented by anti-immigrant, anti–affirmative action, and English-only ballot initiatives in California and elsewhere), and to assert the powerful presence of Americans of Mexican descent. Chicanas and Chicanos continue the struggle, as at once a community unto themselves and a force connected to wider circles of resistance to cooptative forms of multiculturalism prematurely celebrating a diversity not yet rooted in equality of economic, cultural, and political power.

FIVE

Old Cowboys, New Indians

Hollywood Frames the American Indian Movement

Do you remember Leonard Peltier? Do you remember he stood at
the window of the farm house in South Dakota yelling Stella!
Stella! while the FBI surrounded him and the rest of AIM, a cast
of thousands. It was epic, a Cecil B. DeMille production made
intimate when two FBI agents were shot to death.
                                      —Sherman Alexie, from
                      "The Marlon Brando Memorial Swimming Pool"

Native American "red power" warriors moved "like a hurricane" across
the landscape of America in the late 1960s and early 1970s.[1] These new
"Indians" challenged five hundred years of colonial domination by fighting for a return to full sovereign status for native nations, restoration of
lands guaranteed by treaty, just compensation for the minerals exploited
from reservations, and a renaissance of native culture. The most famous
and infamous native organization of the red power era, the American
Indian Movement (AIM), will be my focus here. Despite its name, AIM
was not *the* Indian movement but rather only one organization among
many groups that formed a larger movement. Many other important
Indian resistance groups preceded and ran parallel to AIM, but AIM
was the most visible and media-oriented of the radical Indian movement
groups, and media visibility is very much to the point because the art
form I will pair with the Indian movement in this chapter is the mainstream Hollywood film.

While drawing information from various written sources and two
important documentaries about AIM *(Incident at Oglala* and *The Spirit*

of Crazy Horse) as background, I will focus on the three *fiction* films that deal to one degree or another with the group. After introducing AIM, and talking about its use of and use by the mainstream media during its years of peak activity (1968–73), I will discuss the films in order of release: *Powwow Highway* (1989), *Thunderheart* (1992), and *Lakota Woman: Siege at Wounded Knee* (1994).[2] The discussion will assess and compare the films' strengths and weaknesses as representations of the nature and aims of Indian radicalism to the movie-going U.S. public. The "public," of course, is a very vague, problematic concept, so at points I will try to be more specific about what particular audiences might do with each film. To do this I have supplemented my observations with as many reviews and reactions as I have been able to gather, from both Indian and non-Indian audiences.

The independent Native American documentary and fiction film community is a vital, thriving one, yet so far it has not experienced a breakthrough to the mainstream to equal those of African American, Latino, or Asian American filmmakers.[3] Racism and extremely high production costs have kept Hollywood-style films largely beyond the control of Native Americans, the economically poorest population in North America. This means that the filmed stories about AIM do not emerge directly out of its movement culture, or even out of the native community. This is particularly unfortunate since, as recent studies suggest, a native aesthetics and cultural rhetorics differ in all manner of ways from Hollywood filmmaking.[4]

AIM activists were involved to one degree or another in each of the three narrative films I discuss here, but in none did they have anything approaching control of the final cinematic product. Rather, AIM members made various attempts to influence a movie-making process that was in the hands of mostly sympathetic, but culturally and politically limited white outsiders who were *translating* movement ideas and values, sometimes well, more often poorly. And these outsiders, mostly from that mythical land called Hollywood, attempted this translation within a medium saturated with a history of racial stereotyping totally at odds with the goals of the Indian movement. The AIM activists were trying to get their message out to a wider public whose political unconscious, like that of the filmmakers, was deeply shaped by the "cowboy and Indian" conventions of the Hollywood western.[5]

To further complicate this whole picture, I will suggest that the "real" AIM activists and their "real-life" opponents were to a certain extent acting out their own internalized Hollywood scripts from the beginning of the movement. From the start, for better and for worse, AIM was engaged in a battle over control of its mass-mediated image. Thus, the films about AIM can be viewed as an extension of, not something wholly different from, its movement work. In this chapter I analyze the relationships between a "movement culture" and a sympathetic "cultural formation" within the dominant culture, a formation we could call "pro-Indian Hollywood." The formation began with the early interest in Indian activism of actor Marlon Brando and spread to others, including Jane Fonda, Robert Redford, and Michael Apted. My analysis addresses both the usefulness and the limits of this formation in supporting the work of the movement. Of course, the lines between these two kinds of formation are fluid, not rigid. In other words, the movement was always already partly in Hollywood, and vice versa.

AIMing Indians in New Directions

AIM was founded in Minneapolis in July 1968, with early leadership provided by Anishinabé (Chippewa) organizers like Dennis Banks, Clyde Bellecourt, and Mary Wilson. AIM was not the first name considered for the group, however. They were originally going to call themselves Concerned Indians of America. And while the acronym CIA certainly would have been a resonant one, the choice of American Indian Movement says a good deal about the genius and the arrogance of the group. Robert Warrior and Paul Chaat Smith offer the best chronicle of AIM written thus far, and they stress the sense of drama and the orientation toward the mass media that was both AIM's strength and its weakness. In their excellent book on the Indian movement, *Like a Hurricane*, Warrior and Smith summarize the dramatic flair already apparent in AIM's self-naming:

> [The name was] perfect because it suggested action, purpose, and forward motion. Perfect because it was big, transcending the lesser world of committees and associations and congresses and councils. Organizations had recording secretaries and annual dinners. Movements changed history. The initials—A-I-M—underscored all of that, creating an

active verb rich in power and imagery. You aimed at a target. You could aim for victory, for freedom, for justice. You could also, defiantly, never aim to please. Written vertically and stylized a bit, the acronym became an arrow.[6]

Though they do not say so here, it is clear from the rest of the book that Smith and Warrior also recognized that the name was extremely presumptuous. Imagine what would have happened if the Black Panther Party had tried to name itself *The* Black Power Movement, or if the Brown Berets had called themselves *The* Chicano Movement. AIM's bold naming and equally bold actions certainly got the group the attention they wanted, but in the process did some disservice to those Indian resisters who came before and those alongside whom the group struggled in the 1960s and 1970s.

Two main sources of inspiration shaped AIM in its early years. The first was precisely these other, insufficiently acknowledged Indian activists. Before AIM, a new generation of radicalizing Indians was reforming older Indian organizations like the National Council of American Indians (NCAI), and focusing new grassroots efforts that were emerging from many sites around Indian country. When young Vine Deloria Jr. assumed leadership of NCAI in 1964, he sought to link this older, established organization with new local groups of a more radical bent, and with the National Indian Youth Council (NIYC). Led by figures like the great Ponca organizer Clyde Warrior, the NIYC became the cutting edge of Indian politics in the mid-1960s. Many in NIYC became interested in direct action, inspired in part by actor Marlon Brando, who spoke to them of translating the example of the black civil rights movement into Native American terms.

One key example of a new direct action spirit was the so-called "fish-ins" in the Pacific Northwest. Organized by local Indians, with support from the NIYC and from Brando and other Hollywood activists, these events in the early 1960s called for restoration of traditional fishing rights. In the San Francisco Bay area, local Indian activists had laid groundwork for years that emerged into prominence with a dramatic Indian takeover of Alcatraz Island in 1969.[7]

The other source of inspiration was militant antiracist organizations like the Black Panther Party for Self-Defense. Like the Panthers, AIM was started primarily by victims of the criminal justice system. At the time of AIM's founding, Indians made up 1 percent of the Minnesota population but 50 percent of the state's prison population. Like blacks and Chicanos, urban Indians were (and are) routinely victimized by the police, and early AIM actions included a police observation plan that resembled the one in Oakland set up by the Panthers to resist police harassment and brutality (see chapter 2).

Though AIM was initially peopled largely by Anishinabé men and women from the reservations north and west of the city, the decision to locate its headquarters in Minneapolis and its early focus on urban issues gave the organization an urban image. This was initially a limitation in the context of a city-reservation split. The Native American world had been split asunder by two devastating federal government actions during the 1950s, going by the ominous names "termination" and "relocation." The 1953 Termination Act brought an end to many reservations and entailed the relocation of many Indians to urban areas of the United States, a process carried out under the auspices of the Bureau of Indian Affairs (BIA). Part of AIM's work, along with that of many other Indian activist groups, was an attempt to bridge this growing chasm between the reservations and the cities.

Thus, after initially focusing on providing various daily-life services to Minneapolis Indians and working Panther-style against police brutality in the city, AIM extended its work to actions in white-dominated towns like Custer, South Dakota, that bordered reservations. In such towns Indians were routinely beaten, and sometimes killed, by local racist ranchers (an encounter with "real" cowboys that set a tone for later run-ins). AIM successfully intervened in several of these disputes, forcing local law enforcement to take the cases seriously, and serving notice that Native Americans would not take such abuse anymore. It was largely these actions that first built a following for AIM on the reservations. In addition, AIM's penchant for dramatic media events staged at sites of traditional, nationalist white power spread the word of the group's brash style. For example, at Plymouth Rock, Massachusetts, AIM held an action challenging the Thanksgiving myth, offering evidence that the white settlers were in fact giving thanks for a recent triumph in massacring New England Indians. A similar action was staged at Mount Rushmore, symbol of white desecration of the Black Hills, a sacred site for several native nations. Such well-publicized actions sparked the establishment of AIM "chapters" all over the country, some totally unknown to the central leadership.

AIM also played an important role, along with numerous other Indian activist groups, in the "Trail of Broken Treaties" car caravan that crossed the country from west to east in 1972. The caravan picked up various tribal contingents along the way and stopped at sites that represented the continuing impact of two hundred years of treaties made and broken by the U.S. government. The trail ended in Washington, D.C., with an unplanned occupation of the Bureau of Indian Affairs office. AIM members and others, with help from FBI provocateurs, sacked BIA headquarters, destroying and stealing documents and other government property. The action split the Indian community deeply, greatly increased the notoriety of AIM, and upped the ante of FBI surveillance and counter-attacks against the organization. Whatever its limits as an action, the BIA trashing had great symbolic power to many young Indians who had felt themselves being trashed by Washington bureaucrats their whole lives. And to a nation whose most popular, currently circulating image of Native Americans was Indian actor "Iron Eyes" Cody weeping in a television commercial against littering, the image of young Indian warriors littering the BIA building with the bureaucratic detritus of two hundred years of broken promises was surely startling.

But all this was soon overshadowed by AIM's most notorious and dramatic action, the two-and-a-half-month armed standoff with law enforcement during the Indian occupation of the village of Wounded Knee, South Dakota, in spring 1973. This AIM-led siege is the event most often referred to in all three films, and it amply illustrates my point about the entwining of a cinematic images and "real-life" AIM actions. The occupation started after AIM was invited by elders onto the Oglala reservation to help the tribe in ousting its corrupt leader, Richard "Dickie" Wilson. The village of Wounded Knee was a resonant stage for the action, given its proximity to the site of the last great massacre of Indians by the U.S. cavalry, which took place in 1890 and resulted in the slaughter of three hundred undefended men, women, and children.[8] Ostensibly, the second battle at Wounded Knee, which, in an eerie echo of the first, involved about three hundred Indian resisters, was about wresting tribal governance away from Oglala leader Wilson, who had the backing of the U.S. government, and returning it to a sovereign

Oglala Nation. But beyond the local dispute, this was clearly a symbolic battle to reassert the sovereignty of all Indian nations once guaranteed by government treaties. Real bullets were exchanged in the siege, and two Indians were killed in the course of the action. Still, the war by guerrilla tactics was clearly less important than the war by guerrilla theater. There is more than a little evidence to suggest that the Wounded Knee occupation included much "acting" and "staging" by participants from all sides. Cultural critic Kathleen Turner (not the actress) and historians Robert Warrior and Paul Chaat Smith, among others, have described the AIM actions at Wounded Knee as "theater," arguing that they were a self-conscious attempt to stage a media event that could dramatize claims about broken treaties, continuing economic exploitation of American Indian lands, and an unrepresentative, puppet government on the Pine Ridge Reservation. The FBI and other government forces were equally theatrical in their actions, and generally more successful at manipulating the media. For example, they banned the media initially from any coverage, restricted media access throughout the occupation, and threatened to arrest representatives of the progressive press who offered sympathetic accounts from inside the AIM compound. A careful study by Michelle Dishong of the coverage of Wounded Knee II by "the newspaper of record," the *New York Times,* richly documents the bias of accounts toward the government side of the story.[9]

Comments from the activists and journalists on the scene at the battle of Wounded Knee in 1973 also draw attention to the role the Hollywood imagination played in the action. Indeed, this was probably inevitable since no groups have been more powerfully and archetypically mythologized by U.S. popular culture than cowboys and Indians. Journalistic accounts of AIM/FBI encounters at Wounded Knee reflect this mediation, and the accounts themselves were undoubtedly interpreted in part through reception mechanisms shaped by years of cinematic and televisual images. AIM member John Trudell, for example, has commented that "[if] FBI agents that grew up watching John Wayne and cowboys and Indians come out here and want to play cowboys and Indians, then they [have] got to suffer the consequences, just as we do." In speaking like this, Trudell reveals the extent to which he and his compatriots were also playing out the cowboy and Indian script. And that script was further encouraged by the mainstream media. For example, one journalist on the scene at Wounded Knee recalls that correspondents "wrote good cowboy and Indian stories because that was what they thought the public wanted."[10]

If the occupation of Wounded Knee was a staged production, then AIM leader Russell Means was surely its star. One *Time* magazine reporter recalls that Means could sometimes be seen directing cameras and staging events for the media's benefit.[11] Means's career subsequent to the Wounded Knee siege is also suggestive about the role he played during the occupation. During the last decade Means has appeared in several movies; he recently performed the voice of Powhatan in Disney's travesty of the Pocahontas story. Indeed, Means's career has led one cultural critic to invent a new term for his social role. American Indian studies scholar James Stripes refers to Means as an "actorvist," a term that might fit John Trudell, national leader of AIM in the late 1970s, even better since he appeared in two of the fiction films I will discuss and was interviewed in both of the documentaries as well.[12]

Certainly a case can be made that the role of leader of AIM in the early 1970s was one that trained Russell Means well for a career in "real" acting. More than one historian of the American Indian Movement has spoken of Means's flair for the dramatic. During the occupation of the Bureau of Indian Affairs office in 1972, for example, Means let himself be caught on camera using a confiscated oil portrait of then president Richard Nixon as a shield while engaging police on the steps of the building. Means's "shades and braids" image was enough to get him more than the "fifteen minutes of fame" Andy Warhol suggested all Americans would soon have, and resulted in an actual portrait of Russell done by Warhol himself. More than one detractor in Indian country has used such facts to portray Means as more image than substance, and he was sometimes accused of "impersonating" an Indian even before Hollywood, during his AIM heyday, partly because he spent very little time in Indian country while growing up.

But implying that these AIM "actorvists" sold out to Hollywood or were never real activists is too easy. Both Means and Trudell remain vocal critics of Indian oppression, and both have claimed that they are using, not being used by, the mass media. As Russell Means frames it, "I haven't abandoned the movement for Hollywood. I've brought Hollywood to the movement." I partly agree with his statement, though I would rephrase it to say that Hollywood, for better and for worse, was in the movement from the beginning. In this sense, the fiction films about AIM are a logical extension of a process already at work in AIM actions themselves. Thus, I look at the films as embodying a struggle between the cultural frames offered by movement activists and the cultural frames of the Hollywood film, and I want to suggest that at times those frames overlapped and interacted, fused and confused the picture.

Powwow Highway

Perhaps the most unambiguously positive thing I can say about the films in which AIM is represented is that Kevin Costner (also known as "Dances with Wolves") was not involved in any of them. On the other hand, similarly inclined movie mogul Indian wannabees *were* involved. Ted Turner was behind one of the films, Robert Redford was involved in another, and former Beatle George Harrison produced a third. Whatever limitations these films have, they are an advance over the *Dances with Wolves* version of noble savagery in one important respect: the AIM films attempt to portray *living* American Indians. Costner's film, while arguably a slight improvement over the traditional Hollywood western, reinscribes a contemporary version of the noble savage myth that pervades U.S. culture in the form of nostalgia for what "the Indian" allegedly *was*. This myth takes several forms: pseudo-vision quests in the so-called men's movement; the "New Age" claims of some white women and men who, as native scholar-activist Andrea "Andy" Smith notes, boast of having been Indians in a past life in order to make a great deal of money in their present life through selling images of American Indian spirituality; or liberal guilt about what "the white man" did to the Indians in the past.[13] The sentiments seldom extend in any significant way to concern about the hideous injustices that *continue* to be heaped upon native peoples in the United States today. In Hollywood, the only really good Indian is still the dead Indian. The AIM films, whatever their flaws, are at least among the very few mainstream productions that even attempt to make visible the generally "disappeared" lives of Indians in contemporary America.

Powwow Highway, bankrolled by George Harrison, was an independent film that managed to gain something of a mainstream audience, especially via television and video. As arguably the first widely circulated attempt to present something of the contemporary lives of Native Americans in film, its relatively low-budget and low-tech feel in some

Film poster for *Powwow Highway.*

ways equip it better than the other two, glossier films to convey the low-budget, low-tech lives of most Indians today. At its best, *Powwow High-way* gives a complex sense of some of the intricate struggles between tradition and modernity faced by descendants of first nations, and captures a certain casual resistance to white ways that people in Indian country identify as living on "Indian time." At other moments the film seems little more than a buddy film, a kind of *On the Road*, Indian-style. Indeed, when the highbrow TV network Bravo screened *Powwow Highway*, it characterized the film as "an off-beat road movie," evoking visions of Jack Kerouac in braids, or worse still, Bing Crosby and Bob Hope on the road to Pine Ridge. The film is based on the novel of the same title by former AIM member David Seals, who eventually came to dissociate himself from the movie.

The protagonists are Philbert Bono, a seemingly none-too-bright, gentle, three-hundred-pound Cheyenne who fancies himself a spiritual warrior and refers to his beat-up old car as his "pony," and Philbert's pal Buddy Red Bow. Buddy is a former AIM activist, veteran of Vietnam and Wounded Knee, and a still angry fighter against federal/corporate corruption and exploitation of the reservation. Clearly, the friendship between the two men is weighted with symbolic value. They embody a complicated play between Indian spiritual traditionalism and modern militancy that was part of AIM's history.

When Philbert attempts to get elder wisdom from his great-aunt, she laughs derisively at him and tells him she is sick of young Indians looking for some magic in the past. Undaunted, Philbert begins to cobble together bits of traditional "medicine," filtered through the distorted lens of white Indian fantasy. Author Leslie Marmon Silko suggests in her novel *Ceremony* that traditional rituals have always changed to meet the needs of the present, rather than being lodged in an impossible-to-return-to past. Similarly, *Powwow Highway* suggests that contemporary Indian survival will blend respect for the past with wild improvisation, a making-do with the impure tools of the present (as when Philbert leaves a candy bar as an offering to his ancestors).

We first meet Buddy in a powerful scene in which he challenges a slick presentation to the Cheyenne tribal council by a sell-out Indian "apple" (red on the outside, white on the inside) working for a mining corporation that hopes to further exploit the tribe's mineral wealth. Buddy eloquently rattles off statistics on Native American poverty and compares the rosy promises of the corporation to hundreds of nice-sounding treaties signed and ignored by the U.S. government over the past two hundred years. He ends his speech by rejecting the mineral-rights colonialism being offered as a chance at the American dream, noting that Indian country "isn't America. This here's the Third World."

When Buddy's sister is busted for drugs in New Mexico on what turns out to be an FBI-directed frame-up used to get Buddy off the "rez" in order to push through the uranium deal, Buddy teams up with Philbert, the only person he knows who has a car. The plot meanders as the two travel none-too-directly from Montana to New Mexico to help get Buddy's sister out of jail. The unfolding plot includes a slight mellowing of Buddy's anger in the face of Philbert's gentle but strong faith in his partly improvised spiritual tradition. In this the plot resembles the increasing commitment to traditional spirituality that AIM demonstrated as it evolved.

The most direct treatment of AIM occurs in the middle portion of the film when Philbert, following the "powwow highway" rather than the most efficient route to New Mexico, diverts his trusty Buick pony named Protector to Pine Ridge, South Dakota. There Buddy meets up with some of his old comrades from the Wounded Knee siege. When he arrives, his friends tell Buddy of the terror still being waged against AIM sympathizers on Pine Ridge—"a shooting every day," as one of them remarks. This is hardly an exaggeration, given that close to seventy AIM members and sympathizers were murdered or died under mysterious circumstances in the three-year period following Wounded Knee. Most of these unsolved deaths have been attributed by scholars to AIM's prime enemy, conservative tribal chairman Richard Wilson and his vigilante "goon squad," actively or passively abetted by the FBI.

In *Powwow Highway* Buddy has a brief encounter with the leader of the goon squads who have been harassing his friends. He publicly backs the goon down at a powwow, with the aid of a knife thrown as a warning by a war buddy suffering from post-traumatic stress disorder. This is an important moment because an unusually large number of AIM members were Vietnam veterans who concluded that they had been fighting against the wrong government. They turned their deep anger and their military skills to the service of Indian war against the U.S. government and its tribal puppets, and in so doing they brought the war in Vietnam home in ways that deeply shaped Native American radicalism.[14]

The morning after the powwow, Buddy and Philbert give a ride to a couple of friends who have been besieged by the goons, dropping them off at a suburban tract house. The subplot here involves Buddy claiming that the men have sold out, and his friend replying that Buddy himself has not been living under the constant threats the friend and his wife have been enduring. A kind of respectful standoff is achieved, in which Buddy's ongoing militancy is given greater weight without condemning the difficult choice made by his friend. I read this as a kind of reconciliation narrative working within the orbit of AIM, where many such difficult choices were being made in the years following the internal struggles and savage repression by the FBI and other authorities in the wake of Wounded Knee.

The remainder of *Powwow Highway* never discusses AIM directly, but we do see the FBI's involvement in framing Buddy's sister as a clear indication of the continuing collusion between the federal government and corporations in exploiting mineral rights on Indian lands, one of the key elements of AIM's position. The climactic event of the film suggests a complicated play of media frames. Philbert, with the aid of powerful medicine he gathers along the powwow highway, springs Buddy's sister from jail Old West–style by pulling out the bars of her cell using his Buick "pony's" horsepower. Philbert's inspiration for this Indian liberation moment came while watching an old western on TV. The scene suggests that Indian resistance will require a combination of turning white mass-media culture against itself, Philbert's traditional tribal magic, and Buddy's AIM-inspired militancy.

The final scene of the movie, immediately following the jailbreak, also helps to undermine the "buddy movie" quality somewhat. We see Philbert, his "pony" aflame at the end of a car chase with the police, walking down the road alongside Buddy, Buddy's sister and her two kids, and a white girlfriend who helped with the escape. In the background is the pragmatic Cheyenne tribal chairman whose faith in the more ideologically aggressive Buddy had led him to assist the war party from a distance. The ending is a utopian one, suggesting that forces separating AIM-style militancy from existing tribal governments, Indians from whites, men from women can be easily transcended. It seems at best only a magical resolution, a fantasy projection rooted as much in New Age white imaginations as in serious Indian resistance.

While the film has its moments, reviews by Euro-American critics suggest that much of the subversive potential of the film is recontained for a white audience. The AIM material is given too little context, and either the harmless buddy film or a feel-good-about-Indians, New Age, spiritual reading predominates. Turning to native reactions, reviews and personal accounts suggest that *Powwow Highway* was received with mixed feelings in Indian country. On the one hand, there seems to have been a certain amount of appreciation that living, breathing "rez" Indians were portrayed on screen at all. On the other hand, there was a sense of disappointment that a rather whitewashed, and superficial portrait emerges. Several reactions, including that of author Seals, discuss how the film sanitizes the book, making the Indians too good, as if merely switching black hats for white could undo the limits of the "cowboy and Indian" formula. The novel's Indians are far more ambiguously de-picted, with real human flaws; Buddy's sister, for example, is not just a victim of an FBI frame-up but really is dealing drugs. Seals's response in-cludes having the film appear briefly as a spectral character in his novel-istic sequel to *Powwow Highway*, *Sweet Medicine*, in order to underscore the movie's differences from his novel. Clearly *Powwow Highway* broke some new ground in Hollywood cinema, but ultimately it veers away from tough questions.[15]

Thunderheart

The second of our films, *Thunderheart*, was directed by British film-maker Michael Apted. In the same year, 1992, Apted also directed one of the documentaries about AIM, *Incident at Oglala*, with funding from Robert Redford. *Incident at Oglala* deals with the case of Leonard Peltier's alleged involvement in the murder of two FBI agents in 1976. *Thunder-heart*'s fictional story is a thinly veiled effort to deal with the period of AIM activity after the events at Wounded Knee had passed. The film opens with the following words on the screen: "This film was inspired by events that took place on several Indian reservations during the 1970s." This would seem to be at once a claim for realism and a disclaimer, probably aimed at Justice Department lawyers. "Inspired by" seems to leave enough room to claim poetic license if the FBI took exception to being portrayed in the film as conspiring to commit murder, obstruct justice, and collude with private corporations to steal uranium-rich Indian lands. The director also changes the name of AIM in the film to ARM, "Aboriginal Rights Movement." It also changes the name of the FBI in the film, but in quite a different way.

The FBI's name changes are made by a character in the film named Crow Foot, a local Oglala cop whose skills make him a kind of cross between Hollywood Indian scout and Sherlock Holmes. Played with brilliant humor by Graham Greene, Crow Foot makes a series of revi-

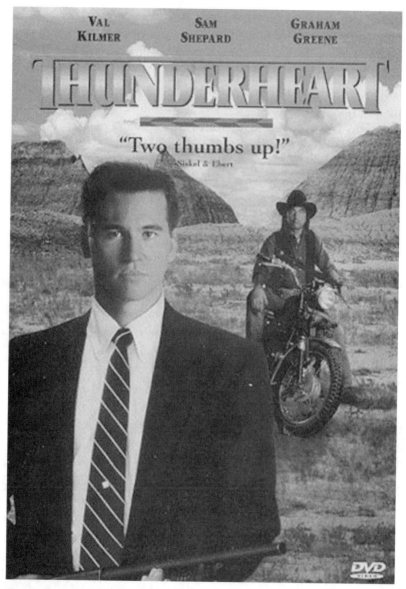

Film poster for *Thunderheart*.

sionist readings on the most famous initials in American law enforcement: from "Federal Bureau of Intimidation" to "Federal Bureau of Interpretation" (here stressing the fictive dimension of interpretation). Finally another Indian points out that on the rez FBI stands for "Full Blooded Indian." This progression from intimidator to interpreter to

Indian also marks the progress of the central character in the film, an FBI agent played by Val Kilmer. Kilmer's character is named Ray LeVoy, a naive young agent who has an American Indian heritage he has deeply and successfully buried, at least until he arrives on the reservation. He is sent there as a token Indian to help legitimate the FBI's attempt to round up an AIM/ARM member who they claim murdered another Indian. The ARM activist is played by AIM "actorvist" John Trudell.

The rather predictable plot revolves around the gradual re-Indianization of Kilmer's FBI character as he is at once seduced by the powers of ARM's tribal elder medicine man, played by Ted Thin Elk, and appalled to find evidence of an FBI plot to frame the ARM activist and abet the sale of uranium-rich lands. *Thunderheart*, like *Powwow Highway* before it, rightly draws attention to the deadly effects, both economically and through water contamination, that illegal mining practices have had on Pine Ridge and other reservations.

One key moment in the film momentarily shatters the Hollywood frame, which dominates this film more than the other two. It occurs when Trudell, playing James Looks Twice, is arrested by Kilmer and his hard-nosed FBI boss, played with aptly laconic flatness by Sam Shepard. Kilmer's character refers to Looks Twice as a militant, to which he replies, "I'm not a militant, I'm a warrior." Shepard's character retorts, "Yeah, and I'm John Wayne." Looks Twice follows up with a quick speech: "[I'm p]art of a five hundred year resistance. Deep voices that have to be heard. You can kill us but you can't break our spirit." These words closely echo ones the actor Trudell has made in his AIM speeches, and it probably matters little to this analysis whether he gave them to or got them from the movie script (though I think it likely was the former). The effect is a momentary crack in the film's melodrama.

As in *Powwow Highway,* there is a strong theme of connection between tradition, spirituality, and warriorhood. In the real-life history of AIM such a connection was often the goal, though one not always achieved. But accounts of the involvement of Sioux elders in the decision to make a stand with AIM at Wounded Knee suggest that that event may have done much to solidify a bond between the mostly urban Indians of AIM and spiritual traditionalists. That bond is one of the most important legacies of the AIM era (even though AIM's often vague pan-Indianism paid too little attention to particular tribal cultural histories).

But no account I know of says anything about a turncoat FBI agent playing a role in any of this. And that is surely among the most disappointing elements of *Thunderheart*. Just as the film *Mississippi Burning* undercuts its important retelling of the history of Freedom Summer by making the FBI, which did so much to try to destroy the civil rights movement, a hero in the film, *Thunderheart*'s use of this turncoat FBI agent sometimes transforms the film into a ridiculous "Mississippi Burning Goes West." But at least in this case the Indian FBI agent is used as a device to expose the FBI, not to make the bureau the unsung hero of another movement it did so much to try to destroy.

In *Thunderheart* the device may work to some extent to lure in the unsympathetic audience member who might initially identify with the FBI position, given its prominence in hegemonic Americanism generally and its reported role in saving the nation from militant "wild Indians" like AIM. But the cost of the device is to undermine the film in many other ways and turn it in some absurd, Hollywood directions. Kilmer's character is revealed to be a descendant of "Thunderheart," a medicine man killed at the original massacre at Wounded Knee in 1890. A kind of blood-essentialism perversely combines with a paternalistic suggestion that only a hero from the outside, trained in the white world, can rescue the Indian nations.

This plot line severely undermines the political pull of the film, and particularly the movement dimension. Too little sense of even symbolic collectivity is suggested around ARM in the movie, and what sense of Indian community there is in the film is undercut by an incongruous ending in which Kilmer's character heads down the road as if this were just one in a series of adventures. In a serious confusion of the "cowboys and Indians" plot, the movie ends with the FBI Indian "riding" off into the sunset alone, cowboy-style. The film thus ends on a rather hazy, nostalgic moment that locks Indian activism in a more recent past as surely as *Dances With Wolves* locks Indian cultures in the nineteenth century.

Lakota Woman: Siege at Wounded Knee

The third and final film I shall examine is *Lakota Woman: Siege at Wounded Knee*, a Ted Turner–Jane Fonda co-production originally shown on television and then released to video stores. The film is based

Poster for *Lakota Woman* video.

on a controversial (auto)biography of AIM activist Mary Crow Dog "as told to" Richard Erdoes. The book is controversial for several reasons, including the question of who "really" wrote it, its sympathetic treatment of AIM, and its long-time failure to find a publisher. This latter point is of interest because the reason given for the initial failure to find a publisher, in the late 1970s, was in effect that Indians were no longer fashionable. This raises the question of why Native Americans became "fashionable" once again in the late 1980s and early 1990s when all these films were produced. One partial answer, which probably mitigates the effects of all the movies, is a pervasive capacity of American culture to nostalgize any topic, even one as initially disturbing as the red power movement. In this case one might speculate that this general nostalgia was augmented by the particular nostalgia of Fonda, who had assisted in airlifting supplies to the Wounded Knee encampment during her more radical youth.

In any event, the passage of time between the original events and their filmic reenactment surely works to the advantage of the "cowboys" in this story since in the intervening years they viciously suppressed the American Indian Movement, using the goon squads when necessary, disinformation campaigns at every opportunity, and the court system continuously. The general strategy was to use trumped-up charges that were later dropped after they had done their damage of keeping key figures tied up in legal battles and movement funds directed toward legal fees rather than organizing. Sometimes the government had greater success in actually framing and incarcerating individuals, such as Leonard Peltier. Though 92 percent of cases that made it to trial were won by AIM, the costs in money, time, jail time while awaiting trial, and movement energy were devastating. While AIM continues to exist to this day, the movement never recovered from this assault.

With those limitations in mind, it is possible to say that *Lakota Woman* is the most complete, and in most respects the best, of the AIM fiction films done so far. Much of the credit must go to the original material, since Mary Crow Dog was for a time at the heart of AIM, and she provided a lucid and compelling story for Erdoes and later the filmmakers to work with. Another key factor is that the story is told from the point of view of an Indian woman. One of the least admirable aspects of AIM, in my judgment, is a tendency toward masculinist posturing that Mary Crow Dog does a nice job of puncturing from time to time in both the book and the film. I read that posturing as in part a product of the Hollywood script in which warriorhood was always just about armed confrontation, rather than about building and protecting community by many means. Putting Mary Crow Dog at the center decenters the "cowboy and Indian" dynamic considerably. It is also important because women have played and continue to play key leadership roles in many parts of native cultures, and they certainly were important in AIM. The film correctly shows, for example, that traditional women of Pine Ridge played a particularly strong role in pushing to invite AIM to take up the occupation at Wounded Knee. When a male leader suggests in the film that women leave the encampment, Mary and the other women present give a resounding response of "hell no!" More generally, a female center is important because, as in most movements of the era, women in AIM did much of the real organizing work while too often male leaders took starring roles in the spotlights. Those starring roles, however, also meant that it was disproportionately the men who ended up in jail. Eventually women in AIM formed their own organization, WARN (Women of All Red Nations), which supported the men of AIM but recognized the need (and the traditional right) of women to form separate groups. WARN remains today one of the most important native resistance organizations.

The character of Mary Crow Dog, played by Irene Bedard (who also performed the voice of Pocahontas in Disney's animated film), is also used to illustrate the ambivalence in AIM about the use of violence. While the women in the film are portrayed as every bit as militant as the men, they do not fetishize guns. On the one hand, the advertisements for the television presentation of the film seem to play up Mary's woman warrior stance by picturing her peering through the scope of a rifle. On the other hand, in the movie itself we learn that when she peers through that scope and gets a government soldier in her crosshairs, she acknowledges his humanity and does not pull the trigger. That is for me an important moment because, looking back on the radicalism of the 1960s and 1970s, it is clear that the FBI "cowboys" tried to provoke violence as often as possible in order to discredit movements. Dismissing movements as "violent" and "extremist" has long been a way for the government to avoid confronting the issues radical movements raise. In the case of AIM, while government agents wanted to avoid a second Wounded Knee massacre, they were pleased whenever they helped the warriors live up to the violent, criminal "renegade" image they and the media had crafted for them. While AIM's official stance was always one of violence only in "self-defense," that proved a difficult distinction to make, as it had been for the Black Panthers. It was made more difficult by law enforcement infiltrators who joined AIM often for the express purpose of pushing for more violent actions.

Mary Crow Dog's involvement with AIM becomes the center of the film even more than in the book, and the movie gives a far more detailed portrait of the spirit, ideas, and goals of AIM than any other film, including the two documentaries. The film is also careful to make clear at the beginning that it is only the story of "Mary Brave Woman [as she was named after she gave birth inside the encampment during the siege] — this is how she saw it." While this may, again, have been written partly as a legal disclaimer, it also makes clear that this is a partial portrait, not a definitive one. Following these opening printed words, the film segues quickly to scenes of the Pine Ridge landscape, as Mary's voice-over tells us that this is the story of how she "finds her soul." She says modestly that it is "only a little story" compared to that of Crazy Horse and other great warriors, but it is hers.

The film is good at giving a quick but textured sense of the background that led Mary and many Indians like her to join the movement. An early scene contrasts her material poverty with a sense of the strength of family in native communities. Mary narrates, "We were poor but I didn't know it and we had love and respect." The story of the first Wounded Knee massacre is also told as both a tribal and a family affair through Mary's grandfather who had witnessed it. This scene of military genocide is soon followed by attempted cultural genocide as symbolized by Mary's Indian braids being cut off in a repressive Christian boarding school, which systematically goes about trying to erase her cultural heritage, as such schools have tried to do for many generations. We also get glimpses of her teenage years, which can perhaps most aptly be described as aimless. We get statistical information on the poverty and unemployment rates on the reservation that contextualizes what in the other films is too often mere background (though both of the other fiction films make remarks about the rez being part of "the Third World"). Mary and her friends court, and in one case meet, death in drunken car chase games. One of the documentary films, *The Spirit of Crazy Horse*, reads alcoholism as a resistance to the life imposed on Native Americans by the dominant culture, and while that view is not made explicit in *Lakota Woman*, it is clear that Mary redirects some of the reckless energy and anger at what has become of her people under white domination into the more creative and active response of working with AIM.

Her involvement is portrayed fairly carefully as developing in stages rather than through some flash of conversion, as too often happens in films about radicals. There is an amusing scene in which she first learns about radical Native American activism from an alternative newspaper given her by a young "hippie chick" who is clearly thrilled to be talking to a real live Indian. Later she gets a more direct lesson in the movement while in jail after one of her drunken adventures, and she gradually drifts into movement circles. A male inmate gives her the gist of AIM philosophy as follows: "We light the spark; we're gonna take it all back, and then we're gonna set it free."

Bedard as Crow Dog offers voice-over narration that allows for a fair amount of discursive development of AIM views and contextualizations, providing useful information for the audience as the film moves rather quickly through most of the major events in the evolution of AIM. The account begins with the intervention into border town killings that first established AIM as a force in the Dakotas. The uprising around the murder of Wesley Bad Heart Bull in Custer, South Dakota, which solidified AIM's reputation, is staged carefully. The narrator tells us that Bad Heart Bull's mother was given three to five years for allegedly inciting a riot outside the courthouse where her son was being tried, while the murderer was set free.

The Mount Rushmore action, where an AIM activist humorously remarks that "we reclaim this piece of bad art in the name of the Lakota people," is also touched upon. Crow Dog's narration adds that while "we had no magic to restore the mountain, the FBI acted like they believed we might," and proceeded to brutalize the protesters. Another scene raises the important issue of archaeological desecration, again with a touch of humor at the expense of white presumptuousness. AIM activists approach a dig overseen by a professor surrounded by graduate students and ask the befuddled prof, "Where's your grandmother buried? We want to dig her up and put *her* in *our* museum." When the archaeologist asks, "Who are you people?" the activists reply: "We are walking scientific specimens. We are quaint tourist attractions. We are living fossils. We are your conscience, if you have one."

When the film turns to the siege at Wounded Knee, which takes up most of its second half, the effort to achieve accuracy is clear. We get scenes of speeches by Russell Means (played by Lawrence Bayne) that give the spirit, if not always the specific content, of AIM ideology. We also get a sense of how the urban members of AIM became acquainted with and were influenced by traditional elders on the reservations. That some of the conservatives among the traditionals opposed AIM is also acknowledged, at least in passing, and one asks a question frequently directed at AIM: Will these outside guys be here when the smoke clears? And in the meeting in which the decision to go to Wounded Knee is made, it is accurately women who take the strongest stance.

Leonard Crow Dog, the young Lakota medicine man who became a spiritual adviser to AIM and whom Mary married after Wounded Knee, has a central role in the latter part of the film. Lakota spirituality and its relation to AIM work is handled with some care and without the heavy-handedness found in the New Age version. While some have argued that any depiction of native spirituality is a sacrilege, Lakota spiritual advisers were hired to assure sensitive handling of the ritual scenes, and humor was used to fight against Hollywood medicine man stereotypes. For example, one elder remarks that "father peyote" will lead AIM back "into the spirit world," "where we'll talk about the great mysteries of life, like where the sunglasses go when you lose them." (This is perhaps also a gentle slap at the "shades and braids" image of the male AIMsters.)

The battle with the forces of Dickie Wilson (played with icy power by August Schellenberg) is also trenchantly portrayed. Direct quotes from Wilson's press conferences, including his famous threat to cut off Russell Means's braids, give a sense of his growing frustration with challenges to his paternalistic authority at Pine Ridge. More seriously, Wilson's campaign to wipe out AIM is referred to appropriately as a "reign of terror," and his collusion with white vigilante cowboys in addition to the federal marshal cowboys is clearly represented. In one scene we overhear putative law enforcers relishing that fighting Indians is giving them a chance to be "real" cowboys. Another scene stresses that, as it was in the past, most of the firepower is on the side of the cowboy cavalry. FBI training of Wilson's goons to use automatic weapons, and details of the far greater firepower of the cowboys, including two armored personnel carriers, is carefully documented, unlike the original coverage in the *New York Times*.

The presence of and limited understanding of events provided by "the media" are also thematized. Mary notes that the reporters "loved our Indian uprising" but suggests that their focus on the "cowboy and Indian" dimensions ignored the subtantive issues, and that they quickly grew tired unless new dramas were produced (which may account for those events the real Russell Means allegedly staged). When Mary herself is asked by reporters to explain the meaning of the siege, she at first tries to defer to the male spokesmen, but then offers her own answer. She lists the names of various tribes—Mohawk, Nisqually, Ojibway, and Cheyenne, among many others—whose members had come together at Wounded Knee. To illustrate what this means, she holds up her hand, fingers spread, then brings the fingers together into a tightly clenched fist. But rather than digging deeper into the meaning of her gesture, the reporters just ask her repeatedly to reenact it. In another scene, the Russell Means character chastises the press for not doing the background work necessary to understand what the occupiers were fighting for. Later the characters of Dennis Banks and Means address the issue of violence as raised by a reporter. Banks says, "The history of AIM is one of action, not violence." When a follow-up question asks about the guns in the AIM compound, Means makes a plea of self-defense by reeling off the names of Indians murdered in recent months, linking the deaths to a long tradition of killing.

There are other points I could detail in which documentary-style information about the Wounded Knee events and the surrounding context are given. One could also point out inaccuracies and distortions in detail, mostly attributable to poetic license. But I want to close my discussion of the film with remarks about a different dimension, its portrayal of the ethos of the AIM encampment. One of the most profound aspects of collective, social movement action, at least from my experience, is the feeling political theorist Hannah Arendt referred to as "public happiness," the sense of exhilaration that comes when one throws one's whole being into a principled cause. This feeling is seldom captured in film, with its bias toward individualized storytelling. But a sense of community, so much a part of native nations as well as social movement cultures, is conveyed relatively well in the film. It is summed up by Mary's remark that she never felt more "free" than when inside the Wounded Knee camp. That one can indeed feel most "free" when in jail for civil disobedience or when surrounded by the trigger-happy federal marshals and FBI agents is a paradox of social activism rarely portrayed in the mass media. The sense of the encampment as a community, one both mundane and extraordinary, comes through powerfully at points. While framed as one woman's story, and thus caught up to a certain degree in Euro-American notions of individuality, the film's narrative moves toward collective power and communal responsibility.

The film ends on a powerful note, one that attempts, not fully success-fully, to fend off the nostalgic move that might lock Indian resistance in the past. Standing in front of the mass grave monument to the 1890 massacre at Wounded Knee, Mary looks directly into the camera and details the ways in which the government lied in its negotiated settle-ment of the occupation, notes the role played by the media in the action, then counts off some of the assassinations that followed in the wake of the occupation, and recites the names of members still in jail. "Once we put down our guns and the television and newspaper reporters went home, the arrests began. They could say anything they wanted. Whatever we said was gone in a cold Pine Ridge wind. Nearly everything is gone now. The government tried to extinguish all signs that Indians once made their stand here. It will do them no good because the world saw, the world heard. Even though in time [some of our people] were murdered by goons. Even though once again the government lied and betrayed us. Even though some of our leaders are still in jail. In the end it will do them no good at all to try to hide it because it happened. Today it is still not ours, but tomorrow it might be. Because of that long moment those short years ago at Wounded Knee. Where we reached out and touched our history. I was there. I saw it. It happened to me." Then in Lakota and English she adds, "So that our people may live," as two Indian chil-dren run across the screen. The ending offers a refusal to have the past erased, and a call to bring the warrior legacy into the future.

The ending is a powerful one, but it is also solidifies for me a feeling that the film has been too perfect, too neat. The Indian-maiden beauty of Bedard herself seems to tie together a film with too few rough edges, too much Hollywooden idealism. The Indian resisters are a bit too good to be true, the black hats on Dick Wilson's Indian cowboys fit a bit too tightly. There is little sense of the internal strife that wracked AIM, little sense that some of the leaders had less pure motives and less admirable characters than they are given in the film. Incarceration and service in Vietnam had deeply wounded many AIM members, some of whom were unstable, not to say just plain crazy. And, as I suggested above, the "shades and braids" corps gave in more than once to a vanity that did not serve the movement. In addition, the film says far too little about the failure of AIM to follow through in the aftermath of its symbolic victories. In their efforts toward sympathy, the filmmakers whitewash AIM, make it too purely a victim. By robbing the AIM activists of their human imperfections, they ironically rob them of much of their human agency. The ending is also problematic in its elegiac tone. Seeing Mary/Irene alone before the site of two Wounded Knee struggles with nothing but the wind blowing undercuts the sense of collective agency of Indian resistance and evokes the vanishing Indian trope; it is as if only a return of the Ghost Dance, rather than concerted tribal action for sovereignty, will lead to a different future.

But looking at *Lakota Woman* from the angle of production rather than product suggests a different ending to the story of Indian resistance through film. One of the more admirable facts about *Lakota Woman*, and one that, along with its woman-centered story, no doubt accounts for many of its strengths, is that the filmmakers went to some lengths to hire Native Americans not only as actors for the film, but as crew members and consultants to assure a degree of accuracy on several levels. In addition to Richard Moves Camp, consultant on Lakota spirituality, the film employed Mary Crow Dog herself as a consultant (on her own life story) and other former AIM members to go over details about the occupation.

More important than the gestures toward authenticity, however, is the hiring of the crew members. For I agree with critic Judy Merritt, novelist David Seals, and many in Indian country that in the future Indian films should be made as much as possible by Native American people. Merritt challenges the Ted Turners and the Robert Redfords to put their money where their mouths are by turning over whole productions to Native American crews. Novelist Seals has said that he will not authorize a sequel to *Powwow Highway* unless it is directed by an Indian. And the Lakota people have recently worked to get Ted Turner to stop production on a proposed film about the figure he calls "Crazy Horse" and whom they know as Ta' Shunke Witko. This is not racial essentialism or "blood quantum" theory at work; it is about the need for a degree of cultural competency Hollywood has again and again fallen short of, and it is a call for the rights AIM aimed at from the beginning: self-determination and self-representation for native people everywhere. Cinematic self-representation, will, of course, be no panacea. It will be subject to all the contradictions that trouble Native American communities today. But it will be an important step in a larger process, just as surely as Wounded Knee itself was a step in a struggle that continues.

In the meantime, we have these films about AIM, which have strengths as well as serious flaws. In this they mirror AIM itself. Perhaps the deepest flaws in AIM were its misogyny and its own excessive reliance upon the mass media, a flaw that my presentation here risks replicating. The misogyny eventually led to brutal acts perpetrated against women in AIM, including in all likelihood the murder of AIM activist Annie Mae Aquash.[16] AIM was spectacularly successful, for brief moments, in drawing attention to Native American issues through effective guerrilla theater. Actions like Wounded Knee awakened members of native nations throughout the United States and around the world. But the often vague, pan-Indian politics of AIM could not address the differing, complicated situations of Indian nations. And while AIM's mass media approach can at best mobilize, it cannot truly organize people or communities. That takes face-to-face, painstaking work.

In the wake of the relative decline of the organization due to internal strife and FBI repression, much of the work of AIM passed on to specific, local political, cultural, and spiritual warriors in the many Indian nations. Great successes in rekindling native pride, cultures, and rights have occurred in the years since AIM's heyday, despite ongoing economic exploitation. This work has been less visible, less spectacular, than AIM's symbolic actions, but it has also gone far deeper. From this deeper base in various indigenous communities, cross-nation and even worldwide native organizations have emerged to continue interlinked struggles for land, sovereignty, and legal redress. At the same time, native art, poetry, fiction, and film have flourished, bringing voices that stir Indian hearts and minds, and address difficult questions to the white world.

But even in this new context, AIM's work is not done. In a time when, as Warrior and Smith note, young Native Americans are growing up with little knowledge of the AIM era, AIM's stories, even these flawed filmed versions, may prove useful. Who knows but that, when encountered by chance on TV, or used by a teacher or organizer who can point to the distortions, one or another of the films might spark some questions, touch off some "Crazy Horse dreams," and ignite new kinds of resistance efforts as the next generation of Indian and non-Indian activists examines and learns from the successes and the failures of the AIM era.

SIX

"We Are [Not] the World"
Famine, Apartheid, and the Politics of Rock Music

Millions of kids are lookin' at you
You say, "Let them drink soda pop"....
From the African nation
to the Pepsi generation...
You're gonna make it rich
as long as some poor bastard in Africa
is lying in a ditch.
    —The Pretenders, "How Much Did You Get [for your soul]"

We're rappers and rockers
United and strong.
We're here to talk about South Africa
We don't like what's goin' on.
    —Artists United against Apartheid, "Sun City"

The mid-1980s saw the rise of a series of globally televised concerts, records, and videos that have been variously called "charity rock," "benefit rock," or, with a nod to a rather different tradition, "agit-pop" (a word play on *agit-prop*, the shorthand term for so-called agitation propaganda used by radicals to characterize movement-based political art in the 1930s).[1] Benefit concerts are hardly a new thing. They are at least as old as the Paterson Pageant of 1912, and have a rich history, especially in the 1930s and 1960s.[2] But the global scale of these events of the 1980s was unprecedented, and they set off a new wave of "rock and roll activism" that continues today.

The archetype and best known of these agit-pop events is the "Live Aid" African famine relief concert of 1985. Following upon Live Aid there have been dozens of such efforts in countries around the world on a host of different issues, from apartheid to the environment to AIDS to political prisoners. These events were especially important because they emerged in that famously conservative and greed-ravaged era of the 1980s, when progressive causes often seemed to be in eclipse. In actuality, several important social movements were under way during that decade, including a strong antimilitarist/antinuclear movement and a host of "solidarity" movements attempting to change U.S. policy toward El Salvador, Nicaragua, and, most relevant to this chapter, South Africa.[3] The "benefit rock" events are important because they are among the most compelling attempts to create moments of "popular global culture," in contrast to "global pop culture." They are riddled with political contradictions and limitations, but they also suggest one possible, progressive axis of transnational communication in this globalizing era.

In this chapter I examine two clusters of these agit-pop events, with the aim of suggesting the possibilities and limits of their use by social movements as a point of entry onto the terrain of the "mass media" or "popular culture." In particular, I analyze these recordings, concerts, and associated books, t-shirts, and so forth as presenting popular ideas about relationships between the so-called "underdeveloped" Third World and the (over)developed First World. In the process I want to suggest a middle ground in two longstanding debates about popular culture and social change. The first debate is between those who find the mass media inherently conservative because of their commercialized nature, and those who see popular culture as a zone of significant political resistance. The second debate is between those who see U.S. pop culture as part of a "cultural imperialism" that dominates and overwhelms other cultures of the world, and those who believe that despite U.S. dominance significant amounts of postmodern "transnational culture" flow from many locations and in many directions. Although I do not address these very large questions directly, my analysis is meant to suggest that both sides of these important debates have at best part of the truth.[4]

To approach these issues, I first look at Live Aid itself, along with the associated "Band Aid" and "We are the World/USA for Africa" famine relief projects. By way of contrast, I then analyze a cluster of musical

texts originating in the United States and Britain in support of resistance
to South African apartheid, in particular the American *Sun City* music/
video project, and the "Nelson Mandela 70th Birthday" tribute concert
in England. I chose the famine and anti-apartheid projects as examples
because they are similar enough to allow certain important political
contrasts to stand out, and because they allow me to examine two different ways that movements can contest for the meanings circulating in
popular culture. The most obvious similarity is that both famine relief
and the struggle against apartheid directly and indirectly comment on
relations between colonial and neocolonial nations (like Britain and the
United States), on one hand, and the emerging, decolonizing nations of
the Southern Hemisphere on the other. A focus on Africa allows me to
analyze both the dangers and the possibilities of Western pop and rock
music as embodiments of and resisters to the domination of "the West"
over "the rest" of the world. It further allows me to show how a global
phenomenon can be attached to local movement sites of action.

The prime difference between these two sets of events is that the
famine project had its politics more or less thrust upon it and thus represents a case of a struggle by movements to *appropriate* an ambiguous
cultural text, while the anti-apartheid project was more or less politically
radical from the beginning and thus represents a test of the limits of an
attempt to *create* a movement text within the confines of the mass media.

Benefit Pop/Rock and African Famine

Let us look at the Live Aid cluster of texts first, through a kind of double
lens: first, a textual analysis that elaborates a composite portrait of highly
negative critical interpretations of the famine benefit; then, a more positive *con*textual analysis that suggests the inadequacy of this first kind of
narrowly text-based analysis. These contrasting readings demonstrate
how the necessary task of analyzing a text as a formal structure needs to
be supplemented by analyzing the ways in which the meanings of texts
change as they are placed into new historical and political frames of
reference.

In the standard story told, the African famine-relief pop/rock benefits
begin with the efforts of the then moderately well known Irish rock
musician Bob Geldof. It is interesting that in this origin story Geldof's
efforts are themselves set in play by the mass media, in this case by a
BBC documentary on the famine that Geldof saw more or less by acci-

dent. The famine, which stretched through Africa's Sahel region from Senegal to Ethiopia, caused an estimated 1 million deaths in the 1980s. Stunned and disturbed by the images and facts presented in the film, Geldof organized British rock and pop stars to produce a record drawing attention to the famine and raising relief money to fight it.

The first result of this project was the song, "Do They Know It's Christmas?" performed by various British artists under the name Band Aid and released late in 1984.[5] This record was followed a few months later by release in the United States of the similar song, "We Are the World." Then, finally, on 13 July 1985, the huge and extremely financially successful Live Aid concerts were held in London and Philadelphia, and were telecast worldwide to more than 1.5 billion people.[6]

Even granting that there are a fair number of Christians in northern Africa, it is difficult to imagine a more culturally insensitive question to ask musically than "Do They Know It's Christmas?" Moreover, how likely is Christmas to be first on the minds of starving people? This dubious question typifies the narcissistic self-importance and ethnocentric disregard for cultural differences that permeate much of this project. An inability to see the very different cultural conditions of Britain and Africa is reinforced by the virtual absence of black artists from the British recording session and from the British half of the concert. This is important not because every record or event has to be racially balanced, but because the absence of blacks served to underscore the emerging, no doubt unintended, racist message that the relief effort was about helpful whites helping helpless blacks. The absence of black artists is especially unforgivable given that the many Rastafarians among black British, Afro-Caribbean, and African American performers view Ethiopia, one of the more devastated of the famine areas, as a spiritual homeland.

From the point of view of fundraising with regard to their target audience, "Do They Know It's Christmas?" was perfectly conceived to play into those seasonal spasms of humanist "good will toward men" that get engraved on Christmas cards and fill the buckets of armies of salvation of various sorts every holiday season in both the United Kingdom and the United States. Indeed, in these terms, the song exceeded all expectations, becoming a Number 1 hit and a gold record, raising more than $11 million.

While this fundraising success is impressive, and while the personal motives of most of those involved were undoubtedly sincere, these initial efforts of Band Aid recycled some of the most problematic humanist ideas, from patronizing, patriarchal "charity" and philanthropy to deeply racist, imperialist echoes of "the white man's burden" (the nineteenth-century notion that the "white man" is bringing "civilization" to the backward peoples of the world). In fact, "modern" agricultural development contributed to undermine the food base, as well as the culture, of the Africans who were experiencing the famine.[7]

When the text of musical famine relief migrates across the Atlantic to the United States, some of its most suspect aspects are mitigated a bit, but not much. Here the origins are significantly different in at least one respect, the race of the prime movers, virtually all of whom were black. Inspired by Geldof's project, the American effort was touched off by Harry Belafonte, an entertainer with a history of political activism, including a long association with Martin Luther King Jr. and involvement in numerous progressive social movements.

Belafonte soon persuaded his friends Lionel Richie, Michael Jackson, and Stevie Wonder to take over work on an American version of the Band Aid record. Unfortunately, Wonder, the only one of this trio with even minimal political knowhow, was forced by other commitments to drop out, and the actual composition fell to Jackson and Richie. The result was the immensely (if briefly) popular song, "We Are the World." Once ubiquitous, still insipid, it remained, until Elton John rerecorded "Candle in the Wind" as a tribute to Princess Di, the biggest-selling single of all time.

In video form *We Are the World* received wide airplay on the then relatively new Music Television network, MTV. Again it was a spectacular success. As in the song "Do They Know It's Christmas?" the text can be characterized as extraordinarily ethnocentric, displaying a self-centeredness reinforced by the video, which shows us no Africans at all, but lots of rich musicians looking and sounding at once sincere and self-satisfied. The extremely static staging of the video visually reinforces a sense of *in*activist self-containment; no one moves from the claustrophobic recording studio, and intercut images of Africans present only victims.

The lyrics play back and forth between identity and difference in such a way as to make it impossible to see Africans as capable social actors, while simultaneously pretending "they" are just like "us." The presumed identification between "the starving children" and the well-fed rock stars is a classic example of how liberal humanism obscures important differences of condition, making political analysis impossible. As the presumptive "we" of the title designates the First World, it serves to remove "our" responsibility by folding us into the Third World as one world. There is no difference or distance from which to construct notions of relative responsibility for the famine. "We" too are its victims. While empathetic connection to those suffering from the famine might be desirable, such a pure identification with "them" erases the distance needed to understand and challenge the sources of their very different political, economic, and cultural conditions. Such an easy sense of connection covers differences of class, race, religion, and political ideology within Africa, and within First World countries (where hunger also exists in the midst of plenty). The problem is that the two worlds come to be conceived as generically prosperous, on the one hand, and generically deprived, on the other.

Even as this too easy sense of connecting the "worlds" is offered, the subtext suggests its opposite, a pure difference between "us" and "them," we the saviors and they the victims. Thus, the most ironically truthful line in the song is the one that goes, "We're saving our own lives." Intended to achieve identification with the "victims," it marks the true distance by suggesting that the "we" who will be saved are not the Africans, but the song's singers and audience, saved from having to think seriously about an "unpleasant thing" by simply giving a few dollars for famine relief. At the same time, it masks the true connection, world and national economies, in which the benefits to people like the musicians and fellow contributors come at the expense of those whose work makes possible the prosperous lives the musicians live.

Taken together, these two records could be said to add up to this message: "We" [in the West] are the world, and "they" [in Africa] don't even know it's Christmas.

The problematic aspects of these two record/video efforts are magnified, but also somewhat diffused by the mega-concert that grows out of them, Live Aid proper. Unlike the records, which make no reference, and the videos, which make minimal reference to the famine itself, the televised concerts did attempt intermittently to address the famine and some of its causes. Recorded vignettes by "experts" in the field of hunger were interspersed with musical performances. But the ideological limits of those vignettes were quite narrow. No one, for example, seriously addressed the relation of hunger to Western agricultural policy or the role played by First World manipulation of the economies of the Third World. Countries throughout the developing world have been forced to borrow money from the World Bank and the International Monetary Fund (both organizations largely controlled by the United States), and in exchange they have been made to develop their economies only in ways acceptable to and profitable for the United States and the other major capitalist nations. The mechanized, chemical-dependent techniques of large-scale agriculture are in many cases less efficient than traditional methods, some of them thousands of years old and based on a rich knowledge of local ecologies. Once having committed themselves to expensive, U.S.–defined modes of modernization, developing countries are often drawn into a web of debt that becomes a way for the First World to shape their politics and cultures. More subtly than in the days when Europe could simply declare the rest of the world to be part of its empire, but often just as devastatingly, the political and cultural independence of the so-called "underdeveloped" Southern Hemisphere is undermined, with a loss of biodiversity and cultural diversity. And, as in the case of the African famines, these political-economic manipulations often cost thousands of lives.

Apart from or combined with philanthropic appeals, most commentaries during the rock aid events coded the famine as either a natural disaster or a technical problem. Coding the problem as "natural" removes all human, political responsibility for the cause. And calling the problem "technical" reinforces a sense of African "backwardness" implicit in the "underdevelopment" notion underpinning the overall story of "victims and saviors." Some of the appeals did move a bit beyond charity or the suggestion that Western technocratic elitism was the answer (rather than part of the problem), but not many. And particularly in the American context of broadcast on commercial television, these gestures seem quite obscene set alongside the perpetual orgy of consumption portrayed and appealed to in commercials.

Moreover, again and again, the north African famine is portrayed in the televised event via pictures of starving "women and children." As these images build upon one another, Africa itself is in effect both feminized and infantilized. One pervasive logo, used throughout the American broadcast of the event, begins with an image of the African continent, which then suddenly and magically becomes transformed into an electric guitar. Indeed, in a curious metamorphosis it appears as though the feminine womb of Africa gives birth to the phallic guitar that will be its savior.

Some critics suggest that as these messages mix with commercials pushing consumption of consumer goods, the American audience starts in effect to consume Africans. One of the logos for the project super-imposes a place setting with a knife, fork, and spoon over a map of the African continent. Cultural theorist Zoë Sofia has argued, only partly tongue in cheek, that the only solution to what she calls the "Cannibal-Eyes" of mass-mediated consumer capitalism is to "eat the rich," prefer-ably on a prime-time game show. Whether or not eating the rich is the solution, surely consuming the poor as a heartwarming television spec-tacle is part of the problem.[8]

Summing up various critical readings of the famine relief benefits I have been paraphrasing, one could say that Live Aid uses a falsely uni-versalizing liberal humanism, robs Africans of their own power, re-inforces Western ethnocentric racism, puts forth a vision of passivity that equates children with women and both with Africa, and obscures the neocolonialist sources of the famine by coding it as a natural disaster or as a technical rather than political problem. Put more colloquially, this analysis views Bob Geldof as a kind of clueless but slightly hipper Jerry Lewis who takes up starving Africans as his "kids" and holds the biggest telethon in history.

As the vicious pleasure with which I have presented this analysis makes clear, I find a good deal of truth in it, particularly as an analysis of some of the likely immediate effects of the event as presented to an Anglo-American audience. But I do *not* think this kind of analysis is the whole or final truth about the events if they are conceived not as one moment in time but as the beginning of a contest over what meanings would be attached to the famine and the relief efforts.

That such a contest over meanings took place is apparent as soon as one moves from examining the texts to considering their historical and political context. As cultural critic Stuart Hall has argued, the relevant historical context is the rise in both the United States and the United Kingdom of a very successful right-wing political project that went by the name of Reaganism in the United States and Thatcherism in Britain (named for the respective national leaders of the day, President Ronald Reagan and Prime Minister Margaret Thatcher). These projects, at the center of the "me decade," included a largely successful effort to wipe out all vestiges of liberal or progressive notions of community or of responsibility to anyone less fortunate than oneself. They promulgated the myth that a "free market" would magically distribute goods fairly, rewarding the hardworking and leaving the lazy to wallow in deserved poverty. People were told all they needed to do was develop enough "character" to pull themselves up by their own bootstraps. Unfortunately, the political impact of this ideology left many without shoes, let alone boots, with or without straps.

In such a context, Hall contends, even read most minimally as liberal philanthropy, the Live Aid events were the single most important counter-moment to the installation of this right-wing orgy of greed and self-interest. Hall calls the famine relief effort "one of the great popular movements of our time," and believes it offered a "direct democratic" challenge to "bureaucratic" power. He even suggests that Live Aid put the "new right" on the defensive, that it represented one of the few significant rips in the seams of its emerging hegemony.[9]

Hall is perhaps exaggerating a bit here to balance what he sees as a kind of knee-jerk left purism that produces the kind of analysis I gave above. But I think the core of his logic has been borne out, both in the evolution of the Live Aid project itself, and more important, in its use as a model for many of the more directly counter-hegemonic musical mega-events that came in its wake.

With regard to Live Aid, let me try to at least partially redeem the rock star and "his" mega-telethon by describing the way in which Geldof responded to critiques like those I leveled above. As the Irish rocker freely admits, he began his project as a political naïf, so much so as to claim that the famine was not a political issue. Finding himself, however, on the covers of the conservative journal *Spectator* and *Marxism Today* during the same week, he soon got the message that his event *was* political, and could be claimed by both the right and the left. Amid this political maelstrom, Geldof learned about Third World debt, defense spending, and world agricultural policies, and eventually found himself before the United Nations, scolding the assembled delegates for not dealing with the effect of Western agricultural policy on Africa, and supporting a call for a total moratorium on African debt, among other things.

Convincing criticism from the left moved Geldof and the project further and further away from charity and its discourses. Policies for disbursal of Live Aid funds were formulated that put only what was absolutely needed into emergency relief, directing the rest to long-term development programs, and eventually to attempts to Africanize all the projects by turning them over to local control by the people affected.[10]

Although millions of people desperately needed these efforts, many on the left (I among them) seemed willing, almost eager, to believe the worst about the disbursal of Live Aid funds and goods. Rumors of corruption and inefficiency spread wildly. But an independent audit found the Live Aid project to have been extremely efficient, above the standard for such work. Indeed, funds were still being distributed years after the concert, from a total raised that approached $250 million in cash, goods, and services.[11]

I dwell on Geldof not to make him heroic but to offer him as an allegory writ large for a process that many of the viewers of Live Aid underwent in a less visible way when they tried to do more than send a check. They joined various ongoing hunger relief projects in droves, and once there they usually began a process of political education that was for many also a process of radicalization. That process did not happen automatically, however, and that is my key point: it happened because some on the left chose to struggle for the meaning that Live Aid would have, to try to reshape it to their analysis and their agenda. Rather than just condemning it as naive, neocolonialist, racist, and so forth, they chose to attempt to decolonize the event, to liberate it into more fruitful political talk and action.

The second, related struggle set off by Live Aid was an effort to use the specific breach it had made in the new right's hegemonic process to open up other spaces of resistance. Hundreds of subsequent musical benefits and mega-benefits in dozen of countries attest to the ongoing impact of Live Aid. Of those the most dramatic, especially in reversing some of the imagery of Live Aid itself, were those projects entwined with the anti-apartheid struggle.

Music against Apartheid

In the United States the most interesting of the efforts to draw upon the precedent set by Live Aid was made by a group of musicians calling themselves Artists United against Apartheid. Their major project was a record and video entitled *Sun City*.[12] Far more politically explicit and aggressive than Live Aid, *Sun City* forms a kind of test case for examining how far it is possible to convey radically progressive ideas through mass-media forms. Far more directly than the relation between AIM and Hollywood discussed in chapter 5, these efforts sought to connect a movement to a pop-culture formation.

The Sun City project was started by "Little Steven" Van Zandt, formerly the lead guitarist for Bruce Springsteen's E-Street Band and later, like Geldof, a moderately successful solo artist and producer. In Van Zandt's telling, after learning from some American anti-apartheid activists about the situation in South Africa, he traveled there himself and spoke with numerous white and black South Africans involved in the liberation movements. Asking different groups what he could do to be most effective, he was told again and again that his appropriate role would be to tell his fellow musicians *not* to play at Sun City, a Las Vegas–like tourist complex set in the middle of one of the barbed-wire-surrounded black ghettos that white South Africans euphemistically called "homelands."

So began the Sun City project, aimed to reinforce and expand the United Nations–sponsored musicians' boycott of South Africa, and to educate the American public via music about the liberation struggle and about conditions of blacks living under racist systems, not only in South Africa but in the United States as well. Eventually the project came to include a single, an album, a video (directed by Jonathan Demme and Hart Perry), and various ancillary texts (including the obligatory t-shirt, as well as glossy picture books and a "rockumentary").[13]

I will discuss the video first because several contrasts with the *We Are the World* video are immediately apparent. The first important difference is that in *Sun City* black people, African American and Afro-Caribbean musicians, and, most important, black South Africans play central roles. They are visible in active not passive roles. Second, the musicians are moving, they are going somewhere; there is movement, perhaps even *a* movement, happening. The sense both lyrically and visually is a demand to act on, not just consume, these images. Third, to reinforce this message, the images themselves are far more kinetic throughout. On the one hand, the piece fits relatively seamlessly into the flow of MTV-style rock video imagery, thus allowing it into that mass-mediated space. On the other hand, what it shows on closer inspection is raised, clenched fists (mostly black ones) ripping away at apartheid and by suggestion ripping away veils of televisual illusion to show some of the realities of

Sun City rock stars superimposed on South African protesters. Scene from *The Making of "Sun City."*

apartheid beneath. It is of key importance that it is clearly Africans, not just the rock stars, who are ripping away at these images.

Van Zandt started his project as a more politically savvy and politically radical individual than Geldof, and thus his project too was more radical from the beginning. When he, like Geldof, eventually found himself at the United Nations, in this case to receive a humanitarian award for his work, he was careful to make explicit his project's distance from charity and its attendant discourse of victimage. His speech said in part: "This is not a benefit record because though the needs of black South Africans are great they do not ask us for our charity, and though the black South African suffering is horrifying, they do not ask us for our pity."[14]

Despite this clear attempt to distance the Sun City project from the discourse of Live Aid, Little Steven has frequently acknowledged that his project would not have been possible without various precedents set by the famine project, from directing focus onto the African continent to disinterring notions of international human rights to politicizing rock musicians (several of whom appear in both projects). The Sun City project's tack was not to totally reject liberal notions of humanitarianism, but instead to try to move its audience through and beyond that position to a more politically engaged one. This is reflected in the distribution of profits from the project, which were more or less equally divided along lines that allowed the project to finesse the ideological border between humanitarianism and political action. Roughly one-third went to the families of political prisoners; one-third to educational centers and colleges set up in Tanzania and Zambia by the prime anti-apartheid force, the African National Congress; and one-third to grassroots educational outreach efforts by the anti-apartheid movement in the United States.[15]

In virtually all the material released by the Sun City project, the finger was pointed not just at South Africa but also at the United States as a prime supporter of South African apartheid and as a site of homemade racism. At every opportunity, Van Zandt was careful to articulate this key point: "I hope that by focusing on the exaggeration of racism in [South Africa], we can realize that racism is very much alive in our own country, and that we can begin to dismantle our own apartheid right here at home."[16]

By apartheid at home, Van Zandt means U.S. racism generally, but this includes apartheid within the musical community, both the segregation of black and Latino music, and the domination of the industry by white producers. He and collaborator Arthur Baker tried to undermine the segregation and segmentation of musical audiences by bringing together the particular mix of musicians used on the session (rappers, rockers, punkers, funksters, reggae singers, salseros, new wave musicians, jazz artists, and significantly, Nigerian and South African musicians, among others). While the music industry likes to talk about diverse musical styles as simply reflecting different, freely chosen "taste cultures," demographic analysis makes clear that race, ethnicity, class, gender, and, of course, age make up the prime determinants of musical subcultures. Music subcultures certainly reflect tastes, but they also serve to reinforce social divisions that doubly serve capitalism: by dividing potential oppositional forces and by economically exploiting and trivializing ethnic diversity commercially. Attempts to bridge these subcultural divisions musically formed an important subtext of the Sun City project. Using the term *musical apartheid* to describe these divisions risked trivializing political apartheid, but was also a key to bringing the issues back home.

This multiple crossover list of artists also had a pragmatic marketing value, to achieve maximum airplay, as the various specialized radio formats would pick up on particular artist(s) representing their genre. But, as I will discuss in a moment, this part of the strategy met limitations.

Rockin' the Grassroots

I find two aspects of the Sun City project particularly suggestive. First, it utilized virtually all the available, relevant mass-mediated forms, pushing them close to their didactic limits, while maintaining enough of the form to keep it recognizable and thus available as a pop(ular) item. And second, the project sought to create substantive links to grassroots activism.

As I have already suggested, the *Sun City* video uses the hyperactive style of rock videos but tries to disconnect that manic energy from the postmodern aimlessness of MTV culture, and connect it to political struggle and direct action.[17] Some critics have suggested that the video does this by making political action look like too much fun, too much like a street party. But I would argue that this is precisely one of its strengths. This objection exemplifies a continuing left puritanism that is deadly to the possibility of a counter-hegemonic project. The inability of recent oppositional movements to articulate (link) politics and pleasure is one of the key factors that has condemned them to marginality even among that notoriously rebellious social category, youth. Indeed, the pleasures of *political* transgression remain one of the better kept, presumably guilty, secrets of the left, and recent attempts to foreground the pleasures of political as well as cultural transgressions seem to me a key area of theorizing activity.

In addition to the music video, the project also used two other video formats, recoding what is perhaps the most banally narcissistic of all popular culture genres, the "Making of..." format. "Making of" videos are designed to take you the viewer "behind the scenes." In the *Sun City* versions, you are indeed taken "behind the scenes," but the pretext of giving glimpses of the recording and filming processes is used to extend the audience's glance behind the scenes of apartheid. *The Making of*

"*Sun City*" video, a ten-minute version of which was shown on MTV while a forty-five-minute version was released for home use, includes charts and graphs illustrating economic conditions in South Africa, interviews with Winnie Mandela and other anti-apartheid activists, and testimony from most of the musicians taking part in the project. These latter comments naturally vary considerably in their level of political insight, but that too may serve a function, as it allows points of connection for viewers who may feel initially too uninformed to act. Thus the star-fan matrix, normally a site for adolescent fantasies, is here used to secure identifications that open the possibility of acting despite not (yet) having an elaborated analysis of South African politics. Space needs to be left in such a project for the less well informed to make a first step, and the inexpert comments of the musicians provide such an opening.

Similar use is made of the "star book" form, the glossy, vacuous genre normally used to provide purchasers with a mini-poster collection, full of pictures and with minimal, usually not very intellectually demanding text.[18] The Sun City project's version of this book genre does have lots of pictures, including obligatory ones of the musical stars who play on the record, but it also includes pictures of Nelson Mandela, of South African miners, of the victims *and* the resisters of apartheid. The glossy book does have enough pictures of self-indulgent star nonsense to draw in fans, but it also has a fairly substantive, though not daunting, text that includes plenty of encouragement to get a more in-depth analysis of apartheid. Indeed, the book, the record, the cassette, and virtually all other associated paraphernalia of the project contain bibliographies on South African history and the anti-apartheid movement, as well as ways to contact anti-apartheid organizations. This leads me to the second dimension of the exemplary actions by the Sun City project.

From its inception, Van Zandt had a sense that having grown out of his contacts with grassroots activists in South Africa, the project should be put to the service of grassroots activists in the United States. He tried to accomplish this in several ways. Most directly, he traveled around the country, offering himself as a speaker and making contact with dozens of local anti-apartheid solidarity groups. He also made the video widely available to these groups for use as an organizing tool, both to draw new people to meetings and to educate them once there.

The Sun City project also created a teaching packet to accompany the video for use both by community groups and in schools. The packet included not only educational materials but also a list of direct political actions from all around the country that had been inspired by the Sun City project, actions that could be emulated or improvised upon locally.[19]

The Sun City project was an ambitious, in many ways successful attempt to mediate between a mass-produced and -distributed cultural text, and local sites of reception. Put more strongly, it set out actively to produce connections to local movement groups, and created more general "reading formations" that would ensure a radical reading of the text.

But if the project reveals several potentially useful approaches to making and distributing oppositional mass-mediated texts, it also suggests some limits likely to be encountered by any such effort.

First, while the anti-apartheid project made a significant financial and educational impact, when compared to the more politically vague famine relief efforts, its impact was less spectacular. The album and single made it onto the Billboard Top Forty but had trouble getting sufficient radio airplay and never moved very far up the charts. This underscores my sense that the project may have pushed near the limit of what a didactic, radical intervention could do within the commercial mass media's terms.

While radio stations offered a variety of plausible nonpolitical reasons for not giving the song more airplay, it seems clear that its political message scared them. Similar difficulties were encountered when the project sought to have *The Making of "Sun City"* documentary aired on PBS. The offer was refused, despite numerous awards given to the video, on the grounds that it would violate the "journalistic integrity" of the network to air a program that simply promoted the ideas and careers of its producers. At the time this statement was offered, PBS was running two Lucasfilm documentaries on the making of those apparently less commercial ventures, *Star Wars* and *Raiders of the Lost Ark*.

As a result of this virtual censorship, the impact of the Sun City project was not on the scale of *We Are the World,* although it is difficult to measure precisely. My own informal poll of my students conducted in the mid-1990s, probably not a scientific sample of 2 billion people, confirmed my sense that *Sun City* is considerably less well known than *We Are the World,* even among progressive students. But more than half of those surveyed had seen the *Sun City* video or heard the song. According to one source, the *Sun City* video received a "heavy rotation" slot on MTV— a serious amount of airplay.[20]

The Sun City project years, 1985 and 1986, were peak years for anti-apartheid activism in the United States, particularly through various divestment campaigns on and around college campuses. The Sun City project certainly did not create this movement, but just as certainly it furthered it, providing a far more powerful outreach tool than those usually available to local activists. The project harmonized with a developing anti-apartheid movement centered on American college campuses. Student activists led the way with divestment campaigns aimed at getting their universities and colleges to remove from their huge investment portfolios corporations that bolstered the apartheid economy of South Africa. Students around the country built cardboard shantytowns, mirroring conditions in many black townships in South Africa, and placed them in prominent locations on campus, often near administration buildings. This street theater was accompanied by educational campaigns detailing investments of the particular school. Some campaigns also included hunger strikes by students, rallies, sit-ins, and a host of other efforts to dramatize the issues. Many shantytown demonstrations were accompanied by a sound track provided by *Sun City*, mimicking the spirited, festive music accompanying black resistance efforts in South Africa itself. The circulation of *Sun City* records and videos was a significant recruiting device, preparing students to hear the messages being offered through the other movement "texts," such as the shantytown installations. Millions of dollars were successfully pulled out of apartheid land by this campus movement, and as part of a worldwide divestment campaign it had an immense impact on the white South African government.[21]

The Sun City project also helped pave the way for the next stage of contestation, a move by the anti-apartheid movement to go after the level of the "spectacle" achieved by that master event, Live Aid. The movement held a "Nelson Mandela 70th Birthday Tribute" concert on 11 June 1988, in the same London stadium that had housed Live Aid, and invited a few hundred million people to join in the celebration.

The Nelson Mandela Concerts

At the level of global spectacle and in terms of sheer numbers, the Nelson Mandela concert rivaled even Live Aid. Its worldwide audience is estimated to have been around 600 million people in some sixty countries.[22] Once again, I would not want to speculate on what these numbers mean across the staggering array of communities in which the event was received, but it is possible to say something about what it meant in the United Kingdom and the United States, which in this case provide interesting contrasts.

Tony Hollingsworth, who produced the birthday tribute, claims that he hoped to make the show act as "a flagship... whereby the local anti-apartheid movements could pick up from the enormous coverage... and run a far more detailed political argument than you could have on stage."[23] Local anti-apartheid groups in Britain at the time of the concert were organizing a "Nelson Mandela: Freedom at Seventy" campaign into which the concert played very effectively. Chitra Karve, a spokesperson for the British anti-apartheid movement, said that given this context, "every second of the [concert] was political."[24] This would seem to be confirmed by the threefold rise in membership in local anti-apartheid groups in the weeks after the concert. A postconcert survey in Britain showed that 75 percent of people between the ages of sixteen and twenty-four knew of Mandela and supported his release.[25]

Such knowledge may not have run very deep, but it was apparently broad enough to effect changes in, among other things, media coverage of South Africa. According to Hollingsworth, the agitational and consciousness-raising elements of the concert combined to alter the terms of media discourse in Britain with regard to the liberation movement. Before the concert, Mandela was routinely referred to on the BBC and in other media as the leader of a "terrorist" organization; after the concert and its attendant publicity, Hollingsworth claims, this kind of representation was no longer possible.[26] Even making allowance for a promoter-activist's exaggeration, there is no doubt that events like the Mandela concert played a key role in transforming the image of Mandela and the African National Congress (ANC), not only in Britain but worldwide.

Perhaps the most eloquent testimony to this claim comes from Nelson Mandela himself who, upon his release from prison twenty months after the concert, chose to make his major public appearance in Britain not in Parliament, but at a rock concert in Wembley stadium. By his presence there and in the speech he delivered on the occasion, Mandela made clear his belief and the belief of the movement that events like the seventieth birthday tribute were playing a role in their struggle.

Did rock songs and musical spectacles lead to the freedom of Nelson Mandela and the end of apartheid? No, of course not. Twenty-seven years of struggle by black South Africans, a worldwide network of solidarity workers, and a complex process of pragmatic gambling on the part of the white South African government did that. Moreover, Mandela is still only relatively free even after serving as the president of his liberated country, because his people are still not free of the poverty, disease, and factionalisms left by apartheid.

But did these spectacles and the work of musicians play any significant role? There I think the answer must be an equally emphatic yes — especially if those events are seen as connected to the vast networks of local organizers who appropriated them for their work at the grassroots. The anti-apartheid projects suggest the possibility that transnational and even global texts can be articulated to particular local political conditions with ideological goals partly outside of mass-mediated frames.

Corporate Mobilization and Rock Organizing

Let me conclude by using the rather different experience of the reception of the Mandela concert in the United States to suggest some limitations, pitfalls, and points of struggle for those attempting to use mass-mediated public cultural forms for movement purposes.

The Mandela concert broadcast in the United States was a significantly deradicalized version of the British concert. The Fox network, which secured American rights to the event, chose to cut out all of the anti-apartheid political speeches, including those by musicians prefacing their songs. Moreover, in a deeply ironic, perhaps intentionally cynical, fashion, several of the sponsors of the American showing were themselves companies doing major business in South Africa. This is a stark example of something that should never be forgotten: because these events and texts occur in a matrix of late capitalist enterprise, commercial sponsors can both subtly and directly undermine projected political meanings.[27] Since the mid-1980s, the number of public events and institutions free of commercial sponsorship has declined drastically.[28]

More generally, such events do not significantly challenge, and in some ways they reinforce, capitalist relations of production. Mega-events require immense amounts of capital, and thus most have required some degree of capitulation to corporate sponsorship.[29] This dependence can be lessened, however, and the potential for oppositional messages heightened, by use of the "ideology of rock." Rock music defines itself against commercial "pop" music by stressing rebellious authenticity.[30] While much of the time this difference is turned into little more than a marketing niche by multimedia conglomerate record companies, this self-definition as rebel music can be built upon by activists. Activists can appeal to rock musicians and other wealthy music industry personnel to take their rebellion more seriously by providing noncorporate funding for alternative political records and events.

The Sun City project's stronger message was made possible in part because it was not a capital-intensive venture, but also because it was conceived in essence through the discourse of "rock" as it defines itself as rebel music against the discourse of tamer "pop" in events like Live Aid. Those who wish to use rock music to carry truly oppositional messages have a built-in ideological advantage that they can draw upon. They have an opportunity to call out rock musicians to be the truly rebellious figures they claim to be by involving them in serious, movement-based rebellion.[31]

So far, the challenge that mega-events offer to late capitalist modes of *consumption* are also relatively weak ones. Their images of normally highly individualistic performers and highly individualistic audiences doing collective work do provide some sense of collective, structural, as opposed to merely personal, power. Without a movement culture connection, however, this power can be folded back into the more empty collective power felt at any large rock concert. Some critics have raised the question of whether consuming images of Nelson Mandela raising his fist is significantly different from consuming images of Michael Jackson raising his.[32] Certainly there is the potential for rock music in benefit contexts to obscure or trivialize the politics they represent. But it is not inevitable, and to make no distinction between the images of Jackson and Mandela is the worst kind of postmodern, postmortem posing.

The *Sun City* video, for example, does address its viewers in different ways than does *We Are the World*, and I think those differences matter politically. But those differences are only weak potentialities when left to float in the vast sea of commercial culture. Until they can be linked to movement cultures around and beyond these media texts, they are easily absorbed back into the dominant system. Certainly, movements are not pure spaces of resistance. Hegemonic forces of the so-called mainstream flow through them as well. But they are spaces where an unusually direct kind of cultural-political literacy can be practiced, where a relatively strong counter-public sphere can shape the reception of mass-mediated messages.

The process of "rock vs. pop" is often carried out at the level of subcultures in contrast to mainstream pop culture, and it is taking place on an increasingly global scale. In the ongoing debates about the meanings of "globalization," thinking through the phenomenon of agit-pop is of great importance. Cultural theorist Fredric Jameson has pointed out that how one makes sense of the globalization of culture depends in great part on the starting point of analysis. Jameson notes that if you focus on the texts of global cultural production, "you will emerge slowly into a postmodern celebration of difference and differentiation: suddenly all the cultures of the world are placed in tolerant contact with each other in a kind of immense cultural pluralism." If you focus on the economic production side of this global culture, "what comes to the fore is increasing identity (rather than difference): the rapid assimilation of hitherto national markets and production zones into a single sphere . . . a picture of standardization on an unparalleled new scale."[33] At the level of cultural theory the question posed is how fully "commodification," the turning of cultural text into a salable item, controls the meaning of that text. But I would argue that that question cannot be answered in the abstract. It can only be answered through political struggle. And that political struggle will in large measure center on attempts to politicize subcultures.

There is a central paradox at the heart of mass culture. On the one hand, it thrives on standardization and reduction of all cultural meaning to marketability. On the other hand, it must have innovation; it must constantly produce newness in order to overcome the boredom inherent in standardization. Innovation can seldom come from inside mass culture. Thus, it is largely dependent for its success on its ability to appropriate energy and style from subcultures (think of the way subcultures like punk, grunge, and hip-hop have been essential to the music industry in the last several decades). Subcultures, by contrast, inherently define themselves against mainstream pop and against commercialization. The trick for those who would bring progressive political power into this process is to convince the inevitably arising subcultures that their vague anticommercialism will not prevent the "selling out" of their values because the pop industry needs them and will selectively appropriate them. Again and again that process has meant diluting and often destroying the subculture's power of self-definition. The argument would be that for "rockers and rappers [to be] united and free," they must develop explicit, full-fledged political and economic analyses of their situation. This entails, in effect, transforming aesthetic or stylistically based subcultures into movement (sub)cultures.

We have a clear example of what is at stake here in the contrast between the parallel stories of the "grunge" and "Riot Grrrlz" subcultures. These two subcultures grew up in the same time period and within a few miles of each other in the state of Washington. Both had strong "scenes" and innovative musical styles that eventually attracted major record companies. But where grunge became almost fully absorbed into the pop mainstream, despite its avowed anticommercialism, riot grrl, despite flirting with the mainstream, largely has maintained itself as a powerfully independent force. The difference, I would argue, is that the third-wave feminism of riot grrl gave it a basis for launching a political and economic analysis that was used to fend off transformation of their politically charged work into mere "style."[34] This is not fundamentally about maintaining purity, but about recognizing that subcultures are inevitably entangled in political-economic struggles with the mainstream that they can turn to their advantage by joining forces with or acting as movement cultures.

Recall that the great civil rights organizer and theorist Ella Baker always made a distinction between mobilizing people and organizing them. Charismatic leaders, whether preachers, politicians, or rock stars, play a role in *mobilizing* people. But *organizing* them is something else. Organizing people to struggle with and for themselves requires deeper, more sustained dialogue and different kinds of actions than those of consuming mass-mediated images.

However, if it is true that mobilizing people is not enough, it is equally true that without mobilization there can be but little organizing. Romantic images of face-to-face contact cannot alone compete with the dramatic visions of the mass-mediated imaginary. A process of moving from the streets to the mass media and back again, mediated (as I will discuss more fully in chapter 9) by the middle space of the Internet, will be essential for movements today to make significant challenges to the dominant order.

The space of social movements and the space of mass media hyperreality are different ones, and that difference is crucially important in creating a radically democratic politics. But for the space of movements to be more than a refuge for the politically correct, we must also create a third space of mediation that attempts to shift that bizarre mass-mediated virtual public sphere in truly democratic directions. Those who believe that the "new world order" of Presidents George H. Bush and George W. Bush looks all too much like the imperial world order of King George III (the one we Americans fought a revolution against) have much work to do.

Just as mobilizing is surely not enough in itself, any social movement that is serious about extending its constituency beyond the margins needs at some level to contest for and with the realm of mass-mediated messages. That kind of politics, as I have been arguing, may need some global counter-spectacles and more than a little of that transnational language known as rock music.

The energy set in motion by Live Aid continued nearly two decades after it began. When Bob Geldof's protégé, U2's Bono, addressed the U.S. Senate on the Third World debt crisis and traveled to Africa with Secretary of Treasury O'Neil in 2002, debating policy all the way, he was building on that legacy. At a time when there are millions of people in Africa with AIDS, and when a new, possibly even more devastating famine is emerging in southern Africa, finding ways to harness the power of global pop culture to assist popular global movements has never been more urgent.

SEVEN

ACTing UP against AIDS

The (Very) Graphic Arts in a Moment of Crisis

In this chapter I explore one of the most dynamic and successful social movement groups of the late 1980s and 1990s, the AIDS Coalition to Unleash Power, or ACT UP. One key argument of this book—that all movement politics involves a degree of *cultural* politics—owes much to recent activist groups like ACT UP, which have made such an insight difficult to ignore. ACT UP, as much as any movement yet invented, has made self-conscious cultural struggle part of its core work. Those of us who now see culture everywhere, even in movements from earlier centuries, owe a great debt to groups like ACT UP, which have brilliantly highlighted the impossibility of fully separating cultural from political dimensions of movement activity.

In examining ACT UP I tell its story as, among other things, an attempt to reinvent the politics of protest in the face of the changed political, economic, and cultural conditions often given the label "postmodern." While I think that claims to a unique, postmodern condition are often exaggerated, they do point to certain cultural developments that have reshaped the terrain on which movements function, and no group has done more to address those developments than ACT UP. Postmodern perspectives call attention to the notion that the cultural landscape is now so media-saturated and commodified, it is hard to tell the real from the virtual, past from present, entertainment from news, resistance from cooptation. One of the many ways in which this media-saturated environment has had an impact on social movements has been through the trope of decade segregation. How often does one hear the media use a phrase like "sixties-style demonstration," which at once trivializes movements as a "style" and suggests that the movement in question is an anachronism (as though it had missed the one decade when movements were apparently allowed, the 1960s). This attempt to ghettoize movements as a phenomenon of one decade forms part of a larger trend in which it has become more and more difficult for movements to get the attention of the public. Part of the genius of ACT UP has been the group's amazing creativity, particularly through use of the visual and performing arts, in challenging the media's packaging of protest and trivialization of movements. As we will see, it did this most effectively through the use of striking, aesthetically rich images, accompanied by witty, sound-bite-worthy slogans. Drawing heavily on *AIDS DemoGraphics,* a remarkable book by Adam Ralston and Douglas Crimp that covers the work of New York City's branch of ACT UP, I will trace the major themes, foci, and actions of the organization primarily through a trail of graphic—sometimes very graphic—slogans and images emblazoned on signs, posters, banners, stickers, t-shirts, buttons, bumper stickers, and other paraphernalia.

Protexts and Contexts

The disease of acquired immune deficiency syndrome, which came to be known as AIDS, emerged in the United States in the early 1980s. By historical accident, in the United States the syndrome arose initially primarily among gay men, a fact that forever colored the response. For the first couple of years of the epidemic, very little attention was paid to it outside the gay community. This was due in no small part to homophobia, a social disease on the rise in a time of right-wing ascendancy in national politics. The far less virulent infection called legionnaires disease, which was identified around the same time when an outbreak occurred among a group of older, white male war veterans, received far more medical attention. When AIDS was first identified, it was given the name gay-related immune deficiency (GRID), a name that obviously reinforced an association of homosexuality and the disease. The religious right, recently emboldened by the election of President Ronald Reagan, quickly seized on the situation to deepen their attack on homosexuality and their promotion of an antifeminist agenda that sought to return sexuality to the control of patriarchal heterosexual men.

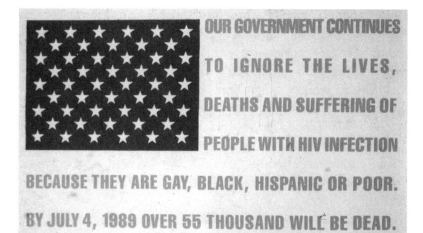

OUR GOVERNMENT CONTINUES TO IGNORE THE LIVES, DEATHS AND SUFFERING OF PEOPLE WITH HIV INFECTION BECAUSE THEY ARE GAY, BLACK, HISPANIC OR POOR. BY JULY 4, 1989 OVER 55 THOUSAND WILL BE DEAD. TAKE DIRECT ACTION NOW. FIGHT BACK. FIGHT AIDS.

ACT UP reworks the U.S. flag. Courtesy of AIDS DemoGraphics.

The response in the gay community moved quickly from confusion and panic to self-organization. In the face of neglect from government and the medical system, service organizations like the Gay Men's Health Crisis (GMHC) emerged in many cities. The GMHC took on the monumental task of lobbying for medical research, while also seeking to attend to the needs of those afflicted with the mysterious disease. GMHC and groups like it gradually became institutionalized as vitally important AIDS service organizations, in effect filling in for the neglect of local, state, and federal governments. They provided the latest medical information, disseminated "safer sex" guidelines, and organized care for those with the disease. By the mid-1980s, with the death count rising, and during the administration of a conservative president who had yet to utter the word *AIDS* in public, let alone offer a policy on the disease, a growing sense of crisis was being felt. In this context, the GMHC and other service organizations seemed too tame, too overworked, and too tied to bureaucracies that still had done far too little to address AIDS. As has happened in so many areas of contemporary society, economic slowdowns and conservative antigovernment politics have forced voluntary, largely self-sustaining organizations to provide the services governments should provide. In providing those services, however, these organizations inadvertently help the interests of a political system that has shown its unwillingness to help them. They thus insulate governments from the demands of those in need. In the case of AIDS, the government's (in)action of pushing responsibility onto impossibly underfunded service organizations like GMHC was having a deadly impact. Sensing the injustice of this situation, a new generation of activists sought to tear away the insulation, provoking confrontation, not compromise, direct action, not accommodation, in the face of government and corporate indifference.

New York Stories

ACT UP was founded in New York City in March 1987 amid a deepening sense of the horrifying extent of the HIV/AIDS epidemic. The group declared themselves a "diverse, non-partisan group united in anger and committed to direct action to end the AIDS crisis."[1] In myth, ACT UP springs up spontaneously during a speech by AIDS activist Larry Kramer. The speech and Kramer's passion were certainly important inspiration. But the origins of ACT UP are multiple and complex, drawing from various elements of the women's health movement, earlier AIDS activist groups like the Silence = Death Project, disgruntled members of the more moderate Gay Men's Health Crisis, and various gay and lesbian liberation groups. ACT UP eventually grew to national and international dimensions. By early 1988 chapters had appeared in various cities throughout the country, including Los Angeles, Boston, Chicago, and San Francisco. By the beginning of 1990 ACT UP had spread throughout the United States and around the globe, with more than a hundred chapters worldwide.

While this growth led to great diversity, ACT UP's New York origins left an indelible mark on the group. One can chart much of the activity and cultural shape of ACT UP via a social geography of New York City. Four of the major targets of ACT UP have a strong historical presence in the city: the mass media (Times Square, home of the national TV networks), corporations (Wall Street, the New York Stock Exchange), advertising (Madison Avenue), and the arts (Soho, Greenwich Village, Broadway). Two other favored targets of ACT UP activists, the Catholic Church and government bureaucracies, also have major New York sites that proved convenient points of focus. And proximity to Washington,

D.C., made a host of federal government sites accessible to ACT UP NYC as well.

ACT UP had an unusual, if not unique, set of material and cultural advantages, as well as substantial disadvantages as an organization. On the negative side, especially in the early years it was lobbying on behalf of several highly stigmatized communities, including gay people, intravenous drug users, and prostitutes. Add to this the stigma of working on the terrain of a disease about which little was known and around which much fear of contagion circled, and formidable obstacles confronted the group. On the positive side of the ledger, the organization drew much of its membership and support from middle- and upper-class professionals and semi-professionals, including people employed in some of the very sites the group would target. This provided unusual amounts of material resources, and unusual kinds of intellectual resources. Of particular relevance for this analysis is that ACT UP's membership included visual artists, advertising copywriters, and media professionals who knew intimately what would and would not work, what would or would not sell in contemporary U.S. culture. They understood, for example, that modern mass-media news most often takes narrative form; thus, ACT UP's dramatic demonstrations always sought to tell good, carefully plotted stories.

Theorizing in an Epidemic of Words and Images

ACT UP's somewhat atypical constituency also included an unusually large number of academics, artists, and others who were conversant with, if not enmeshed in, contemporary cultural theory. Cultural critic/AIDS activist Cindy Patton claims that:

> ACT UP, especially the New York City group ... provides an interesting example of emerging postmodern political praxis using deconstructionist analyses and tactics. A number of key people in the group are artists or intellectuals with deconstruction politics. To many people actively involved in gay and now AIDS anarchist politics, deconstructionist, cultural marxist, and post-structuralist methods and jargon are fairly familiar, whether coming directly from Derrida, Gramsci, or Foucault, or simply as part of a zeitgeist. In addition, particular postmodernist texts form the reading list of the ACT UP New York group, which holds discussions of the relationship between their particular praxis and their experience/politics.[2]

Allowing for the likelihood that Patton is exaggerating the influence of her own preferred theoretical-political style in the organization, it is clear that ACT UP is informed by postmodern theory in some significant ways. This is manifested particularly through a stronger than average sense that, in Michel Foucault's terms, power and knowledge are inseparable. This leads to great sensitivity to the ways in which even the most factual, scientific knowledge is a cultural construct caught in politically inf(l)ected webs of language. This has aided ACT UP especially in taking on socially constructed medical knowledge, and in analyzing and using mass media framings of the "real."

In the same year as the founding of ACT UP, cultural critic Paula Treichler published an essay that did much to bring theory into the orbit of AIDS activism. Treichler noted that AIDS was not only a disease of epidemic proportions, but a phenomenon that had spawned an "epidemic of signification." Her essay offered a kind of primer for a postmodern understanding of language as implicated in the process of creating AIDS: "The name AIDS in part constructs the disease and helps make it intelligible. We cannot therefore look 'through' language to determine what AIDS 'really' is. Rather we must explore the site where such determinations really occur and intervene at the point where meaning is created: in language." Treichler quickly refutes the common misunderstanding of postmodern theory that sees it as claiming that nothing is real, or that any story is as good as any other. Rather, she writes: "Of course AIDS is a real disease syndrome, damaging and killing real human beings. Because of this, it is tempting—perhaps in some instances imperative—to view science and medicine as providing a discourse about AIDS that is closer to its 'reality' than what we can provide ourselves. [But] try as we may to treat AIDS as 'an infectious disease' and nothing more, meanings continue to multiply wildly."[3]

After demonstrating brilliantly how even the most elemental scientific "facts" about AIDS are infected with cultural assumptions, Treichler calls for an approach to the medical knowledge about AIDS that is neither dismissive nor submissive: "We need to use what science gives us in ways that are selective, self-conscious, and pragmatic ('as though' they were true). We need to understand that AIDS is and will remain a provisional and deeply problematic signifier."[4] This understanding of knowledge about AIDS as "provisional" and "problematic" was crucial to giving ACT UP the power to challenge the proliferation of questionable cultural meanings imposed on the disease by the medical community, the government, and the media.

What became clear, with the aid of cultural theorists like Treichler, Michel Foucault, Jan Grover, Cindy Patton, Simon Watney, Douglas Crimp, and many others, was that homophobia, racism, and sexism were deadly social diseases that needed to be fought along with the virus, not only in the outside world but inside ACT UP as well. Prejudice against gays, people of color, drug users, and women set back the process of treating and seeking a cure for AIDS and its causative agent, the human immunodeficiency virus (HIV). The country's longstanding puritanical sexual attitudes made it difficult to talk publicly about a sexually transmitted disease. It became clear that in an "information age" and a "knowledge economy," more than ever knowledge was power, power knowledge. The war over HIV/AIDS was going to be very much a "discursive" battle, a battle over the meaning of words and images. This was surely not something wholly new in a social movement, but the extent to which "semiotic" warfare became self-conscious and central to the work of ACT UP was unprecedented.

The postmodernist element in ACT UP politics reinforced a strong preference for decentralized, antihierarchical organizational forms that the group inherited from other movements, most directly from the antinuclear direct action movement of the late 1970s and early 1980s. ACT UP was structured in a set of "affinity groups" (typically consisting of five to fifteen individuals), each of which maintained a strong degree of autonomy within the organization. Few rules or overarching ideas, other than a general commitment to nonviolence and a desire to bring an end to the AIDS crisis, limited ACT UP activists. Mobility and flexibility were deemed crucial resources in a cultural environment constantly in motion.

ACT UP's postmodernist tendencies are also manifested in the group's complicated relation to so-called "identity politics"—the efforts of groups to organize around specific racial, ethnic, gender, sexual, or other characteristics. On the one hand, the group understood the necessity to deploy a "gay" identity at times as an organizing tool. But even as it demonstrated a willingness to use "identity" politically, members incessantly questioned the assumptions through which identities often devolve into static, homogenizing essences. ACT UP put into play the complexly ambiguous identity, "queer," an identity that at once reminds those using it of its oppressive origins as a homophobic epithet, resignifies it as a positive identity, and articulates a queering (blurring) of the lines between gay and straight, normative and oppositional. Thus ACT UP members learned to see identity formation as an ongoing collective and strategic practice, not an unchanging essence.

Postmodern perspectives on the instability of identities also proved useful, as Joshua Gamson has argued, in dealing with one of the central contradictions faced by ACT UP: the need to challenge the mainstream, homophobic view that AIDS was a "gay disease," on the one hand, and, on the other hand, the need to mobilize the gay community to see the AIDS crisis as a community crisis tied to the politics of lesbian and gay liberation. Rather than becoming stymied by this seeming double-bind, ACT UP was able, thanks to its postmodern critique of such easy dichotomies as gay/straight, to treat this contradiction as a useful one that could challenge dangerous oversimplifications perpetrated by the mainstream media.[5]

More generally, ACT UP's theoretical understanding means that its members recognize that in addition to fighting government bureaucracies, media bias, and corporate self-interest, they are also fighting, as Gamson phrases it, an "invisible" force: social norms that define what is normal, natural, and appropriate versus what is abnormal, unnatural, and deviant. The power of these norms lies precisely in their invisibility, their deep embeddedness in culture such that they are taken utterly for granted. ACT UP developed several strategies for bringing these invisible norms out of the closet and into the open where they could be challenged.

Cultural Que(e)ries

While it was never an exclusively gay organization, the movement culture of ACT UP drew heavily upon institutions, forms, and styles within gay male and lesbian communities. In turn, ACT UP played a significant role in transforming those communities. A gay culture that had previously remained largely underground had been strengthened, extended, and moved above ground by successive waves of movement activity from the 1950s onwards. Three overlapping waves of activism preceded the emergence of the ACT UP generation: a "homophile" phase in the late 1950s and early 1960s that established baseline positions in a style reminiscent of the NAACP; a more radical "gay liberation" and "lesbian-feminist" phase in the late 1960s to mid-1970s, shaped by revolutionary models provided by feminist and ethnic radicals; and a "gay and lesbian rights" phase from the mid-1970s to the mid-1980s that consolidated and institutionalized what the radical movement had begun. In this context, ACT UP and spin-off gay groups Queer Nation and Lesbian Avengers represent a fourth phase, a reradicalization aimed at both the AIDS crisis and assimilationist elements in lesbian and gay communities. As the rise of AIDS fueled a new demonization of gays that showed signs of reversing the modest but important gains of the gay rights era, ACT UP pushed back on the political and cultural fronts simultaneously.

Each movement phase not only strengthened semi-autonomous gay culture(s), but also contributed to a process that brought greater visibility to elements of queer culture that were deeply embedded in key terrains of U.S. high and popular culture. Even as each emergent wave created new, interwoven institutions for gay people, it also complicated gay/queer community life by revealing internal differences in race, class, gender, political orientation, and sexual practices. As waves crash against the shore, they dissolve and re-form into new configurations; just so, lines between radical and reformist, integrationist and separatist are seldom neatly traceable in highly fluid situations. Thus, ACT UP emerged at a highly complex moment, and its actions were never less than controversial across various lesbian/gay/queer subcultures.

Despite and because of this complexity, it is clear that queer cultural connections and styles enabled and shaped virtually all dimensions of ACT UP, from the social networks that it recruited from, to the sites chosen for meetings, to fundraising sources, to, most pertinently, its graphic images, slogans, costumes, and highly theatrical demonstration style. The rise of gay, lesbian, and queer studies in the universities; the creation of gay bookstores, coffeehouses, movie theaters, and health clinics; the expansion of the gay press: all these provided material-intellectual resources of great importance to ACT UP. These institutions made more available a set of gay cultural codes that could be deployed positively in organizing and parodically used against a mainstream "white, male, heterosexual" world.

A sense of how a playfully gay cultural coding worked in the movement is apparent in the group's name itself. The acronym *ACT UP* has multiple meanings. It clearly signals a sense of the need to act, to act defiantly, and to stand up against oppression. At the same time, this rather macho sense of activism is undercut both by an echo of the phrase *acting up* (in the sense of not working right) and *acting up* (in the sense of a child behaving badly). And, of course, the emphasis on *acting* clearly signals a sense of performing or pretending that is supposedly the opposite of serious political action. The name thus suggests a characteristic political seriousness in ACT UP that was entangled with an equally serious and equally political playfulness (for example, wrapping antigay Senator Jesse Helms's home in a giant yellow condom).

A pointed example of how gayness played politically appears in one of ACT UP's first demonstrations. During the Washington demonstration in June 1987, District of Columbia police officers displayed their homophobia and hysteria about "catching" AIDS (or gayness?) through casual contact, by wearing bright-yellow rubber gloves as they arrested several dozen ACT UP members who were engaging in civil disobedience. As Crimp and Ralston report it, the "activists, many looking unusually respectable in conservative business clothes, raised a very queer chant, 'Your gloves don't match your shoes! You'll see it on the news!'" Amid the campy humor, the chant is perfectly designed to "out" the police hysteria. The point is made more memorable through its catchy, rhymed phrasing. It was just the kind of chant (connected to a visual image) that would make sure that not just the police, but also the protesters, would see themselves "on the news."

Another contribution of gay culture to ACT UP actions is hinted at by the reference to "conservative business suits" in the passage above. This particular costume in part reflects the professional class and business world in which many members spent their "day jobs." Some activists sometimes used this mode of dress straightforwardly, as it were, to reflect their class similarity to those they were protesting against. At other times, however, group members used this costume as a disguise, as what they called "Republican drag." This ability to "pass" sent a message about the ubiquity of gayness and the contingency of "normal" identity. It also served activists well in such efforts as "zapping" the New York Stock Exchange or "crashing" international AIDS medical conferences. In conservative drag ACT UP could infiltrate the audience, for example, and pepper gathered scientists with the kind of troubling questions from which they were often insulated in their academic or corporate ivory towers. At still other times, the drag employed was the more traditional, cross-dressing kind, and was used to express an unrepentant otherness in gay culture and gay humor, symbolized by the favorite chant of ACT UP's cousin Queer Nation: "We're here, we're queer, get used to it."

Campy humor informed other dimensions of the organization as well. Affinity groups, the core units used to organize ACT UP, have a long history of clever self-naming. In ACT UP, this self-naming frequently took on a decidedly queer quality. For example, one group's acronym was CHER, in homage to one of the favorite divas of a segment of the gay male community. The meaning of the acronym changed frequently, but one explication is particularly rich: Commie Homos Engaged in Revolution. This version of CHER at once sends up homophobia and expresses solidarity with the long-suffering American left against which the label "commie" had been hurled to dismiss anyone so "deviant" as to question the U.S. political system. In similar fashion, another colorful affinity group called themselves the Pinkos. Both names hint at the hysterical connection drawn during the "un-American activities" witch hunts of the 1950s between deviant politics and deviant sexuality, between the allegedly "contagious" "spread" of communism and sexual perversity.[6]

The campy humor of ACT UP underlines the impossibility of separating "political" from "cultural" dimensions of a movement. The group's humor was both an effective tactic and a mode of defiant assertion of identity. And even the "expressive" mode was political in that it deepened solidarity in the movement. ACT UP understood that humor could be disarming and used wit strategically to counter half-witted messages circulating in the mainstream (when protesting the Catholic Church's deadly stand against condom use, members chanted, "Curb your dogma"). Sometimes, as in the acronym ACT UP itself, they used humor to make fun of their own emerging ideological rigidities. They also used it just for fun. But as Crimp and Ralston put it, "ACT UP's humor is no joke. It has given us the courage to maintain our exuberant sense of life while every day coping with disease and death, and it has defended us against the pessimism endemic to other Left movements, from which we have otherwise taken so much."[7]

Silence = Death

ACT UP's media savvy and aesthetic sophistication combined to form a series of remarkably catchy images and slogans, texts to catch both the media's and the public's attention. The group understood that in an image-saturated, sound-bite culture, getting people's attention was no easy task. But many ACT UP activists were media veterans, and their expertise helped the group gain an unprecedented amount of media coverage.

While the slogan and image "Silence = Death" precedes the birth of ACT UP, the group quickly adopted the phrase and its accompanying image, a pink triangle on a black background, which became its most identifiable image-text. As political slogans go, it is certainly a strange one, alerting us that there was from the beginning something different about this particular group of activists. While most traditional activists would view as a liability the lack of immediate clarity about what the phrase might mean, to ACT UP that ambiguity was precisely the point. ACT UP created many brilliantly clear, pointed slogans. But the group also understood the importance of strategic ambiguity. In this case, the equation was meant to, and on countless occasions did, evoke the question: "What does that mean?" As such, it became an invitation to a prolonged discussion of the AIDS crisis. Various answers to the question were possible, but many would begin by saying that the pink triangle was fastened on gay prisoners as they were marched to Nazi concentration camps. Silence about those camps led to millions of deaths. By analogy, fearful silence about the extent of the AIDS crisis, including fearful self-silencing by gays and other stigmatized groups, deepened a crisis they believed would soon reach Holocaust proportions. But this pink triangle inverted the one gays were forced to wear by the Nazis; this one pointed up in hope, not down in despair. If silence equaled death, speaking out and acting up could equal new chances for life.

Art Is Not Enough

The Silence = Death graphic eventually found its way into an exhibit at the New Museum of Contemporary Art in Soho in 1988. By that time the Silence = Death collective was metamorphosing into the key ACT UP graphic collective, Gran Fury (named after the kind of cruising car favored by the gay-harassing police). Entitled "Let the Record Show," the exhibition demonstrates both ACT UP's early targeting of some and support from others in the art community. As noted above, the presence of many visual artists, advertising professionals, actors, and playwrights in ACT UP seeded the group with aesthetic powers and a visual-theatrical orientation that proved crucial to its successes. And a particular, "postmodern" aesthetic then prevalent in part of the art world lent itself well to activism. Much postmodern art and criticism was deemphasizing the individual artist of genius in favor of a sense of art as a social process embedded in political contexts. This attitude assisted ACT UP in quickly recruiting artists and appropriating whatever aesthetic styles the group believed would further the visibility of the movement. Appropriation itself had the imprimatur of the avant-garde, since "appropriation art," in which the myth of utter originality was being challenged by artists deliberately imitating or directly copying works by earlier artists, was all the rage. ACT UP shifted register to the other, emotional definition of *rage*, but kept the aesthetic possibilities.

But the art community did not automatically or fully embrace the fight against AIDS. That support had to be gained by organizing and acting. ACT UP protested, for example, an exhibit of protest graphics at the Museum of Modern Art (MOMA) in New York that included no examples of AIDS activist graphics. They believed the museum exhibit perpetuated a sense of art as above the political fray by emphasizing formal elements of the protest graphics on display, and by embalming art objects while excluding living activist-artists like the Silence = Death/ Gran Fury Collective. "Let the Record Show" was a counter to this more mainstream art tradition and became the first of many shows raising awareness of and, in benefit form, raising money for AIDS activism. The exhibit title itself plays on the distinction between "mere" documentation ("the record") and "true" art (worthy of a "show"). This counter-exhibit and the MOMA protest both challenged the sense that real art was about form and abstract, universal human experience, and sought to break down the complacent distinction between art as representation and art as action: acts of representation were held politically accountable, and political acts were celebrated for the terrible beauty of the crisis they brought into view. At the same time, as seen in a Gran Fury ACT UP poster produced near the beginning of the crisis, art, however useful, is "not enough." In striking white letters on a mournful black background, the poster declaims: "WITH 42,000 DEAD, ART IS NOT ENOUGH. TAKE COLLECTIVE DIRECT ACTION TO END THE AIDS CRISIS."

Medicinal Civil Disobedience

The central targets on ACT UP's initial agenda were the intertwined issues of health education, medical research, drug availability, and disease treatment. Following the kind of position articulated by Treichler

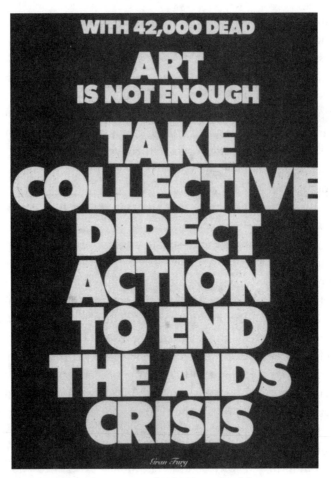

Art Is Not Enough. Courtesy of AIDS DemoGraphics.

and others, ACT UP members became skeptical medical consumers and, often, amateur medical researchers themselves. The group's professional membership included doctors and medical researchers, but beyond that many other members took up the task of learning about the process and substance of drug development, testing, and distribution. Their understanding of the social construction of disease and their analysis of the corporate-government process of drug approval led them into several kinds of civil disobedience. This included what we might call medicinal civil disobedience in the form of publicizing, making available, and using illegal or not-yet-legal medicines. It also took the more traditional form of demonstrations against pharmaceutical corporations and the federal drug bureaucracy, and aggressive actions invading medical conferences. It also took the form of imagining theatrical actions like wearing lab coats and presenting "guerrilla" slide shows that parodied conference presentations, or doctoring real slide shows by inserting slides stating, "He's lying" or "This is voodoo epidemiology."[8]

ACT UP actions also challenged health educators, from the surgeon general on down. The group called for education about AIDS that was frank, not euphemistic, unprejudiced, not homophobic, and targeted in culturally sensitive ways to particular communities, rather than blandly generic. This included challenging the dominant model of medical expertise in which the opinions, experience, and cultural location of the client-patient had been deemed largely irrelevant. Drawing inspiration from the women's health movement that grew out of second-wave feminism, and wielding the privilege embodied in their highly educated constituency, ACT UP had grudging but substantial success in changing attitudes and practices inside and outside the medical establishment.

ACT UP's basic strategy might be called the politics of shaming. Through demonstrations, flyers, posters, informational media actions, newspaper advertisements, letter-writing campaigns, civil disobedience, and sit-ins and small "zap" actions in corporate, government and media offices, the group sought to draw attention to shameful government sluggishness, shameful corporate profiteering, and shameful media bias. Faster drug approval, lower drug costs, community-targeted health information, more humane treatment programs, easier availability of experimental drugs, more money for medical research: all these goals were furthered by ACT UP action and negotiation, and all prolonged or saved lives. These victories had ramifications beyond the context of AIDS, benefiting all users of the health care system.

AIDS: It's Big Business, But Who's Making a Killing?

Given these concerns, it is no surprise that the first major ACT UP "demo" (demonstration) targeted pharmaceutical corporations and their allies in the federal government. Specifically, the demonstration was aimed at Burroughs Wellcome, maker of the first important anti-AIDS drug, AZT, and its relationship with the federal Food and Drug Administration (FDA). Burroughs Wellcome had proposed to charge more than $12,000 per year for this critical drug. For ACT UP, in a country without universal health care this was tantamount to condemning

AIDS Is [still] Big Business! Courtesy of AIDS DemoGraphics.

to death all but the wealthiest people with AIDS. Noting the heavy sub-
sidizing of medical research by the federal government, and the exclusive contract given Burroughs by the FDA, ACT UP argued that there
was outrageous price-fixing collusion between government and pharmaceutical companies. ACT UP descended on Wall Street at 7 a.m. on
Thursday, 4 March 1987, to protest the alliance between the FDA and
Burroughs Wellcome. Protesters tied up busy commuter traffic for several hours. "The demonstration made national news, and several weeks
later, when [the FDA] Commissioner announced a speed-up of the FDA's
drug approval process, CBS anchor Dan Rather credited ACT UP's pressure."[9] The action also proved a recruitment device; stock trader Peter
Staley, for example, was so impressed by the demo and so disturbed by
the homophobic reaction to it by his fellow traders that he started "living a double life, trading by day, going to ACT UP meetings at night,"
till eventually he devoted himself to the group full time. He became a
stalwart member of ACT UP, and later a founder of the spin-off group
TAG (Treatment Action Group).[10] Corporate targeting included a brilliantly innovative use of the sticker graphic. ACT UP designed small
stickers with the words "AIDS Profiteer" that members affixed to cold
care medicines and other medical products from Burroughs Wellcome
Corporation as they moved through pharmacies. A later continuation of
this action included a poster with a slogan that at once called for a new

type of boycott, selling stocks, and paid witty homage to the tradition of campaigns to free political prisoners: "Sell Wellcome, Free AZT." ACT UP took on other pharmaceutical corporations as AIDS medicine evolved; one effective tactic was backing up the label "AIDS Profiteer" with strategically placed ads detailing the price of particular drugs and the yearly profits of the company making them. This politics of shaming often proved quite effective as in the dip in Burroughs stock that had followed the demonstration against the firm.

The Government Has Blood on Its Hands

As part of its targeting of government inaction, ACT UP went after the FDA itself, and the agency's cumbersome process for getting new drugs and treatments approved. Activists challenged what they saw as the deadly neglect entailed by long-delayed approvals of experimental drugs. In the group's inimitable style, an ACT UP graphic proclaims: "Time Isn't the Only Thing the FDA is Killing." A tactic developed to dramatize this problem and used in numerous ACT UP actions was the "die-in." Adapted from antinuclear activism, ACT UP's version is interpreted by Gamson as not only a direct commentary on drug policy, but also a swipe at normalizing: "A 'die-in,' in which activists draw police-style chalk outlines around each other's 'dead' bodies, gives death another meaning by shifting responsibility: these are deaths likened to murders, victims not of their own 'deviance,' but shot down by the people controlling the definition of normality."[11] Moreover, these "living dead" protest their relegation to the hospice and the cemetery or to the silence that equals death. By moving "death" out into public space, they resist the death sentences written by normative discourse and social indifference to the search for treatment and cure.

In a similar vein, a good deal of the cultural struggle around AIDS has focused on blood. Where "contaminated" blood was used to separate the innocent from the guilty, an ACT UP graphic declares that "the government has blood on its hands," above a huge bloody handprint. A still more dramatic and imaginative use of blood symbolism was embodied in the infamous "Dannemeyer Vampire." Rep. William Dannemeyer was a California politician whose Proposition 102 would have required all doctors to report to authorities all those infected, or even suspected of being infected, with HIV. In response, San Francisco's ACT UP chapter built a huge puppet effigy of Dannemeyer, with a vampire head, black cape, and blood dripping from its fangs. As Gamson reads it, "ACT UP activates another popular code in which blood has meaning—the gore horror movies—and reframes blood testing as blood sucking. It's not the blood that is monstrous, but the vampire [politician] who would take it."[12]

The issue of blood testing and violation of patient confidentiality led ACT UP to take on another corporate antagonist, the insurance industry. The actions against the insurance industry, sometimes including throwing blood or bloodlike liquids at corporate offices, opened out to a host of efforts to guarantee the privacy of people with AIDS, secure their rights to employment and housing, and force the extension of other basic human rights to these individuals.

Reading the "New York Crimes"

Many ACT UP activists were in the media or had friends in the media, and they understood that the mass media are not neutral reporters of reality, but active agents in the social creation of what counts as truth, reality, and news. Not surprisingly, given their location, the nation's "newspaper of record," the *New York Times*, early became a target. ACT UP undertook a prolonged struggle to get the *Times* to cover the AIDS crisis more fully, and to reshape the discourse used in that coverage. In the process, the group used some of their more inventive techniques and slogans. They created, for example, a mock-up of the *Times* front page, renamed the *New York Crimes*, in which they detailed how the paper had neglected to cover the crisis. They noted, for example, that during the first year and a half of the AIDS epidemic, when close to a thousand cases had already been reported, the *Times* carried only seven articles about it, none on the front page. In contrast, ACT UP counted fifty-four articles about a Tylenol contamination scandal over a three-month period, despite only seven reported cases. The group traced this neglect to a longstanding, deep-seated homophobia in the paper.

The last straw for ACT UP in relation to the *Times* came in June 1989, when the paper published an editorial suggesting that AIDS activist groups were exaggerating the seriousness of the disease. According to this editorial, at a point when a hundred thousand cases had been reported, the disease was "leveling off" because AIDS is "still very largely confined to specific risk groups. Once all susceptible members are infected, the numbers of new victims will decline." ACT UP's translation was "Soon all the fags and junkies will be dead, and we'll be rid of AIDS." Outraged, ACT UP organized a demonstration in front of *Times* publisher "Punch" Sulzberger's Fifth Avenue residence that included painting white outlines of bodies and the inscription "All the News That's Fit to Kill" (an allusion to the newspaper's motto, "All the News That's Fit to Print") on the street in front of the apartment. The organization also launched a boycott of the paper that included the brilliant touch of placing stickers on newspaper vending machines that read: "*The New York Times* AIDS Reporting is OUT OF ORDER," with the last phrase printed large enough to discourage potential users of the machines. Another sticker read: "Buy Your Lies Here. The New York Times Reports Half the Truth about AIDS. ACT UP FIGHT BACK FIGHT AIDS." In addition to the typically catchy, sound-bite-length slogans, ACT UP handed out a flyer with statistics on the paper's (lack of) coverage, and raised specific questions about AIDS issues the paper had not addressed. In a comparison clearly designed to embarrass the prestigious newspaper, ACT UP pointed out that the *Times* had sent only one reporter to cover the twelve-thousand-delegate Fifth International AIDS Conference earlier that year, while even the tabloid *New York Newsday* had sent five. Not only that, the *Times* reporter failed to attend the most exciting event of the conference, the opening ceremonies, which were taken over by hundreds of international AIDS activists.

ACT UP's media assault often focused on terminology, keywords in the AIDS cultural battle. Perhaps because ACT UP's core constituency of gay people had been historically sensitized to the power of negative labeling, the organization quickly zeroed in on issues of naming. The first and strongest assault was on the expression "AIDS victim," common in the media. The group argued persuasively that the term *victim* not only implied passivity but encouraged a fatalistic sense that the inevitable result of AIDS was death. ACT UP countered with two alternative phrases: the more neutral sounding "people with AIDS," and the more pointed "people living with AIDS." This second expression emphasized that dying was not the sole occupation of those infected with the HIV virus—people were "living with" the disease.

ACT UP understood that images spoke as loudly as words in this context. A year after the founding of ACT UP, the Museum of Modern Art once again became a target when it exhibited a collection of photographs of AIDS "victims" taken by Nicholas Nixon. Nixon's images were almost invariably of emaciated, darkly lit figures in late stages of AIDS-related diseases. From the point of view of ACT UP, they evoked at best pity, not activating anger, and rendered the "victims" complacently silent. They reinforced the message that one died from but did not live with AIDS. Picketing the exhibit once again raised the level of awareness in one of AIDS activists' most sympathetic communities, the art world.

A similar struggle surrounded the expression "risk groups." Given the environment of prejudice surrounding AIDS, the Centers for Disease Control's designation of certain people, in particular gay men and intravenous drug users, as members of "high risk groups" was bound to deepen the stigma. ACT UP argued that such labeling not only increased stigmatization but also worsened the health danger by misdirecting attention away from the source of HIV infection—certain practices, not certain people. As an alternative, ACT UP and other activists promoted the phrase "risk behaviors." This move helped force a break through the censorship that made it difficult to talk about such things as unprotected anal sex. Over time and through numerous demos, boycotts, press releases, articles, and direct pressure on reporters, medical professionals, and bureaucrats, ACT UP succeeded in changing the discourse around AIDS, and that in turn changed the climate for research, testing, and treatment.

ACT UP also took on the way in which even the term *victim* was dichotomized. Well-publicized cases like that of Ryan White, an adolescent hemophiliac who contracted HIV through blood transfusion, led the media to invent the category of "innocent AIDS victim." The phrase inevitably if subtly suggests its opposite, the "guilty" victim. Given the social prejudices unleashed by the epidemic, it was not hard to figure out who these other, not-innocent victims were—queers, drug abusers, and sex workers. The religious right was the most extreme force in this construction, arguing that AIDS was God's vengeance on sinful people: deviants, the promiscuous, and drug-addled criminals. But in ACT UP's analysis, mainstream America embraced an only slightly less vicious version of this kind of thought whenever people unquestioningly accepted wording like "innocent victim." ACT UP's assault on this kind of discourse is epitomized by the slogan and graphic: "All people with AIDS are innocent." Designed by the Gran Fury collective for a nine-day campaign of actions in spring 1998, this graphic appropriated the caduceus, the image of twin serpents encircling a staff that symbolizes the medical profession. Use of this symbol at once targeted the way victim prejudice had infected the medical community and associated ACT UP's position with the Hippocratic medical model of treating all patients equally.

Not So Cosmopolitan

A different kind of media action was directed against a specific article in a well-known women's magazine. *Cosmopolitan* published a piece in January 1988 entitled "Reassuring News about AIDS: A Doctor Tells Why You May Not Be at Risk." In addition to furthering the notion of AIDS as a "gay disease," the misinformation contained in the article was potentially deadly to women or anyone else taking it as truth about HIV/AIDS. Clearly aimed to soothe a presumed female readership, the article by a psychiatrist named Robert E. Gould offered the lethally misinforming advice that straight women had little to worry about, even if they had unprotected sex with infected partners, unless they had vaginal lacerations. Adding racist assumptions to baseline homophobia, Gould dismissed the high incidence of heterosexually transmitted HIV/AIDS in Africa as the result of brutal, near-rape sexual practices claimed to be typical on the continent.

The actions against *Cosmo* were led by women and marked the emergence in ACT UP of a stronger female and feminist presence. Women in the group, especially lesbians, had been meeting informally for some time, but the *Cosmo* event catalyzed the formation of a women's committee in ACT UP. Although they were among those least at risk for contracting HIV/AIDS, lesbians had gotten deeply involved in AIDS activism from the beginning, for reasons ranging from personal connections with gay men to solidarity in the face of the homophobia that had done so much to worsen the crisis. But the solidarity of women in ACT UP was not always fully reciprocated. Larger numbers, louder voices, and bigger egos had often made ACT UP a male-dominated, sexist organization. Thus, in attacking sexist assumptions in mainstream media, the women's committee was also addressing ACT UP itself.

The women's committee turned out more than a hundred fifty demonstrators at the headquarters of *Cosmo* in the Hearst Magazine Building on a cold January day in 1988. They called for a boycott of the magazine and its advertisers (handing out a list of the latter), and they followed up with a national media campaign, using the particular issue to raise a wider set of concerns regarding poor coverage of women and AIDS.

After being ejected or blocked from appearing on some mainstream talk shows, the women's committee turned to direct media action, producing their own video, "Doctors, Liars, and Women: AIDS Activists Say No to *Cosmo*." The video was widely shown on cable television and at video festivals, museums, and universities, and included information on a range of AIDS issues affecting women. It even gave tips on how to create a demonstration. Like all ACT UP activities, the video stressed a sense of "do it yourself" organizing, free from stifling desire for central control.

At the time of the *Cosmo* action, the Gran Fury collective produced the poster, "AIDS: 1 in 61," which reads in part, "One in every sixty-one babies in New York City is born with AIDS or born HIV positive. So why is the media telling us that heterosexuals are not at risk?" This arresting statistic on HIV-positive babies arose overwhelmingly from black and Latino neighborhoods. Done in both English and Spanish, the poster addressed both neglect of women with AIDS and the racism that often accompanied that indifference: "Ignoring color ignores the facts of AIDS. STOP RACISM: FIGHT AIDS." Both because of its ideological complexity and its proximity to the crisis, ACT UP was among the first groups to notice the changing demographic of the disease, and to act upon that knowledge. But the group's ability to address the impact of HIV/AIDS on communities other than the gay community ran up against serious challenges.

Kiss-ins, Ball Games, and Other Invasions of Public Space

Like the artists of the mural movement, ACT UP graphic artists and theatrical demo designers sought to reclaim public space. This reclamation was crucially important because the longstanding, puritanical practice of keeping sex talk private was proving deadly. While American culture is one of the more sex-obsessed cultures in the world, using sex to sell everything from cars to household cleansers, certain kinds of sex talk are taboo in certain public arenas. The most obviously relevant silence concerns "deviant" same-sex relations. Beyond this, America's sex phobias were limiting delivery of crucial information about HIV/AIDS. ACT UP's assault on public spaces ranged from politicizing baseball games to crashing medical conferences to its most notorious variation on the sit-in tactic, public same-sex "kiss-ins."

Same-sex kiss-ins also demonstrated the continued link within ACT UP of gay/lesbian liberation and HIV/AIDS activism. The first large-scale kiss-ins were held in conjunction with the 1987 March on Washington for Lesbian and Gay Rights. The materials handed out at the public kiss-ins clearly articulated their motivations, including their intent to confront that invisible force of normalization: "We kiss to protest the cruel and painful bigotry that affects the lives of lesbians and gay men. We kiss so that all who see us will be forced to confront their own homophobia. We kiss to challenge repressive conventions that prohibit displays of love between persons of the same sex." The handout goes on to link this general homophobia to the AIDS crisis: "The Helms Amendment, preventing federal funding for any AIDS educational materials that could be construed to promote lesbian or gay sex, passed in the Senate by a vote of 96 to 2. The federal government has been unconscionably slow to react to the AIDS crisis, a slowness tantamount to condoning the deaths of tens of thousands of gay men."[13]

The essence of the kiss-ins found its way into public space via a different vehicle as well. Gran Fury produced a take-off on a famous Benetton clothing advertisement. The ad, placed on buses circulating throughout the city, carefully mimicked the style and content of Benetton ads that featured kissing couples, making only two slight alterations: two of the three couples kissing were same-sex couples, and the accompanying copy was not from Benetton but from ACT UP and read: "Kissing Doesn't Kill, Greed and Indifference Do. Corporate greed, government inaction and public indifference make AIDS a political crisis." With characteristically brilliant brevity of wit, the images and copy counter the notion that HIV can be transmitted by casual contact, assault homophobia, and separately target pharmaceutical corporations, the government, and the general public reading the ad.

A different invasion of public space took place during a baseball game in New York's Shea Stadium. Like the *Cosmo* demo, it was aimed especially at correcting misinformation about putative heterosexual immunity to AIDS, and, like the *Cosmo* demo, it was organized by the women's committee. Activists bought out four hundred seats in three large sections of the stands from which they could unfurl banners with typically ACT UPitty but site-appropriate slogans like "No Glove, No Love" (that is, no condom, no sex), "AIDS Is Not a Ball Game," "Strike Out AIDS,"

"Don't Balk at Safe Sex," and, most graphically, "AIDS Kills Women" and "Men: Use Condoms or Beat It." ACT UP also handed out informational "score card" flyers that also utilized baseball metaphors: "*Single:* Only one woman has been included in government-sponsored tests for new drugs for AIDS. *Double:* Women diagnosed with AIDS die *twice* as fast as men. *Triple:* The number of women with AIDS has *tripled* as a result of sexual contact with men in New York City since the 1984 World Series. *The Grand Slam:* Most men still don't use condoms." Aiming to hit its target audience in their ball(s)park, the action was directed at straight men who refused to take responsibility for safer sex. ACT UP purposely chose to be inappropriate, to coopt a space from which politics is supposed (or presumed) to be absent. But in cultural war, symbols like "America's pastime" are precisely the points where (hetero)normativity is constructed, where the lines between normal, innocent victims of tainted blood get distinguished from virus-spreading sissies who probably never even played baseball!

These are merely a few among the dozens of actions ACT UP has performed over the years, from single-person or small-group "zap" actions to elaborate demos with hundreds of people committing acts of civil disobedience.

"Facing" the Crisis

One of the key questions facing a social movement is how to represent the forces against which the movement is struggling. As sociologist William Gamson points out, this process entails a paradox. On one hand, if the forces against which the movement is arrayed are portrayed too abstractly, both potential recruits and movement members may find it difficult to identify with the struggle. On the other hand, if a movement personalizes the struggle too much by naming particular individuals as the opponent, the important insight that structural factors, not just individuals, are the ultimate target is lost. A parallel problem exists on the other side of the equation. If a movement imagines itself too fully in collective terms, the sense of agency in the individual members of the group may wane; they may feel they are replaceable. Conversely, placing too much emphasis on individual commitment plays into the process by which the dominant society undermines collective opposition by personalizing and individualizing all social problems. That process, of course, is the very thing against which movements are organized. ACT UP dealt seriously and creatively with both of these dilemmas.

A significant part of ACT UP's power came from the mobilization of anger; recall that its self-definition included the phrase "a group united in anger and committed to direct action to end the AIDS crisis." Direct action is a collective activity, but anger is a very personal emotion. While one may analyze a structure to the point of anger, it is far easier to express anger toward a person than a system. ACT UP graphics suggest a very balanced approach to the dynamic of personalization versus emphasis on structural causation. Their targeting suggests an understanding that while political and bureaucratic systems function abstractly, they also depend in part upon the decisions of individuals in authority. ACT UP posters present the faces of opponents, associating them through written texts with various "crimes" contributing to the AIDS crisis. President Reagan ("AIDSgate," "He Kills Me"), Cardinal James O'Connor ("Public Health Menace"), New York mayor Ed Koch ("10,000 New York City AIDS Deaths: How'm I Doin'?"), New York health commissioner Stephen Joseph ("Deadlier than the Virus"), and Burroughs Wellcome CEO A. J. Shepperd ("AIDS Profiteer") were among those singled out in the early years of ACT UP. That singling out took the form of using the faces of these individuals, but in ways that made them more abstract.

Because a straightforward photolike representation might risk humanizing the opponent in ways that made it more difficult to sustain anger, the images were variously colorized, blurred, or rendered grainy in ways that abstracted the individual. The "AIDSgate" poster by the Silence = Death Collective, for example, which is credited by some with recruiting many new members to ACT UP at the national demonstration for lesbian and gay rights in the summer of 1987, featured a head shot of President Reagan done in a garish green with demonic red where the whites of the eyes would normally be. Another poster of Reagan made in the same year by Donald Moffett images a head and torso shot of a smirking president in sepia tones on the right side, juxtaposed to a red and black targetlike set of concentric circles on the left. Over Reagan's chest, in the same color as the red in the target, are the words "He Kills Me." The phrase at once evokes and trashes the public image of Reagan as an allegedly charming, old-boy humorist, and pointedly suggests that Reagan's indifference to the AIDS crisis is deadly. The deadliness is at once general and concrete; the phrase "He Kills Me" personalizes the threat. Where superimposing the target over Reagan might have seemed a violation of the nonviolence code (if not a provocation to the Secret Service), separating the two images makes ambiguous the question of who is the targeted and who is the targeter. The implication that "he," the president, is targeting "me," the person with AIDS, at the same time evokes an anger that is retargeted at Reagan and his policies.

Two uses of pharmaceutical CEOs offer a contrast in regard to giving and not giving a face to the opposition. The first image features "Mr. A. J. Shepperd, Chairman—WELLCOME PLC." Once again a head shot, the face is rendered in abstracted, very grainy black and white, with Shepperd's name and title given in a subliminally threatening diagonal slash across the chairman's necktie. Stamped in larger letters across his receding hairline are the words "AIDS Profiteer." A second, quite famous poster eschews giving face to the "enemy." Again a black and white image, this one features several petrie dishes and a syringe held by a gloved hand in the foreground, and a medical masked head. Presented with *noir*-style contrast, the lab technician's facial features are washed out totally into a black backdrop. On the head of the shadowy figure the following quotation appears: "One million [people with AIDS] isn't a market that's exciting. Sure it's growing, but it's not asthma." Below the quote is the attribution "Patrick Gage, Hoffman-LaRoche, Inc." This contrast of facelessness with the facefulness of the Shepperd poster makes perfect tactical sense. Where Burroughs Wellcome was a direct target of ACT UP, a company whose policies the group specifically wanted to change, Hoffman-LaRoche, as the quotation suggests, was not interested at the time in the "AIDS business." Thus the point of the attack here was to represent the callous indifference of the pharmaceutical industry in general, so that abstract, faceless indifference was the point. At the bottom of the poster are the words "This is to enrage you." This direct evoking of emotion was a common technique in ACT UP posters, and it again embodies a kind of postmodern complexity: it at once tells viewers what to feel ("rage") and tells them that they are being manipulated, "This is [engineered] to enrage you." Through such complicated yet direct image-texts, ACT UP posters managed to personalize and generalize, attack individuals and target the structures in which they are embedded, while simultaneously evoking a collective but personal "you."

Acting Out: Extending the Issue Frame

ACT UP has shown amazing adaptability when the contexts of AIDS as disease and social construction have shifted, partly in response to its own efforts. While remaining a predominantly white male organization, ACT UP has developed, with much pushing by others inside and out of the organization, a rich analysis of the intersections of race, class, gender, sexuality, and nationality. The list of issues it has taken up includes housing for homeless people with AIDS, free needle exchange programs for intravenous drug users, issues of AIDS in prison, underfunded public hospitals in the inner city, the spread of AIDS in the Third World, health insurance for low-income people, and treatment protocols for women, for lesbians, and for people of color (and for people fitting two or more of those categories). Some of this work has been done via ACT NOW (the AIDS Coalition to Network, Organize and Win), a national, and later international, forum created to extend the range of issues addressed by ACT UP and to offer widespread coordination while maintaining a decentralized structure. But coalition building has been far from easy.

One way to mark the shifting forces in and around ACT UP is to compare two major national marches in which the group was a significant force. The first, the 1987 March on Washington for Lesbian and Gay Rights, attracted six hundred thousand people and was, among other things, a coming-out party for ACT UP and for the wider field of AIDS activism. The march was led by people with AIDS, and the event included the first public display of the enormous AIDS Quilt, another, differently inflected part of AIDS cultural activism that marshaled mourning and remembrance as effectively as ACT UP mobilized anger.[14] It was also the moment when ACT UP received national exposure through its colorful graphics, dancing dragon mobile picket line, and large-scale civil disobedience. AIDS was on the agenda in various others ways throughout the march and surrounding events, and thus the Washington, D.C., rally marks the moment when it became clear how much lesbian and gay rights organizing would be changed by the AIDS crisis.

Seven years later, a Lesbian, Gay, Bisexual and Transgender March on Washington drew close to 1 million people. By this time it was clear that both ACT UP and the wider queer movement were increasingly connected to larger circuits of social justice; both linked movements were acknowledging far more fully than before the extent of diversity within their own ranks. There are many reasons for this, including increasing attacks from the Christian fundamentalists and others on the right who were using an antigay agenda as a wedge against all strands of progressive social action. The preamble to the march platform states: "The Lesbian, Gay, Bisexual and Transgender movement recognizes that our quest for social justice fundamentally links us to the struggles against racism and sexism, class bias, economic injustice, and religious intolerance. We must realize if one of us is oppressed we are all oppressed. The diversity of our movement requires and compels us to stand in opposition to all forms of oppression that diminish the quality of life for all people."

This preamble, and the shape of the march overall, were the result of much internal struggle between those wishing for a narrower, simpler "gay rights" agenda, and those pushing for this larger vision. And note how those who won out phrased the larger vision. It is the "diversity of our movement" that "requires and compels" this wider understanding. In other words, as more and more people came out, as more and more histories were written, as more and more complicated lesbian, gay, bisexual, and transgender studies emerged, it was impossible to deny the diversity within and across various gay or queer communities. At the same time, there is a recognition, beyond celebrating and protecting this diversity within, that "all forms of oppression that diminish the quality of life" for one group threaten others. ACT UP was both driven by and a driving force in this dual recognition of internal gay diversity and external connection to other communities. Because AIDS cut its swath widely (but not "indiscriminately") across the entire gay, lesbian, and bisexual communities, and beyond those communities, AIDS activism was a key site for this transformation.

From the group's beginnings, many in ACT UP were quite serious in attempting to reach out beyond their gay white male and lesbian core constituency. Because of its closeness to the crisis, ACT UP was among the first to recognize that the crisis had moved beyond the gay community. In trying to assist other communities, however, the group ran up against external and internal obstacles. One might have expected that ACT UP, with its sensitivity to the need for community-specific AIDS education, might have been better prepared for how not only the meanings, but the very course of the disease, differed from community to community, especially across lines of race, gender, and class. But those lines proved very difficult to cross.

As we have already seen, it took years and much prodding for women within ACT UP to convince men in the organization to take seriously the independent educational and medical needs of women generally and lesbians more specifically. Similar blindness emerged around economic and social factors affecting the course of the disease and its recognition and treatment in particular nonwhite, nongay, and/or poor communities. AIDS deaths among intravenous drug users were not recorded as such by authorities for some time, partly because symptoms tended to blend in with other "side effects" of substance abuse and were often different than those affecting middle-class gay men, and partly because the "gay disease" stereotype blinded health officers. As noted above, ACT UP did much to bring this other population of people with AIDS to light, but not always in the most effective or useful ways. ACT UP's rhetoric of crisis, for example, did not necessarily match the understanding of poor people of color for whom crisis mode is just everyday life. Many blacks and Latinos in inner cities saw the advent of AIDS not as a transformative event, but as one more in an ongoing series of assaults on their communities. Where middle-class white professionals felt a deep sense of entitlement to a health care system geared to their needs, blacks and Latinos were often inured to a system utterly indifferent to theirs.

At the same time, both media stereotypes and homophobia, which communities of color were no more immune to than white communities, made gay people of color invisible in AIDS iconography. By stereotype, if you were black or Latino and HIV-positive, you were a drug user, if you were white and HIV-positive, you were gay. These and similarly stereotypical assumptions at work both inside and outside of ACT UP meant that the group's efforts to reach out to communities of color were often received with suspicion. Intensive work on racism within the group, the presence of more gay and straight people of color in the organization, and a shift in national movement priorities gradually lessened these tensions. But ACT UP has seldom significantly crossed the color line (though as of 2002, ACT UP Philadelphia reported that more than half its membership was of color). Nevertheless, many in ACT UP worked diligently to deepen analyses of the ways in which homophobia, sexism, racism, and class oppression are inextricably interwoven into the AIDS crisis, and argued that all must be fought simultaneously if the crisis is to be ended.

(De)Constructing Ideologies

To talk about the "overall" ideology of any complex movement is risky business at best. But for ACT UP, to offer such a generalizing characterization would be not only risky but a violation of one of the ideological principles of the (dis)organization itself. The highly decentralized, profoundly anarchistic nature of ACT UP makes an attempt to characterize its general political position extremely problematic and a violation of the members' ideologically self-conscious agreement to disagree ideologically. One student of the movement characterizes the central ACT UP goals as "greater access to treatments and drugs for AIDS-related diseases; culturally sensitive, widely available and explicit safe-sex education; and well-funded research that is publicly accountable to the communities most affected."[15] The life-and-death stakes of an initially mysterious and terrifying disease certainly gave the group a very concrete focus. As one member put it: "People have been fighting for social justice in this country for centuries . . . We're going to get aerosol pentamidnine [a treatment drug for pneumocystis pneumonia] a lot quicker than we're going to get social justice."[16] Yet even many of the most pragmatic members of ACT UP soon realized that their concrete goals were inseparable from larger issues of social justice.

At the other ideological extreme from the pragmatists in the organization, but not necessarily inconsistent with their goals, is the radically "deconstructive" position articulated by members like Cindy Patton: "ACT UP groups do not protest or demonstrate; rather they perform, and in their 'actions' they identify the unspoken, inaudible linkages in the power system which are obscured by both the unitary notion of power ('get a government response') and the network notion of power ('decentralize'). . . . Coalition, and even agreement, may not be a desirable goal, but only a strategic or tactical moment in denaturalizing identities and the systems of power which construct them in order to control us."[17] For other members, a broad, radically democratic, decentralized but still recognizably "progressive left" perspective was the core ideology of

ACT UP. This element, while wary, worried less than Patton about being absorbed back into the various power systems, and took most seriously the second letter in the acronym, for *coalition*.

Part of ACT UP's ideology was an understanding that all "cultural texts," including actions, are open to widely variant interpretations. Applying this analysis to its own actions meant that ACT UP performed "social texts" that were explicitly designed to leave room for multiple interpretations. This was not to promote some "anything goes," utterly relativistic position—a common misunderstanding of postmodernism—but rather to acknowledge that analyzing the always partly open-ended nature of communication could make one more effective in challenging dominant rhetorics and the social positionings from whence they were articulated. In other words, the postmodernism of ACT UP actors challenged universal claims to truth and representation that they believed often embodied not universal but particular straight, white, middle-class male positions. They opened themselves instead to studying and understanding other, insurgent particularities of race, ethnicity, class, generation, gender, sexual preference, and their intersections. Crimp and Ralston acknowledge the collective nature of ACT UP graphics, and note that the multiple audiences to which they are directed always include themselves: "AIDS activist art is grounded in the accumulated knowledge and political analysis of the AIDS crisis produced collectively by the entire movement. The graphics not only reflect that knowledge, but actively contribute to its articulation as well. . . . They function as an organizing tool, by conveying, in compressed form, information and political positions to others affected by the epidemic, to onlookers at demonstrations, and to the dominant media. But their primary audience is the movement itself. AIDS activist graphics enunciate AIDS politics to and for all of us in the movement."[18] This last point is crucial, for it acknowledges that rather than accepting self-limiting ideas of "preaching to the choir," ACT UP understands that ongoing internal political education and a willingness to grow and change ideologically are critical to a movement's success. Indeed, a healthy if not always pleasant fractiousness has been a hallmark of the organization. The strong decentralist structure that allows room for difference has been crucial in assuring that this contentious ongoing learning process has been more often a resource rather than a threat. Of course, those who would forestall movements can also be fast learners. And as some critics have argued, a similarly decentralized set of interlocking but semi-autonomous forces of domination characterizes postmodern capitalist society, and those forces are not easily challenged.[19]

Outside-in Strategies, F(r)actions and Spin-off Groups

ACT UP was from the beginning known best for its uncompromising, in-your-face tactics. Given that its origins lay partly in critique of AIDS service organizations like the Gay Men's Health Crisis, which ACT UP believed had gotten too close to mainstream medical and government institutions, and given its confrontational style, this reputation is well earned. But the picture is also more complicated. Many in ACT UP understood that their pressure was making space for insiders in AIDS medical and government bureaucracies to maneuver. This situation, which I call the outside-in, or push-pull strategy, is common in many movements. Just as Malcolm X proved a useful foil for Martin Luther King Jr., ACT UP served those very organizations, such as GMHC, that it criticized as too moderate.[20] ACT UP members engaged in letter writing, petitioning, and lobbying, in addition to taking direct action. And they often used direct action itself, as had the civil rights movement, to force open a process that led to the kind of negotiation more moderate forces had been unable to initiate.

The complexity of political factions and fractions within ACT UP is also revealed in the number of spin-off organizations it generated. These spin-offs spun in two rather opposite directions: new groups less oriented toward direct action, on one hand, and new radical queer groups that were very direct action–oriented.

As we have seen, women in ACT UP had to struggle to get the gay male–dominated movement to address issues of particular concern to women. The work of women in ACT UP to bring out the issues of HIV-positive women in general, and lesbians in particular, played a key role in seeding a strong, widespread, and diverse lesbian health movement. That effort has led to increased medical attention to a lesbian demographic with regard to breast cancer, sexually transmitted diseases, and a host of other concerns. Some lesbians frustrated by ACT UP's gay male focus spun off to form Women's Health Action and Mobilization (WHAM), a "direct action group committed to demanding, securing, and defending absolute reproductive freedom and quality health care for all women." Like ACT UP, WHAM and other radical women's health and reproductive rights activists sought more targeted medical research, inclusion of women and lesbians in drug trials, better and more widespread health information for women and lesbian communities, and full reproductive rights. Like ACT UP's bad cop, good cop routine with regard to more mainstream AIDS advocacy groups, these new women's and lesbians' health movement groups brought renewed radical energy and pressure to a scene that had become routinized and limited by institutionalization.

In another vein, because ACT UP was centrally involved in a politics of scientific knowledge, some members moved ever deeper into the arcane dimensions of medical research, developing personal contacts within the medical field whom they influenced through far lower-key tactics (like conversation over coffee) than the image of ACT UP usually conjures. Some in the movement gained through this process a deeper understanding of, if not sympathy for, those who work in AIDS research institutions. Thus, it is not surprising that ACT UP's growing expertise and increasing intimacy with AIDS bureaucracies led some members to form a spin-off organization called the Treatment Action Group (TAG) in 1992. TAG was a far different organization, not only in focus but also in form. A small group formed by invitation only, it eschewed openness and democracy in favor of expertise and traditional political clout. It became a "parallel institution" of sorts, mediating between AIDS bureaucracies and radical activist critique. TAG's difference from ACT UP is perhaps most dramatically shown by the group's acceptance of a $1 million donation from Burroughs Wellcome. While criticized by many in ACT UP for elitism and for growing too close to the enemy, TAG has been credited by others with great success in lobbying the government to release promising AIDS drugs more quickly, to improve the FDA clinical trial process, and to better coordinate research activities at the National Institutes of Health through an Office of AIDS Research. That success, however, could not have occured without, and, indeed, is indivisible from, ACT UP work. But TAG is far more likely to receive official credit for these advances, since the most radical elements in a force field of influence never receive credit from those institutions they influence.

Among the spin-offs of ACT UP that spun rather in the opposite direction, the most notorious is no doubt Queer Nation. Founded in 1990, this short-lived but highly dramatic and influential group sought to take ACT UP's confrontational style back into lesbian and gay organizing.

Queer Nation took some of the radical energy, internal diversity, and tactics of ACT UP into attempts to empower bisexuals, transgendered people, and others who had been excluded from, marginalized by, or toned down by the mainstreaming of aspects of the lesbian and gay movement. Queer Nation's signature actions, often aimed at "queering" public places, included kiss-ins in shopping malls and straight bars, same-sex marriages on the steps of Catholic cathedrals, and "pink panther" patrols bashing back against antigay violence. Like ACT UP, Queer Nation grew rapidly both in cities around the United States and internationally. Though the contradiction between the inclusiveness implied by *queer* and the exclusiveness implied by *nation* wore down many chapters after a few years, the organization's colorful style and imaginative actions did much to bring the category "queer" and some of the theory behind it more fully out into the public sphere.

A second, similar spin-off group, the Lesbian Avengers, founded in 1992, took the energy, style, and direct-action emphasis of ACT UP into an attempt to radicalize lesbian activism. The group's handbook for the New York chapter (like ACT UP and Queer Nation, the group was founded in New York City, but soon spread nationally) speaks in terms that clearly echo its origin. One section of the handbook is titled "Demo-Graphics," in homage to the ACT UP book of the same name, and the group's self-description suggests both its ACT UP style and the targets of some of its actions:

> Props, floats, shrines, burning torches, papier mache bombs, plaster statues whatever! Demo-graphics need to be eye-catching, meaningful, and visually exciting.
>
> We try to never use a cliché or tired old rhetoric. . . . When we built a shrine to the two gay people burned to death in Oregon, our demo posters said, "Do Not Let Them Rest in Peace." When we dogged the mayor of Denver for 48 hours the signs said "Boycott the Hate State." When we held our New Year's Eve Party, the poster featured a picture of seventies Blaxploitation film star Pam Grier, in hot pants, loading a rifle. The poster advertised "Activist a Go-Go." Our Valentine's Day Action honoring Gertrude Stein and Alice Toklas celebrated "Politically Incorrect Domestic Bliss.". . . So whether the theme is whimsical or angry, our slogans have been clear.[21]

Clearly, the Avengers, like Queer Nation, focused on in-your-face confrontations around a variety of issues affecting their community. Both Queer Nation and Lesbian Avengers appealed especially to a younger generation of gays, lesbians, and other queers who, raised in a more "out" world made possible by generations of activists who preceded them, pushed further "out," bringing their defiantly deviant selves out into the streets, the malls, the schools, the talk shows.

The various spin-off groups of ACT UP mark both a positive diffusion of energy and internal fault lines in the organization. On the negative side, despite ACT UP's antihierarchical, decentralized form that could contain many positions, both its failures and its successes created some internally irresolvable tensions that could only find resolution in the formation of new groups. On the positive side, ACT UP set off a chain reaction that radicalized communities and fostered a host of new groups. Indeed, a proliferation of both health advocacy groups and radical queer groups constitutes small-scale "cycles of protest" set in motion by ACT UP.[22]

Most followers of ACT UP argue that the group peaked in the early 1990s and declined somewhat in effectiveness thereafter. Urvashi Vaid, one of the most perceptive observers of contemporary movements and a major figure in lesbian, gay, queer organizing, and a sometime member of ACT UP, credits the group with bringing a new generation of activists into their own, but is critical of the lack of follow-up behind ACT UP's spectacular actions:

> Direct-action activism emerged in part as a reaction to the conservatism of the gay mainstream, and significantly affected gay movement strategy from 1986 to 1992. ACT UP marked the first (and only) time that this strategy took center stage in national gay politics. A new generation of activists, committed solely and principally to being queer and promoting queer freedom, came into its own.... [But] the direct action strategy focused on the glamorous and neglected the obvious. We sought (and got) media visibility, but after our fifteen minutes in the sun, we were left with another round of silence and the need to repeat the old actions, with diminished effectiveness each time. Our coercive moralism and guerilla tactics eventually alienated and angered the people whose decisions we tried to shape. Ultimately, our neglect of dull systematic political organizing left us in 1993 without the political capacity to fight the right locally for our national policy agenda.[23]

ACT UP's very strength—the imaginative, novel, and telegenic aspects of its demonstration—became a liability, both because novelty always wears off, and because being high on direct action can distract from grassroots "dull systematic political organizing."

Mainstreaming Reappropriations

As I have argued throughout this book, one clear sign of the success of a movement is diffusion/defusion of aspects of its culture into mainstream cultures. In the case of ACT UP the very brilliance of its graphic sense and its theatrical flair no doubt hastened this process. But this is hardly surprising, since ACT UP's own analysis of how the process of cultural politics works anticipated that even the group's opponents would reappropriate their "texts." The group also understood that the process of reappropriation was not a wholly negative one. As in the fable of the wolf that ate the tasty stones proffered by the sheep it planned to eat, eventually the stones limit the mobility and options of the predator.

A key example of this appropriation was the rise of what some have called "AIDS chic." The most ubiquitous emblem of this was the wearing of red ribbons by people in the entertainment industry. Started by an activist group calling itself Visual AIDS, the ribbon moved fairly quickly from a brilliant device to draw attention to AIDS by associating the fight against it with figures in popular culture to a complacency-deepening symbol of how easy it was to feel good about AIDS: just pin on a red ribbon! The more selective and effective version of AIDS chic took the form of fashion shows, art exhibits, and musical concerts that raised millions of dollars for AIDS research and treatment. This kind of mainstreaming, as I argued in chapter 6 regarding what we might dub "famine chic," was viewed skeptically by many in ACT UP but was also recognized as a necessary source of funds that might perhaps be put to more radical uses than the funders may have intended.

Surely, the clearest, most ironic example of mainstream appropriation involves the graphics of the Silence = Death project and the Gran Fury collective being taken up and resignified by pharmaceutical companies. The rise in recent years of ever more specific niche marketing led inevitably to "gay people with AIDS" being moved from "risk group" to "target audience." As Sarah Schulman articulates it in her important book *Stagestruck: Theater, AIDS, and the Marketing of Gay America*: "advertising relies on a philosophy of niche marketing that has become so precise that Puerto Rican girls, poor alcoholics, Christian fundamentalist rock fans, punks of Arab descent, teenagers wanting cigarettes, and terminally ill gay men all have their own interactive relationship with some area of advertising."[24] In other words, with or without the aid of postmodern theory, advertisers too have learned the virtues of understanding specific "positionalities" and their rhetorical preferences. The powerful images created around anti-AIDS activism proved too tempting for markete(e)rs seeking to consume people with AIDS. Magazines like *POZ*, aimed at HIV-positive readers, complete a circle when they publish pharmaceutical ads that incorporate pink triangles and other aspects of the "AIDS activist aesthetic" to sell their products. In appropriating images that ACT UP activists themselves had often appropriated from mainstream advertising styles, these ads remind us of the ongoing, irresolvable problem of resignification that ACT UP's postmodern graphic identity so brilliantly embodied. There is no such thing as a radical image or message; there are only radical "contextualizations" that in turn become "texts" that can be resignified back into the mainstream. This is not a cause for cynicism, just a caution against complacency and a call for ongoing acts of imaginative engagement.

The AIDS Crisis Is Not Over

As early as 1988 ACT UP felt it necessary to create a poster reading, "The AIDS Crisis Is Not Over," and ever since the group has periodically had to fight the sense that new treatments, new funding, new political promises had brought the crisis to an end. The mainstreaming of AIDS, its normalization, has brought with it another version of this old problem. Though ACT UP groups are still acting up all over the world, they struggle with a new wave of indifference resulting in part from their successes. Positions considered outrageous when articulated by ACT UP a decade ago seem like common sense today. For those who know nothing of the activist organization, this common sense appears from nowhere, while those who give credit to ACT UP sometimes do so in a romanticizing way that mythologizes the movement's past at the expense of its present. Consistent with their very process-oriented sense of social movement, many original members of ACT UP have moved on, and many new positions have been articulated. The development of relatively effective AIDS drug treatments has greatly extended the lives of some people with AIDS, and ACT UP deserves a good portion of the credit for speeding the development of these drugs. Anthony Fauci, director of the National Institutes of Health during the rise of ACT UP, noted in 2002 that activism profoundly changed not only the process of developing AIDS drugs but also the whole federal approach to drug development.[25]

Sociologist William Gamson observes that "the trick for activists is to bridge public discourse and people's experiential knowledge, integrating them in a coherent frame that supports and sustains collective action."[26] In this process, for a while, time is on the side of movements. Claims that by definition always initially come from outside some mainstream frame become less strange through multiple iterations. Over time the chances of those iterations resonating with experiential knowledge grow. In the case of AIDS, the terrible, exponential spread of the disease itself meant that more and more people had the opportunity to match what groups like ACT UP were saying about AIDS and people with AIDS to their experience with someone they knew personally. This too led to normalization of the disease and, sometimes, to greater sympathy for protesters.

But within some of the most deeply affected communities, it also led to a different kind of normalization of disease. In some sectors of some gay urban communities, where infection rates sometimes exceeded half of the population, a deeply romanticized fatalism set in, one that went so far at times as to stigmatize HIV-negative individuals in the community as less authentic, thereby undermining safer sex practices. Hence, another kind of full circle turns, as attempts to undermine stigma inadvertently contribute to the transformation of stigma into a "red badge of courage" that ironically puts new persons at risk.[27]

All of the issues ACT UP has faced over the years remain, in sometimes altered, but distressingly recognizable form: AIDS "profiteering" has only increased as the numbers of potential "customers" have grown; inadequate attention from the federal government has worsened under President Bill Clinton's and President George W. Bush's continued downsizing of government; and public indifference, for a time lessened by the power of direct action, has reasserted itself in the face of the illusion that better treatment has ended the crisis. Add to this the problem of dealing with the new wave of desperate, romanticized high-risk behaviors, and you have a formidable set of issues at home. In addition, currently much ACT UP activity in the United States and elsewhere is focused on AIDS in the Third World where infection statistics are staggering, resources far scarcer than in the United States, and racist indifference again apparent. Of the 40 million people in the world currently diagnosed with HIV/AIDS, 70 percent are on the African continent. Rather than simply enjoying the relative advantages of access to life-prolonging treatments provided by their often privileged economic and social location, to their credit, U.S. AIDS activists have moved their critique of AIDS policy more and more into the realm of international politics. This is at once a tribute to the ideological openness and willingness to grow within ACT UP, and part of a more general sense among participants in many progressive movements that they must work on an integrated set of issues and on a truly global stage, even as they attend to the particulars of their place and the specifics of their issues. As we will see in chapter 9, this process of "globalization from below" represents a new wave of activism nationally, transnationally, and internationally.

EIGHT

Environmental Justice Ecocriticism
Race, Class, Gender, and Literary Ecologies

In previous chapters I have focused primarily on cultural texts and cultural formations, but my goal now is to examine an academic "intellectual formation." By "intellectual formation" I mean a set of theories and practices stable enough to make a significant influence on social thought, primarily through academic writing and teaching. Intellectual formations arise from different social locations—from within science, industry, the arts, academe, and, not infrequently, social movements. Indeed, one strand of social movement theory argues that an important dimension of social movements is their engagement in "cognitive praxis" that changes the way we think about the world.[1]

The concept "cognitive praxis" (literally, "thought-action-theory") reminds us that consciousness is a material social force. Movements have sometimes been translated into full-fledged academic fields. We have noted in earlier chapters that ethnic studies arose out of racial nationalist movements of the 1960s, and women's studies emerged out of the feminist movement in the 1970s. The science/social science field of environmental studies is another, more directly relevant example. The creation of a new academic department is only one of many ways movements shape academia and intellectual life; more often, movements shape the general intellectual context in which scholarly debate takes place.

The intellectual formation I will examine in this chapter is a recently emergent strand, "environmental justice cultural criticism," part of a larger formation known as "ecocriticism." Ecocriticism consists of a body of work that studies links between literature, culture, and the natural environment. Ecocriticism arose from the influence of the environmental movement, and is the foremost contribution of the humanities to environmentalist thought and action. It directs itself primarily to the field of literary studies, but also seeks more broadly to give humanities scholarship a place in environmental studies, a field thus far dominated by the sciences and social sciences. The overall ecocritical intellectual formation is now quite elaborate, with several distinct schools or approaches. In addition to dozens of books and hundreds of articles, the formation includes an organization, the Association for the Study of Literature and Environment (ASLE), with more than a thousand members. There are also several journals, including the house journal of ASLE, *Interdisciplinary Studies of Literature and Environment (ISLE)*, as well as academic courses offered in colleges and universities around the country, and a variety of other signs of a developed intellectual formation.

The field of ecocriticism could only have come into being as a result of the rise of environmental movements, especially those during the wave of social movements in the 1960s. But as with any movement-initiated intellectual formation, its relation to ongoing movements is somewhat indirect. Intellectual formations are often seen by grassroots activists as a selling out or watering down of a movement, because the long march through the academic institutions is seldom as exciting as street fighting. But both are arguably equally important in furthering the work of social change. Especially in the contemporary world where higher education has become a form of mass culture in the United States, the struggle to bring movement-generated social critique into universities is crucially important. To be sure, this process, like all processes of movement diffusion, entails losses as well as gains. Often over time movement-generated cognitive praxis tends to become more "cognitive" and less "praxis" in orientation. That is, it tends to become more and more tenuously connected to the kinds of action-oriented questions emerging from the grassroots. But continuing pressure from movements can often assure that the intellectual formation is shaped and reshaped to meet the changing needs and perspectives coming from the level of movement action. As we saw in chapter 3, the women's movement provides a particularly rich example of how changing forces within a movement, such as the voices of constituencies previously marginalized (by race, class, and sexual orientation, in this case), have reshaped the agenda of cultural and academic formations. I suggest that a similar force has been at work with regard to the relationships between environmental movements and the field of academic literary and cultural criticism.

To illustrate this process in action, this chapter describes an emerging strand of the ecocritical formation that demonstrates the increasing impact of a previously marginalized sector of environmentalism. I call this emerging strand "environmental justice ecocriticism," or more broadly, "environmental justice cultural criticism." While the term is my invention, the field it names has been developing for some time. I mention my own involvement in this field to underscore a point I made in the introduction about the inevitable partisanship that intellectuals bring to their pursuits. While that is implicit in all the chapters of this book, it is more explicit in this chapter, which began as an active contribution to, or "intervention" in, the field it is describing. Thus, in this chapter I am advocating for, not merely commenting upon, the phenomenon of environmental justice cultural criticism.

Environmental Justice and Academic Criticism

Environmental justice is the branch of the environmental movement that most fully challenges the ways in which racism, class hierarchy, sexism, and other elements of social injustice have unevenly shaped people's experiences of environmental degradation and their access to environmental pleasures.[2] The environmental justice movement has been developing inside and outside of the "mainstream" environmental movement since at least the late 1970s. Likewise, ecocriticism has been developing since the 1970s. But until recently the two fields of activity were not often placed in relation to each other. Ecocriticism has had very little to say about issues of race and class in regard to the environment. Conversely, the environmental justice movement has largely ignored questions of cultural context, focusing narrowly on environmental law, science, and public policy.

Environmental justice ecocriticism argues the need to attend to the cultural contexts in which environmental racism and working-class exploitation have developed. At the same time, the study of issues of race and racism in literature has largely ignored environmental questions. This is largely because mainstream environmentalism has been presented in ways that have coded it as a "white issue," a perspective that the environmental justice movement has been at pains to change. Environmental justice ecocriticism is thus seeking to bridge several intellectual divides. In so doing, it offers a model of a movement influencing an academic field, while in turn the field seeks to offer resources back to the movement proper.

The environmental justice movement gained public attention in the early 1990s, though its origins go back much further. The First National People of Color Environmental Leadership Summit in Washington, D.C., in 1991 is often seen as the moment when the movement came to define itself as a large-scale national effort. But that moment grew out of countless local efforts over more than a decade. Moreover, once the concept was established, it became possible to further trace the links between environmentalism and social justice. At the base for the modern movement was the disease, death, and discomfort experienced by thousands of people of color and low-income whites across the United States and around the world. When activists began collecting data to move beyond anecdotal evidence, a clear pattern emerged showing that the most dangerous toxic chemicals, incinerators, nuclear waste facilities, uranium mines, and other environmental hazards were disproportionately sited in the vicinity of poor white communities and communities of color. These data provided a rationale for intense community action, underwriting legal struggles and scientific debates that have been at the core of the environmental justice movement.

The environmental justice movement includes many different groups. For example, African American, Asian American, and Latino groups are fighting landfills, incinerators, smokestacks, toxic dumps, and other sources of a poisoned environment. Antitoxics campaigns have grown out of the Love Canal fight, led by Lois Gibbs and other working-class women, which resulted in the creation of groups like the Citizens Clearinghouse for Toxic Waste. Native American activists are fighting against the devastating impact of uranium mining and nuclear dumping on tribal communities. Sometimes portrayed as a civil rights movement, sometimes as an environmental movement, environmental justice aims to show that the two are often one.

In all strands of the environmental justice movement, women have played central roles, such that gender must be central to any full analysis. This is even more pertinent in the field of environmental justice ecocriticism, where forms of feminist environmentalism have played a path-breaking role in linking constructions of nature to social issues. Ecofeminists have also been important in demonstrating that connections between social injustice and environmental damage are not new but centuries old.

Whose History of Environmentalism?

Histories of the environmental movement told from the perspective of the white middle class often stress literary origins nicely compatible with the rise of environmentalism's literary branch, ecocriticism. But from the perspective of environmental justice ecocriticism, a very different origin story is possible. The traditional story of modern environmental consciousness often focuses on literary precursors like the English and American Romantic poets, and on literary naturalists like Henry David Thoreau and, a little later, John Muir. This story then moves into the formation of environmental concerns in the form of "preservationism" and "conservationism" in the early twentieth century.

But suppose the origin story is retold from the perspective of environmental justice.[3] Then, alongside the story of Wordsworth appreciating the beauty of Britain's Lake District, you would have William Blake "appreciating" the devastating environmental impact of England's "dark satanic mills." Alongside Thoreau's sojourn around Walden Pond, you would have tales of New England "factory girls" fighting against the health-shattering effects of textile dust and dyes so corrosive many died of poisoning. This story would also point out that the Romantic nature-loving Thoreau was also the radical antislavery advocate and a major figure in the history of civil disobedience. It would also point out that alongside his environmentalist virtues, John Muir was a racist and an anti-Semite.

When this story enters the twentieth century, the traditional version focuses on the rivalry of the "preservationists" like Muir and the "conservationists" like Gifford Pinchot and his boss, Theodore Roosevelt. Pinchot represents a utilitarian, resource-management approach to nature. In contrast, naturalist Muir, for whom the goal was not management of nature but absolute protection of wilderness, championed the preservationist cause. Most of the national park system resulted from the compromise between these two otherwise antagonistic forces. The preservationist branch is perhaps best represented by one of the biggest and longest running environmental groups in America, the Sierra Club, or by other major groups like the Audubon Society.

Environmental justice criticism would insist that alongside this story of attempts to preserve wilderness and wild species, there must be stories of the environmental hazards faced by workers and slum dwellers in this same era. It would point out that sometimes the same progressive-era activists who fought for protection of wilderness also fought for worker preservation. But it would also point out that some of these same wilderness advocates were vicious racists like Madison Grant, co-founder of the California Save the Redwoods League, who propounded Anglo-Saxon superiority and championed eugenics campaigns to weed out "weaker" races. While some mainstream environmentalists would say these were historical accidents of no consequence to the truth of those individuals' environmental vision, environmental justice advocates would say there is an intimate and ongoing connection that must be addressed.

The great wave of environmentalism arising out of the social movements of the 1960s also has to be rewritten in light of environmental justice criticism. More needs to be said about the roots of the new environmental movement of those years in strategies and tactics from the civil rights and other social justice movements. Long-trumpeted conspiracy theories claiming that Richard Nixon encouraged the environmental movement as a way to distract dissenters from more troubling social issues like racism and the war in Vietnam are simplistic. Still, there is a parallel truth: environmental movement historians have sometimes distracted themselves from the enabling fact of social justice movements as models for ecological activism. Without the social justice activism that preceded it, the environmental movement that emerged in the late 1960s never would have taken the forms it did or have been as strong.

The shift from wilderness preservation to a wider agenda of concern, including air and water pollution, industrial waste, and pesticides, which occurred in the mid-1960s, was deeply indebted to the social justice movements of that era. Established groups like the Sierra Club and National Audubon Society broadened their agenda. More active new groups, such as Friends of the Earth, League of Conservation Voters, Environmental Defense Fund, and Natural Resources Defense Council, emerged or solidified during this era. All benefited from the social movement activity of the times, and that influence appears stronger and stronger as one moves out into branches like the antinuclear movement, radical Greens, or Earth First!

A history of the environmental movement sensitive to environmental justice would also recognize that it was the entrance of human health impacts into the equation that turned a small movement into a mass one. Rachel Carson's *Silent Spring* (1962) served as a catalyst when it drew causal links between the impact of DDT and other chemicals on animals, and their likely impact on human beings. Likewise, the stories of pollution, nuclear waste, and atomic tests in the atmosphere played a major role in a developing environmental consciousness. Yet, as this consciousness expanded, the mostly male, mostly white, mostly middle-class leaders of the movement paid little attention to the unequal impact of these phenomena, failing to note that working-class soldiers, Native Americans, and Pacific Islanders bore the brunt of atmospheric nuclear testing; that pesticides hurt Latino and Filipino farmworkers far more than consumers; and that escape from the degraded conditions of blighted cities was far easier for white suburbanites than for the people of color and poor whites who were left there by "white flight" in the 1950s and 1960s. Indeed, the not-in-my-backyard attitude that prevailed in parts of the mainstream movement directly contributed to further degradation of communities of color and poor white communities when polluters, including the U.S. government, made decisions to locate their environmental waste in poorer communities with fewer resources of resistance. Thus, it is not simply that traditional histories of environmentalism leave out parallel stories dealing with "social justice" concerns, but that without examination of those concerns, the impact of both mainstream environmentalism and more radical strands represented by groups like Greenpeace and Earth First! is distorted.

Environmental Movements and Schools of Ecocriticism

Just as the history of environmentalism is being rethought and rewritten in the light of environmental justice questions, so too must the story of environmentalism's literary critical branch, ecocriticism, be remade. To understand environmental justice ecocriticism, it is necessary to see it against the background of this wider formation. So let me offer a brief typology of ecocritical approaches as a way of mapping the field. Along the way, by suggesting how each school relates to a part of the environmental movement, I can also say more about the history of environmental movements generally.

Much, if not most, ecocriticism in practice combines two or more of these "schools," and some strands fit none of these rubrics perfectly. The schools listed roughly correspond to major sectors in past and present environmental movements. This mirrors the environmental movement more broadly, where the same group or individual activist may work on issues that cross more than one environmentalist position. Since all of these schools are still relatively undefined, they can best be characterized by the issues they seek to address, rather than by the definitive positions they take.

Preservationist Ecocriticism

As mentioned above, preservationism is often seen as emerging in part from a literary sensibility and practice, traced back via Muir to such mid-nineteenth-century figures as Thoreau, and sometimes to the Romantic poets. A focus on writers already in the canon of "great literature" eased the task of bringing the environment into literary study, but bringing in the wider body of natural history and other forms of nature writing has been more challenging.

In ecocritical form, the preservationist strand asks: What can studying literature and nonfiction nature writing do to enhance appreciation and improve stewardship of the natural environment? What can literature and criticism do to help preserve and extend wilderness, protect endangered species, and otherwise assist in the preservation of the natural world? How can literature and criticism strengthen the transcendent dimension of the human/nature relationship?

Ecological Ecocriticism

The school of ecological ecocriticism, emerging from the second wave of the environmental movement in the late 1960s and early 1970s, builds on the notion of "ecology." While having a base in biological science, the term *ecology* became widely used in the movement to signal the interdependent and systemic relationship between human beings and the wider natural world. Its typical documents include Rachel Carson's groundbreaking book *Silent Spring*, a work that traced the long, "ecological" connection between pesticide pollution, animals, plants, and human disease. The first great event of this new phase is often cited as Earth Day 1970 with its popularization of the "whole earth" image of a globe connected through a web of natural relationships. This branch of the movement spawned a host of new social institutions, including a huge array of movement groups, along with the intellectual formation "environmental studies."

The kinds of ecocriticism growing out of ecological frameworks vary considerably, but tend to ask questions like these: How can the ecosystem idea (or metaphor) be extended to a poetics of the literary system in relation to nature? How can literature and criticism be placed within ecosystems, or be used to elucidate the nature and needs of ecosystems? How can a sense of rootedness in place, in particular ecosystems or bioregions, be enhanced when examining literary works? How can the insights of the science of ecology be used to analyze literary texts and other cultural representations of the natural world in ways that better connect people to environments?

Biocentric/Deep Ecological Ecocriticism

The deep ecology movement arose in the late 1970s and early 1980s and became identified with a position of uncompromising "biocentrism," as opposed to the "anthropocentrism" that puts humans at the center of and above the rest of terrestrial life. As the name implies, this position claims to take the principle of ecology to a deeper level, by which proponents mean both a deeper spiritual level (the Earth as "sacred" space) and a deeper level of commitment to protecting nonhuman creation. The main prophets of deep ecology, figures like Arne Naess, Bill Devall, and George Sessions, argued that nothing less than a new whole earth–based worldview would constitute true environmentalism.

Translated into ecocritical terms, deep ecological ecocriticism asks questions like these: How can literature and criticism be used to displace "man" and place a natural equality of all living entities at the center of concern? How can literature and criticism be used to show the limits of "humanism" and the benefits of a wider biocentrism? How can the independent existence and rights of the nonhuman "biotic" (living) and "abiotic" (inert) realms be protected and extended through literary and critical acts? How can a deeper, biocentric spirituality be furthered by literature and criticism? Some deep ecologists go so far as to ask how we can return to a preindustrial world where intimate contact with nature was an inevitable part of daily life, and seek out utopian projects of such a past-future.

Ecofeminist Ecocriticism

Ecofeminism is a more radically political strand of environmentalism that emerged in the early 1980s. In essence, it argues that the traditional position of women in society has often paralleled the position of "nature" as one of subservience. It argues that both nature and women suffer from a comparison in which the latter are deemed closer to the former and thus further from the higher realm of culture. Ecofeminists have pioneered the field of linking the sociocultural with the natural, and by identifying issues of gender as inextricably tied to issues of race, class, and sexuality, they have contributed the most of any existing school to the emergence of an environmental justice ecocriticism.

Ecofeminist ecocritics ask: How have women and nature been linked in literature and criticism? How has nature been "feminized"? How have women been "naturalized"? In what other ways has the gendering of nature been written and with what effects? How are the liberation of women and the liberation of nature linked? How do interrelations of race, class, and sexuality complicate the imagined and real relations between women and nature? Is there a separate, different history of women's "nature writing" and other writings about nature?

A more nuanced analysis could identify many other strands of ecocriticism. But this typology should be enough to give some sense of the variety of the field and the ways in which it has developed in interactive relationship with evolving schools within the environmental movement(s).

What Is Environmental Justice Ecocriticism?

How does environmental justice ecocriticism position itself in relation to these other schools? Perhaps the best way to characterize it is, again, through the kinds of questions it addresses. Environmental justice ecocriticism asks: How can literary and cultural criticism further efforts of the environmental justice movement to bring attention to ways in which environmental degradation and environmental hazards unequally affect poor people and people of color? How has racism domestically and internationally made possible greater environmental irresponsibility, and how are these truths manifested in literature and other kinds of cultural texts? What are the different traditions in nature writing by the poor, by people of color in the United States, and by cultures outside the United States? How will an understanding of those differing traditions deepen our capacity to imagine better solutions to environmental problems and the social problems with which they are inextricably intertwined? How have issues like toxic waste, incinerators, lead poisoning, uranium mining and tailings, and other environmental health issues been manifested in cultural texts, and how can criticism further our understanding of the cultural dimensions of these issues? How can issues of worker safety and environmental safety be brought together in cultural criticism in such a way that labor movements and environmental movements can be seen as positively connected, not antagonistic?

More broadly, the field asks how ecocriticism can encourage justice and "sustainable development" in the Third World and among native people where racism and imperialism combine to worsen environmental injustice? And, finally, looking self-critically at existing mainstream ecocriticism, to what extent and in what ways have other schools of ecocriticism been ethnocentric or ignored questions of race and class as they intersect with environmental questions? These and a host of related questions have forged new connections between academic critique and movement struggles by strengthening a sense of the cultural struggle surrounding the legal and medical battles that have thus far been at the core of the environmental justice movement.

Criticizing the Critics

When I first coined the term "environmental justice ecocriticism" in 1997, I was naming a largely nonexistent field.[4] Today the kind of work I was calling for is well under way. This is not due to the influence of my naming process but rather indicates that a certain set of intellectual preconditions was in place to allow a new formation to emerge. One of those key conditions was the prior existence of the general field of ecocriticism. Thus, while the new strand is highly critical of aspects of the earlier one, it is also dialectically indebted to it. It emerged partly in the gaps of the earlier field. But once created, the formation calls us to reorient the whole terrain of ecocriticism, just as environmental justice calls us the rethink the entire environmental movement.

Both the problems environmental justice criticism is seeking to remedy and some hints toward the solution of those problems can be found in the collection of essays entitled *The Ecocriticism Reader: Landmarks in Literary Ecology,* edited by Cheryll Burgess Glotfelty and Harold Fromm.[5] As the title suggests, this volume was intended as the defining text for its field, and to a large degree it has become that. As stated in the introduction, "These are the essays with which anyone wishing to undertake ecocritical scholarship ought to be familiar."[6] While there are some gestures noting the incompleteness of the project of ecocriticism — mention of its "evolving nature" for example — to the extent that this text is representative (and in many respects I believe it is), it suggests that ecocriticism is in danger of recapitulating the sad history of environmentalism generally, wherein unwillingness to grapple with questions of racial and class privilege has severely undermined the powerful critique of ecological devastation. Where a certain type of ecocritic worries about "social issues" watering down ecological critique, mounting evidence makes clear that the opposite has been the case. Pretending to isolate the environment from its necessary interrelation with society and culture has severely limited the appeal of environmental thought, to the detriment of both the natural and social worlds.

The problems I am addressing can be seen clearly in a remark in a section of the introduction to *The Ecocriticism Reader* entitled "The Future of Ecocriticism." Co-editor Cheryll Burgess Glotfelty names the problem and exhibits it in the same breath. She writes: "Ecocriticism has been a predominantly white movement. It will become a multiethnic movement when stronger connections are made between the environment and issues of social justice, and when a diversity of voices are encouraged to contribute to the discussion."[7] Notwithstanding the good intentions no doubt present in this statement, it is a remarkably complacent and politically insensitive one. Offered as a series of passive constructions, it acknowledges that the "whiteness" of the movement can appear to be a problem, but shows little sense of urgency about making connections between "the environment and issues of social justice." We are presumably to wait until those connections "are made" (as if they had not been made for years by environmental justice workers), and there is more than a hint that "we" will have to wait for those connections to be made after "a diversity of voices are encouraged to contribute to the discussion." Again, why do "we" have to wait? Why does Glotfelty not feel an urgent need not merely to encourage but actively to seek out those voices for the collection? And why are issues of racial justice not seen as a "white" problem, rather than one that must await diverse voices? A vast body of literature now available on the racialization of "whiteness" is utterly ignored in that formulation. The content of the rest of the volume unfortunately reinforces the problems and gaps in this initial formulation.

Not a single essay in the volume deals seriously with environmental racism. The two essays that seem most clearly chosen to introduce something of the "diversity of voices" Glotfelty mentions are essays by mixed-race American Indian authors Paula Gunn Allen and Leslie Marmon Silko. Both attempt to elucidate aspects of Native American relationships to the natural world, and however admirable each may be on its own terms, in context they seem to play into the myth that Indians of the past were noble, in this case noble keepers of the land, while contemporary Indians remain invisible or useful only as symbols of a degraded present. I hasten to add that this is not an attitude I attribute to Gunn Allen or to Silko, but rather to the discursive context in which I fear they will be set in the absence of serious environmental justice perspectives.

Taking this text as representative, its problems can to a great extent suggest problems in mainstream ecocriticism generally. While the mainstream has surely flowed in some new directions since 1997, the problems embodied in this exemplary anthology are still very much alive. The impact of a new body of work with a stronger social justice emphasis can certainly be seen in some mainstream ecocritical works. Lawrence Buell's *Writing for an Endangered World*, for example, clearly shows the marks of what I am calling environmental justice ecocriticism. But his way of treating that movement is primarily to incorporate it into his own grand design. True transformation would entail a rethinking of all the premises of the field through the lens of social justice, not the mere addition of such concerns. Buell's work, however well intentioned, seems more appropriative of than deeply engaged with questions of social justice.[8]

Two articles that appear back to back in *The Ecocriticism Reader* illustrate the central problem of much ecocriticism, and the beginnings of a way out. The first essay, by Scott Russell Sanders, is entitled "Speaking a Word for Nature."[9] The presumptuousness of the title is matched by the content, which in essence condemns virtually all of contemporary American literature as unnatural, or even antinatural. Sanders cites several examples of this alleged unnaturalness, but one will suffice for present purposes. Sanders writes: "In Don DeLillo's *White Noise*—the most honored novel of 1985—the only time you are reminded that nature exists is when his characters pause on the expressway to watch a sunset, and even the sunset interests them only because a release of toxic gases from a nearby plant has poisoned it into technicolor" (193). For Sanders this points up the utter lack of appreciation for or sense of connection to "nature" in DeLillo's novel. Tellingly, this passage comes soon after Sanders reports that his own attempt to view a lovely sunset in the Great Smoky Mountains has been interrupted by a rumbling camper van that clearly reminds him of the gross insensitivity of city folks to nature. From Sanders's *ecological* ecocritical perspective, DeLillo's "unnatural" novel is a tragedy and a travesty. But if we look at the novel from an environmental justice perspective, we gain quite a different sense of *White Noise.*

Clearly what is at stake here is what counts as "nature" or "the environment." Sunsets apparently count, while toxic gases do not. It would be hard to find a more succinct statement of the problem in much ecocriticism. DeLillo's novel brilliantly shows how the toxic gas cloud aesthetically "improved" the sunset, a biting critique of the limits of an aestheticizing, pastoral form of environmentalism. The problem with Sanders's perspective is not that it is ecological, but that it is not ecological enough. The ecosystem and "nature" seem to end at the edge of the city or the national park or the wilderness. Sanders argues that much contemporary literature is superficial because it does not treat seriously human connectedness to nature. But his own analysis remains equally superficial in that it fails to connect the social realm to the "natural" (defined too narrowly), including what those toxic gases are doing to all of us, but to low-income communities especially. It remains deeply embedded in a Romanticist notion of nature as the nonhuman and the relatively pristine.

Left out are human beings as natural beings and as beings connected to nature not only through appreciation but also through destruction. To privilege the first without dealing seriously with the second is a recipe for continued ecological disaster. The kind of nature appreciation writing Sanders thinks we need more of has been the dominant form at least since the Transcendentalists of the nineteenth century. Despite the great virtues of this tradition, it is not the primary source of modern environmentalism. That source is work like Rachel Carson's, which brought to the world's attention the link between human damage to nature and human damage to humans. The toxic chain she traces is powerful in its evocation of a silenced spring, but the ultimate power and impact of the book come from placing people in that chain.

The next essay in *The Ecocriticism Reader* also discusses *White Noise*, but in a very different way that opens toward my environmental justice interpretation. Cynthia Deitering's "The Postnatural Novel: Toxic Consciousness in Fiction of the 1980s" places *White Noise* in the context of numerous works of the last several decades that have made the traditional "wasteland" literary trope more concrete and specific by pointing to various kinds of real waste—toxics, garbage, landfills, industrial debris—that are so much a part of the contemporary "landscape." Where Sanders saw DeLillo's novel as antinatural, Deitering sees DeLillo as pointing us toward greater awareness of a toxic environment that is leading to ecological and social disaster. This seems to me the beginning of a better understanding of a work like DeLillo's, but an environmental justice ecocritic would push the analysis further in two interrelated ways.[10]

First, Deitering's essay misses the opportunity to raise more directly the nature and causes of the toxic crisis. And second, in doing so, it would be crucially important to see that crisis related in part to the whiteness of the world depicted in *White Noise*. "Noise" in technical jargon is that which distorts communication. And the "white noise" that is the background or subtext of U.S. culture includes a racially coded distortion of environmental reality. The whiteness of the world in DeLillo's novel is one studded with privilege and the capacity to bury consciousness of toxicity along with all other signs of human vulnerability. The novel is in part about flight from death and the search for reality in a wholly simulated environment. The sunset whose observation Sanders mocks is part of an ecosystem of commodified representations parodied most directly in tourists flocking to photograph "the most photographed barn in America." The commodification of this picturesque rural America is merely an extension and condensation of an ideology of the picturesque that has pervaded European and American apprehension of "nature" since the late eighteenth century. And that process of commodification has been inadvertently furthered by the kind of aestheticization found in much ecocriticism. What the environmental justice ecocritic would bring to the fore here is the invasive, pervasive effects of corporate capitalism on this process, and the racial-class dynamic that has permitted that process to continue. Aesthetic appreciation of nature has been a class-coded activity; moreover, the insulation of the middle and upper classes from the most brutal effects of industrialization has played a crucial role in environmental devastation. Aesthetic appreciation of nature has precisely masked the effects of environmental degradation. In the case of this novel, that dynamic can be seen most richly in the way in which the white suburban characters have been so protected by privilege that they literally cannot see the toxic danger in front of them: the "airborne toxic event" is something that happens only to others, to lower-class people in ghettos or inner cities or squalid Third World villages.

Building Environmental Justice Ecocriticism

Let me turn now from my critique of mainstream ecocritcism to a sketch of some directions in which environmental justice ecocriticism is developing. Three main "levels" are currently developing simultaneously: (1) identifying images/stereotypes that link environment, race, and class; (2) uncovering and mapping counter-traditions to white mainstream literary environmentalism; and (3) bringing various kinds of cultural theory to bear to expand our understanding of the myriad connections between racism, colonialism, and the environment.

On level one, the task is to discover and uncover particular relations between representations of race and class and representations of nature. Some of this work is already under way in ecofeminist writings, among other places, and environmental justice ecocritics can learn much from feminist analysis of how gender stereotypes like "Mother Nature" have facilitated environmental degradation.[11] Since the vast majority of environmental justice activists are women, questions of gender should be very much tied to questions of race and class in this field anyway. Such work would range from tracing the history of racist metaphors like "savage wilderness" or "urban jungle" to examining the class and racial cultural biases that disallow the environmental knowledge produced by non-elites, whether women in the projects documenting lead poisoning in their buildings, or tribal elders on reservations observing the effects of uranium tailings on their communities and landscapes.[12] This work will also incorporate a rich body of work on the racist history of biology that analyzes ways in which the racialization of science has played into the racialization of environmental science.[13] It will also examine the cultural assumptions in various environmental rhetorics, both texts and images, that have enabled environmental racism to flourish, and alternative texts and images that have undercut environmental racism.[14]

The second level of new work in the field will further efforts to define other traditions than middle-class white ones in nonfiction nature writing, as well as in works of fiction, poetry, the visual arts, theater, and pop culture that open up environmental justice questions.[15] As Patrick Murphy has pointed out, a preference for nonfiction "nature writing" has limited the range of literary ecocriticism.[16] This limit is especially problematic with regard to writers of color, both in the United States and around the world, who have for the most part been excluded or felt alienated from the Euro-American male-centered tradition of natural history writing and the nature experience essay. The process of recovering earlier work and inventing a tradition of environmental justice literature will parallel similar efforts to recover women's literature, various ethnic literatures, and gay/lesbian literature. It will mean uncovering buried writers and rereading known writers in the light of new questions.

How might an environmental justice ecocritic comment, for example, on these lines from the famous "A Poem about My Rights" by the late June Jordan, African American "womanist" author?

> I am the wrong
> sex the wrong age the wrong skin and
> suppose it was not here in the city but down on the beach
> or far into the woods and I wanted to go
> there by myself thinking about God
> or thinking about children or thinking about the world
> all of it disclosed by the stars and the silence
> I could not go and I could not think and I could not stay there
> alone[17]

Jordan here is asserting, with and against the Thoreau nature writing tradition, a "right" to enter the literal and literary "woods" of America as an equal partner, free from the fear of rape attendant upon her race, her class, her gender. Where, she asks, does the gendered part of her being begin and the racialized part end? Where does her natural body enter into its cultural moment? How does the nature of colonialism reinforce the colonization of nature? How might a privileged enjoyment of wilderness blind the seer to the nature of injustices inflicted on the less privileged? Jordan reminds us throughout the poem that her "natural" body is a colonized site, one colonized *with* and *as a part of* the natural world; that the rape of an African country, an environment, an African American woman's body are all entwined; that each violation of rights shapes the others, reinforcing mutually. Just as surely, she reminds us that only a mutually reinforcing resistance on all these levels will bring liberation to any part.

How might an environmental justice ecocritic look at this quite different, equally influential poem by Adrienne Rich, "Trying to Talk with a Man"?

> Out in this desert we are testing bombs,
> that's why we came here.
>
> Sometimes I feel an underground river
> forcing its way between deformed cliffs
> moving itself like a locus of the sun
> into this condemned scenery....
>
> ... Coming out to this desert
> we meant to change the face of
> driving among dull green succulents
> . . .
> surrounded by a silence
> that sounds like the silence of the place
> except that it came with us
> . . .
> talking of the danger
> as if it were not ourselves
> as if we were testing anything else.[18]

A formalist critic or a psychological critic would approach this setting as metaphor, an externalization of a barren relationship (and that it surely is, in part). Feminist critics have read it as a critique of patriarchal power embedded in verbal reticence. What could ecocritics add? Ecological ecocritics could link lack of respect for the delicate desert ecosystem with the other character flaws suggested in the poem. Eco-feminist critics would extend this to the patriarchal power and arrogance that threatens the world with the bombs being putatively "tested" on this landscape. An environmental justice ecocritic would use these analyses of power, and then point also to what is left out of the poem. Such a critic would work to re-place the indigenous Paiute and Western Shoshone back onto this Nevada Test Site region, for it is they who have suffered most directly the effects that the patriarchal military-corporate-scientific complex have inflicted on this particular landscape. They are present as the absence that calls this place a wasteland. Seeing that this wasteland is inside the "man" of the title allows an opening toward what "he" does not see: the desert and the people who have lived on it for several thousand years.[19]

A research-oriented, second level of analysis would include a long-range study of how nature has been figured in different cultural traditions within the United States. American slaves, for example, saw the "wilderness" not as the Puritans had, as a place of evil, but rather as a place of refuge from captivity, or as a frightening territory that had to be crossed to achieve freedom.[20] More recently, there are those cultural texts that Joni Adamson has called the "literature of environmental justice."[21] Adamson uses the word *literature* with intentional ambiguity, pointing us primarily to a body of poetry and fictional prose directly treating environmental justice issues, but also keeping open the wider meaning of the term as any writing on a subject. A range of U.S. writers, including DeLillo, Ana Castillo, Leslie Marmon Silko, Toni Cade Bambara, Octavia Bulter, Audre Lorde, Linda Hogan, Ursula LeGuin, Barbara Neely, Gerald Vizenor, Alice Walker, Simon Ortiz, Barbara Kingsolver, Joy Harjo, Winona LaDuke, and Karen Yamashita, among many others, offer direct critiques of environmental racism in their poetry and fiction. With regard to the larger meaning of literature, environmental justice ecocritical work could also include reading the nonfiction writing about environmental justice, from movement manifestos to EPA documents, with an eye toward their cultural meanings, contexts, and influence.[22] This work can be of real political usefulness in that the environmental justice movement as currently constituted has often worked with a rather thin sense of culture, and has not utilized cultural workers as much as it might.

In addition to looking for the most direct sources for an environmental justice ecocriticism, theoretical imagination should encourage us to approach texts where the links are not immediately present. To take a less well-known work, Muriel Rukeyser's epic poem of 1938, *The Book of the Dead,* might be read through an environmental justice lens.

A work of terrible beauty, the poem chronicles the worst "industrial accident" in U.S. history, the Gauley Tunnel tragedy of the early 1930s in which hundreds of workers, whites as well as blacks, died. Union Carbide not only forced the workers to mine silica without protective gear and without warning about known health hazards, they actively covered up the hundreds of resulting deaths from acute silica poisoning. Rukeyser parallels the exploited, disposable lives of the workers to the exploitation of the land they labored under. She offers the stark image of dead workers, most of them African American migrants, further blackened by their labors, but whitened by the inhaled "white powder" that has killed them. Her metaphors unite the workers to the earth in their blackness and to the white bosses who sacrificed them via the white silica dust.

In another vein, Mary Wood offers an imaginative reading of immigrant writer Mary Antin's "natural history" of mice in her early twentieth-century tenement as a reflection on gender, ethnicity, racial privilege, and the coding of nature.[23] Wood asks seriously playful questions about what counts as nature and natural history. Why does the idea of studying the habits of urban mice seem funny to us, while observing more "wild" creatures is seen as the utmost in enlightenment? In a similar vein, Giovanna Di Chiro has contrasted the aestheticized mode of "eco-tourism," which in many ways parallels traditional ecocriticism, with the "toxic tourism" organized by some environmental justice groups.[24]

Finally, level three would seek to bring together theoretical tools from political ecology, cultural studies, Marxist theories of the production of nature, racial formation and critical race theory, postcolonial theory, and multiethnic literary theory, among other sites. Bringing materials from these sources will move environmental justice ecocritical analysis in new directions, and help build bridges to other movements linked to these critical approaches. Works by Laura Pulido and Devon Peña, for example, are highly suggestive of ways to bring environmental justice issues together with a theorized "cultural poetics" sensitive to dimensions of race, class, gender, and sexuality.[25] Neo-Marxist work on the "capitalist production of nature" can be vital to understanding the links between political economy and political ecology.[26] Cultural studies approaches to environmental issues are many and varied, and often bring critical questions to bear from postmodern theory.[27] One key facet of this work is a growing body of *urban* ecocriticism that makes the crucial but often ignored point that the natural environment does not end at the edge of cities.[28] Since suburbia, from which a great many wilderness lovers hail, has proven a far more environmentally destructive place than cities, we need also to develop a sense of suburban ecologies and theorize more fully their role in environmental, gender, class, and race politics. There is also a body of work in political ecology that links up national and transnational questions of culture and environmental justice in crucial ways, and could provide the basis for comparative environmental justice ecocritical work sensitive to varied cultural traditions, political economic conditions, and geopolitical contexts.[29] The potential usefulness of postcolonial theory is suggested in David Mazel's essay "American Literary Environmentalism as Domestic Orientalism."[30] Mazel's insights might well be adapted to link environmental colonialism to racialized and gendered colonialism more fully and extensively, thereby joining other work that has pointed out the political dangers of a romanticized, feminized, alienated nature.[31]

Just as a reformulated environmentalism may well prove to be a movement capable of bringing into coalition a wide array of progressive social movements nationally and internationally, environmental justice ecocriticism could do much to overcome what Chicana feminist critic Chela Sandoval has called the "apartheid" of theory that has divided related academic discourses all aimed at supporting vital social and environmental change.[32]

Bringing environmental justice into ecocriticism entails a fundamental rethinking and reworking of the field as a whole, just as environmental justice theory and practice is leading to a fundamental rethinking of the environmental movement. Ecocriticism, like the environmental movement generally, cannot afford to be seen as a domain structured by white privilege, as a place where white people go to play with wilderness, while others are locked into urban "jungles" (as the racist construction of inner cities is often phrased). The alliances between labor and environmentalists at the WTO demonstrations in Seattle in late 1999 made clear beyond a doubt how much more powerful an environmental critique can be when it works with, not against, working people and people of color, at home and around the world.

While I have focused my critique thus far primarily on ecocriticism, I want to touch on two other sides of this dynamic. First, as I mentioned in the beginning of the chapter, the environmental justice movement itself has had little to say about culture and has made too little use of it.

A focus on issues of the law, of environmental science, and of public policy certainly should be at the center of movement concerns. But all those issues are themselves cultural in the sense that they are embedded in and expressive of cultural knowledge and cultural process. The battle to gain respect for ordinary, everyday knowledge as against scientific expertise is a cultural struggle, and those who practice environmental justice ecocriticism have insights to offer that struggle. A better understanding of how cultural hegemony works will be crucial to expanding the legal, scientific, and public policy terrains in ways beneficial to the environmental justice cause. Environmental justice ecocritics can and should bring their work with them into grassroots contexts, putting cultural knowledge to work in more pragmatic ways.

Second is the resounding silence about environmentalism in much ethnic studies and ethnic literary-critical work. Because of the failures of mainstream environmentalism and the limitations of mainstream ecocriticism, scholars of multiethnic literatures have felt comfortable largely ignoring crucial environmental issues, even when the authors they study have raised such issues. Environmental justice is a critical issue in communities of color around the United States and around the world, and race- and ethnicity-centered literary and cultural critics ignore this at their peril. Those who study ethnic literatures and cultures can learn much from ecocriticism about ways to read the environment, and can in turn contribute to this crucial dimension of political, economic, and cultural struggle.

I have tried to show in this chapter how an intellectual formation emerging out of a social movement has evolved alongside that movement. And I have suggested ways to create new forms of intellectual work and new connections among academic fields to further those efforts. The next step is to bring forth more of the vital insights emerging from academic environmental justice ecocriticism to become important components of a new, expanded movement for social justice and environmental health. If the famous "ivory tower" exists, it is not located at my university or any other I have visited. Movements do not stop at the edge of campuses. Indeed, campuses have long been among the key sites of movement formation and growth. Both through their impact on the students they help to form, and through their own direct engagement with movements, academic critics have as much chance as anyone to be on the frontlines.

NINE

Will the Revolution Be Cybercast?

New Media, the Battle of Seattle, and Global Justice

A helmeted police officer kicks a young man in the groin, then shoots him pointblank with a concussion bullet. A mother pours water from a canteen to wash the pepper spray from her teenage daughter's eyes and the blood from the gash on her head. A dozen women and men blockade an intersection by forming a human chain, their arms linked by metal tubes. Hundreds surround the intersection to protect their compatriots from assault by Darth Vader–like police with shields and clubs. Thousands of labor unionists leave behind the leaders of a planned march, turning instead to march to the support of the blockaders. Millions watch on television around the nation and the world, and wonder why the streets of one of America's most beautiful cities are filled with thousands of people protesting something they call "corporate globalization."

Between forty thousand and sixty thousand people, representing some seven hundred organizations worldwide, took part in the "Battle of Seattle" in November 1999. The immediate target was the World Trade Organization as it tried to hold its ministerial meeting in the "Emerald City." But the real targets were many, the grievances manifold, and the alternative vision that of a "democratic globalization" to set against the "corporate globalization" embodied in the WTO. The link between these hundreds of organizations was what they saw as a drastically unbalanced world economy in which the two hundred richest corporations have twice the wealth of the pooled assets of 80 percent of the world's population, and in which fifty of the one hundred wealthiest economies are not nations but corporations.

I will use the "Battle of Seattle" as a way to discuss the transnational movement against corporate globalization in which the protests played a pivotal role. But since the Seattle events cannot encapsulate the whole movement, I will also move backward and forward from that moment in history to trace the trajectory of anti–corporate globalization activities. Seattle's mobilization was not the beginning of this new movement against global inequalities, but for many, especially those in privileged seats in the United States, it was the first taste of how strong and varied were the forces arrayed against the global imbalances of wealth, power, rights, and resources. As the *Washington Post* noted, "The WTO meeting was merely the place where these people burst onto the American public's radar. Social movements around the world had already linked into grass-roots networks, made possible by the astounding speed at which they can communicate in the Internet era."[1] It provides a fitting end to this book because it is at once the culmination of the history of U.S. social movements in the second half of the twentieth century, and a transformation for the twenty-first century. It is a culmination because it bears the marks of all the movements surveyed in this book (among many others), and it is a transformation in that it shows how movements are interlinked both nationally and internationally—deepening a theme stressed throughout this book.

At the risk of engaging in cultural imperialism by giving too much emphasis to the Battle of Seattle, I center my discussion on those events because they represent both a moment of convergence for U.S. movements and a moment in which U.S. movements were decentered in the context of a global struggle. Many analysts see Seattle as the site where various related antiglobalization movements felt themselves becoming a single movement. While not all would agree that the shift was that dramatic, most agree that the actions in Seattle represent a turning point at which the forces arrayed against corporate globalization took on a new level of self-awareness and confidence. In addition to being a successful direct action, it served as a kind of de facto summit meeting of hundreds of groups critical of the impact of the "neoliberal" economic policies they saw devastating the planet and increasing the chasm between the rich and the poor. As I examine this movement turning point, I'll also look at the ways in which Seattle was a turning point with regard to the Internet and other "new media." As with the movement generally, the independent media movement took a great leap forward in Seattle as it took full advantage of the radical new possibilities provided by that cultural site known as "cyberspace."

Globalization and Its Discontents

The citizens of the world assembled in the streets of Seattle were labor unionists and environmentalists, lumber workers and forest activists, students and teachers, farmers and cheese makers, Germans and Ukrainians, Africans and Asians, North Americans and Latin Americans, Johannesburgers and Seattleites, gays and straights, human rights activists and animal rights activists, AIDS activists and antinuclear activists, debt relief advocates and consumer advocates, feminists and womanists, computer hackers and meat packers, children and elders, indigenous people and white urban professionals, Muslims and Jews, Christians and Buddhists, atheists and pantheists, anarchists and advocates of one world government. Some wore business suits, some overalls, some wore sea turtle costumes, some leather and piercings, some wore almost nothing at all. All wore a look of determination that later shifted wildly between joy and terror, confusion and triumph. By the time the tear gas clouds and pepper spray winds had begun to clear in the late afternoon of 30 November 1999, the thousands gathered gradually learned the news that they had accomplished their central goal: they had shut down the convention of one of the world's most powerful organizations.

So how is it that, at a time when many on the left were certain that movements had fragmented into a thousand, unconnected single-issue constituencies, a single action brought together people from hundreds of activist groups not only from all over the United States but from all over the world? What did these people want? And what role did new cultural media like the Internet, laptop computers, and cell phones bring to the task of mobilizing, carrying out, and publicizing this massive, complicated new network of movements stretching around the globe?

To answer these questions, we must first answer another one: what kind of "globalization" were the protesters protesting? Some degree of globalization, in both economic and cultural terms, has existed for at least the last five hundred years (since Europeans set out on their colonial "adventures"). Because of this long history, critics disagree about the extent to which the most recent manifestation of globalization is wholly new, but most agree that over the last twenty-five years or so certain novel features of a transnational political, economic, and cultural system have emerged.[2] Particularly when viewed in combination, these new features represent a significant change in global power relations. The key elements of globalization include the increased role played by transnational organizations like the World Bank, the International Monetary Fund (IMF), and the WTO; a weakened role for national governments and an increase in the power of multi- or transnational corporate power; new economic practices that greatly intensify the segmenting of the labor force by distributing various parts of the production process around the globe rather than centralizing it in one nation; and new global communications networks. These various processes are then rationalized through a new version of free market political-economic ideology known as "neoliberalism."

Critics of globalization argue that these interlocking institutions and practices have intensified environmental degradation, undermined worker rights and civil rights, exacerbated a worldwide health crisis, and facilitated cultural domination by the corporate media of the United States. They argue that transnational corporations, located primarily in the seven most developed nations (the United States, Canada, France, Germany, Japan, Italy, and Britain), have used organizations like the WTO and IMF to undermine democratic citizenship in order to serve their profit interests. By acting transnationally or globally, these corporations have been able to circumvent basic human rights once guaranteed by national governments, and sink standards of worker and environmental protection to the lowest level available—a "race to the bottom."

The main mechanism through which a neoliberal corporate order has been imposed on the developing world has been *structural adjustment programs* (SAPs). In structural adjustment, a developing nation's government is obligated to transform its economy to better serve First World corporations if it wants to receive loans from the World Bank or IMF, or avoid trade sanctions from the WTO. Corporate globalizers call this a necessary transition. Critics call it multinational blackmail. This process of imposed structural adjustment has included devaluing national currencies, turning government-run industries over to private corporations, lowering environmental standards, limiting or eliminating workers' right to unionize or strike for better conditions, and cutting social services, such as child care, public education, health care, or unemployment insurance. Critics argue that while the worst impact of these processes has been vastly increased poverty in the Third World or the Southern Hemisphere, globalization has also rebounded back on the industrialized Northern Hemisphere, hurting workers and virtually all other citizens who are not corporate executives. The collusion of the Democrats with Republican attacks on so-called "big government" in the United States, for example, has meant an attack on basic environmental and human rights in the name of unrestrained corporate profits that should instead be balanced against other social goods.

Most observers see the process of corporate globalization as intensifying greatly after the fall of the Soviet Union and its satellites in 1989. Critics argue that the collapse of communism brought with it the collapse of the welfare state in the developed world and virtually all other ameliorating social mechanisms in the rest of the world. The presence of an alternative economic system, however deeply problematic it was, forced the capitalist world to provide services, basic rights, and a social safety net that have now been removed. In the developing world, various nationalist and socialist efforts to lessen the impact of unrestrained markets were eliminated through structural adjustment. In the over-developed world, similar benefits were eliminated through the deregulation of industry and the shrinking of government services. According to neoliberal theory, "freer markets" should increase market power and eventually raise everyone's level of income. According to critics of corporate globalization, what has happened instead is a "global race to the bottom," in which countries competing for the most exploitable, least expensive labor force have progressively degraded the environment, undercut local self-sufficiency, lowered the quality of life for most workers, and left more than 1 billion people without any work at all.

The mainstream press describes this movement as "antiglobalization," but relatively few activists express wholesale opposition to globalization. The activists are more likely to say that they oppose "corporate globalization" and advocate "critical globalization," "democratic globalization," or "globalization from below." Each of these modifiers suggests key elements of the critique: that current forms of globalization are "uncritically" procorporate, that they are "undemocratic" in their lack of representative institutions, and that they are imposed hierarchically from "above" rather than being decided with citizen participation from "below." Most of the activists say they are not against the global economy, but against the damage to people and the environment done by this particular version of globalization, a version embodied in the current rules set down by the WTO and other representatives of transnational corporate capitalism. The protesters believe there is another way to do it, or rather many other ways to do it, based on the principle that the millions of people currently excluded from decisions that dramatically affect their lives should have a say in what a global network of economies, governments, and cultures should look like. They argue that without economic democracy, political democracy, where it exists, is severely undermined. And they argue that far from bringing democracy with it, as promised, "free trade" has more often undermined democracy in the developing world as governments use increasingly repressive measures to manage the social disruption caused by structural adjustment.

Globalize Liberation, Not Corporate Power

The movement or movements attacking corporate globalization consist of hundreds of groups targeting a host of specific issues and/or the larger system. Students of the movement(s) generally sort out the overarching positions into three major ones. First are those who seek to reform globalization and its key institutions like the WTO, IMF, and World Bank. Second are those who call for more radically democratic alternative forms of grassroots globalization ("globalization from below").[3] Third are those who call for an end to globalization through one or another process of transition toward smaller scale, semi-autonomous political economic units.[4] Partly it is a question of which level of governance one trusts most: "Some emphasize the need for a global system that provides minimum rights and standards and new forms of global economic regulation. Others emphasize the need to restore the power of the nation state to control national economics. Still others portray localization—the economic empowerment of local communities—as the true alternative to globalization."[5] Given this range of positions and the host of differing groups under these rubrics, the issue of whether these efforts can be characterized as a single movement, or should more properly be considered a set of movements, is open to question. But most participants and observers, especially after the events in Seattle, speak of a single movement with many elements. Indeed, not since the 1960s have so many social movements been able to rally around a common set of concerns.

The complexity of the movement also means that it has many origins (and as many origin stories). As Naomi Klein quipped, "The movement began 500 years ago, or on November 30, 1999, depending on who you ask."[6] Most would say that its origins lie in a slow process of linking movement groups and nongovernmental organizations into coalitions. This array of movements and social forces had been combining or "networking" in a variety of ways for at least a decade or so before coming together in an even larger coalition in Seattle. Important large-scale, international grassroots movement activities that set precedents for the Seattle action include the following:

- The environmentally focused but multi-issue Earth Summit in Rio in 1992
- The broad coalition fighting in the early 1990s against the North American Free Trade Agreement (NAFTA)
- The "Fifty Years Is Enough" protests at the World Bank's anniversary meeting in 1994
- The International Women's Conference in Beijing in 1995
- The international support for the Zapatista struggles in Chiapas, Mexico, and the *encuentro* convocations the indigenous activists hosted in 1996 and 1997
- The 1998 campaign of environmentalists and consumer advocates that helped sink the Multilateral Agreement on Investment (MAI), a draft treaty that sought to loosen controls on international finance
- The global debt relief campaign coordinated by Jubilee 2000 that during the last half of the 1990s played a major role in bringing about a significant reduction of debt claims against Third World nations

Other international organizing efforts in the 1990s that were important in building elements of the network include the global antisweatshops movement, with its U.S. base on college campuses, and the successful campaign to ban the use of land mines. Earlier groundwork had been laid in the 1980s by the international movement against nuclear weapons, and by the transnational solidarity movements against South African apartheid and U.S. policy in Latin America. The significant presence in the Battle of Seattle of CISPES (Committee in Solidarity with the People of El Salvador) exemplifies the ways in which this earlier movement history folds into the anti–corporate globalization movement. El Salvador, having been made safe for exploitation by U.S. policy, now has 225 "free-trade-zone factories" set up like prisons with cinderblock walls topped by razor wire, armed guards, and locked metal gates. The textile factories employ about seventy thousand young women who are fired if seen congregating in groups, must ask permission for their two allowed bathroom breaks a day, and are dismissed if found pregnant after one of the periodic pregnancy tests they are forced to endure.[7]

The various constituencies (human rights, environmental, farmers, workers, feminists, debt relief advocates, and many others) were organized into two main components: nongovernmental organizations (NGOs) and direct action–oriented movement groups. The term *nongovernmental organization* was created by the United Nations to describe all those groups working outside of official government institutions to effect social change. Many, but not all, NGOs are registered as such with the U.N. But the name encompasses a wide variety of groups, both ideologically and in terms of focus, from environment to human rights to women to health advocacy and so on. Some NGOs are more service-oriented, others lobby to affect policy, and still others are virtually indistinguishable from direct action social movement groups. Direct actionists tend to see NGOs as more moderate and formal, if not bureaucratic, and NGOs tend to see direct actionists as disorganized and overly confrontational. Still, the borders between the two types of organizing are often porous. The Direct Action Network (DAN) that coordinated the blockade dimension of the Seattle activities, for example, was sponsored by groups that fell into both of these categories.

In the general flow of the movement against corporate capitalist globalization, many NGOs form a mediating space between formal governments and the disruptive power of direct actionists. In an overall strategy, the two sectors often benefit each other, with NGOs proposing much needed temporary reforms while the direct actionists push for deeper transformations. But this mutual benefit is not often felt or acknowledged by partisans of the respective modes of political activity.

The Battle(s) of Seattle

Both NGOs and the direct actionists came to Seattle already organized into various larger networks. Friends of the Earth International, Public Citizen, Jubilee 2000, and Fifty Years Is Enough, for example, provided very important umbrella structures for a wide variety of NGOs focused on trade, Third World debt, the environment, human rights, women's issues, and many other concerns. The Peoples Global Action (PGA) played a similar role for direct action–oriented groups from around the world. And many similar, sometimes overlapping, coalitional formations existed for both types of organization. In addition, coalitions organized around issue areas—agriculture, indigenous rights, women—often cut across the direct action/NGO distinction. The weeklong events in Seattle in late November and early December 1999 brought all these forces into a new array. In a sense, the real Battle of Seattle was fought by hundreds of activists logging thousands of hours of organizing time in the weeks and months leading up to the WTO confrontation. That all these diverse elements came together to share ideas and feel their collective strength was already a triumph before the actions began. At the risk of splitting apart a simultaneous, interacting set of activities, I will present the "battle" in three acts: education, culture, and blockading. To note the simultaneity, I have blended the acts in some parts.

Act One: The Anticorporate University

Seattle's "festival of resistance" began officially on Saturday, 27 November, marked by prayers, meditation, and education (sides of the action not much covered by the "corporate" media).[8] Teach-ins on dozens of aspects of globalization and social justice, sponsored by groups like the International Forum on Globalization, Global Exchange, Indigenous Environmental Network, and Public Citizen, took place at venues throughout Seattle beginning on Saturday and continuing all week long. Local Seattle activists had created an interest in globalization issues in the city through a series of lectures, debates, workshops, and public forums in the weeks and months preceding the WTO conference. This local interest, added to that of thousands of protesters, made every event virtually a sold-out, standing-room-only affair. In contrast to *New York Times* critic Thomas Friedman's characterization of the protesters as know-nothing "flat earthers," these were well-informed people hungry for further knowledge.

Many of the most prominent intellectuals of the movement against corporate globalization, including Vandana Shiva, Noam Chomsky, Lori Wallach, Ralph Nader, Medea Benjamin, Jose Bové, Naomi Klein, and Walden Bello, were on hand. These people and others play an important role in translating immensely complicated academic discourses on global economics, trade issues, international law, and so on into terms more useful to the movement. Each day of the week was dedicated to a theme that linked at least two issue areas—for example, "Food and Agriculture Day" and "Environment and Health Day." While education was emphasized, various cultural events—concerts, street dances, theater—

and some preliminary direct actions were woven into the more academic presentations. There were talks on "Alternatives to Corporate Globalization"; "The Human Face of Trade"; "The Need to Advance the People's Resistance against Imperialist Globalization"; "Genetically Modified Organisms"; "Trading Away Public Health"; "Forests, Fisheries, Toxics"; "Global Trade Unionism"; "Trade Related Intellectual Property Rights"; and dozens of other dimensions of corporate domination of world trade.

The following issue areas represent many of the key constituencies brought into dialogue in Seattle.

Debt Elimination/Economic Development Groups

IMF, World Bank, and WTO policies have led most countries in the Third World or the Southern Hemisphere into a vicious cycle of debt. The promised economic development has not come (except for transnational corporations with headquarters in the First World/Northern Hemisphere), and the gap between rich and poor has grown, as revealed by the World Bank's own statistics. One former World Bank economist notes that despite "repeated promises of poverty reduction ... the actual number of people living in poverty ... increased by almost 100 million" during the 1990s.[9] Hundreds of NGOs and movements in the Third World have fought against the "austerity" imposed by international debt and structural adjustment programs. In addition to national and local resistance groups, several large coalitions were formed, such as Jubilee 2000, with its network of Third and First World peoples of color calling for the canceling of debt in developing countries. Between its founding in 1995 and its refocusing in its target year 2000, the Jubilee campaign (named to parallel the "abolition of debt" to the jubilee that came with the abolition of slavery in the United States) gathered more than 24 million signatures worldwide, and successfully reduced debt in many countries, though falling far short of its goal of total debt elimination. The other side of this process, the development of alternative "fair trade" economic structures, was represented in Seattle by NGOs like Global Exchange and Third World Network.

In the United States Jubilee is led by faith-based groups, particularly African American ones. It was founded very much in the spirit of the civil rights movement, and drew upon the legacy of spiritual power and practical organizing of many civil rights movement veterans. Jubilee led the prayer vigil on Sunday, and on Monday the group held an afternoon rally featuring SNCC Freedom Singers veteran Bernice Johnson Reagon and her a capella ensemble Sweet Honey in the Rock. This was followed by Jubilee's own kind of blockade. The group's supporters, at least five thousand strong, formed a human chain around the Seattle Expo center where WTO delegates were attending a champagne gala with executives from Boeing and Microsoft, Seattle's financial infrastructure. Engaging in a type of action they had performed in other locations around the world, they encircled the delegates in a call "to break the circle of debt."

Farmers

One effect of "freer markets" has been the further penetration of First World agribusiness into the developing world, and into remaining pockets of family farming in the developed world. Small-scale farmers throughout the world have fought these efforts, arguing on behalf of the public's interest in better, safer, and more varied food; food produced with fewer dangerous chemicals; and stores free of genetically engineered "Frankenfoods." Some small-scale farmers, including many indigenous people, have a long history of harvesting medicinal herbs and plants that are now being "discovered' and patented by pharmaceutical companies through a process some have called "biopiracy."[10] French cheese maker Jose Bové, famous for his verbal and physical assaults on McDonald's restaurants in his home country, led a similar protest in Seattle. In an act of civil disobedience, he handed out chunks of smuggled Roquefort in front of the McDonald's at Third and Pine, and talked to assembled crowds about WTO rules that protected fast food chains and devastated local producers. Some jostling by reporters led to a broken window on a side door to the restaurant, but the sometimes tense demonstration was kept from exploding by humor and some good-natured local police.

Indigenous People

Corporate globalization has had a devastating impact on the Fourth World of native peoples. To many, WTO's agreements are just one more set in a long line of "betrayals by treaty." Shaky indigenous sovereignty is being threatened, from the rain forests of Brazil to the deserts of the American Southwest wherever "Indians" stand in the way of the profits of pharmaceutical companies, logging operations, or mining conglomerates. Not only native herbs and plants are being "pharmed," but also the very DNA in native bodies is being "harvested," often without knowledge or consent, through blood extraction. Any unusual DNA components found are being catalogued and patented for potential medical profit. At the time of the protests in Seattle, a WTO "free logging" agreement threatening millions of acres of forest on sacred indigenous lands in the United States and Latin America was under consideration by the corporate globalizers. There was an Indigenous Forum attended by native elders and native activists from all over the country and the world that, among other things, used this key issue to strengthen links between native activists and environmentalists.

Environmentalists

Because environmental problems know no national borders, environmentalists have long held global perspectives. Those perspectives have been deepened as global institutions like the WTO weaken or eliminate already inadequate environmental laws in the name of freeing up trade. This process is also taking the form of turning the environment into a product to be bought and sold, not only through biopiracy but also through such actions as selling the water supply of Third World nations to First World corporations, an act resisted fiercely and stopped by indigenous activists when attempted in the Cochabamba region of Bolivia.[11] More generally, environmentalists believe that imposing the industrialization process of the First World on the Third World is far from the best or only route to development. Many argue that more environmentally sound, locally self-sufficient development will mutually benefit people and the environment. Radical environmental groups like Rainforest Action Network, EarthFirst! and Greenpeace contributed tactical innovations to the movement in Seattle, especially by scaling tall buildings and other structures to hang anti-WTO banners with messages like "Globalize Liberation, Not Corporate Power."

Human Rights

Human rights advocates, both locally and internationally, played a key role in the coalition because they see the link between structural adjustment and repressive regimes. Nations have to be "made safe" for investment, and this has often meant regimes violently repressing existing resistance movements, even as new ones spring up in opposition to the "austerity measures" accompanying investment. Global human rights advocates argue that trade rights have too often replaced the civil rights of workers and dissidents. Groups like Amnesty International, which has more than 1 million members worldwide, have fought diligently to counter the neoliberal trend toward loosening human rights guarantees. The impact of neoliberalism in the United States also includes the human rights abuses embodied in the "prison-industrial complex," the vast growth of prisons, many now privately run for profit, filled disproportionately by men and women of color. Many antiglobalization activists view these inmates as political prisoners in the war against corporate greed, driven to desperation by a devastated welfare system, increasing unemployment, and capital flight from the cities to white suburbs.

Public Health and Consumer Advocates

Austerity measures imposed by neoliberal debt policies have severely limited often already very sparse public health funding. In places like Africa, where 70 percent of the world's 40 million people with HIV/AIDS reside, this has often meant a death sentence for the poorest elements of the population. Thus, many international public health workers align themselves with the movement. Advocates for the rights of consumers have also been active in the movement because they see decisions made by the WTO and other organizations as lowering the quality and safety of food and other products by gutting national standards and safeguards. Consumer advocates have also joined with labor in raising issues about the production process, fighting WTO rules that make it virtually impossible to block import of a product based on its production by exploited or child labor. In Seattle, U.S.–based advocacy networks like Public Citizen played a key role, as did international public health groups like Doctors without Borders and ACT UP.

Women's Rights

Women's movements were increasingly globalized throughout the 1970s, 1980s, and 1990s. One measure of this growth is the ever increasing size of the women's world congresses: 6,000 women in Mexico City in 1975, 14,000 in Nairobi in 1985, and 30,000 in Beijing in 1995. The scope of the Beijing conference of 1995 demonstrated that sisterhood had not only been made "global" itself, but had expanded to address a host of issues on the broad agenda of anticorporate globalization efforts. In the years leading up to Beijing, for example, women's groups met under U.N. sponsorship to address links between environment and development (Brazil, 1992), human rights (Vienna, 1993), reproductive rights and population (Cairo, 1994), and social development (Copenhagen, 1995). All these issues and many more were on the agenda at Beijing and in the dozens of global feminist networks represented there. Structural adjustment policies affecting the environment have often been felt first by women, leading to the growth of numerous feminist environmental efforts; the search for ever cheaper and more malleable labor forces has played a role in the "feminization of the labor force"; SAPs have strengthened an existing trend toward the "feminization of poverty" as joblessness and underemployment break up increasing numbers of family households; and this poverty, combined with the lowering of human rights standards, has increased such insidious practices as the transnational "traffic in women" (women sold or traded into prostitution or into slavelike domestic relationships).[12] An International Women Workers Forum in Seattle drove home these issues, and specifically linked women's groups and the labor movement.

Labor

Workers and labor unions form a very significant force in the anticorporate movement. There were more general strikes around the world in the second half of the 1990s than at any time during the twentieth century, including during the world depression of the 1930s.[13] This newly militant international labor movement has also inspired many in the United States. A steady decline of union membership and the power of workers over the last several decades due to weak leadership and complacency has begun to be reversed. Longstanding attempts to play off workers against environmentalists, and to blame the loss of "American jobs" on low-wage Third World workers, are being challenged. An alliance of environmentalists and steelworkers pioneered by activist Judi Bari in the redwood country of California proved the wedge needed to open a dialogue between these once antagonistic forces. The coming together of labor and environmentalists in Seattle symbolized a new generation unwilling to make a devil's bargain between jobs, on the one hand, and clean air, safe water, and a livable environment, on the other. In the aftermath of Seattle, the AFL-CIO Executive Council passed a new resolution emphasizing rights of workers in the developing world, the need for debt relief, and reform of WTO policies detrimental to development.[14]

Students

Students have been a key component of protest movements for many, many generations, and so it is with the movement against corporate globalization. Students are a special force because they have the time to reflect and do research, are less socialized into complacency, and have less to lose in terms of family income. The most visible student activists are those associated with United Students against Sweatshops (USAS). USAS has branches on the campuses of more than one hundred fifty U.S. colleges and universities. Like most elements of this new movement, students combine close attention to the local with a global perspective. This branch of the wider antisweatshop movement began when students investigated the production process behind the t-shirts and other clothing created for their schools. Most found that built into the slick Yale Bulldog or Penn State Lion logo was the exploited labor of a Third World worker. They discovered that that might be true even if the label said "Made in the U.S.A," since many textile manufacturers set up shop in places like Saipan, an American "protectorate" in the Pacific that is technically U.S. soil but where wages are low and labor conditions are horrendous. Increased numbers of sweatshops on the mainland in cities like Los Angeles, San Diego, and New York offer another indication of how some shots taken at the Third World ricochet to hit the First.

The Center for Campus Organizing, an umbrella group for students fighting on a variety of fronts including unionization of student workers (teaching and research assistants), suggests how the antisweatshop movement has expanded outward. In Seattle students became the most dynamic force for the blockades and for the cultural actions entwined with them.

Act Two: The No Logo Costume Ball and Carnival against Capital

The festive turtle action came from a different sector of the movement but was in keeping with the spirit of cultural resistance that was a key part of the Direct Action Network's strategy. Protest art groups like Art and Revolution had been at the center of the organizing from the beginning. David Solnit, one of the group's founders and also a co-founder of

Direct Action Network, had long insisted "that art shouldn't just be an ornament, but rather an integral part of the movement. Everything is theatrical. Traditional protest—the march, the rally, the chants—is just bad theater."[15] Festive trainings for the action run by Art and Revolution included not only civil disobedience tactics, but also hands-on work in puppetry and street theater. The "DAN Handbook for N30," the key organizing document for the blockade, reflects this cultural emphasis:

> In this ever shrinking world where corporations are attempting to homogenize us into passive, unquestioning consumers, our culture is our greatest weapon of resistance. Traditional demonstrations and protests, while essential, oftentimes alienate the general public, are disregarded by corporate media, bore many of the participants, and are ignored by policy makers. Taking to the streets with giant puppet theater, dance, graffiti art, music, poetry and the spontaneous eruption of joy breaks through the numbing isolation. . . . We must strive to use all our skills in harmony to create an enduring symphony of resistance. The cacophony against capital will be deafening when nine days of large-scale street theater preparations culminate in the largest festival of resistance the world has ever seen. We will make revolution irresistible.

The cultural resistance began several days before the main blockade and continued throughout the "battle" despite, as we will see, rather critical reviews from certain helmeted representatives of the Seattle government. The streets were filled not only with the ubiquitous sea turtles but dancing Santas, jugglers, stilt-walkers, fire-eaters, clowns, drag queens and kings, wood nymphs, Statues of Liberty with "Stop the WTO" pins, thirty-foot-tall puppets, and self-described "radikal cheerleaders" chanting jingles like "Ho, Ho, Ho, the WTO's got to Go!" Youth predominated, but the Raging Grannnies and others of more mature years were on the streets as well.

Many costumes parodied the military-corporate culture the street festival was offering itself as an alternative to: General Warren D. Struction, under the banner "Incredible Feats of Stupidity," dramatized that "free trade" includes selling U.S.–made weapons to every repressive regime in the world; a giant tennis shoe handed out flyers about the joys of sweatshops; a red devil with a chainsaw looked around for trees to clearcut. Some particularly adventurous protesters also scaled the city's skyscrapers to attach huge banners covered in pointedly humorous attacks on globalization. One of the most memorable consisted of

WTO = Death. Courtesy of Linda Wolf.

two huge arrows hanging atop a 170-foot-tall construction crane: one arrow said "Democracy," the other, WTO, and they pointed in opposite directions.

The cultural resistance actions built upon a growing tradition of "festive resistance" on the left, much of it connected to the reclamation of public space. One key part of this movement has been the network called Reclaim the Streets (RTS). Begun in the United Kingdom, Reclaim the Streets groups have spread their style of political-cultural action in the

WTO protesters on high. Scene from *This Is What Democracy Looks Like.*

streets around the world. As one activist notes, "By the time of Seattle, RTS-style protest had taken hold of the activist imagination."[16]

Andrew Boyd remembers that there "was one sublime moment in Seattle when [I] realized that the wild yet focused energies in the streets could never be resolved into a folk song—we were now part of Hip-Hop nation. The rhythms of the chants were rougher, more percussive. The energy was fierce and playful."[17] A range of youthful (and not so youthful) subcultures, including ravers, grungers, post-punks, rastas, neo-hippies, and hip-hoppers, partied together against the consumer culture that is consuming the globe. Whether they identified with any of these subcultures or not, young people especially brought a new power to the actions. Inspired by books like movement activist Naomi Klein's *No Logo: Money, Marketing, and the Growing Anti-Corporate*

Movement, young people were fed up with their bodies being turned into billboards for exploitative clothing lines, their jobs subject to McDomination, their culture Disneyfied, their schools "branded" and sold out to corporations like Channel One.[18] And they were fed up with their own unintended complicity in the ways all these phenomena form part of America's "CocaColonization" of the rest of the world. As one participant from Boston put it, "We were in Seattle for the world and for justice. But we were also there for ourselves, to create a new culture."[19]

Act Three: Marches, Blockades, and the Action Factions

Monday, 29 November, designated as Environment and Human Health Day, brought further education through teach-ins, lectures, workshops, and open forums. It also saw the first march of the infamous sea turtle brigade. The march got under way at noon, led by Ben White of Earth Island Institute alongside Steelworker Don Kegley, followed by hundreds of children, youths, adults, and elders in costumes representing one of the hundreds of creatures threatened with extinction by WTO policies. Thirty-five hundred people—university students, union activists, and street theater players—joined them in the streets. Traffic came to a stop with turtles dancing in the streets. Drawing upon the gentle energy of "turtle power" invoked by organizer White, the action was a peaceful one with everyone, apparently even the police, enjoying the events.[20]

All these educational and cultural events and smaller marches were a vital part of the action, but what most people think of as the Battle of Seattle began on Tuesday morning, 30 November. Two main events were planned for that day, an AFL-CIO–sponsored, labor-centered rally and march scheduled to begin at 10 a.m., and the direct action blockade of the delegates organized by the Direct Action Network. In solidarity with the labor march and the protests, the longshoremen's union had closed down virtually every port on the West Coast for the day, one of the largest shutdown actions in decades. The original plan for the labor march called for participants to join the blockaders after the rally, but a last-minute deal worked out with the Clinton administration, purportedly giving labor a "seat at the table" for future global trade discussions, split the labor march off from the planned direct action. The rally in Seattle's Memorial Stadium, featuring speeches by leaders from a host of local, national, and international labor unions, drew between thirty-five thousand and fifty thousand participants and went off with only

Turtle Power! Courtesy of Linda Wolf.

minor hitches. The event, especially in association with the wider array of issues represented in Seattle, was viewed by many as an important moment of revitalization for a beleaguered and complacent labor movement that had once been the core element of U.S. progressive politics.

The Direct Action Network, coordinator of the WTO blockade, was a coalition formed in the months leading up to "N30" (as activist shorthand designated this protest). DAN was sponsored by a range of environmental, student, labor, debt relief, solidarity, and animal rights groups:

Global Exchange
Rainforest Action Network
Project Underground
Ruckus Society
Mexico Solidarity Network
Fifty Years Is Enough

Institute for Social Ecology
Adbusters
National Lawyers Guild
War Resisters League
Earth First! (Seattle)
Industrial Workers of the World (IWW)
Green Party of Seattle
Animal Welfare Institute
Center for Campus Organizing

People's Global Action, the largest international network of grassroots activists, and steelworkers joining environmentalists in the recently formed Alliance for Sustainable Jobs and the Environment, also endorsed the action.

The central features of the DAN blockade were developed and openly publicized months in advance. Everyone in the world seemed to know what to expect, except, apparently, the Seattle police department. The plan was to shut down the WTO meeting by nonviolently preventing access to delegates by blockading key streets and intersections around the Convention Center. The organizers believed they had agreement with police on two key elements: that the blockaders would be arrested without violence, and that medical personnel and legal observers would not be arrested at all. On both counts police actions proved otherwise.

The handbook DAN produced for the action announced the vision of the action: "Thousands of people theatrically processing through Seattle with giant images and puppets graphically showing the economic and ecological devastation left in the wake of global capital. Mass nonviolent direct action and blockades shutting down roads and arteries leading to the ministerial of the WTO. Simple theater skits for people on the streets breaking down corporate globalization and showing glimpses of the world as it could be—global liberation. Reclaiming the streets with celebration: Mardi Gras style marching band, street parties, West African dance, sounds of topical spoken word and hip hop."[21]

The structure of the blockade of the streets of downtown Seattle followed the network model of the movement overall. It is no accident that the main coordinating group called itself the Direct Action Network. The actions were built around a web of affinity groups of between eight and twenty people who chose their own mode and site of action within an overall plan agreed to by the consensus (unanimous agreement) of representatives from each of the affinity groups. The essence of the plan was to form a wall of humanity between the Convention Center hotel where most of the WTO delegates were staying and the Paramount Theater a few blocks away, where the opening session of the WTO ministerial was scheduled to be held.

Participant Paul Hawken notes that while the Direct Action Network hoped that fifteen hundred people would show up, close to ten thousand did. Thousands more eventually joined the two thousand people who began the march to the Convention Center at 7 a.m. from Victor Steinbrueck Park and Seattle Central Community College. The protesters "were composed of affinity groups and clusters whose responsibility was to block key intersections and entrances. Participants had trained for many weeks in some cases, for many hours in others. Each affinity group had its own mission and was self-organized. The streets around the Convention Center were divided into 13 sections and individual groups and clusters were responsible for holding these sections. There were also 'flying groups' that moved from section to section, backing up groups under attack as needed. The groups were further divided into those willing to be arrested and those who were not."[22]

Near Seattle Community College, the Denny Street warehouse became the assembly ground or "staging area" for much of the direct action protest, especially for the substantial contingent of youths. As one observer notes, "The Denny Street warehouse was far more than a meeting place; it was part factory, part barracks, part command and control center, part mosh pit. Later on it would become an infirmary."[23] The blockaders included priests, rabbis, monks, ministers, steelworkers, lawyers, doctors, and professors, but the majority were students and other youth. The ranks of those intentionally risking arrest were especially heavy with youthful protesters. In addition to drums, a boombox soundtrack was provided by the likes of British post-punk band Chumbawumba, the metal-rap group Rage against the Machine, and such local Seattle groups as the Farts to account for that "mosh pit" atmosphere in the Denny warehouse. Hip-hop, punk, and rave music scenes are increasingly being drawn into the movement, and Seattle was no exception.

On Tuesday morning, 30 November, the street actionists were up early, before the police. Most report that the atmosphere was tense but still festive as the day began with a march. As left journalist Alexander Cockburn reports, "Steelworkers and EarthFirst!ers led the way, carrying a banner with the image of a redwood tree and a spotted owl. The march featured giant puppets, hundreds of signs, the ubiquitous sea turtles, singing, chanting, drumming and nervous laughter. There was an atmosphere of carnival to the gathering. New Orleans during Mardi Gras. Juarez on the Day of the Dead. A carnival with an ominous edge."[24]

Cockburn found himself next to a group of black men and women trailing behind the Rap Wagon, a white van with a powerful sound system blasting a "nasty improvised rap called 'TKO the WTO.'" The atmosphere of carnival was dampened but not dissipated by mid-morning when brutal police assaults on the nonviolent blockaders began. Around 10 a.m., Cockburn and a friend found themselves at one of the key intersections, Sixth and Union.

> A band of about 200 protesters had occupied the intersection and refused to move after the police gave an order to disperse. About ten minutes later, [a black armored personnel carrier, misnamed Peacekeeper] arrived. Tear gas canisters were unloaded and then five or six of them were fired into the crowd. One of the protesters nearest the cops was a young, petite woman. She rose up, obviously disoriented from the gas, and a Seattle policeman, crouched less than 10 feet away, shot her in the knee with a rubber bullet. She fell to the pavement, grabbing her leg and screaming in pain. Then, moments later, one of her comrades, maddened by the unprovoked attack, charged the police line, Kamikaze-style. Two cops beat him to the ground with their batons, hitting him at least 20 times. As the cops flailed away with their four-foot-long clubs, the crowd chanted, "the whole world is watching, the whole world is watching." Soon the man started to rise and he was immediately shot in the back by a cop who was standing over him, cuffed and hauled away.[25]

Cockburn adds that "the so-called rubber bullets are meant to be fired at areas of the body with large muscle mass. Like the thighs and ass. But over the next two days Seattle cops would fire off thousands of rounds without exhibiting any caution. Dozens of people, none of them threatening the cops with harm, were shot in the back, in the neck, in the groin, in the face, in places that the ammunition's manufacturers, ever conscious of liability questions, warn could cause severe trauma or death."[26] To their credit, the Seattle fire department did not join in this melee by refusing an order to use fire hoses on the protesters.

Instead of attempts at arrest that the protesters had been led to expect, the pattern of police assaults was repeated again and again throughout the day and into the night. But using a variety of techniques, sometimes

retreating, then reappearing, affinity groups successfully held all intersections and key areas downtown. When they were gassed, sprayed, shot,
clubbed, or pushed back, a new affinity group would quickly replace them.

Not all encounters with the forces of global law and order entailed
violence. A group of students from Portland's Lewis and Clark College
worked the intersection of Fourth and Olive, on the periphery of the
blockade, and though threatened by police and occasionally stung by
drifting tear gas, they were not directly assaulted or arrested. Mid-
morning, however, they were asked by coordinators to move to Fourth
and Pine. Amid the noise of traffic and street celebrations, the affinity
group held a twenty-minute meeting in the middle of the street before
agreeing to relocate. When they arrived and settled into the new intersection, the police presence was much more dramatic. Soon a tractor
with a huge scoop in front appeared and headed toward the affinity
group. As one of the students, Sarah Joy Staude, recalls it: "We got all of
our supporters in line in front of it. The driver claimed he was lost." Their
protective strategy apparently worked, and police were soon diverted to
other hot spots in the action.[27]

The central focus of the blockade was the Paramount Theater, the
site chosen for opening ceremonies of the ministerial. As Hawken reports,
"Police had ringed the theater with Metro buses touching bumper to
bumper. The protesters surrounded the outside of that steel circle. Only
a few hundred of the 5,000 delegates made it inside, as police were unable
to provide safe corridors for members and ambassadors. The theater
was virtually empty when U.S. trade representative and meeting co-chair
Charlene Barshevsky was to have delivered the opening keynote."[28] WTO
head Michael Moore, and then President Clinton's representative, Secretary of State Madeleine Albright, both locked in their rooms unable to
leave, were said to be apoplectic in the face of the blockade's success.

The level of violence directed against the nonviolent protesters grew
throughout the day. When a small splinter group, the Black Bloc, broke
some windows in the downtown shopping center, strategically targeting
stores with direct connections to the worst excesses of globalization,
the violence against protesters finally had a cover story, but not a very
convincing one. About the best one can say on behalf of the forces
defending the WTO against democratic citizens is that they had been
lied to by their superiors, taught to believe the protesters were terrorists,
capable of unleashing chemical warfare or worse.[29]

In point of fact, all the chemical warfare came from the side of the forces of "law and order," in the form of tear gas and the most excruciatingly painful pepper spray ever used against nonviolent protesters. The pepper spray used in the action, MK-46, is manufactured by Def-Tech technologies. As Cockburn notes, the corporation cautions that it should only be used defensively and should not be sprayed at range closer than three feet. Throughout the action the spray was used offensively and shot right in the faces of protesters.[30] Hawken describes the effect such abuse of the spray had on one protester: "When I was able to open my eyes, I saw lying next to me a young man, 19, maybe 20 at the oldest. He was in shock, twitching and shivering uncontrollably from being tear-gassed and pepper-sprayed at close range. His burned eyes were tightly closed, and he was panting irregularly. Then he passed out. He went from excruciating pain to unconsciousness on a sidewalk wet from the water that a medic had poured over him to flush his eyes."[31]

This was not an isolated event. Fortunately, protesters and sympathetic bystanders showed great generosity and cooperation. Hawken recalls that "as I tried to find my way down Sixth Avenue after the tear gas and pepper spray, I couldn't see. The person who found and guided me was Anita Roddick, the founder of the Body Shop, and probably the only CEO in the world who wanted to be on the streets of Seattle helping people that day. I could hear acutely. When your eyes fail, your ears take over. What I heard was anger, dismay, shock. For many people, including the police, this was their first direct action. Demonstrators who had taken nonviolence training were astonished at the police brutality. The demonstrators were students, professors, clergy, lawyers, and medical personnel. They held signs against Burma and violence. They dressed as butterflies."[32]

Arrayed against this apparently threatening butterfly brigade were a wide array of perhaps overequipped law enforcement personnel:

> The police were anonymous. No facial expressions, no face. You could not see their eyes. They were masked Hollywood caricatures burdened with 60 to 70 pounds of weaponry. These were not the men and women of the 6th precinct. They were the Gang Squads and the SWAT teams of the Tactical Operations Divisions, closer in their training to soldiers from the School of the Americas than to local cops on the beat. Behind them and around were special forces from the FBI, the Secret Service, even the CIA.

The police were almost motionless. They were equipped with US military standard M40A1 double-canister gas masks, uncalibrated, semi-automatic, high velocity Autocockers loaded with solid plastic shot, Monadnock disposable plastic cuffs, Nomex slash-resistant gloves, Commando boots, Centurion tactical leg guards, combat harnesses, DK5-H pivot-and-lock riot face shields, black Monadnock P24 polycarbonate riot batons with Trumbull stop side handles, No. 2 continuous discharge CS (ortho-chlorobenzylidene-malononitrile) chemical grenades, M651 CN (chloroacetophenone) pyrotechnic grenades, T16 Flameless OC Expulsion Grenades, DTCA rubber bullet grenades (Stingers), M-203 (40mm) grenade launchers, First Defense MK-46 oleoresin capsicum (OC) aerosol tanks with hose and wands, .60 caliber rubber ball impact munitions, lightweight tactical Kevlar composite ballistic helmets, combat butt packs, .30 cal. 30-round magazine pouches, and Kevlar body armor. None of the police had visible badges or forms of identification. The demonstrators seated in front of the black-clad ranks were equipped with hooded jackets for protection against rain and chemicals. They carried toothpaste and baking powder for protection of their skin, and wet cotton cloths impregnated with vinegar to cover their mouths and noses after a tear gas release. In their backpacks were bottled water and food for the day ahead.[33]

The vinegar cloths, unfortunately, got much use. So much tear gas and pepper spray, and so many concussion grenades and rubber bullets were used that the force ran out and had to seek out more from around the region.

There was a brief lull in the afternoon, but then the assaults began again. The labor march, which many hoped would join up with the direct actionists, was diverted away from them by the parade leaders. But many rank-and-file marchers felt closer to the more active form of protest, and thousands marched instead into the blockade zone to add support. According to Tico Almeida, "Eventually, the marchers split in two directions: tens of thousands heading towards the WTO meeting with the hopes of 'shutting it down'; and other tens of thousands favoring a peaceful sit-down protest in the streets surrounding the hotel where many of the WTO delegates were stuck waiting while the events played out further downtown. This second action was particularly important because it created a safe protest option for families who had brought children, for senior citizens, and for those who hoped to re-form, but not [abolish] the international trade system."[34] Through all the assaults, the protesters held onto their objectives at both sites. By late afternoon word reached the streets that the ministerial session had been canceled for the day. To the surprise of almost everyone, the protesters had won.

The victory was soon overshadowed, however, by another action taking place away from the blockade. The notorious Black Bloc, a black-clad group of women and men identified with the anarchist political tradition and a "nix it, don't fix it" attitude toward globalization, had begun to break windows and spray-paint slogans on certain carefully chosen global businesses. Unlike the vast majority of protesters who had committed to absolute (no property damage) nonviolence, the police knew well in advance that this was the intention of the small Bloc. DAN had requested that the Bloc not hold its action on the same day as DAN's, precisely to avoid the muddling of issues that came in its wake. Some in the corporate media seized on the events to try to discredit the whole protest action with talk of "chaos in the streets" and "senseless, random violence" all over the city. But what exactly had happened? Seattle participant-observer Cockburn asks, "In the end, what was vandalized? Mainly the boutiques of Sweatshop Row: Nordstrom's, Adidas, the Gap, Bank of America, Niketown, Old Navy, Banana Republic and Starbucks. The expressions of destructive outrage weren't anarchic, but extremely well targeted. The manager of Starbucks whined about how 'mindless vandals' destroyed his window and tossed bags of French Roast onto the street. But the vandals weren't mindless. They didn't bother the independent streetside coffee shop across the way. Instead they lined up and bought cup after cup. No good riot in Seattle could proceed without a shot of espresso."[35] Soon-to-be-ex Seattle mayor Paul Schell and some mainstream reporters noted the relatively small number of "anarchists" (always said to be from Eugene, never from Seattle where some in fact resided), but in a curious rhetoric. They argued that this "handful" of people "ruined" the protest. Ruined it for whom? Who was so quick to see in these relatively few acts the "ruin" of a week of articulate, pointed, and successful (in shutting down the WTO meeting) protests? Who, if not the corporate media, made the choice to concentrate on these acts?

The Black Bloc actions heightened the level of police violence and divided the protesters. The crowds thinned out in the evening, but a presence was maintained by a couple of thousand activists. A decision was made to drive them out to enforce a 7 p.m. curfew law put in effect through a declaration of emergency. The clearing out forced the protesters into the nearby Capitol Hill district where assaults were so indiscriminate that many bystanding residents of the area were gassed, sprayed, or clubbed.

The next day, 1 December, a "no protest" zone, 25 blocks square and of dubious legality, was set up by the police around the ministerial sites. The wave of protesters attempting in the morning to reassert their blockade were met at the edge of the zone by police promising to use lead, not rubber, bullets this time. Later in the day, Steelworkers organized a march along the waterfront to protest police brutality and reassert the freedom to assemble. They invited students and environmentalists to the podium to talk about what had happened.

Sporadic street skirmishes continued for the next several days. Police violence continued as well, but gradually lessened as the police were advised by city officials to change their tactic to the one the protesters had expected from the beginning—arrest. There were eventually more than six hundred arrests during the ministerial protests, of which only two came to trial and ended in convictions. Violence against protesters continued in jail, where more than three hundred incidents of abuse were reported. At one point a ring of demonstrators surrounded the courthouse to protest the treatment and express support for those continuing the battle in jail. In the wake of the police violence and jail treatment, Chief of Police Norm Stamper was forced to resign. Years later the city of Seattle is still awash in a sea of lawsuits. Victories in the courts will no doubt contribute money to the movement's sparse coffers. But no legal victories will remove lasting marks from the bodies (or the minds) of those whose "festival of resistance" grew less festive as it was forced to grow more resistive.

Journalist Peter Costantini, who writes for MSNBC News and Rome's Inter Press, summed up his surreal experience of Seattle:

> In more than three decades of protesting and covering protests in the
> United States, Europe, and Latin America, I had never been gassed.
> Finally, in my 50th year, the Seattle Police Department helped me lose
> my lachrymogenous virginity as photographer Casey Nelson and I
> strolled cluelessly up Pike Street, looking for anarchists or diplomats to

interview. As our lungs burned and eyes gushed, some wit on a balcony of a highrise condo cranked up a powerful sound system and blasted [Jimi] Hendrix's deconstruction of "The Star-Spangled Banner" over the melee below.

I looked around, but Oliver Stone was nowhere to be seen. Maybe Francis Ford Coppola had a hand in the festivities—I could almost hear Robert Duvall rasping, "I love the smell of pepper spray in the morning." Whoever produced it, the premise was implausible: laid-back, flannel-clad, latte-swilling, overcast, exports-driven Seattle—goosed by a generous dose of international organizing—looses a psychotropic shit storm that leaves the pin-striped proconsuls of the WTO dumbfounded and, with the connivance of frustrated Third World envoys on the inside, thwarts their plans for a new Millennium Round of trade talks.[36]

Assessments

Virtually all the protesters viewed the Battle of Seattle as a success, but they differed somewhat about the nature or source of the success. Most agreed with Costantini that one major success was that the protests seemed to have emboldened delegates from the undeveloped world to assert themselves against dominant Northern Hemisphere proposals in the ministerial. But people differed as to which protesters, and which tactics, were key to the victory. Labor activist Tico Almeida saw it this way: "In the end, I think it was the series of teach-ins and marches and peaceful protests—at times with slightly different messages, but with a common goal of democratizing the global economy—that made the 'Battle of Seattle' such an important event. Those who focused only on broken glass, tear-gas and rubber bullets missed the story entirely."[37]

In contrast, Cockburn was among those who believed the "street fighters" were the key to the protest's impact:

> Beyond the wildest hopes of the street warriors, five days in Seattle brought one victory after another. Protesters initially shunned and denounced by the respectable "inside strategists," scorned by the press, gassed and bloodied by the cops and national guard: shut down the opening ceremony; prevented Clinton from addressing the WTO dele-gates at Wednesday night gala; turned the corporate press from prim denunciations of "mindless anarchy" to bitter criticisms of police bru-tality; forced the WTO to cancel its closing ceremonies and to adjourn in disorder and confusion, without an agenda for the next round.
>
> In the annals of popular protest in America, these were shining hours, achieved entirely outside the conventional arena of orderly

protest, white paper activism and the timid bleats of professional leadership of big labor and establishment greens. This truly was an insurgency from below.[38]

The question of whether or not property destruction constitutes violence, and whether or not it can be an effective tactic, has been an issue in the direct action movement at least since the Seabrook nuclear power protests of the late 1970s. In the immediate aftermath of the battle, after the exhilaration wore off, the question of violence again took center stage. For the mainstream press, the primary issue was the broken windows downtown. For domestic and international human rights groups like the ACLU and Amnesty International, the primary issue was the police violence against peaceful protesters. For the movement, the prime issues were tactical and strategic: were the acts of property destruction responsible for negative coverage in the mainstream media, or were they the only way the events got any press coverage at all? Most insisted that before any discussion the window smashing had to be put in perspective. By most estimates, the number of "rioters" was somewhere between thirty and one hundred, out of a total number of protesters in excess of fifty thousand. And even among those thirty to one hundred, a significant number were Seattle petty criminals not involved in the protest, but merely jumping on the bandwagon as looting opportunists.

Whatever credit or discredit one gives to particular elements in the action, it is clear that Seattle was a turning point in the corporate antiglobalization movement(s). Paul Hawken goes so far as to offer a rather daunting historical parallel: the "American revolution occurred because of crown-chartered corporate abuse, a 'remote tyranny' in Thomas Jefferson's words. To see Seattle as a singular event, as did most of the media, is to look at the battles of Concord and Lexington as meaningless skirmishes."[39] While it remains to be seen whether the "Seattle espresso party" will match the "Boston tea party" in historical significance, it is clear that Seattle was no isolated happening. Rather, it proved a pivotal moment both in the terms of strengthening connections among the component groups of the actions, and in the protesters' use of new media to spread the word to the world about what had occurred in the Emerald City. For U.S. activists it also proved a key step in moving beyond so-called identity politics. As one participant phrased it, people bring their identities to the movement, but the identities are not the movement. The worldwide proliferation of groups involving dozens of ethnicities, sexualities, genders, and religions in a dizzying array of combination has meant that no identity can stay centered for long. The U.S. left mantra of race, class, gender, sexuality has been truly melded into a more complex configuration on a global scale.

A Network of Networks

The organizational pattern by which the disparate groups and interests were linked into the Battle of Seattle and into a movement is essentially a network of networks. Writer Naomi Klein relates that structure to a new medium of communication: "What emerged on the streets of Seattle . . . was an activist model that mirrors the organic, decentralized, interlinked pathways of the Internet—the Internet come to life."[40] Networks can be more or less formal, more or less permanent, but they generally tend toward the informal and impermanent. As the net (or web) metaphor suggests, networks are organized horizontally, not vertically or hierarchically, and their lines of connection can shift quickly from one path to another. Herself one of the most prominent figures in this network of movements, Naomi Klein writes:

> Despite this common ground, these [anti–corporate globalization] campaigns have not coalesced into a single movement. Rather, they are intricately and tightly linked to one another, much as 'hotlinks' connect their websites on the Internet. This analogy is more than coincidental and is in fact key to understanding the changing nature of political organizing. Although many have observed that the recent mass protests would have been impossible without the Internet, what has been overlooked is how the communication technology that facilitates these campaigns is shaping the movement in its own image. Thanks to the Net, mobilizations are able to unfold with sparse bureaucracy and minimal hierarchy; forced consensus and labored manifestoes are fading into the background, replaced instead by a culture of constant, loosely structured and sometimes compulsive information-swapping."[41]

Klein's analogy is useful, but perhaps a bit too tidy. It ignores, for example, that the network pattern of the action had been a tried-and-true structure for many direct action movement groups since the late 1970s. It is also not a universally accepted structure among all components of this (non)movement. Some worry that the structure mirrors the chaos engendered by, and works to the benefit of, the current system of domination that social theorist Manuel Castells calls "networked capitalism."[42] But Klein's analogy does point to a crucial cultural dimension of the movement. The connection between the movement and new cybercultures of the Internet is undeniable. Like the flow of information along the Internet, movement networks form and re-form in many different configurations depending upon the need. Social scientists who have long attempted to divide the landscape precisely into SMOs (social movement organizations), SMSs (social movement sectors), and SMIs (social movement industries), will no doubt be given many headaches by this form of organizing, but it may be only a difference in scale, not kind, from earlier intermovement structures.

Some activists suggest that the structure of the network is itself a model of what "globalization from below" might look like. No one denies the great complexity of the global economy, but all deny that management by corporate executives and their ministerial representatives is the only way to run it. For these activists, the organizational power of groups able to reach various kinds of short- and long-term agreements suggests the capacity of ordinary citizens to manage global problems while maintaining local autonomies. Meanwhile, the "global culture" of the Internet does not replace local cultures, but it does supplement them in ways that may prove crucial to the success of the movement.

This does not mean that ethnicity ceases to exist, but that it is changed and challenged. As cultural critic Lisa Lowe has noted, "The current global restructuring—that moves well beyond the nation-state and entails the differentiation of labor forces internationally—constitutes a shift in the mode of production that now necessitates alternative forms of cultural practice that integrate yet move beyond those of cultural nationalism."[43] Ethnicities are at once for sale as commodities, sites of resistance to white, male European domination, and easily crossed, ignored boundaries in the new economy. For ethnicities to remain sites of resistance, they cannot be trapped in essences and outmoded modes of nationalism, nor can they be lost in cyberspace. They will need to be "strategically translated," in Rey Chow's terms, sites where "difference" resists appropriation by capital and becomes instead resistant intercultural connection. The movement will be one of the key sites where cultural translations occur without fully succumbing to the market logic of capitalism.

Arguments will continue as to how far to take the movement/Internet analogy, but no one denies the importance of new media to the Seattle events and to the movement overall. The movement in its current global form would not be possible without the low-cost, instantaneous communication and the rich research possibilities of the Internet. The Internet provides groups with access to hundreds of corporate and government documents vital to understanding and strategizing against neoliberal policy, and it is the only mass medium currently available without a built-in bias toward the status quo. Indeed, given the anticorporate ethic among many computing subcultures, it may even have something of a bias against hegemony.

Participation in Seattle was mobilized largely through an extensive Internet campaign, driven by hundreds of listservs and thousands of personalized e-mails traveling virtually instantaneously around the globe. Typical of the many calls circulated around the world on-line was this one from People's Global Action (PGA). It is a call not only to Seattle but for local support actions worldwide (of which there turned out to be dozens):

> The November 30th global day of action would be organized in a non-hierarchical way, as a decentralized and informal network of autonomous groups that struggle for solidarity and co-operation while employing non-authoritarian, grassroots democratic forms of organization. Each event or action would be organized autonomously by each group, while coalitions of various movements and groups could be formed at the local, regional, and national levels. A strategy that may be useful at the local level is that various groups co-operate in creating a surrounding atmosphere of carnival and festivity as a setting for their various actions.[44]

The call also authorized and encouraged translation into many languages and posting to any and all relevant on-line bulletin boards, Web sites, and listservs. The great face-to-face encounter that was Seattle demonstrates the continued importance of direct person-to-person contact, but it was made possible by the virtual contacts of cyberspace. Use of computers to mobilize for the event was matched by the use of new media (laptops, camcorders, cell phones, Palm Pilots, and so on) during the event.[45]

This web of alternative communications also proved a spur to another kind of new media action, showcased in cyberspace but linked to Seattle: the "virtual sit-in." Coordinated by a British group calling itself the Electronic Hippies Collective, and supported by "hacktivists" from around the world, this new medium of protest consisted of thousands of visits to the official WTO Web site, designed to tie up its traffic the way a traditional sit-in might tie up access to an intersection, a lunch counter, or a politician's office. Pioneered by groups like Electronic Disturbance Theater, the virtual sit-in has become a component of many actions, along with other kinds of electronic civil disobedience. The Electronic Hippies claim to have mobilized more than a hundred thousand blockading "hits" per day on the first two days of the Battle of Seattle, thus allowing virtual participation in a symbolic attempt to replace corporate-ministerial speech with the free speech of ordinary citizens of the world.

A related, more controversial practice, the creation of fake or "shadow" Web sites, was also used around the Seattle actions. These sites mimic the design of official sites like the WTO's main site, and then put in their own, rather different content. One site, for example, using as its URL the acronym of WTO's predecessor organization (www.gatt.org) announced that the Seattle ministerial had been cancelled (days before the actual shutdown). (More recently one of these shadow sites announced, "The WTO Secretariat approved a schedule by which the WTO in its current form will be disbanded and transformed into the Trade Regulation Organization [TRO], whose charter will be based on the Universal Declaration of Human Rights.") This practice has been used often against corporations through such acts as putting a Nike logo on one's site so that when viewers click on it, it leads them a site critiquing Nike sweatshop practices. The problem with fake sites, however, from the point of view of some activists, is that the practice can set up an endless cycle of disinformation that ultimately undermines not only the official information of the corporate globalizers but the credibility of the protesters' own counter-information. For a movement critical of the lack of "transparency" (bureaucrat talk for open and accessible information) in organizations like the WTO, such actions may be perceived as hypocritical.

Another kind of new media played an unexpected role in the Battle of Seattle. When police managed to shut down part of the Direct Action Network's communications system, the protesters improvised by going out and buying a cache of cell phones.[46] Used by activists spread strategically around the demonstration sites, the phones proved essential for such tasks as coordinating blockades, informing protesters of police positions and tactics, and letting protesters know when reinforcements from the labor march would arrive. They also gave independent media reporters another means for filing their reports.

Will the Revolution Be Cybercast?

Black nationalist rapper-before-the-fact Gil Scott-Heron opined in 1968, at the height of a worldwide wave of social movements, "the revolution will not be televised." Computer "hacktivists" in Seattle thirty years later agreed with Scott-Heron that the mainstream media would not televise their revolution, so they were determined to "cybercast" their worldwide web of a revolution themselves. In doing so, they set in motion a growth and coordination of independent media that perfectly paralleled the growth and transformation of the movement overall during and after Seattle.

One month before the Seattle events, a group of alternative media organizations, independent journalists, and activists conceived the idea of a space where they could edit and disseminate their own coverage of the protests. The main impetus came from another network, in this case of independent media groups like Free Radio Berkeley, Deep Dish TV, Paper Tiger Television, Fairness and Accuracy in Reporting, Media Island International, Radio for Peace International, and Free Speech TV. They combined existing media of print, photo, video, and audio with the Internet savvy to create an interactive Web site (www.indymedia.org) that allows users not only to read, watch, or listen to stories, but also to post their own works of media as well. According to the Web monitors, during the week of the Seattle protests the site received over 1 million hits, more than CNN during the same five days.[47]

During the action it was possible to view simultaneously up to nine live Webcams overlooking key points of protest activity. From the Indymedia Web site, video and audio feeds "streamed" the images and sounds of unfolding events in the streets of Seattle to a worldwide audience. Up-to-the-minute written reports and digital still images, some sent directly from the street via laptop computers and Palm Pilots with wireless modems, were available as well. A daily half-hour video was produced and fed via satellite to community access TV centers. And a Webcast radio station, Studio X (Voices of Occupied Seattle), provided live running commentary and reports from the field to a global audience. Adding to this rich media mix were several micropower broadcast stations, one operating in Seattle and one beaming in a signal from the nearby Olympic Peninsula. These broadcasts could be picked up anywhere in the world by anyone with a computer and Internet access. Local support actions in dozens of cities around the world got information from the Web site about what was going in Seattle, and sent back reports on what linked protesters were doing in London, Berlin, São Paulo, Prague, Johannesburg, and dozens of other cities.

Recognizing that the Internet was not accessible to everyone, the Indymedia collective found ways it could be used to generate access for those without computers. As one member, Jeff Perlstein, recalls, there was great concern about the "digital divide" that has meant many of the world's poor have no way to connect to the Internet. Thus from the beginning Indymedia "set about [to link] high and low technologies, or old and new technologies." The Internet and the Web site were "the backbone of our distribution" but not the only options. Rather than relying on Internet access alone, they used the Internet to send audio files around the world that were then rebroadcast to millions of listeners on local radio stations, and text files that were downloaded into flyers and newsletters circulated the old-fashioned way—by hand.[48] They also put out a daily newsletter both locally and in key sites around the world.

To their credit, the protesters seemed to know when not to use networked computing. There was no bank of computers to be found at the action site that might get protesters caught up in a circle of narcissism. People seemed to realize that the face-to-face encounter should be just that for participants, and that the mediated version was for those who could not, or chose not to, attend.

In the wake of Seattle and in several subsequent actions, the footage taken by the independent media has also been used in court to document police brutality or illegal arrest or false charges, as well as in movement documentaries. Much of the content created during the Seattle actions remains available on-line and thus continues to offer an alternative to mainstream, corporate media reporting on the event. More important, following the Seattle events, more than fifty autonomous but linked Indymedia branches have sprung up on six continents, and all major actions, such as those in Quebec, Washington, D.C., Genoa, Prague, and New York, have had active live reporting over the Internet.

The Indymedia network of sites has become a major source of information, linking activists and providing a sophisticated, easy-to-use alternative to CNN and other corporate media. Indymedia collectives work

Independent media on the job. Scene from *This Is What Democracy Looks Like.*

by consensus and are open-access publishers so that anyone who wishes to can post news. The emphasis is on reports from the grassroots ignored by the main media's search for "leaders" and known authorities. Many of the groups run workshops for anyone wishing to learn more about computers and the other components of independent media, or for people without access who just need to use their resources. In both the content and their process of creation, they offer a rich alternative to the homogenized information provided by the mainstream. Operating on "copyleft" (as opposed to "copyright") principles, the groups have made both the content and innovative software used on the sites freely available to be recirculated by anyone.

Indymedia centers also use "open source" programs, the free alternatives to costly corporate software, and in so doing support the movement to keep the Internet itself from falling fully into corporate hands. If corporate media have their way, the Internet will be turned into a broadcast medium like television rather than the relatively open-ended, interactive medium it remains today. Moving to more and more sophisticated broadband production would also make the cost of putting content on the Web prohibitive for all but the wealthiest media companies. The struggle to keep this crucial organizing medium relatively free will be an essential component of the movement against corporate globalization generally.

Says Indymedia "code warrior" Ana Noguera, "IMC has boundless potential for breaking the corporate media blockade" of information.[49] Indymedia folks also realize that since the only motive driving corporate media is profit, they can sometimes sneak their message onto that stage by offering "exclusive" material. They are finding more and more ways to get their views into the mainstream, while maintaining their independence and their base in the everyday lives of those whose voices never make it onto CNN, CBS, or even PBS.

Few activists forget that, as Iain A. Boal put it, the new media's "liberatory functioning as a tool for 'organizing from below' flourishes in the shade of its dominant use as essential support for the global transmission of administrative, military and commercial intelligence, and the enhanced surveillance of labor."[50] The activists are not among the naïve utopian technological determinists who see the Internet as the world's savior. Rather, they see it as a site of struggle where with mobility, flexibility, imagination, and daring they may actually have some tactical advantages over their often stodgy, bureaucracy-bound opponents. Hacktivists, camcorder commandoes, data dancers, code warriors, digital deviants: a new media culture of resistance has become a vital part of the movement.

But this Indymedia revolution does not lack its critics and problems. For one thing, despite significant efforts to spread Indymedia around the globe, it remains a North-dominated sector and contributes to a suspicion in the Third and Fourth Worlds that the movement against corporate globalization is too much controlled by First World activists. The problem of access is also far from solved. Moving beyond dependence on the Internet and openness to more widely available media like radio is only a start. The extraordinary situation of relatively equal access by forces of opposition to a medium dominated by corporations is of great importance. That the Indymedia sites look as professional as the CNN site is a great gift in the struggle over control of information. But it could lull the movement into two kinds of complacency. First, it can distract from the ongoing need to contest for the rest of the electronic public sphere. It is not enough to offer an alternative; there also must be serious efforts to engage the still dominant mainstream corporate media like television as well. Second, the situation can change. As I mentioned above, much corporate energy is currently being directed toward the transformation of the Web into a broadcast, as opposed to an interactive, medium. As this process intensifies, it will be more and more expensive, and therefore more and more difficult, for Indymedia efforts to compete for the attention of what will increasingly become "viewers" rather than "users." None of these problems is insurmountable, but much movement energy needs to go into "surmounting" them.

The Battles Continue

What were the effects of the Seattle protests on the immediate adversary, the WTO, and what was the impact on the movement(s)? There is no doubt that the "tear gas ministerial" was a disaster for the corporate trade advocates. Third World delegates, emboldened, as many reports indicate, by the presence of so many dedicated activists, including so many Americans, raised objections to the millennial round that doomed the agenda of the dominant nations of the Northern Hemisphere.[51] The WTO has yet to fully recover from the battle, and subsequent protests that followed its meetings as they moved around the world have kept the WTO on the defensive.

In the immediate wake of Seattle, virtually all the coalitions and groups involved reported an upsurge of interest and activity. The movement against genetically engineered foods, for example, was able to turn out more than a thousand protesters for an FDA hearing in Oakland, California, in December 1999, the largest antibiotechnology action yet. Large-scale actions for the movement followed in rapid succession in Washington, D.C., Quebec City, Prague, and Genoa, all involving thousands of protesters. Like the Seattle action, they were often met by police violence, but this only emboldened the movement further.

Testimony to the effectiveness of this series of actions has come from some unexpected sources: "it is the trade unionists, students, environmentalists—ordinary citizens—marching in the streets of Prague, Seattle, Washington, and Genoa who have put the need for reform on the agenda of the developed world."[52] These are not the self-serving claims of an activist, but the frank assessment of former World Bank economist and Nobel prizewinner for economics Joseph Stiglitz. Stiglitz makes clear that, whatever they may say publicly, the major world financial and trade organizations have been deeply shaken by the protests.

Internal Tensions

In the wake of the battle, Chicana feminist activist Betita Martinez asked, "Where was the color in Seattle?" and her question continues to echo in the movement. Subsequent efforts to bring communities of color more fully into the U.S. wing of the movement have proved only partly successful.[53] Several factors account for this, including failure to fully confront white privilege within the movement and the far greater cost of the arrest strategy to people of color given their treatment by the prison system. In a related critique, some activists began to wonder if parts of the movement were falling into the classic trap of direct action—the need to make each new demo larger, more spectacular, more militant than the last. Some also asked if the "action hopping" protesters were becoming an elite corps of direct action tourists, leaving behind the millions without the means to travel the world in protest. Thoughtful critics like Chris Dixon reminded the "action junkies" that the strength of a movement is its grassroots, and those roots grow best in home soil.[54] Ratcheting up the stakes so the movement would consist only of those who could join globetrotting actionists would be a disaster. These summit actions have also sometimes drawn attention away from local protests, which have taken place in over one hundred countries in the world.[55]

Most activists continued to work in their particular corner of the world on the particular issues most immediately relevant to them: farmers on genetically engineered crops, workers on labor rights, environmentalists on toxic waste, students on the sweatshops that produced their college t-shirts. All agreed that the powerful coming-together in Seattle and similar actions elsewhere are important in invigorating the movement, in giving activists worldwide a sense that they are part of something larger, a movement, not a series of isolated issues. But those actions, critics argued, are part of the movement, not the essence of the movement.

Yutaka Dirks offers related criticisms in regard to plans to protest the summit meeting of the "G8" (eight industrialized nations) in Kananaskis, Alberta, Canada, in June 2002. Dirks, like Dixon, questions the efficacy and the accessibility of jet-set protesting. "If we are serious about changing the world," she writes, "about putting a halt to the latest phase of capitalist globalization, we need to re-evaluate our strategies. The distance between community based struggles and the 'summit hopping anti-globalization movement' needs to be addressed. We need to reflect on our past organizing." Noting that the people most affected by globalization are the least likely to be able to follow protests around the world, she calls for more focus on local organizing, especially working with poor people and people of color: "We need to listen to and learn from those most affected by globalization, those who are talking about the racist/sexist/oppressive ways we have been organizing. We need to take the work of organizing in inclusive ways and confronting oppression within our movement seriously." Dirks goes so far as to ask protesters from afar not to come. It is the classic argument that mere mobilizing was undercutting serious organizing. As it turned out, a small, festive gathering in Alberta did balance local and global concerns (including the "glocal," as some call it), and also avoided assaults by the "Blue Bloc" (the police). The protesters held a series of nonviolent, imaginative actions, many focused on local issues, and greatly embarrassed local officials who had spent millions of dollars on unneeded defense forces.[56]

Another key development in the movement, and one that also moves away from reactive focus on the summits of the globalizers, was the creation of the World Social Forum (WSF). The World Social Forum met first in 2001 in Porto Alegre, Brazil, partly as a symbolic challenge to the World Economic Forum of corporate leaders and trade ministers. In 2002 the second WSF meeting in Porto Alegre drew 12,274 delegates representing close to 5,000 civil society organizations and movements (political parties and military units are not allowed), plus another 50,000 participant-observers.[57] All thought of "shadowing" the WEF was replaced by focus on the movement's plan. The WSF has become an annual event, the major counter-summit of the "movement for global justice," as many now call it. This important renaming clearly suggests a move from the defense to the offense, from reacting to globalization to building alternatives. The global justice summit is formed, like its predecessors, as a network of networks, not a hierarchical organization. WSF does not itself take positions (beyond its charter), but serves rather as a place for movement groups to meet on an annual basis to educate, assess, strategize, network, and plan.[58] The WSF charter reads in part: "The alternatives proposed at the World Social Forum stand in opposition to a process of globalization commanded by the large multinational corporations and by the governments and international institutions at the service of those corporations' interests, with the complicity of national governments. They are designed to ensure that globalization in solidarity will prevail as a new stage in world history. This will respect universal human rights, and those of all citizens—men and women—of all nations and the environment and will rest on democratic international systems and institutions at the service of social justice, equality and the sovereignty of peoples."

Within these broad principles, there is certainly a wide array of ideological positions, running the gamut from A to Z, anarchism to *Zapatismo*. But ideological certainty is largely anathema, both because of a predominating spirit of experimentalism and because of the commitment to respect local conditions. The sheer complexity of ethnicities, positions, and ideas makes it unlikely that any one faction could dominate, but sectarian efforts to do so will no doubt continue. The choice of Porto Alegre, site of a regionalist and localist challenge to Brazilian central state power, represents a continuing commitment to a diversity of solutions focused on particularities, even as it builds global networks.

Terror! Greed! Corruption! and the New Millennium Blues: From the World Trade Center to WorldCom to World Dom

In the wake of the terrible events of September 11, 2001, in the words of radical journalist L. A. Kaufman, "all has changed." In an article under that title published on 17 September 2001, Kaufman was already aware of how profoundly the attack on the World Trade Center and the Pentagon would affect the movement. A great symbol of corporate world trade had been transformed into a symbol of innocent victimhood. She writes:

> The September 11 attacks definitively interrupted the unfolding logic of the movements for global justice. The IMF/World Bank protests in D.C. were going to be simultaneously broader, more diverse, and more intense than any demonstrations in recent U.S. history. The AFL-CIO was pouring unprecedented resources into the events, mobilizing its membership on a massive scale, and faith-based and non-governmental organizations were activating thousands of people who had never come to a globalization protest before. Meanwhile, more and more people were embracing the philosophy of "diversity of tactics," shifting away from the strict nonviolence guidelines that have been the hallmark of large-scale direct actions for two decades, and agreeing to respect those who chose to engage in more confrontational or property-destroying tactics, so long as they didn't directly endanger other protesters.
>
> "Diverse tactics" are clearly off the table for the time being, especially in New York and Washington, where the sound of breaking glass connotes death and devastation, and the masked uniform of the Black Bloc will only inspire fear.

And with the world's greatest symbol of global capitalism having been reduced to a smoldering mass grave, it's going to be difficult for a while to present anti-capitalist critiques in a way that will resonate broadly, and not seem to justify an unjustifiable atrocity.

Our movements' vision of global justice is needed now more than ever; we will simply need to take great care in presenting that vision in a way people can hear.

... Action is essential: May it be prudent, strategic, and effective.[59]

It is hard to imagine two groups more different than the Al Qaeda terrorists and the antiglobalization activists, but a conservative administration in the United States quickly passed a "Patriot Act" so sweeping that it promised to turn all dissent into a pretext for the terrorist label.

In the rest of the world, the movement had a bit more room to move tactically, but a particularly brutal suppression of demonstrators in Genoa, Italy, in the summer of 2001, including one death and hundreds of injuries, had already put the European branch of the movement into a reassessment phase when the September 11 attacks shocked the world. In February 2002, the sixty thousand activists from around the world who attended the second World Social Forum in Porto Alegre reaffirmed the movement's commitment to nonviolence. Soon thereafter, in March 2002, close to 2 million people protested in Rome over labor issues, and half a million in Barcelona protested an international trade meeting.[60]

One key sign of the shifting post–September 11 tactics occurred during these protests in Barcelona on 15–16 March 2002. Both the terrorist attacks and the death of protester Carlo Giuliano, along with severe injuries to hundreds more during the Genoa protests a year earlier, had convinced protesters that a new approach was necessary. The Spanish anarchist union CGT, never a group to fear confrontation when useful, put out a call to "walk out on the script, for using direct action and civil disobedience as mechanisms for struggle that go beyond violent confrontations with the police." They argued that "we have to regain the furiously festive and subversive nature of our activity, breaking military frameworks (summit-blockade-clash with police), the powers want to confine us to."[61] When half a million protesters held a two-day festival involving more than twenty-five decentralized actions but no confrontations with police, the new vision was solidified. The streets had been reclaimed, the educational process had gone on, and the gathered ministers knew of yet another city where they were not welcome. They felt the force of half a million people not "buying into" their rhetoric of free market globalization.

In the United States and around the world it was clear that street fighting was a recipe for disastrous amounts of repression. More imaginative tactics are now the order of the day. Instead of breaking windows at Starbucks, what if demonstrators tied up their business for hours by forming long lines in and around their cafes, requesting fair-trade espresso when they made it to the counter, then leaving, slowly, when they couldn't get it? Similar large actions in clothing stores could make the same point about labor conditions in the textile industry. That situation is so pervasive that traditional boycotts would be hard to put into effect; other than going naked, there is virtually no way to avoid sweatshop-produced clothes. Indeed, at the protests in Alberta in June 2002, protesters shed their clothes in a protest under the banner "I'd Rather Be Naked Than Wear Gap Clothes." This action was modeled on an earlier clothing-optional party organized by antisweatshop activists at the University of North Carolina. Lisa Featherstone saw that action as an example of a larger tendency, noting that the "militant, theatrical and often campy direct action [tactics] ... of early nineties groups like ACT UP and Queer Nation have clearly influenced the new crew of student activists."[62] This spirit, uncompromising but imaginative enough to draw media attention, and riddled with serious humor to disarm authorities, is the mode most likely to be effective at this historical moment. It is also likely that the tactical reconsideration forced upon the movement by the September 11 attacks will keep the moderate, policy-oriented branch and the direct actionists in closer contact. Property damage tactics had the potential to drive a wider wedge between these two components of the movement, which too seldom saw their work as mutually supportive.

The U.S. branch of the movement returned to life when between seventy-five thousand and two hundred thousand people (estimates ranged widely) protested peacefully in April 2002 in Washington, D.C., against the IMF and World Bank. The aftermath of Seattle continues to be one that empowers groups. The corporate media often speak of the antiglobalization movement as nothing but a "laundry list" of disconnected issues. But just the opposite is the case. Seattle and subsequent events turned a laundry list of groups focused on the environment, genetically engineered foods, human rights, consumer protections, women's rights, labor issues, poverty, and debt relief into a far more coherent force focused on a common enemy—neoliberal policies underwriting corporate power. At the same time as it gave a greater sense of connection to a host of U.S. groups, it allowed those groups to see themselves as a small part of a larger, worldwide movement. The way for these connections had been paved by several generations of activists, from civil rights and black power groups linking to African anticolonialism, to Chicana/os expanding "America" southward, to U.S involvement in international campaigns against nuclear weapons and against apartheid, to ACT UP's move beyond the United States. But this movement for global justice has taken this process much further out of isolation and into a truly international perspective. Seattle was important in demonstrating resistance inside the nation most responsible for the horrors of corporate globalization, but the lesson learned has been that U.S. groups must often follow the lead of those most affected by U.S.–engendered policies. To do otherwise is to add "movement cultural imperialism" to the long list of problems to be overcome.

The crisis of September 11 was quickly followed by a different crisis that turned instead to the benefit of the movement. Corporate scandals around Enron, WorldCom, and a host of other companies seemed to confirm what protesters had been saying about the hypocrisies of neoliberal free trade. Though it seemed unlikely that "corporate terrorism" would be added to the list of targets in the "war on terror," it also seemed clear that the latter could not fully deflect attention from the former.

War and Peace(s)

Despite the complexities offered by the post–September 11 situation domestically and around the world, the movement for global justice continued to grow into the twenty-first century, taking with it the legacy of a half-century of extraordinary social movement action on behalf of economic, social, and environmental justice. Alongside this growth, American power also flexed its muscles as never before. The U.S. war on Iraq generated the largest antiwar movement in the history of the world. On 15 February 2003, to cite one example, between 8 million and 11 million people demonstrated across the globe against the then impending war. This, the largest "focus group" (as President George W. Bush dismissively called it) ever assembled, rested to a great extent on the cyber and face-to-face networks forged by the movement(s) for global justice. Public opinion in 189 of the world's 191 nations was against U.S. intervention (Israel and the United States the only exceptions), suggesting that U.S.–based activists have much work to do to catch up with the rest of the world and to fight the clouding of domestic vision that accompanies imperial power (see online bonus chapter). While stopping the war proved impossible in the face of a U.S. president contemptuous of the views of anyone beyond his small circle of advisers, the actions mobilized against the war strengthened the worldwide forces aligned to create rich new alternatives to the ecological devastation, brutal poverty, and human exploitation produced by neoliberal capitalism run amok.

TEN

Reflections on the Cultural Study
of Social Movements

Let me tell you a new version of an old story. Let's call our version "Blindness, Insight, Elephants, and Sufi Social Science":

Once upon a time, a group of social movement theorists was on safari in search of the elephant. Their search took them out on a dark, moonless night, and they spread out across the jungle. When they returned to camp, each reported their findings. The first theorist to encounter the elephant was a *collective behaviorist*. He had heard an elephant charging through the jungle and, after having nearly been trampled, declared that elephants were dangerous, anarchic things, prone to rioting and mob actions. The next safarist, a *resource mobilization* theorist, walked right into the side of a sleeping elephant. Her report declared the creature to be a solid, well-organized thing, rather like a carefully built wall. A third theorist, from the *political process* camp, followed an elephant as it moved about its habitat, and declared that the most interesting thing about elephants is how their behavior is determined by the shifting opportunities for food found in their part of the jungle. Another, fanciful theorist, from the *social constructionist* school, became fascinated by the elephant's large, fanlike ears. She opined that elephant ears functioned rather like satellite dishes, taking in information about the jungle, processing it in uniquely elephantine ways, then transmitting it anew into the wider jungle. Throughout these reports, another theorist, of the *historical materialist* persuasion, was looking mildly perturbed. When his turn came, he declared it self-evident that the elephant's large, tree-trunk-like legs were the foundation on which all other elements of elephantness ultimately depended. Finally, the *cultural studies* practitioner took the floor, speaking eloquently of the loud but lovely trumpet sounds emanating from the elephant's trunk. This theorist felt certain of having begun to decipher the most important aspect of the elephant, its discourse, declaring that in essence elephants were singers, artfully shaping the jungle purely through the power and beauty of their voices; those tree-trunk legs, the massive torso, satellite-dish ears, and unpredictably whiplike tail were merely secondary enablers of the performance.[1]

Just as I have attempted in the preceding chapters to synthesize and give new angles of vision on particular movements, by way of conclusion I will synthesize and try to provide a new spin to social movement theory, especially *cultural* approaches to movement analysis. My much belabored revision of the famous Sufi allegory of the "blind men and the elephant" is homage to, not a put down of, fellow movement theorists. It is meant to acknowledge succinctly some of the rich body of work done on movements over the past half-century. But it is also a cautionary tale about the beastly complexity of movements, one suggesting that no one will ever capture one (alive) for their particular, private movement zoo.

The Sufi tale, in my reading, is not a call for a total theory of elephants (or movements), but rather a call to respect the integrity of the creature and to recognize the inevitable partialness of perspective. What I offer here, instead of a total theory, is a series of observations that I hope will illuminate certain key aspects of the beast. In my view, the great variety of movements makes any attempt to find their essence both futile and dangerous. The main danger lies in inadvertently missing (or indirectly stifling) the creativity of movements, missing their rich variety, and being inattentive to their ability to shift shape in response to new conditions.

One of the curious things about the cultural study of social movements is that scholars of social movements have, until rather recently, had little to say about culture, while cultural studies scholars have had, with a few exceptions, surprisingly little to say about movements. During the 1990s some sociologists, due to the influence of cultural studies scholars and an increasing emphasis on culture within movements themselves, began to take the cultural dimension of movements more seriously.[2] Indeed, some feared that the "pendulum" was swinging too much in the direction of culture, though the continued dominance of sociology by quantification and limited forms of qualitative study makes this very unlikely.

A few scholars have begun to synthesize the most relevant portions of the social science and the cultural studies traditions. Verta Taylor and Nancy Whittier, for example, in one of the most cogent and useful discussions of movements and culture, offer this summary of some of the main schools relevant to thinking about the movement/culture matrix: "Major approaches to the analysis of culture advance different concepts, based on distinct epistemological frameworks, for analyzing the relationship between symbolic forms and the structure of social relations. For functionalists, culture is conceived as values and norms, while Marxists and neo-Marxists analyze culture as ideology and class consciousness. Symbolic interactionists emphasize intersubjective meaning, focusing on the subjective dimension—beliefs, goals, normative expectations, states, and motivations—that underlie social interaction, while dramaturgical approaches think of culture as ritual. A new generation of cultural theorists, influenced by poststructuralism and postmodernism, construe culture as discourse."[3] Taylor and Whittier go on to show through case study analysis of feminist groups that despite their bases in "distinct epistemological frameworks," each of these approaches offers insight into movements that can, to some degree at least, be synthesized. Nevertheless, significant tensions continue to exist among movement theorists on questions of culture.

Sociologist Amy Swidler has cogently argued that part of the problem is that sociologists have drawn primarily upon one strand of cultural theory, Max Weber's, to the neglect of another, more promising strand, that of Marcel Mauss. Swidler argues that Weber's thin theory of culture helps account for empirical sociology's relative neglect of cultural factors. Even those schools of movement analysis like frame analysis that do examine cultural factors are limited by certain Weberian assumptions about the centrality of individuals and the beliefs they hold. She argues that Maussian approaches (in which she includes most cultural studies work) can lead to much useful empirical research by focusing not on fuzzy notions of culture as "ideas in people's heads" but rather on structural notions of culture. Swidler suggests four guidelines for such work. First, focus on culture not as individually held beliefs but as structures embedded in practices relatively independent of the beliefs held by individual actors. Second, focus less on culture as what actors themselves really think and more on culture as their "knowledge of how others will interpret their actions." Third, focus on "public contexts in which cultural understandings are brought to bear," often in ways that are functioning above the level of individual belief in ways that unite diverse actors with diverse opinions. Fourth and finally, focus on cultural institutions as sites that set limits and possibilities for movement activity. This last would in effect be a cultural analogue to the political process model in which what we might call "cultural opportunity structures" are analyzed for how they shape movement actors and actions.[4]

Some of the problem, then, arises from vastly different theories and definitions of "culture" in play in movement analysis.[5] Another key source of tension stems from the fact that social scientists have tended to reduce culture to politics, while cultural studies scholars have tended to reduce politics to culture. These are gross generalizations, to be sure, but they point to an important conceptual problem. Regardless of what theory of culture we deploy, we need to take greater care in thinking about the relationships between the terms *political* and *cultural*. A term much in use these days, *cultural politics,* will not help much because it is often part of the problem of subsuming the political into the cultural. As Cindy Patton notes, much neo-Marxist and poststructuralist theory "has produced an incoherent set of critical practices in which the 'social' is deconstructed and evacuated, but a 'cultural' (albeit more fun to study) is reinserted in the same place."[6] *Cultural politics* can be a useful term— indeed, it may be a crucial one—but not in the too often vague way in which it is currently used. Cultural politics, as I have argued throughout this book, works best when it is embedded in or at least strongly connected to specific social movement cultures. Michael Denning has expressed a view close to mine that movements should be seen as sites not only of cultural production but of cultural reception: "Subaltern experience does not necessarily generate social criticism and cultural resistance; the possibility of popular readings of cultural commodities depends on the cultivation, organization, and mobilization of audiences by oppositional subcultures and social movements."[7]

On the other side, an older term, *political culture,* refers to the culture surrounding traditionally defined political activity. But *political culture* is far too circumscribed to be of much use in this context. It can be put to good use, especially if expanded to include a more serious discussion of the ways in which broader cultural contexts shape traditional forms of political activity (voting, lobbying, and so on). But it certainly cannot encompass all the political impacts of culture. The inadequacy of the various meanings surrounding the key concepts of "politics" and "culture" suggests that any discussion of "the cultural study of social movements" must entail some struggle around and expansion of the terrain of terminology.

Culture, Politics, and the Political-Cultural

Differing from those who would collapse politics into culture, or culture into politics, I believe there are good (political and cultural) reasons for keeping the two concepts analytically distinct. Certain scientistic versions of sociological theory have tended to reduce culture to politics by viewing it either as merely *expressive*, and thereby decorative rather than efficacious, or by viewing it as efficacious but in only an *instrumental* way, counting as significant only when producing directly measurable effects on traditionally defined political terrains. Some social scientists have remained trapped by these limiting assumptions, while others have shown more flexibility. Aldon Morris's important early work on the civil rights movement, for example, dealt with the overwhelming evidence that church culture played a key role in the movement by treating that culture primarily as a resource to be instrumentally mobilized. He also suggested, however, that his findings to some extent challenged the limits of the resource mobilization theory in which his work was embedded at the time. More generally, students of movements across a range of ideological positions, from conservative to liberal pluralist to Marxist, have sometimes assumed an unexamined traditional notion of state power that inherently privileges certain terrains as truly political, while others have implicitly or explicitly acknowledged the complexity of the cultural-political.

On the other side of this admittedly too neatly bifurcated ledger are some cultural studies scholars who see cultural resistance everywhere, turning all culture into politics. The problem is not so much the concept of "cultural politics" deployed by these critics, but the frequent failure to distinguish degrees or levels of cultural politics, or to think carefully about the relative scale of impact of a given practice or discourse. Lack of specificity leads to wild swings from assuming absolutely seamless cultural hegemony to "reading" resistance into every "text" that comes along. One dimension of this problem is a slippage between the two most common meanings of culture: culture as a particular realm (the high culture of the arts, mass-mediated popular culture, and homespun folk cultures), and culture as the meaning patterns in whole ways of life. This latter definition has a strange way of absorbing all it touches; rather than seeing culture as a process that shapes all other levels (the economic, the social, the political), it absorbs those other levels in ways that reduce the complexity of the system. French sociologist Pierre Bourdieu's careful work on the specificity of the "cultural field" as semi-autonomous but intricately connected to the general "field of power" and other key fields of the social, the economic, and the political provides one suggestive model of how to think through complicated relations in a nonreductive way.[8]

Social movement theorist Steven Buechler's discussion of these terms offers another excellent starting point for developing a flexible, multifaceted sense of the political-cultural:

> Much confusion about the political dimension of social movements may be traced to inconsistent definitions of the term "political" and the underlying conceptions of power implied by such definitions. As an initial sorting device, we may distinguish between at least two senses of "the political." The term "state politics" will be used to refer to the more conventional type of power struggle in which social activism is directed toward influencing state policy and leaders, including broad revolutionary challenges to the political order. In this conception, power is centralized and hierarchical, although it can be challenged under the right circumstances by sustained opposition. The term "social politics" will be used to refer to a less conventional type of power struggle in which collective action is directed toward altering power relations inscribed in diverse social institutions and cultural practices, including the seemingly "personal" aspects of everyday life. In this conception, power is diffuse and decentralized, and challenges to this form of power take a wider variety of tactical, strategic and expressive forms. Both types of politics contain a mixture of oppositional and transformative elements that qualify them as "political." Although social politics are more likely to be designated as "cultural" and sometimes opposed to "political," it would be more productive to recognize the cultural dimensions of state politics as well as the political aspects of social politics.[9]

This is a succinct and useful statement of the issues that must be considered by anyone seeking to sort out the political from the cultural.

Ironically, however, Buechler's own analysis seems to invoke at least three dimensions—the state-political, the social-political, and the cultural-political—but ends up with only two. If we conceptualize instead four domains—the social, the political, the economic, and the cultural (in the narrow sense)—each of which is shaped, in part, by the meaning-making processes we call "cultural" in the larger sense, we can be clearer about those extra-cultural determining forces like economic activity, social institutions, and political decisions, without reducing any one to another.

The economic, the social, and the political never fully determine the shape of culture, but they do set conditions of possibility and limit that no amount of cultural action can shift. At the same time, culture is always involved dialectically with the goings-on at the level of economics and politics, contesting for the meanings that can be made from the raw material of economic and political event-texts. Movements cannot culturally dissolve an economic upturn or downturn; such events produce new conditions. But they can shape the response to these conditions. This means that economic and political forces are always subject to cultural direction and redirection, but it does not mean that economic and political force can be equated with or reduced to culture or textuality. That we can never isolate an economic event from its textualization, from the meaning-making process it sets in motion, is not equivalent to saying the event itself has no force and that the text has all force. In Raymond Williams's terms, the event is not determinative, but it is determining; it does not create one, inevitable response but it does condition the range of responses. This means, in practical terms, that the cultural analysis of social movements can never be isolated from these other levels.

The dynamics of ACT UP offer a particularly cogent example of how this conceptual problematic works itself out in movements. The practices of ACT UP were frequently directed simultaneously at the political-economic realm in the form of federal drug funding policy, at the socio-economic realm in the form of nonstate institutions (like pharmaceutical corporations), and at the cultural realm in the form of discursive practices in the mass media and in aesthetic texts. Few in ACT UP argued for exclusive focus on only one of these levels—though, as we saw in chapter 7, internal debates did emerge around which of these targets was more important, and eventually spin-off groups sought to focus more intensely on one or another of these dimensions. ACT UP's experience suggests that a continuum across state, social, and cultural "politics" often exists not only among different movements, but also within particular movements. Some movements may fit more fully into one location across this continuum, but more often analysis must attend to considerable slippage in a given movement along this continuum. Clearly, this task becomes even more imperative when examining complexly coalitional movements like the one against state-corporate globalization (see chapter 9).

My argument, then, is that while purely cultural, purely social, purely economic, and purely political domains do not actually exist, it is nevertheless useful at points to deploy these distinctions. For one thing, culture can be a *more* or *less* politicized terrain, and even state politics or socioeconomic activities have *more* and *less* cultural dimensions. It would be a great irony for any student of social movements to insist on these absolute distinctions, since no force has done more than social movements to challenge the borders separating these arenas. Much social movement activity has demonstrated, insisted upon, and enacted a political critique of culture and a cultural critique of the social, the economic, and the political that challenges these boundaries: the working-class cultural institutions so vital to early labor movement, attempts by Marxist movements to politicize the economy, the civil rights movement's attacks on racist social and cultural institutions, the insistence of the women's movement that the "personal is political," and the gay and lesbian movement's "outing" of queer cultural subtexts. Political economy, cultural politics, social cultural studies: these and similar mediating terms are needed to remind students of movements of the dangers of reifying these domains.

As second-wave feminist Gloria Steinem once quipped, "culture is the name they give to the politics that wins." This neatly encapsulates the now commonplace theoretical insight that culture often functions for those in power as a space to be legitimated as "transcending" politics, and suggests why insurgent groups must insist that the cultural realm is shot through with the political. But revealing the political uses of culture is not the same thing as proving that all culture is "merely" politics. What needs to be analyzed is the process by which some cultural texts are politicized—by those in power, on the one hand, and by those challenging that power, on the other. One must also remember that the political uses of aesthetic texts never exhaust their meanings. As I argued about the role of music in the civil rights movement (see chapter 1), movement cultures function best when they both express and move beyond ideology. Ideologies—elaborated key ideas and values—are crucially important to any movement. But they are also often the points of contention that pull movements apart. The very vagueness of "culture" that has kept many social scientists from examining it seriously as a movement force is precisely one of its virtues.

While terminological consistency across the range of social movement theorists might help sort out this problem, that is unlikely to occur and seems ultimately less important than encouraging two kinds of self-reflexivity. First, theorists across a range of positions need to be sufficiently clear about their own assumptions regarding the political-social-economic-cultural spectrum to limit the occasions when movements are judged as failing to engage in a level of political or cultural or social action that it is not their intention to engage. And second, as a corollary, those who study movements need to develop as clear a notion as possible of the internal self-understanding of movements as to their targeting along this spectrum of domains. This movement self-understanding is an evolving (cultural) phenomenon because, as one group of veteran activist-theorists noted, "No movement is born knowing what it thinks, what it wants, and how to achieve its goals. . . . [But] any movement develops a self-understanding, whether a tacit set of assumptions expressed primarily in action, a formalized theory, or something in between."[10] With regard to ACT UP, for example, a strict poststructuralist theorist might look at the range of the group's activity and declare that it offers evidence that a Foucauldian-Derridean cultural politics can challenge state power (contra those who claim it has "merely cultural" impacts). In contrast, a more traditionally trained empirical theorist might argue that pragmatically oriented voices within ACT UP "saved" it from the irrelevance of a cultural politics by directing some of the group's actions toward state power. My own reading, from an ideologically and methodologically less purist position, suggests that an ideological mix within ACT UP itself left these questions strategically unresolved in ways that may have contributed to its successes.

The very permeability of domain borders is precisely the reason why one must insist upon their separability, for both analytical and strategic reasons. Part of the work of movements is to identify and strategically target only certain objects, texts, fields, and assumptions. Therefore, when every aspect of the terrain becomes *equally* politicized, nothing is politicized, for no *strategic* targeting is possible. This is the prime danger with the concept of "cultural politics." An essential concept, it is most useful in circumscribed and targeted use. Similar problems emerge when any other realm—economic, political, social—becomes exaggerated: careful thinking about the particular mix of these forces is undermined.

The Problem of Postmodernity

Much of the conceptual imperialism of the term *culture* comes from various debates about the extent to which or the way in which we currently inhabit a "postmodern condition" that has allegedly blurred the boundaries of the cultural and the political. These theorizations include Jürgen Habermas's antipostmodernist claim that the political-economic "system world" has so "colonized" the sociocultural "life world" that the latter is threatened by a total absorption into the instrumentalizing logic of a commodified life. Habermas, however, does not portray this process as complete or inevitable, and believes it could still be resisted by application of traditional (Enlightenment or modernist) political values. Moving between modernist and postmodernist positions on these matters is critic Fredric Jameson, who argues that a commodification of cultural realms in our late-capitalist, mass-mediated "consumer society" has made it difficult, but not impossible, to map the cultural-political system. In this view, the tendency of postmodern forms to absorb politics into spectacle requires a combination of traditional Marxist and *new* postmodern forms of cultural and political resistance.

Further along this postmodernizing spectrum are figures like Michel Foucault, arguing that traditional state politics has declined from its modernist peak of importance toward a postmodern condition in which power is diffused across the political-social-cultural field through discursive practices and disciplinary regimes of power/knowledge. For Foucault, new forms of resistance that largely eschew direct contestations with the political state are the only forms likely not to be absorbed back into domination. At the far end of this range are critics like Jean Baudrillard, who see this process of collapsing of the political and cultural as having evolved into a mess of simulations and virtualities from which all possibility of noncomplicity, let alone resistance, has been eliminated. Critics working from one or another or some combination of these critical positions have created both useful and reductive versions of cultural politics, just as those working with more traditional notions of politics have proven more or less flexible in analyzing the complexities of contemporary movement cultural-political practices. In general, they raise a question to keep in mind as we turn to look more closely at the various roles played by culture in and around movements: how have those roles changed as a result of ongoing historical processes, processes in which movements have themselves been active players?

Movements in Culture

Much of the cultural study of social movements can be clarified by thinking in terms of three elements: movements in culture, movement cultures, and culture in movements. By *movements in culture,* I mean the processes by which movements emerge from, and return to, broad cultural contexts. By *movement cultures* I mean the general meaning-making patterns that develop among participants in the subculture formed by a given movement. And by *culture in movements,* I mean those specific aesthetic-cultural artifacts (songs, poems, murals, and so forth) deployed within the shifting orbit of a movement culture.

One of the best general outlines we have of the overall process of culture working through movements can be found in an essay by political process movement theorist Doug McAdam.[11] I share McAdam's view that the cultural impact of movements is best conceptualized through a long-range, three-stage dialectical process. First, movements emerge out of a given cultural context, then they evolve novel cultural features, and finally, they diffuse elements of novelty back into the wider culture. Even among the most conservative "consensus movements" (like Mothers against Drunk Driving), the very act of stepping outside conventional politics to express a grievance opens up possibilities for re-viewing the wider culture. As we move across the spectrum toward ever more deeply oppositional or radical movements, that re-viewing and questioning process grows more intensive and extensive. The questioning process evolves over time, and in varying degrees, into a movement culture with its own norms, ideas, and forms. Over the course of the movement and in its aftermath, elements of the movement culture are diffused back into the wider culture.

This diffusion of movement culture back into mainstream culture can at times be the most important impact a given movement may have. Yet it is among the least studied aspects of movements, and it is not difficult to see why. Culture is a messy business; it is clearly a less easily measured object of analysis than Supreme Court rulings, congressional bills, or income patterns. But for social scientists to ignore a whole terrain and its impact just because it is not easily quantifiable seems highly unscientific. As Doug McAdam notes, "Given the entrenched political and economic opposition movements are likely to encounter, it is often true that their biggest impact is more cultural than narrowly political and economic."[12] One key reason for this is that cultural institutions tend to be relatively more open and less defensive than these other realms. Indeed, since at least the rise of modernism in the arts, innovation has been an imperative in much cultural production. Particularly since the mid-twentieth century, this has meant a very active search for new cultural forms that has sometimes played to the advantage of movements. At the same time, it has initiated a process of cultural appropriation that often entails a reduction of the political power of forms emerging from oppositional contexts. While it is important to be as precise as possible in characterizing the impact of culture on movements and movements on culture, we should not let a "rigor" often bordering on rigor mortis remove us from the most significant impacts of movements. Later in this chapter I will return to this key issue of how movement cultures are diffused into the wider society, but here I will note that often the greatest impact is through a general transgression of cultural codes. Swidler puts it this way: "Even without conscious efforts at publicity, one of the most important effects social movements have is publicly enacting images that confound existing cultural codings. From the punk subculture's deliberate embrace of 'ugly' styles . . . to the Black Panthers' display of militant, disciplined, armed black revolutionaries to the New Left spectacle of middle-class college students being beaten by the police . . . altering cultural codings is one of the most powerful ways social movements actually bring about change."[13] While the particulars of each of these cultural code transgressions matter, there is also a more general level on which the extra-institutional nature of movements and the contestatory nature of their practices constitute an ongoing message that the status quo is open to change.

Movement Cultures: Measuring Intensity and Elaborateness

At the center of these three dimensions of the movement/culture dynamic are the discourses and practices most directly embedded in movements, the structures I call *movement cultures*. Movement cultures can be more or less intensive or elaborated, and more or less bounded or porous. They seldom correspond fully to social movement organizations (SMOs). More often they include what Buechler has termed "social movement *communities*"—"informal networks of activists with fluid boundaries."[14] Often they bleed out into more amorphous but influential formations like the "cultures of solidarity" Rick Fantasia sees as feeding into the labor movement.[15] Movement cultures not only have shifty boundaries, but they vary immensely in degree and extent.

John Lofland has offered a schema for measuring movement culture intensity that, whatever one thinks of its particulars, provides a useful starting point for thinking about the component parts and qualities of such entities.[16] Lofland divides the terrain of movement culture into six *dimensions:* values, objects (material culture), stories, occasions (particular rituals, events), roles (specialized to create, perform, and disseminate movement ideas and values), and personae (modelers of movement identities). He further suggests that each of these elements should be examined for intensity across six *qualities:* sharing (how widely the elements are held in common), distinctiveness (how close or distant from mainstream culture or other movement cultures), scope (narrow to wide focus of cultural alternatives offered), elaboration (degree of complexity of interaction among cultural elements), quantity (sheer volume of objects, forms, ideas), and expressiveness (degree of emotional depth evoked in group members). A model like this can generate a continuum between extremes of strong and weak movement cultures, and can help isolate the impact of degrees of movement culture strength on other aspects of movement activity. In what ways, for what kinds of movements, is a strong cultural base important? In what ways, and for what kinds of movements, is a strong cultural base less important or even counter-productive? A "consensus movement," for example, might be adversely affected in its search for the broadest possible constituency by a developed cultural formation, while strong cultural bases often have been crucial to the recruitment of people to ethnic movements. Sometimes the intensity of movement culture furthers its diffusion, and sometimes it hinders it. In the case of the civil rights movement, one could argue that it did both. While the African American musical culture examined in chapter 1 traveled into other movements—"We Shall Overcome," for example, became virtually universally available—that change of context undercut much of the music's specific power and may at times have strained race relations when seen as white appropriation (one factor in the rise of separatist black movements).

The Function(s) of Culture in Movements

Alongside, or as part of, any schema for measuring movement culture intensity, it is also important to look at the *functions* of cultural forms within movements. I have identified ten primary functions (functions that overlap and interact in various configurations):

- Encourage. Individuals should feel the strength of the group. Singing in mass rallies can move a person out of the individual self to feel the strength of the group.
- Empower. Individuals should feel their own strength. Responsibility for performing a movement text can empower an individual to feel more deeply his or her own particular commitment.
- Harmonize. Smooth differences among diverse constituencies. Cultural forms can sometimes cut across lines of age, class, region, even ideology, providing a sense of overarching connection that, at least for a time, subordinates differences.
- Inform internally. Express or reinforce movement values, ideas, and tactics. Movement cultural texts provide information in compact, often highly memorable and emotionally charged ways, both to educate new recruits and to refocus veterans.
- Inform externally. Express movement values, ideas, and tactics to potential recruits, opponents, and undecided bystanders. Movement cultural texts can often be a more effective and affective means of promoting movement ideas to people outside the movement. This can take place either directly in the moment of action (through a chant or a song), or in more indirect form, such as the formation of a traveling movement culture group (SNCC's Freedom Singers or the feminist art movement's "Guerrilla Girls").
- Enact movement goals. This entails art that actively intervenes directly to achieve values. Examples include eco-active art that helps restore an

ecosystem, or a movement mural that improves the appearance of a neighborhood.

- Historicize. Invent, tell, and retell the history of the movement. This might range from songs like "Ballad of the Sit-ins" to a self-produced documentary about an action like Indymedia's *This Is What Democracy Looks Like: The Battle of Seattle.*
- Transform affect or tactics. Set a new emotional tone (for example, diffuse tension from anger to focused resistance, or from fear to calm resolve), or redirect the attention of the group (use a song or image to signal a new stage of a demonstration).
- Critique movement ideology. Challenge dominant ideas, values, and tactics or undercut tendencies toward dogma by evoking emotions and meanings not reducible to narrowly ideological terms.
- Make room for pleasure. Provide respite from the rigors of movement work through aesthetic joy.

While most of these elements should be easy to grasp, the last two, related elements, the pleasurable and the contra-ideological, may need explication. Hard-nosed critics, outside and inside movements, are often most impatient with aspects of movement cultures they see as "merely expressive"—that is, without any direct relevance to the "struggle" at hand. Within social movement theory, this is "instrumentalism." Within movements, it often manifests itself as the insistence that all participants behave at all times in a manner consistent with movement goals and values. In terms of movement theory, this tendency misses the ways in which expressive culture shapes movements, sometimes even instrumentally. And in movement practice, this tendency eventually evolves into a perfect movement of one. Movement growth is often dependent upon an openness that allows novices a space to learn, and veterans a space to escape from, movement values. Movement growth is often dependent upon a capacity to shift values, strategies, tactics, and even goals that can be served by counter-dogmatic cultural play.

Culture in movements is, of course, never pure, never purely the creation of a movement. Various mainstream cultural forces continue to play through movement cultures. For one thing, it is neither possible nor desirable to invent a full culture out of hand (not every element of mainstream culture is ideologically "tainted"). For another, it is impossible to remain isolated from the continuing flow of mainstream culture (even deeply separatist movements maintain some reliance on the dominant system). The mid-movement adoption of some elements of a movement culture by the mainstream may require the movement culture to reshape itself to retain its otherness. For example, blue jeans were first adopted by nonfarmer white youth during SNCC's Freedom Summer. When the garments became fashionable in the late 1960s, they ceased to function as a marker of movement solidarity.

Conversely, one way to keep mainstream culture at bay is through appropriation via parody. Movements frequently take elements of mainstream culture and put a movement twist on them. The most common form is the appropriation and parody of mainstream music found in many movements. It is also present in ACT UP's use of mainstream advertising techniques, a practice elaborated into a full-fledged movement unto itself in the form of groups like Adbusters and others of the "culture jamming" school of social action.[17] This process of appropriation and counter-appropriation can become quite elaborate over time. Nike Corporation, for example, at the height of protests against its allegedly exploitative labor practices, invited consumer rights advocate Ralph Nader to appear in one of its television ads, presumably on the calculated gamble that any corporation hip enough to incorporate one of its prime critics could not be all bad (Nader refused).[18] We can understand the relations of movement cultures to the wider cultural terrain by looking at two other mediating forces placed between movements and dominant cultural forms.

Subcultures and Cultural Formations in Relation to Movement Cultures

The cultural study of social movements also needs to take notice of various relationships between and among *movement cultures* (with their relatively well-defined, ideologically self-conscious, but usually narrow core constituencies), *cultural formations* (with their more diffuse, less ideologically conscious, but often broader constituencies), and *subcultures* (with their more or less political elements mediating between the other two). Here I will suggest some of the ways these latter two cultural entities can interact with social movements.

Cultural (and intellectual) formations begin in the arts or in other intellectual circles.[19] Like movement cultures, they can have a wide or a narrow agenda in terms of opposition to dominant cultural forms, but unlike them, their first concern is usually thought of as aesthetic, rather than political (though often their work includes questioning the aesthetic/

political dichotomy). Often, through a preceding process of movement culture diffusion, formations have some part of their origins in social movements, but generally they do not know of or acknowledge those origins. Cultural formations are at times virtually co-extensive with a movement culture, as was the case with what Michael Denning has called the "cultural front" formation that emerged out of the radical labor and communist movements in the United States in the 1930s, or with much of the black arts movement of the 1960s. That period also spawned the intellectual formation, black studies, closely aligned initially with the movement. Cultural formations also can be shaped or reshaped by emergent social movement cultures less directly, as I have argued is the case with certain types of academic ecocriticism, or with writers like Toni Morrison or Maxine Hong Kingston who show a strong debt to women-of-color feminisms. On some occasions, parts of a cultural formation can be absorbed fully into a social movement (as with those European dadaists who joined the communist movement). But usually the process is more mixed, as in the case of rap music, which has a range from more overtly political "message" rap to implicitly oppositional forms to coopted commercial modes.

Denning makes a useful distinction between "cultural politics" and "aesthetic ideologies" when discussing cultural formations. He uses the term *cultural politics* to name the complex of political and institutional affiliations, "the politics of letterheads and petitions, the stances taken by artists and intellectuals," and the history of the cultural-political institutions in which the new formation is embedded. *Aesthetic ideologies,* on the other hand, refers to the politics of form, the actual aesthetic practices, the forms, styles, genres, and conventions that emerge to embody the cultural politics.[20] Depending on the degree of autonomy insisted upon by the artists and intellectuals involved, the cultural politics and the aesthetic ideologies range from close alignment to considerable disjunction. Some politically committed artists have seen their art as a "weapon" in the struggle, some equally committed ones have insisted that their politics and their art are fully separable, and most have found positions between these poles. Frequently within the same cultural formation there are several different aesthetic ideologies that need to be sorted out and judged by specific aesthetico-political criteria. Judging forms ranging from ephemeral works of agit-prop to complex works of art by the same criteria has often led to dismissive evaluations of all political art. In the 1930s the cultural front contributed significantly to both major works of art like the film *Citizen Kane* and ephemeral works designed only for a very specific audience of workers on a picket line. Similarly, the cultural formations of the 1960s produced both street theater works meant to be effective for a few days, and contributed to the creation of brilliant works of literary art by Toni Morrison that will be read for hundreds of years.

This raises the difficult question of the relation between politics and aesthetics. There is no space to tackle that extremely complicated terrain here, but let me offer a general principle that scholars as different as Raymond Williams and Pierre Bourdieu agree upon: the logic of politics and the logic of aesthetic objects seldom, if ever, perfectly coincide. In Bourdieu's terms, the economies of culture and the economies of politics overlap and interact in a variety of ways, but are never simply co-extensive. Each "field," as Bourdieu calls them, is subject to internal rules and regularities that are peculiarly its own. The fields meet in that over-arching terrain he names the "field of power," but the meeting points in the field of power never exhaust the meaning of the work of art, and political meanings are always also in excess of aesthetic ones on their own terms. Put differently, any aesthetic text can be put to political ends, and all aesthetic texts have political implications, but no aesthetic text is reducible to its political meanings. Two paradoxical observations by important thinkers of the political-aesthetic dynamic can perhaps reinforce this point: "The [ideological] tendency of a work of literature can be politically correct only if it is also correct in the literary sense" (Walter Benjamin); "The conflict between politics and art...cannot and must not be solved" (Hannah Arendt).

In my view, one crucial dimension of the role of art (as opposed to more purely instrumental cultural forms) in movements is to critique and transcend ideology. As I suggested, aesthetic texts are always both ideological and in excess of ideology, and their role in and around movements can be to remind activists, who often are tempted by the pressures of political struggle into ideologically reductive positions, that the full lived complexity of cultural life cannot be reduced to any ideological system.

Mediating between movement cultures and cultural formations are *subcultures*. Subcultures may be ethnic, class-based, generational, aesthetic, or social in various combinations. Like formations, they can be more or less overtly political in orientation. But they differ from movement cultures proper to the extent that they do not centrally employ strategies that directly challenge the existing political, economic, and social system. Some cultural formations, like punk rock, for example, are deeply tied to subcultures. Others are more diffusely spread through the culture. Some subcultures are, rhetorically at least, overtly *oppositional* with regard to the dominant culture, while others are content to be *alternative*, that is, to live and let live. Both the field of cultural studies and the field of sociology have done much to explore the nature and meaning(s) of subcultures.[21] But each shows some of the same biases that mar their work generally in relation to social movement study. That is, some cultural studies work presumes a degree of political contestation built in, as it were, to primarily aesthetically oriented subcultures that exaggerates their political impact. Conversely, much of the sociological study of subcultures has had far too little to say about their semiotic activity, the symbolic challenge that even relatively nonpolitical subcultures offer, at least potentially.

Because subcultures exist, by definition, in some degree of distance from mainstream cultures (with the prefix *sub-* suggesting their lower status from the point of view of the dominant), they always exist as *potentially* political forces. Rastafarian religion in Jamaica, for example, always had the potential to be turned from alternative to oppositional to openly political form, but it took the influence of the new black nationalist movement cultures of the late 1960s and the conscious work of figures like Bob Marley to bring forth that potential. Subcultural force has to be mobilized or folded into social movements to reach its full disruptive potential. Ethnic subcultures have played particularly important roles in recent movements. Ethno-racialized people in a U.S. context can be said in some sense to form an overarching subculture due to their marginalization within white dominant America, but these larger formations never translate fully into a movement culture. To take but one example from this book, in chapter 4 we saw how *selected elements* of Mexican and Mexican-American ethnic subcultures were adopted and adapted by and for the movement culture of the Chicano/a *movimiento*. And the adoption of the politicized ethnic label *Chicano*, in place of more neutral or assimilated terms like *Mexican American* or *Hispanic*, itself sought with some success to claim this movement-bred identity as the definition of the ethnic group more broadly.

The political valence of subcultures is also shaped by the degree of tolerance for alternatives that exists in a given society. In totalitarian or highly controlled societies, any form of subcultural activity (religious, aesthetic, ethnic) can be perceived as threatening. Conversely, most putatively open, democratic societies tolerate a great deal of subcultural activity, so long as hegemony is not threatened. When that point of threat is reached, however, subcultures can sometimes be politicized rapidly. This process was at work, for example, at the Stonewall Bar in Greenwich Village in 1969 when police, by pushing some "queers" too far, drove an underground subculture to the surface, igniting a gay liberation movement. While occasionally entire subcultures may transform into movement culture, more often only some members of a given group come to the conclusion that they wish to expand their subculture into a wider frame, or that the existence of their subculture can only be sustained by political action. This situation varies greatly from society to society even within the democratic West. The United States, for example, has had far fewer and far less elaborated subcultures than England or Western Europe. This helps to account for the far greater emphasis placed on subcultures as movement cultures or sites for the launching of movements in the work of European theorists like Alberto Melucci.

More generally, on a less dramatic level, subcultures are often important recruitment networks for movements. This was true for certain elements of the hippie subculture with regard to the new left student movement of the 1960s, and for certain elements of both New Age and neo-punk subcultures with respect to the antiglobalization movement. In traditional terms, some movement cultures may function more instrumentally, others more expressively, but these dimensions are never fully separable. At times, movements become almost indistinguishable from subcultures in their degree of elaboration, and in doing so make more active the symbolic challenge implicit in many subcultures. At other times this process can reverse itself such that a movement culture evolves into a subculture. While often criticized by activists as a devolution, at times—as Verta Taylor points out with regard to groups during the "doldrums period" of the women's movement—the transformation of a movement community into a subculture with a less overtly political agenda can provide an "abeyance structure" that keeps movement values and goals alive until a new phase of movement activity proper can emerge.[22]

Clearly, as with the boundaries between and among the political, the social, the economic, and the cultural, boundaries between subcultures, cultural formations, and movement cultures (and the dominant culture) are in practice often quite fluid. Moreover, no cultural form can remain wholly oppositional or become wholly coopted; context is everything in terms of the political valence of a cultural text. But in any full examination of cultural activity in and around social movements, it is analytically useful to work through something like this range of more or less distinct components.

Residual, Emergent, and Dominant Cultural Elements

In the life cycle of a given movement, and in terms of larger cycles of protest, cultural formations, subcultures, and movement cultures undergo various processes of evolution and interaction. Much of this dynamic can be analyzed well through Raymond Williams's notion of "residual, emergent, and dominant" cultural processes.[23] Cultural formations, subcultures, and movement cultures all draw upon elements from each of these processes of cultural evolution in the wider society, and each passes through these stages in the process of its own development.

The civil rights movement, for example, drew upon a residual folk cultural form, the spiritual, and turned it into a major resource for the movement. The black power movement, on the other hand, harnessed an emergent pop cultural form, soul music, and turned it to its purposes. On a different scale, the black liberation struggle overall can be said to have shifted gears to a black power phase when the civil rights movement had passed from an emergent into a dominant movement culture form that was felt as a constraint on some current and many new members of the movement community. At that same historical moment, however, as the civil rights "master frame" was passing from dominant to residual for some black activists, it was being transcribed by analogy into emergent movements for civil rights among women and homosexuals.

Similar logics are at play in the ways in which subcultures and cultural formations move in and out of movement culture orbits. Sometimes a movement culture can revive a subculture, as the antiglobalization movement has to some extent done with some punk subcultures. And sometimes an emergent subculture or cultural formation can reinvigorate a movement culture, as when the emerging hippie subculture expanded the boundaries of the anti–Vietnam war movement. Often this process is so mutually reinforcing that it is difficult to tell which force is the dynamic one in the relationship, but that determination is often less important than understanding how they work in a symbiosis that furthers the aims of each.

Movements as Messages, Codes, and Theorizing Entities

The most important cultural impact of a social movement may not come from particular cultural values, ideas, or forms, but from its overall structure. Recently, several movement scholars have attempted to view the overall structure of movements as "messages," "symbolic actions," "direct theory," or "social texts" that speak beyond their particular issues. All movements, even the most consensus-oriented ones in societies that legitimate certain kinds of protest, offer some degree of symbolic challenge to the dominant order just by their existence outside normalized political activity. But obviously the degree and kind of symbolic challenge offered by particular movements vary immensely. Wini Breines has analyzed, for example, how the "prefigurative politics" of the new left movement of the 1960s was embodied in its movement culture as it sought to enact within itself the radically different values and forms it sought to create throughout the wider world.[24] Feminist scholar Noël Sturgeon has offered a deeper semiotic reading of the organizational structures (like small-scale affinity groups and consensus process) of the antinuclear direct action movement of the 1980s. She argues that movement structures not only expressed movement values, but also embodied the movement's theories about social change. Sturgeon offers the term *direct theory* to characterize the way in which the movement's organizational form embodied a point-by-point theoretical and symbolic alternative to the dominant order's notions of legitimate power.[25] Italian movement theorist Alberto Melucci has written of the "symbolic challenge of movements," in which movement cultural codes counter the cultural codes of the dominant society through a sometimes direct, sometimes indirect semiotic warfare.[26] In my own earlier work, *Fifteen Jugglers, Five Believers*, I argued that movements both create new "social texts" and are themselves "texts." Movements are at once sites from which particular alternative stories about the culture emerge, and a kind of meta-narrative about an alternative way to live in the wider world.[27] Though differing in emphasis and case study examples, all these theorists have shown how movement cultures become messages of resistance and embodiments of alternative social arrangements.

Questions of (Collective) Identity

One of the more developed areas in the cultural study of movements has dealt with issues of *collective identity formation*.[28] I will not rehearse this work here, but I will point to some directions in which it might be further elaborated. While much attention has focused rightly on the "collective identities" produced in movements, far less has been given to how cultural forms in and around movements help shape movement identities that later become available as general, cultural identities in the larger society. The black power movement and its aligned black arts cultural formation, for example, invented a militant black self that eventually became widely diffused as a key element of a more autonomous, empowered "Afro-American" identity. As I suggested with regard to the Black Panthers, this process included something like the transformation of the tough street-corner "black dudes" and "nasty gals" into "badass revolutionaries," a move that carried over into the wider black world, strengthening self-esteem and raising the level of resistance a notch even among those not consciously self-identifying as political.

This process of identity transformation is a complicated one inadequately theorized by such concepts as "identity politics." Movement-bred identities are neither true selves to be defended nor disabling essences to be avoided. They are strategically necessary creations that change as movements change. It is primarily from outside movements, or in moments of movement decline, that they are turned into static forms defended in essentialist terms. Much social science study of social movements is based in a "rational actor" model of the individual subject. Whatever limited utility this model of identity may have had for understanding the modern, industrial actor, it has very little application to the postmodern, electronic subject of most "new" social movements. Identities are not frozen forms into which new content can be poured. Nor are they individual creations. All identities are collective identities. And social movements are among the key forces transforming/creating new cultural identities. I want to suggest that a more nuanced understanding of the construction of identities within movements can benefit future movements, but can also explain more generally the nature of contemporary culture. Tracing mediation mechanisms is key here—

especially, in our time, mass media mechanisms. The move from print to broadcast media to networked computing and other new media has shaped identity generally and movement identities specifically. Alongside and entwined with new media, movements have been major forces in the creation of the contemporary emphasis on identities.

At the same time, a proper understanding of social movement identities can be a useful corrective to the limits of so-called identity politics. The inherent paradox is that "identity politics" can exist only when identities are in question. Identity becomes an issue only when it is no longer presumed, taken for granted. This means that identities emerging from self-conscious political struggles are always unstable formations. This should be clear immediately from reflection on the evolution and proliferation of identities over the last few decades. To illustrate this simply through self-naming, one could show how a superficially stable racial signifier changes through the politically evolving sense of self embodied in a succession of terms: "Negro," "black," "Afro-American," "African American," "member of the African diaspora." Each of these successive identities could be shown to indicate not only ideological shifts, but also the conflicting influence of various interacting class, gender, regional, and sexual identities. Assertions of essential black identity in the face of these changes, embedded as they are in shifts in racial formations of the culture at large, have never gone unchallenged, particularly when emerging in the dynamic context of a movement.

These issues are particularly important if, as Sidney Tarrow has argued, we are becoming "movement societies" in which social movements play an increasingly central role in defining collective identities.[29] Movements are surely one of the main sources for the phenomena that have led some postmodern theorists to claim that identities are more fluid and variable than ever before. One need not embrace this notion uncritically to agree that movements as sources of identity are likely to continue to be a major social force.

Ideology, Consciousness, and Material-Discursive Processes

Much of the most important cultural action in movements occurs on that notoriously fuzzy terrain called consciousness. Movements generate new ways of thinking, new ways of being, new norms of behavior, new styles of living (as opposed to mere "lifestyles"), all of which contain an element of what has historically been classified as the "subjective."

These new ways of being are expressed in the formal political realm of parties, elections, legal decisions, and legislation, but often in indirect ways for which movements seldom get the credit (from the society at large or from scholars of movements). Beneath the more studied level of formal ideologies, or even elaborated cognitive "frames," are levels of often contradictory but always socially meaningful layers of consciousness that neither empiricists nor historical materialists are very comfortable with.

But to leave these dimensions unexplored is to do damage, even violence, to movements and to the deeply aggrieved lives out of which movements often arise. Recent social and cultural theories have given us better tools to challenge simplistic dichotomies between objective and subjective, the materialist and the idealist. The crucial focus on political-economic structures, or empirically measurable behavior patterns, cannot capture all of social life. Cultural factors of meaning-making are always semi-autonomous with regard to material conditions. In not taking seriously qualities like pride, dignity, hope, faith, self-esteem, and related elements of consciousness, or by reducing them to "merely" psychological or subjective factors, we may miss key dimensions of a movement's impact. We may also rob subordinated groups of one of their most valuable resources—their ability to see themselves differently from how they are seen by their oppressors.

Perhaps the best way to illustrate this is in relation to the most extreme cases of material deprivation. In *Domination and the Arts of Resistance*, James C. Scott shows convincingly that even in the most extreme conditions of deprivation and unfreedom—slavery, serfdom, indentured servitude, rigid caste cultures, concentration camps, prisons, and so on—people have shown an amazing capacity to control their consciousness and resist the imposition of dominant views. Scott has shown, moreover, that the "hidden transcripts" that demonstrate this resistance often take a cultural form as folktales, songs, jokes, and theater.[30] Surely, then, we do a disservice to movement actors when we fail to acknowledge that part of their experience takes the form of "subjective" transformations not easily visible in external structures or behaviors. Not only is it possible to talk about a more (or less) subjectively free member of an oppressed group, it is often essential to do so if we are to understand how change happens (or fails to happen). Movement analysts should be encouraged to become skilled not only in interpreting explicit movement culture texts, but also in getting at "hidden transcripts" in the interstices of cultural documents. These are not individual experiences but "structures of feeling" every bit as efficacious as political or economic structures.[31] The "freedom high" experienced by many activists working in the southern civil rights struggle, for example, proved to be a materially important force in propelling the movement forward.

At the same time, any argument that so-called subjective factors have become more important than ever in our putatively "information age" must be made with caution. Without that caution, we get statements like this: "In the contemporary context, we can define exploitation as a form of dependent participation in the information flow, as the deprivation of control over the construction of meaning. The true exploitation is not the deprivation of information; even in the shantytowns of the cities of the Third World people are today widely exposed to the media, only they do not have any power to organize this information according to their own needs. Thus the real domination is today the exclusion from the power of naming."[32] This is hyperbole bordering on nonsense. The "real" power is the power of naming? This takes the now self-evident insight that cultural coding is important, and turns it into the *only* important power. The material conditions of those shantytowns are unimportant? Does the lack of hygiene and nutrition, or the opportunity to go to school or the material quality of schools, play no role in the conditions in which power is organized?

To argue, as I just have, that material conditions do not tell the whole story is far different from leaving them out of the story altogether. The power to name reality for others has always been a component of exploitation. That it is more so today is at best debatable. This is the kind of argument that draws attention away from, for example, the material conditions of the production of computers and focuses it exclusively on the information flows made possible by computers and their networks. In place of the swing between fully determining material conditions, and free-floating/flowing information, we need to conceptualize the *material-discursive* in more careful ways. Not only do "ideas become a material force when they are gripped by the masses" (Marx), but in various more subtle, daily ways language as a material force is always entangled with institutions and extra-linguistic structures that are reduced to "signs" only at the peril of analytic obfuscation and moral obtuseness.[33]

The Diffusion and Defusion of Movement Culture

Putting the various elements discussed above back together into their lived complexity, we can see that the most important dimension of a social movement's impact may be the diffusion of its culture out into the putative cultural "mainstream." This reality is obscured by the inherent contestation between normative institutions and extra-institutional movements (not to mention normative social science), which means that movements almost never get much credit for the political, social, or cultural changes to which they contribute. Those changes are almost always highly mediated and indirect. And when they are not indirect, they tend to be superficial, since only those forms and norms seen as unthreatening are openly adopted (as when, for example, black power cultural forms are reduced to Afro hairstyles and a preference for pseudo-African dress style). Nevertheless, even these *defusing* appropriations often carry with them supplemental elements of the more politically charged contexts in which they initially appear (an interest in Africa occasioned by curiosity about that *dashiki* robe might just lead to serious political revelations).

Perhaps the clearest examples of these processes arise from contemporary women's movements. Anyone looking at gender norms in the 1950s and the 1990s would see an immense change at every possible level. The impact of feminism, significant as it has been on legislation and on formal institutions, is still greater at the level of personal interaction. Most of the differences between gender norms in those two decades bear the imprint of feminist ideas. Yet few of the individuals affected by those changes would call themselves feminists and few had direct contact with a women's movement group. A widely used women's studies classroom experiment reveals how this process manifests itself. The professor writes on the chalkboard a list of women's movement issues: equal pay for equal work, equity in sports access, right to reproductive freedom, equality in male-female personal relations, better rape prevention and victim rights, and so on. The instructor then asks who in the class supports each of these items. In most classrooms, even in relatively conservative communities, the response to virtually all the items is one of overwhelming support. Then the professor asks the next question: How many of the students in the class are feminists? The hands raised, even in relatively liberal communities, are usually very, very few.

Every one of the issues listed emerged out of feminist social movement struggle. Yet virtually no one among those supporting the issues identifies with the movement that put them forth.

This story illustrates what I call the *paradox of diffusion and defusion.* The women's movement ideas have been diffused with striking success out into the wider culture, but they have been detached from their movement origins (and, in varying degrees, defused from their most challenging form). Just as it is axiomatic that movements seldom get credit for changes they force upon government and nongovernment institutions, it is axiomatic that changes in norms initiated by social movement activity pass through enough levels of mediation to make that origin invisible. The underlying reason is the same in both cases: most institutions, whether political or cultural, are invested in their own stability, while movements thrive on engendering *in*stability.

Movement cultures are diffused into the wider culture on several different levels reflecting the layers of culture within the movement itself. In the broadest sense, we can talk about culture being diffused through *folk culture* (as was the case with civil rights music), *popular culture* (as in the case of rock music's relation to the antiwar movement of the 1960s or the anti-apartheid movement of the 1980s), and/or through *high culture* (as in the case of the profusion of feminist-inflected women-of-color literary production since the 1970s).

The central paradox is that the energies of radical movement cultures and the cultural forms they generate have their greatest impact when they are *diffused* in a less overtly ideological way into the larger social arena via cultural movements. But that impact is largely *defused* unless self-consciously ideological social movements continue their work. This ongoing, irresolvable, creative tension between defusion and diffusion should be a key point of study for the cultural analysis of movements. Movement cultures are partly implicated in, not wholly immune to, these processes of appropriation, cooptation, and defusion. But the chapters of this book show that they are the primary means of resisting the totalizing forces that would reduce all culture to economic exchange in the course of instantiating a tragically inegalitarian and unjust globalized capitalist system.

As the new media struggle around the Battle of Seattle (discussed in chapter 9) illustrates particularly well, the diffusing and defusing of movement texts and movements as texts entails an increasingly intricate dance between mainstream and alternative media. The increasing speed and intensity of processes that commodify or otherwise appropriate dissent has complicated the articulation of cultural politics and alternative political cultures. A cultural studies practice that continues to speak very vaguely of cultural politics and negotiated readings of social texts is not enough. We need to analyze more fully the processes by which movements help create contexts of cultural reception and production of alternative cultures. The work of the social construction "frame" theorists, and of certain "social cultural studies" advocates, is suggestive in this regard, but far more work needs to be done

Political Economy, Cultural Autonomy, and Historical (Con)Texts

I have argued for the vital importance of culture to social movements and of social movements to culture. But this is not an argument to view culture as somehow autonomous from, or more important than, the other social forces that have more often been studied in relation to movements. The primary focus until recently on organizational patterns, political processes, economic resources, leadership styles, and so on is extremely important. These are profoundly important aspects of movements and must remain at the core of any full agenda for analyzing movements. Culture is always entwined with social, economic, and political forces, but they in turn are entwined with culture.

Steven Buechler offers a layered conception of the force fields around movements that is crucial to keep in sight as one attempts to think about, and to a limited degree isolate, the cultural dimension. In *Social Movements in Advanced Capitalism,* Buechler sets up a model that places movements in systems that move from global to national to regional to local, and argues that each embedded level is capable of redounding back on the other levels. This version of a macro-, meso-, and micro-level analysis clearly shows how no one level can be understood independently of the others. While the model is, as Buechler readily admits, susceptible to overly schematic use, and is subject to challenge in its particulars, it provides a very useful framework for thinking about movements in their wider contexts. It reminds us that global political-economic structures are lived locally (and culturally), that each level is simultaneously global-local and political-cultural. This is, of course, also the insight of what may well become the defining social movement of the twenty-first century, the movement to shift globalizing capitalism in radically democratic, egalitarian, and environmentally sustainable directions.

It takes nothing away from other important dimensions of analysis to say that we need far more work on the cultural forms active within movements and the cultural forces movements unleash. Again, my intent is not to argue for the *greater* importance of culture, just for its importance alongside of and entangled with political, social, and economic forces that have traditionally gained more attention. These divisions themselves—social, economic, political, cultural—are, after all, themselves socially constructed, cultural concepts, not real things neatly dividing the world. Giving culture a stronger footing in this list will allow us to better understand the interactions of all these interwoven forces. But, in turn, without addressing structural forces, particularly political economy, analysis of the cultural dimension is itself radically incomplete.

Notes

Introduction

1. See Charles Tilly, "From Interactions to Outcomes in Social Movements," in Marco Giugni, Doug McAdam, and Charles Tilly, eds., *How Social Movements Matter* (Minneapolis: University of Minnesota Press, 1999), 253–70.

2. I am paraphrasing these lines from Hughes's poem, "Let America Be America Again": "O, let America be America again / The land that has never been yet / And yet must be—the land where *every* [one] is free."

3. Stewart Burns's rich book *Social Movements of the 1960s* (New York: Twayne, 1990), which includes a fair amount of information on the cultural dimensions of the three movements it covers, is a partial exception to this claim, and was an inspiration in the early stages of my work on this book.

4. I first encountered the phrase *social cultural studies* in the work of Steven Seidman. See, for example, Steven Seidman and Linda Nicholson, eds., *Social Postmodernism: Beyond Identity Politics* (Cambridge, UK: Cambridge University Press, 1995).

1. Singing Civil Rights

1. Kerran L. Sanger, *"When the Spirit Says Sing!": The Role of Freedom Songs in the Civil Rights Movement* (New York: Garland, 1995), 46–47. I am most indebted, as is anyone writing about music in the movement, to the life and work of Bernice Johnson Reagon, whose life lived in singing struggle inspired not only the chapter but this book as a whole. Her particular contributions to the ideas in this chapter are cited in the notes below as appropriate.

2. The standard biography of King is David Garrow, *Bearing the Cross: Martin Luther King, Jr., and the Southern Christian Leadership Conference* (New York: Morrow, 1986).

3. The best history of SNCC is Clayborne Carson, *In Struggle: SNCC and the Black Awakening of the 1960s* (Cambridge, MA: Harvard University Press, 1981). See also Charles Payne, *"I've Got the Light of Freedom": The Organizing Tradition and the*

Mississippi Freedom Struggle (Berkeley: University of California Press, 1994); and John Dittmer, *Local People: The Struggle for Civil Rights in Mississippi* (Urbana: University of Illinois Press, 1995).

4. On women in the movement, see Vicki Crawford, Jacqueline Rouse, and Barbara Woods, eds., *Black Women in the Civil Rights Movement: Trailblazers and Torchbearers* (Bloomington: Indiana University Press, 1993); and Bettye Collier-Thomas, ed., *Sisters in Struggle: African-American Women of the Civil Rights–Black Power Movements* (New York: New York University Press, 2001). A longer range view can be found in Lynne Olson, *Freedom's Daughters: Unsung Heroines of the Civil Rights Movement, 1830–1970* (New York: Touchstone Books, 2002). For biographies of three key women, see Joanne Grant, *Ella Baker: Freedom Bound* (New York: John Wiley and Sons, 1998); Cynthia Brown, ed., *Ready from Within: A First Person Narrative: Septima Clark and the Civil Rights Movement* (Navarro, CA: Wild Trees Press, 1986); Chana Kai Lee, *For Freedom's Sake: The Life of Fannie Lou Hamer* (Urbana: University of Illinois, 2000); and Kay Mills, *This Little Light of Mine: The Life of Fannie Lou Hamer* (New York: Plume, 1994).

5. See, for example, John D'Emilio, "Homophobia and the Trajectory of Postwar American Radicalism: The Case of Bayard Rustin," *Radical History Review* 62 (1995): 80–103; and John Howard, *Men Like That: A Southern Queer History* (Chicago: University of Chicago Press, 1999). While lesbians of color like Audre Lorde and June Jordan have brilliantly connected racial, gender, and sexuality oppression in their writings, and the contributions of the civil rights movement to gay liberation have been much noted, there is much more work to be done on the less explored contributions of gay men and lesbians to the civil rights movement in the 1950s and 1960s.

6. For a rich discussion of nonviolence as a powerful tool for change, see Gene Sharp, *The Power of Nonviolent Action*, 3 vols. (Boston: Porter Sargent, 1974, 1975, 1985); and Peter Ackerman and Christopher Kruegler, *Strategic Nonviolent Conflict* (New York: Praeger, 1993).

7. On the Highlander Folk School (later Highlander Center), see Frank Adams, with Myles Horton, *Unearthing Seeds of Fire: The Idea of Highlander* (Winston-Salem, NC: John F. Blair, 1975); Myles Horton, with Judith and Herbert Kohl, *The Long Haul: An Autobiography* (New York: Doubleday, 1990); and John Glen, *Highlander: No Ordinary School, 1932–1962* (Louisville: University of Kentucky Press, 1988).

8. For a brilliant analysis of the ongoing influence of the labor-centered popular front social movement emerging in the 1930s and continuing well into the 1950s, see Michael Denning, *The Cultural Front: The Laboring of American Culture in the Twentieth Century* (New York: Verso, 1996). For a rich analysis of the dynamic of race, gender, culture, and labor in the 1940s, see George Lipsitz, *Rainbow at Midnight* (Urbana: University of Illinois Press, 1994).

9. Quoted in Bernice Johnson Reagon, "Songs of the Civil Rights Movement, 1955–1965: A Study in Culture History," Ph.D. diss., Howard University, 1975 (Ann Arbor, MI: Xerox University Microfilms, 1975), 159.

10. The pioneering book on the "political process model" of social movement analysis focuses on the civil rights/black power movement. See Doug McAdam, *The Political Process and the Development of Black Insurgency, 1930–1970* (Chicago: University of Chicago Press, 1982).

11. Quoted in Steven Kasher, *The Civil Rights Movement: A Photographic History, 1954–68* (New York: Abbeville Press, 1996), 78.

12. King's education in nonviolence by Lawson, Rustin, Smiley, Farmer, and others is important to understand because he is sometimes mistakenly credited with *inventing* a tradition he was in fact translating, though with telling brilliance and effectiveness. In this, as in many other matters, King's genius was that of a rhetorician, a persuader, and an inspirer, more than a strategist.

13. The most important study of the role of church culture is Aldon Morris, *Origins of the Civil Rights Movement: Black Communities Organizing for Change* (New York: Free Press, 1984).

14. Baker's thoughts on organizing, including gender implications, are brilliantly and usefully summarized by Charles Payne, "Ella Baker and Models of Social Change," *Signs* 14 (1989): 885–99.

15. The work of these activists anticipates what academics now call "critical pedagogy." In the history of this school of teaching theory, Brazilian Paulo Freire has often overshadowed the U.S. homegrown critical pedagogues, Clark, Horton, and Baker. For the connections between these traditions, see Myles Horton and Paulo Freire, *We Make the Road by Walking: Conversations on Education and Social Change* (Philadelphia: Temple University Press, 1990).

16. Reagon, "Songs of Civil Rights," 24.

17. Sanger, "*When the Spirit Says Sing*," 106.

18. On the Montgomery bus boycott, see Stewart Burns, ed., *Daybreak of Freedom: The Montgomery Bus Boycott* (Chapel Hill: University of North Carolina Press, 1997); Jo Ann Gibson Robinson, *The Montgomery Bus Boycott and the Women Who Started It* (Knoxville: University of Tennessee Press, 1987).

19. Quoted in Reagon, "Songs of Civil Rights," 15.

20. On the sit-ins, see Carson, *In Struggle*.

21. Reagon, "Songs of Civil Rights," 106–8.

22. Pete Seeger and Bob Reiser, *Everybody Says Freedom: The Story of the Civil Rights Movement in Songs and Pictures* (New York: W.W. Norton, 1989), 72.

23. See Doug McAdam, *Freedom Summer* (New York: Oxford University Press, 1988).

24. Bernice Reagon quoted in Seeger and Reiser, *Everybody Says Freedom*, 82.

25. Payne, "*I've Got the Light of Freedom*," 262.

26. Guy Carawan and Candie Carawan, *We Shall Overcome: Songs of the Southern Freedom Movement* (New York: Oak Publications, 1963), 74.

27. A visual record of these lynching "texts" can be found in James Allen, ed., *Without Sanctuary: Lynching Photography in America* (Santa Fe, NM: Twin Palms, 2000).

28. Quoted in Stewart Burns, *Social Movements of the 1960s* (New York: Twayne, 1990).

29. See Payne, "*I've Got the Light of Freedom*," 34–35.

30. Joyce Ladner, in Payne, "*I've Got the Light of Freedom*," 54.

31. Ibid., 15.

32. Bruce Hartford quoted in Sanger, "*When the Spirit Says Sing!*" 127.

33. Cordell Reagon quoted in Seeger and Reiser, *Everybody Says Freedom*, 77.

34. James Farmer quoted in ibid., 61.

35. Both parodies in Payne, "*I've Got the Light of Freedom*," 263.

36. Ibid., 261.

37. Ibid., 146.

38. Sanger, *"When the Spirit Says Sing!"* 106.

39. Quoted in Seeger and Reiser, *Everybody Says Freedom*, 85.

40. Quoted in Reagon, "Songs of Civil Rights," 16.

41. Carawan, *We Shall Overcome*, 71.

42. Payne, *"I've Got the Light of Freedom,"* 63.

43. Quoted in Juan Williams, *Eyes on the Prize* (New York: Viking, 1987), 163.

44. Quoted in Sanger, *"When the Spirit Says Sing!"* 9.

45. Payne, *"I've Got the Light of Freedom,"* 263.

46. Carawan, *We Shall Overcome*, 69. For more on religion see Sanger, *"When the Spirit Says Sing!"* 91–94.

47. Cordell Reagon quoted in Seeger and Reiser, *Everybody Says Freedom*, 61.

48. Zellner quoted in Carawan, *We Shall Overcome*, 92.

49. John Lewis, *Walking with the Wind: A Memoir of the Movement* (New York: Harvest Books, 1999), 268–69.

50. Bob Cohen quoted in Sanger, *"When the Spirit Says Sing!"* 19.

51. On Ricks and Carmichael, see Carson, *In Struggle*, 209–10.

2. Scenarios for Revolution

1. Seale, *Seize the Time: The Story of the Black Panther Party and Huey P. Newton* (Baltimore: Black Classic Press, 1991 [1970]), 161–62. A video clip of the capitol action can be found at bobbyseale.com/sixtiesvideo.html.

2. When a Shakespearean character declaims that "all the world's a stage," the playwright was drawing upon a traditional notion of *theatrum mundi* (theater of the world) that was already hundreds of years old. What made the 1960s stage unusual was the power of the still emerging medium of television to make the world stage truly projectable across the world.

3. Van Deburg, *New Day in Babylon: The Black Power Movement and American Culture, 1965–1975* (Chicago: University of Chicago Press, 1992), 195.

4. Ibid., 10.

5. Otto Kerner et al., *Report of the National Advisory Commission on Civil Disorders (1968)* (New York: Pantheon, 1988). The notion of "black rage" was popularized in the 1960s by Price Cobbs and William Grier, *Black Rage* (New York: Bantam Books, 1969), to describe a survival mechanism of blacks in which individuals take on parts of the violent stereotype imposed by the dominant society.

6. See Malcolm X, *By Any Means Necessary: The Speeches, Interviews, and a Letter* (New York: Pathfinder Press, 1970), for many of his key speeches.

7. Williams, *Black Theater in the 1960s and 1970s* (Westport, CT: Greenwood Publishing Group, 1985), 20–21.

8. Baraka, in *Liberator* (July 1965), 4–6.

9. Huey P. Newton, *To Die for the People*, ed. Toni Morrison (New York: Vintage, 1971), 92.

10. For a summary of Bullins's years as a radical playwright, see Genevieve Fabre, *Drumbeats, Masks, and Metaphors* (Cambridge, MA: Harvard University Press, 1983), 168–89.

11. Williams, *Black Theater in the 1960s and 1970s*, 25.

12. See David Hilliard and Donald Weise, eds., *The Huey P. Newton Reader* (New York: Seven Stories Press, 2002), 46.

13. Williams, *Black Theater in the 1960s and 1970s*, 116–17.

14. Angela Y. Davis, "Black Nationalism: The Sixties and the Nineties," in Gina Dent, ed., *Black Popular Culture* (Seattle: Bay Press, 1992), 317–33.

15. For the Ten-Point Program of the Black Panther Party, see the appendix at the end of this chapter.

16. Philip S. Foner, ed., *The Black Panthers Speak* (Philadelphia: J. B. Lippincott Company, 1970), 19.

17. Quoted in ibid., xvi.

18. Ibid., 133–34.

19. Ibid., 268.

20. Nikhil Pal Singh, "The Black Panthers and the 'Undeveloped Country' of the Left," in Charles E. Jones, ed., *Black Panther Party Reconsidered* (Baltimore: Black Classic Press, 1998), 57–105, especially 63.

21. Van Deburg, *New Day in Babylon*, 307.

22. Hilliard and Weise, *Huey P. Newton Reader*, 169–70.

23. The pamphlet is reprinted in Newton, *To Die for the People*, 152–55.

24. Panther performances in the homes of rich white sympathizers as an effort to raise money are chronicled cynically by journalist/novelist Tom Wolfe in *Radical Chic and Mau-Mauing the Flak Catchers* (New York: Bantam Books, 1970).

25. Details of the COINTELPRO activities and their ongoing impact can be found in Winston A. Grady-Willis, "The Black Panther Party: State Repression and Political Prisoners," in Jones, ed., *Black Panther Party Reconsidered*, 362–89; Ward Churchill and Jim Vander Wall, *Agents of Repression: The FBI's Secret Wars against the Black Panther Party and the American Indian Movement* (Boston: South End Press, 1988); and Huey P. Newton, *War against the Panthers: A Study of Repression in America* (New York: Harlem River Press, 1996 [based on Newton's Ph.D. dissertation in the history of consciousness program at the University of California, Santa Cruz, completed in 1980]).

26. Foner, *Black Panthers Speak*, 19.

27. Cited in Akinyele Omowale Umoja, "Repression Breeds Resistance," in Kathleen Cleaver and George Katsiaficas, eds., *Liberation, Imagination, and the Black Panther Party* (New York: Routledge, 2001), 8.

28. The cause of some of these imprisoned Panthers is still being fought. In the late 1990s appeals of the case of Geronimo ji Jaga (Elmer Pratt) successfully led to his conviction being overturned after twenty-seven years in jail. The fate of former Panther Mumia Abu-Jamal, currently on death row, and several others still behind bars, remains uncertain. Despite the congressional Church Commission's findings of countless illegalities in the operation of COINTELPRO, no one in the FBI or any other law enforcement body has served a day in prison for their crimes against the Panthers, AIM, and other groups, including the murders of Fred Hampton and Mark Clark. The Patriot Act, passed by Congress in the hysterical aftermath of the tragedy of September 11, 2001, swept away generations of constitutional rights and may give rise to another wave of law enforcement repression of legitimate protest that is likely to become riddled with the kind of gross illegality and injustice found in COINTELPRO.

29. Singh, "Black Panthers and the 'Undeveloped Country' of the Left," 62.

30. For a view of this decline focusing especially on the personal pathologies of Huey Newton, see Hugh Pearson, *The Shadow of a Panther* (Reading, MA: Addison-

Wesley, 1994). For a critical analysis of the limitations of Pearson's book, see Errol Anthony Henderson, "Shadow of a Clue," in Cleaver and Katsiaficas, *Liberation,* 197–207.

31. Ollie A. Johnson III, "Explaining the Demise of the Black Panther Party: The Role of Internal Factors," in Jones, ed., *Black Panther Party Reconsidered,* 391–414, especially 408.

32. For an assessment of the role of women in the Panthers, see Kathleen Cleaver, "Women, Power, and Revolution," in Cleaver and Katsiaficas, *Liberation,* 123–27; and essays by Regina Jennings, Trayce Matthews, and Angela D. LeBlanc-Ernest in the "Gender Dynamics" section of Jones, ed., *Black Panther Party Reconsidered.* Elaine Brown also addresses this topic extensively in her autobiography, *A Taste of Power: A Black Woman's Story* (New York: Anchor/Doubleday, 1994). The classic broader critique of black male sexism in this period is Michelle Wallace, *Black Macho and the Myth of the Superwoman* (New York: Dial Press, 1978).

33. On the rationale for the survival programs, see Foner, *Black Panthers Speak,* section 9.

34. Van Deburg, *New Day in Babylon,* 308.

35. Kobena Mercer acknowledges the contagious power of the Panther vision and the ways in which its power was defused and even used by the right.

36. Jean Genet, *Prisoner of Love* (Middletown, CT: Wesleyan University Press, 1992), 85.

37. Frantz Fanon, *The Wretched of the Earth* (New York: Grove Press, 1963), 36.

38. See Wahneema Lubiano, "Black Nationalism and Common Sense: Policing Ourselves and Others," in Lubiano, ed., *The House That Race Built* (New York: Vintage, 1998), 232–52. For similar arguments, see Ann duCille, *Skin Trade* (Cambridge, MA: Harvard University Press, 1996).

39. The best book on rap and hip-hop culture remains Tricia Rose, *Black Noise* (Middletown, CT: Wesleyan University Press, 1994).

40. For a reading of Tupac's "Keep Ya Head Up" in the context of a brilliant analysis of the limitations of current forms of black nationalism as black community "common sense," see Lubiano, "Black Nationalism and Common Sense."

41. Davis, "Black Nationalism: The Sixties and the Nineties," 317–24. Excellent discussions of black nationalism in rap can be found in Rose, *Black Noise;* Errol A. Henderson, "Black Nationalism and Rap Music," *Journal of Black Studies* 26 (November 1996): 309–39 (also available online at www.nbufront.org/html/fvwin98/erroli.html); and Kristal Brent Zook, "Reconstructions of Nationalism in Black Music and Culture," in Reebee Garafolo, ed., *Mass Music: Mass Movements* (Boston: South End Press, 1992), 256–66. See also Min Paul Scott, "How Hip Hop Destroyed Black Power," available on-line at http://www.daveyd.com/hiphopdestroysblackarticle.html (accessed 3/15/05). Scott portrays white hip-hop producers as the "new missionaries" buying the black natives with Courvoisier and gold chains.

3. The Poetical Is the Political

1. Among the most important and useful social scientific and historical studies of the women's movement are the following: Jo Freeman, *The Politics of Women's Liberation* (New York: Longman, 1975); Myra Marx Feree and Beth B. Hess, *Contro-*

versy and Coalition: The New Feminist Movement across Three Decades of Change, 2d ed. (Boston: Twayne, 1994); Alice Echols, *Daring to Be Bad: Radical Feminism in America, 1967–1975* (Minneapolis: University of Minnesota Press, 1989); and Barbara Ryan, *Feminism and the Women's Movement* (New York: Routledge, 1992). Stacey Young offers an important critique of the limits of social science approaches to the women's movement in *Changing the Wor(l)d: Discourse, Politics and the Feminist Movement* (New York: Routledge, 1997), especially chap. 4. Katie King likewise offers important analyses of the power struggles at play in defining and telling the histories of feminisms in *Theory in Its Feminist Travels: Conversations in U.S. Women's Movements* (Bloomington: Indiana University Press, 1994).

2. The body of traditional social science work that has tried to analyze this process is the movement "frame analysis" school, represented by David Snow and Robert Benford. See, for example, Snow et al., "Frame Alignment Processes, Micromobilization, and Movement Participation," *American Sociological Review* 51 (August 1986): 464–81.

3. Steven Buechler, *Women's Movements in the United States: Woman Suffrage, Equal Rights, and Beyond* (New Brunswick, NJ: Rutgers University Press, 1990), offers one of the best long-range studies of the movement(s) in the nineteenth and twentieth centuries. See also Nancy Cott, *The Grounding of Modern Feminism* (New Haven, CT: Yale University Press, 1987).

4. Key texts in the emergence of women-of-color feminist positions include the following: Cherríe Moraga and Gloria Anzaldúa, eds., *This Bridge Called My Back: Writings of Radical Women of Color* (Watertown, MA: Persephone Press, 1981); Angela Davis, *Women, Race, and Class* (New York: Random House, 1981); Chela Sandoval, "Women Respond to Racism: A Report on the National Women's Studies Association Conference" (Oakland, CA: Center for Third World Organizing, n.d. [1982]); Gloria Hull, Patricia Bell Scott, and Barbara Smith, eds., *All the Women Are White, All the Blacks Are Men, But Some of Us Are Brave: Black Women's Studies* (Old Westbury, CT: Feminist Press, 1982); Barbara Smith, ed., *Home Girls: A Black Feminist Anthology* (New York: Kitchen Table Press, 1983); Bonnie Thorton Dill, "Race, Class, and Gender: Prospects for an All-Inclusive Sisterhood," *Feminist Studies* 9, no. 1 (Spring 1983): 131–50; bell hooks, *Ain't I a Woman: Black Women and Feminism* (Boston: South End Press, 1981); hooks, *Feminist Theory: From Margin to Center* (Boston: South End Press, 1984); and Gloria Anzaldúa, ed., *Making Face, Making Soul: Haciendo Caras* (San Francisco: Aunt Lute, 1990).

5. See Ednie Kaeh Garrison, "The Third Wave and the Cultural Predicament of Feminst Consciousness in the United States," Ph.D. diss., Washington State University, 2000.

6. Feree and Hess, *Controversy and Coalition*, 49.

7. See King, *Theory in Its Feminist Travels*.

8. Buechler, *Women's Movements in the United States*.

9. See Chela Sandoval, *Methodology of the Oppressed* (Minneapolis: University of Minnesota Press, 2001).

10. See Nancy Naples, ed., *Community Activism and Feminist Politics* (New York: Routledge, 1998), especially the essay by Sherna Berger Gluck et al., "Whose Feminism, Whose History?" 31–56.

11. This essay, entitled "Double Jeopardy: To Be Black and Female," appears both in Toni Cade [Bambara], ed., *The Black Woman* (New York: New American Library,

1970), and in Robin Morgan, *Sisterhood Is Powerful: An Anthology of Writings from the Women's Liberation Movement* (New York: Vintage, 1970), 340–52.

12. The classic popular critique of this redomestication was Betty Friedan's immensely influential book, *The Feminine Mystique* (New York: Dell, 1963).

13. See, for example, Leila Rupp and Verta Taylor, *Survival in the Doldrums* (New York: Oxford University Press, 1987).

14. On the origins of the "women's liberation" strand in other movements, see Sara Evans, *Personal Politics: The Roots of Women's Liberation in the Civil Rights Movement and the New Left* (New York: Random/Vintage, 1979).

15. The best study of the 1960s white radical student and antiwar movement, known collectively as the new left, remains Wini Breines, *Community and Organization in the New Left, 1962–1968* (New Brunswick, NJ: Rutgers University Press, 1989). Also useful are Kirkpatrick Sale, *SDS* (New York: Random House, 1973); James Miller, *"Democracy Is in the Streets"* (Cambridge, MA: Harvard University Press, 1994); and Todd Gitlin, *The Sixties: Years of Hope, Days of Rage*, rev. ed. (New York: Bantam, 1993). The latter two books are good on the new left but wrongheaded about the role of the women's movement and black radicalism, blaming them for mistakes made by the new left itself. Gitlin's earlier book, *"The Whole World Is Watching"* (Berkeley: University of California Press, 1981), is insightful on the new left and is one of the best studies yet done of the impact of the media on an emerging movement.

16. For a later example of these recurring dialogues, see Gloria I. Joseph and Jill Lewis, eds., *Common Differences: Conflicts in Black and White Feminist Perspectives* (Garden City, NY: Anchor/Doubleday, 1981).

17. Hull et al., *All the Women Are White, All the Blacks Are Men, but Some of Us Are Brave.*

18. Kennedy's self-description can be found in the contributor notes to *Sisterhood Is Powerful,* 597. Connections to the new left, civil rights, antiwar, nationalist, and anticolonial struggles can be found throughout those notes, as well as throughout the analyses in this classic collection.

19. Some feminists, like Catherine MacKinnon, have claimed that CR is *the* feminist method of making social change, but I believe Patricia Yaeger is closer to the mark in arguing that it is one among several major feminist methods. See Yaeger, *Honey-Mad Women: Emancipatory Strategies in Women's Writing* (New York: Columbia University Press, 1988). MacKinnon's claim for the centrality of CR was made, among other places, in her influential, controversial essay, "Feminism, Marxism, Method, and the State," in Nannerl Keohane et al., eds., *Feminist Theory: A Critique of Ideology* (Chicago: University of Chicago Press, 1982). Discussions of the relative usefulness of consciousness-raising partly involve historical arguments as to what CR originally was, ranging from claims that it was little more than personal venting (relating CR to "encounter" or therapy groups) to arguments that it focused on revolutionary strategy (relating CR to Maoist criticism/self-criticism cadre sessions). For an analysis of the ways in which consciousness-raising has been written and rewritten from various interested feminist political standpoints, see Katie King, "The Situation of Lesbianism as Feminism's Magical Sign: Contests for Meaning and the U.S. Women's Movement, 1968–1972," *Communication* 9 (1986): 65–91, revised and expanded in *Theory in Its Feminist Travels.* On the nature and history of CR see also Pamela Allen, *Free Space: A Perspective on the Small Group in the Women's Movement* (New York: Times Change Press, 1970); Nancy McWilliams, "Contempo-

rary Feminism, Consciousness-Raising, and Changing Views of the Political," in Jane Jaquette, ed., *Women and Politics* (New York: John Wiley and Sons, 1974); and Sandra Bartky, *Femininity and Domination: Studies in the Phenomenology of Gender* (New York: Routledge, 1990), especially chap. 1. T.V. Reed also addresses the role of CR as public ritual in *Fifteen Jugglers, Five Believers* (Berkeley: University of California Press, 1992).

20. Cade, *Black Woman*, 9.

21. Among the still relatively few local studies of the women's liberation movement, see especially Nancy Whittier's study of Columbus, Ohio, *Feminist Generations: The Persistence of the Radical Women's Movement* (Philadelphia: Temple University Press, 1995). In addition to its admirable localism (outside New York, Washington, D.C., Chicago, and San Francisco), the book shows clearly how the women's movement persisted as a force through several generations, from the 1960s through the 1990s, in great part through institutions, practices, and structures that might best be labeled cultural.

22. Cellestine Ware, *Woman Power* (New York: Tower, 1970). King analyzes this text astutely in *Theory in Its Feminist Travels*, 126–30.

23. King, *Theory in Its Feminist Travels*, 127.

24. As important as these feminist groups were, they were only as strong ultimately as the diversity within them. And many were not very diverse racially. The preference of women of color for struggling within ethnic nationalist movements during the early years left many early feminist groups all white in composition. While questions of racism are addressed in the radical, white-centered anthologies, for the most part a full encounter with racism in the women's movement was delayed by these separated (and often separatist) lines of development. In recent years, CR has been implicated in the essentialism debates, because it seemed to be based on naively empirical notions of a common "woman's experience" that glosses over differences of race, class, nationality, and sexuality among women. These critiques have come especially from feminist theorists influenced by poststructuralist and postmodern forms of cultural theory that emphasize the value of "decentered," radically open-ended identities. These critiques have been crucial for the development of feminisms, but there is another way of formulating them, especially given that consciousness-raising has proven at least as important for women of color as for white women. As argued perhaps most cogently by feminist historian Joan Scott, "experience" is not an adequate base of knowledge because it is not the site of personal truth, but rather the site of the impact of ideology on a subject individual. This is certainly "true," but it is only a problem if one assumes that personal truth is what people claim when talking about their "experience." Critiques of CR should be aimed more at limited experiences, rather than at the limits of experience-based theorizing *per se*. Another feminist theorist deeply influenced by poststructuralism, Teresa De Lauretis, comes to a more useful conclusion, stating that "experience" is always the starting point for a consciousness-transforming process of analyzing the representations and self-representations that make up an ongoing process of collective/individual identity formation. See Joan Scott, "Experience," in Judith Butler and Joan Scott, eds., *Feminists Theorize the Political* (New York: Routledge, 1992), 22–40. For reconceptualization of women's experience as ongoing meaning-making process, see Teresa De Lauretis, *Alice Doesn't: Feminism, Semiotics, Cinema* (Bloomington: Indiana University Press, 1984), especially chap. 6.

25. Essentialism in this case means positing some unchanging womanly essence (biologically given, or cross-culturally embedded), as opposed to a view of women's identities as changing, culturally relative social constructions. Two books that are particularly useful in examining the question of essentialism in feminism are Diana Fuss, *Essentially Speaking: Feminism, Nature, and Difference* (New York: Routledge, 1989); and Elizabeth Spelman, *Inessential Woman: Problems of Exclusion in Feminist Thought* (Boston: Beacon Press, 1988). Among other interesting attempts to mediate the essentialist/constructionist debate, see Linda Alcoff, "Cultural Feminism versus Post-structuralism: The Identity Crisis in Feminist Theory," *Signs* 13 (Spring 1988): 405–36; and several of the articles in the special issue "The Essential Difference: Another Look at Essentialism," *Differences* 1, no. 2 (Summer 1989). Alice Echols in *Daring to Be Bad* implicates CR groups and "cultural feminism" in the rise of essentialism. For a rethinking of this claim, see King, *Theory in Its Feminist Travels*.

26. I am indebted throughout this section to Kim Whitehead, *The Feminist Poetry Movement* (Jackson: University Press of Mississippi, 1996). See also Jan Montefiore, *Feminism and Poetry* (London: Pandora, 1995).

27. King, *Theory in Its Feminist Travels*, 122.

28. Audre Lorde, *Zami* (Watertown, MA: Persephone, 1982); Gloria Anzaldúa, *Borderlands/La Frontera* (San Francisco: Aunt Lute, 1987); Cherríe Moraga, *Loving in the War Years* (Boston: South End, 1983).

29. Lorde, *Sister Outsider: Essays and Speeches* (Freedom, CA: Crossing Press, 1984), 116.

30. Gloria Anzaldúa, ed., *Making Face, Making Soul: Haciendo Caras* (San Francisco: Aunt Lute, 1990); Cade, ed., *Black Woman;* Smith, ed. *Home Girls;* Joy Harjo and Gloria Bird, eds., *Reinventing the Enemy's Language: Contemporary Native American Women's Writings of North America* (New York: W.W. Norton, 1998); Diane Yen-Mei Wong and Emilya Cachapero, eds., *Making Waves: An Anthology of Writings by and about Asian American Women* (Boston: Beacon Press, 1989); and Evelyn Tortow Beck, ed., *Nice Jewish Girls: A Lesbian Anthology* (New York: Crossing Press, 1984).

31. See Susan Griffin, *Women and Nature* (San Francisco: Harper and Row, 1978); and Irene Diamond and Gloria Orenstein, eds., *Reweaving the World: The Emergence of Ecofeminism* (San Francisco: Sierra Club Books, 1990). The best treatment of the strengths and weaknesses of this school of feminism is Noël Sturgeon, *Ecofeminist Natures: Race, Gender, Feminist Theory, and Political Action* (New York: Routledge, 1997).

32. See Trinh T. Minh-ha, *Woman/Native/Other* (Bloomington: Indiana University Press, 1989); and Gayatri Chakravarty Spivak, *In Other Wor(l)ds: Essays in Cultural Politics* (New York: Routledge, 1988). Many of the founding essays in this line of critique are gathered in Chandra Mohanty, Ann Russo, and Lourdes Torres, eds., *Third World Women and the Politics of Feminism* (Bloomington: Indiana University Press, 1991).

33. See Kim Whitehead, *The Feminist Poetry Movement* (Jackson: University Press of Mississippi, 1996).

34. Raymond Williams, *Marxism and Literature* (Oxford: Oxford University Press, 1977), 117.

35. Whitehead, *Feminist Poetry Movement*, 3.

36. Florence Howe and Ellen Bass, eds., *No More Masks! An Anthology of Poems by Women* (New York: Anchor/Doubleday, 1973).

37. Howe, in the preface to the revised and expanded edition of *No More Masks!* (New York: Harper Collins, 1993). The subtitle of this revised edition, "An Anthology of *Twentieth Century American* Women Poets," acknowledges the historical and national boundaries of the collection not noted by the earlier subtitle "Poems by Women."

38. Howe and Bass, *No More Masks!* (1973), xxviii.

39. Laura Chester and Sharon Barba, eds., *Rising Tides: Twentieth-Century American Women Poets* (New York: Pocket Books, 1973), i.

40. Stacey Young in *Changing the Wor(l)d* details how feminist editors and publishers, by carefully brokering this process, continue to move work originally associated with movement contexts out into wider public spaces and then into more mainstream locations.

41. Statistics from Chesman and Joan's *Guide to Women's Publishing*, cited in Whitehead, *Feminist Poetry Movement*, 19.

42. The reaction against feminism in the 1980s is accessibly chronicled in journalist Susan Faludi's *Backlash: The Undeclared War against American Women* (New York: Anchor, 1992).

43. The best study of the term *third wave* and its variant meanings is Garrison, "Third Wave and the Cultural Predicament of Feminist Consciousness."

4. Revolutionary Walls

1. George Sánchez, *Becoming Mexican American: Ethnicity, Culture, and Identity in Chicano Los Angeles, 1900–1945* (Oxford: Oxford University Press, 1993).

2. On the popular front social movement and its long-range cultural impact, see Michael Denning, *The Cultural Front: The Laboring of American Culture in the Twentieth Century* (New York: Verso, 1996).

3. In addition to Sánchez, *Becoming Mexican American*, the work of Mexican American activists before the Chicano generation is chronicled in Vicki Ruiz, *Cannery Women, Cannery Lives: Mexican Women, Unionization, and the California Food Processing Industry, 1930–1950* (Albuquerque: University of New Mexico Press, 1987); Mario T. Garcia, *Mexican Americans: Leadership, Ideology and Identity, 1930–1960* (New Haven, CT: Yale University Press, 1989); and Mario T. Garcia, *Memories of Chicano History: The Life and Narrative of Bert Corona* (Berkeley: University of California Press, 1995).

4. See Carlos Muñoz, *Youth, Identity, Power: The Chicano Movement* (New York: Verso, 1989), 51.

5. Among the most important works on the Chicano/a movement are: Muñoz, *Youth, Identity, Power;* Ernesto Chavez, *"¡Mi Raza Primero!" (My People First!): Nationalism, Identity, and Insurgency in the Chicano Movement in Los Angeles, 1966–1978* (Berkeley: University of California Press, 2002); Ignacio Garcia, *Chicanismo: The Forging of a Militant Ethos among Mexican Americans* (Tucson: University of Arizona Press, 1997); Ignacio Garcia, *United We Win: The Rise and Fall of La Raza Unida Party* (Tucson: University of Arizona Press, 1989); David G. Gutiérrez, *Walls and Mirrors: Mexican Americans, Mexican Immigrants, and the Politics of Identity* (Berkeley: University of California Press, 1995); Reies Lopez Tijerino and Jose Angel Gutierrez, *They Called Me "King Tiger": My Struggle for the Land and Our Rights*

(Houston: Arte Público Press, 2001); Rodolfo "Corky" Gonzales, *Message to Aztlán: Selected Writings* (Houston: Arte Público, 2001); Armando Narvarro, *Mexican American Youth Organization: Avant-Garde of the Chicano Movement in Texas* (Austin: University of Texas Press, 1995); Angie Chabram-Dernersesian, "I Throw Punches for My Race But I Don't Want to Be a Man: Writing Us—Chica-Nos (Girl, Us) Chicanas—into the Movement Script," in Lawrence Grossberg, ed., *Cultural Studies* (New York: Routledge, 1992), 81–96; F. Arturo Rosales, *Chicano! The History of the Mexican American Civil Rights Movement* (Houston: Arte Público Press, 1996); and Ernesto Vigil, *The Crusade for Justice: Chicano Miltancy and the Government's War on Dissent* (Madison: University of Wisconsin Press, 1999). Key elements of Chicanas in movement history and in their own "herstory" can be found in Alma M. Garcia and Mario T. Garcia, eds., *Chicana Feminist Thought: The Basic Historical Writings* (New York: Routledge, 1997); Gloria Anzaldúa, ed., *Making Face, Making Soul/ Haciendo Caras: Creative and Critical Perspectives by Women of Color* (San Francisco: Aunt Lute, 1990); and in longer historical context, Emma Perez, *The Decolonial Imaginary: Writing Chicanas into History* (Bloomington: Indiana University Press, 1999). Elizabeth (Bettita) Martinez strategizes the future of Chicana/Latina activism in *"De Colores" Means All of Us: Latina Views for a Multi-Colored Century* (Boston: South End Press, 1998).

6. I am profoundly indebted to the Social and Public Art Resource Center (SPARC) in Venice, California, not only for the mural photographs reproduced here and for much of the information about the murals, but also for its role as a major force in the production and preservation of murals. SPARC is a major ongoing resource for the creation and study of murals and other public art, one deserving of support from anyone who values radically multicultural public art. The center can be reached on the Web at www.sparc.org. SPARC also put together the most useful single resource on Chicano/a murals, Eva Sperling Cockcroft and Holly Barnet-Sánchez, eds., *Signs from the Heart: California Chicano Murals* (Venice, CA and Albuquerque, NM: Social and Public Art Resource Center and University of New Mexico Press, 1990); together with Eva Cockcroft, *Signs from the Heart: Slide Set,* with educational text (Venice, CA: SPARC, 1990). Other important work on Chicano/a murals and the community mural movement includes the following: Eva Sperling, "The Story of Chicano Park," *Atzlán* 15, no. 1 (1984): 79–103; Judith F. Baca, "Our People Are Internal Exiles," an interview conducted by Diane Neumaier, in Douglas Kahn and Diane Neumaier, eds., *Cultures in Contention* (Seattle: Real Comet Press, 1985), 62–75. Connections between Chicana/o, Latino/a, and Latin American muralism can be found in Shifra Goldman, *Dimensions of the Americas: Art and Social Change in Latin America and the United States* (Chicago: University of Chicago Press, 1994); Tomás Ybarra Fausto, "The Chicano Movement / The Movement of Chicano Art," in Ivan Karp and Steven Levine, eds., *Exhibiting Cultures: The Poetics and Politics of Museum Display* (Washington, DC: Smithsonian Institution Press, 1993); and Jeffrey J. Rangel, "Art and Activism in the Chicano Movement: Judith F. Baca, Youth, and the Politics of Cultural Work," in Joe Austin and Michael Nevin Willard, eds., *Generations of Youth: Youth Cultures and History in Twentieth Century America* (New York: New York University Press, 1998), 223–39. The role of murals in the wider context of Chicano/a visual arts is explored in the record of the crucial CARA exhibition of the early 1990s, catalogued in Richard Griswold del Castillo, Teresa McKenna, and Yvonne Yabro-Bejarano, eds., *Chicano Art: Resistance and Affirmation, 1965–*

1985 (Los Angeles: UCLA Wright Gallery, 1991). The exhibit itself is brilliantly analyzed in Alicia Gaspar de Alba, *Chicano Art inside/outside the Master's House: Cultural Politics and the CARA Exhibition* (Austin: University of Texas Press, 1998). Contextual studies of the wider community mural movement and multicultural contemporary art can be found in Alan W. Barnett, *Community Murals* (Cranbury, NJ: Associated University Presses, 1984); John Weber and Jim Cockcroft, *Toward a People's Art: The Contemporary Mural Movement* (Albuquerque: University of New Mexico Press, 1998 [1977]); Erika Doss, *Spirit Poles and Flying Pigs: Public Art and Cultural Democracy in American Communities* (Washington, DC: Smithsonian Institution Press, 1995); and Lucy Lippard, *Mixed Blessings: New Art in a Multicultural America* (New York: Pantheon, 1990). Angie Chabram-Dernersesian also addresses Chicana art in relation to the movement in "I Throw Punches for My Race." See also Raúl Villa, *Barrio-Logos: Space and Place in Urban Chicano Literature and Culture* (Austin: University of Texas Press, 2000), for a brilliant analysis of murals in the context of geographic displacement and resistance.

7. See Yolanda Broyles-González, *El Teatro Campesino in the Chicano Movement* (Austin: University of Texas Press, 1994).

8. For studies of each of these regional variations on a movement theme, see note 5 above.

9. Theorizing around this notion of moving from "representation" to "articulation" can be found in Ernesto Laclau and Chantal Mouffe, *Hegemony and Socialist Strategy* (London: Verso, 1985); Miami Theory Collective, eds., *Community at Loose Ends* (Minneapolis: University of Minnesota Press, 1991); and Iris Marion Young, *Justice and the Politics of Difference* (Princeton, NJ: Princeton University Press, 1990).

10. For an extended discussion of various kinds of multiculturalism, from conservative to critical/left, see David Theo Goldberg, ed., *Multiculturalism: A Critical Reader* (Oxford: Blackwell, 1994), especially the essays by the Peter McLaren, Lauren Berlant and Michael Warner, and the Chicago Cultural Studies Group; and Avery F. Gordon and Christopher Newfield, eds., *Mapping Multiculturalism* (Minneapolis: University of Minnesota Press, 1996), especially the essays in Part I.

5. Old Cowboys, New Indians

1. The most complete study to date of "red power" activism is Paul Chaat Smith and Robert Warrior, *Like a Hurricane: The Indian Movement from Alcatraz to Wounded Knee* (New York: New Press, 1996). Some of the key movement documents of the era are collected in Alvin Josephy et al., eds., *Red Power: The American Indians' Fight for Freedom*, 2d ed. (Lincoln: University of Nebraska Press, 1999). The most immediate coverage and firsthand accounts of Indian activism can be found in *Voices from Wounded Knee, 1973: In the Words of the Participants* (Roosevelt, NY: Akwesasne Notes, 1974). The U.S. Senate investigation of the events of Wounded Knee II is included in *Wounded Knee Massacre: Hearings before the Committee on the Judiciary, United States Senate, Ninety-fourth Congress, Second Session, on S. 1147 and S. 2900, February 5 and 6, 1976* (Washington, DC: U.S. Government Printing Office, 1976). Additional accounts of Wounded Knee and native activism include the following: Edward Milligan (He Topa), *Wounded Knee 1973 and the Fort Laramie Treaty of 1868* (Bottineau, ND: Bottineau Courant Press, 1973); Rolland Dewing, *Wounded*

Knee II (Chadron, NE: Great Plains Network and Pine Hills Press, 1995); Robert Burnette and John Koster, *The Road to Wounded Knee* (New York: Bantam Books, 1974); Peter Matthiessen, *In the Spirit of Crazy Horse* (New York: Viking Press, 1983); Mary Crow Dog, as told to Richard Erdoes, *Lakota Woman* (New York: Grove Weidenfeld, 1990); Stanley Lyman, *Wounded Knee: A Personal Account* (Lincoln: University of Nebraska Press, 1991); Russell Means, with Marvin J. Wolf, *Where White Men Fear to Tread: The Autobiography of Russell Means* (New York: St. Martin's Press, 1995); Joanne Nagel, *American Indian Ethnic Renewal: Red Power and the Resurgence of Identity and Culture* (New York: Oxford University Press, 1996); Troy Johnson, *The Occupation of Alcatraz Island* (Urbana: University of Illinois Press,1996); John William Sayer, *Ghost Dancing the Law: The Wounded Knee Trials* (Cambridge, MA: Harvard University Press, 1997); and Leonard Peltier, *Prison Writings: My Life Is My Sun Dance* (New York: St. Martin's Press, 1999).

2. *Powwow Highway,* dir. Joanelle Nadine Romero and Jonathan Wacks (Handmade Films/Warner Bros., 1989); *Thunderheart,* dir. Michael Apted (Tristar Pictures, 1992); *Lakota Woman: Siege at Wounded Knee,* dir. Frank Pierson (Turner Films, 1994 [made for television with video release]).

3. One exception to this statement was the relative commercial success of the independent Indian-made film *Smoke Signals,* dir. Chris Eyre (Miramax, 1998). This film by a Cheyenne-Arapaho director was scripted by Sherman Alexie (Spokane-Coeur d'Alene) and starred Indian actors Irene Bedard, Evan Adams, Gary Farmers, and Tantoo Cardinal. It remains to be seen whether this film signals a breakthrough for Native American film production, but the initial experiences of the director and screenwriter in trying to find significant Hollywood backing for subsequent projects are not encouraging.

4. The complexities of native aesthetics and cultural politics are ably presented in two important works: Beverly Singer, *Wiping the Warpaint off the Lens: Native American Film and Video* (Minneapolis: University of Minnesota Press, 2001); and Steve Leuthold, *Indigenous Aesthetics: Native Art, Media and Identity* (Austin: University of Texas Press, 1998).

5. Of the voluminous literature on native representation in the traditional Hollywood film, the following works are among the most useful: Peter C. Rollins and John O'Connor, eds., *Hollywood's Indian: The Portrayal of the Native American in Film* (Lexington: University of Kentucky Press, 1998); Michael Hilger, *From Savage to Nobleman: Images of Native Americans in Film* (London: Scarecrow Press, 1995); S. Elizabeth Bird, *Dressing in Feathers: The Construction of the Indian in American Popular Culture* (Boulder, CO: Westview Press, 1996); Ward Churchill, *Fantasies of the Master Race: Literature, Cinema and the Colonization of American Indians* (San Francisco: City Lights Books, 1998); and Jacquelyn Kilpatrick, *Celluloid Indians: Native Americans and Film* (Lincoln: University of Nebraska Press, 1999). The longer historical context for these portrayals is presented in Robert Berkhofer, *The White Man's Indian: Images of the American Indian from Columbus to the Present* (New York: Knopf, 1978).

6. Smith and Warrior, *Like a Hurricane,* 127.

7. See Johnson, *The Occupation of Alcatraz.*

8. Mario Gonzalez and Elizabeth Cook-Lynn, *The Politics of Hallowed Ground: Wounded Knee and the Struggle for Indian Sovereignty* (Urbana: University of Illinois Press, 1999), place the 1973 Wounded Knee events in the context of the long struggle

to get the U.S. government to acknowledge the injustice of the 1890 Wounded Knee massacre.

9. Michelle Dishong, "New York Times Coverage of the Occupation of Wounded Knee," master's thesis, Washington State University, 1996.

10. Cited in ibid.

11. "Trap at Wounded Knee," *Time* (26 March 1973), 67.

12. See James Stripes, "A Strategy of Resistance: The 'Actorvism' of Russell Means, from Plymouth Rock to the Disney Studios," *Wicazo Sa Review* 14, no. 1 (1999): 87–101.

13. Andrea Smith, "For All Those Who Were Indian in a Former Life," *Ms.* (November–December 1994), 44–45; reprinted in Carol Adams, ed., *Ecofeminism and the Sacred* (New York: Continuum Press, 1993).

14. See Tom Holm, *Strong Hearts, Wounded Souls: Native American Veterans of the Vietnam War* (Austin: University of Texas Press, 1996), which looks at the forty-three thousand Native Americans who served in Vietnam.

15. David Seals, *Powwow Highway* (New York: Plume Books, 1990 [1979]); Seals, *Sweet Medicine* (New York: Orion Books, 1992).

16. On sexism in AIM, including the death of Aquash, see Devon Mihesuah, *Indigenous American Women: Decolonization, Empowerment, Activism* (Lincoln: University of Nebraska Press, 2003).

6. "We Are [Not] the World"

1. Perspectives on this phenomenon and related issues in the politics of rock can be found in the following works: Mark Coleman, "The Revival of Conscience," *Rolling Stone* (15 November 1990), 69–80; Robin Deneslow, *When the Music's Over: The Story of Political Pop* (Boston: Faber and Faber, 1989); Simon Frith, ed., *World Music, Politics, and Social Change* (Manchester, UK: University of Manchester Press, 1989); Lawrence Grossberg, "Is There Rock after Punk?" in Colin Frith and Andrew Goodwin, eds., *On Record: Rock, Pop, and the Written Word* (New York: Pantheon, 1990), 111–23; Reebee Garofalo, ed., *Rockin' the Boat: Mass Music and Mass Movements* (Boston: South End Press, 1992); Reebee Garofalo, "Nelson Mandela, the Concert: Mass Culture as Contested Terrain," in Mark O'Brien and Craig Little, eds., *Reimaging America: The Arts of Social Change* (Santa Cruz, CA: New Society Publishers, 1990), 340–49 (see also an expanded version in Garofalo, ed., *Rockin' the Boat*); Reebee Garofolo, "Understanding Mega-Events: If We Are the World, Then How Do We Change It?" in Garofalo, ed., *Rockin' the Boat*, 15–36; Michael Omi, "A Positive Noise: The Charity Rock Phenomenon," *Socialist Review* 16, no. 2 (1986): 107–14; Rob Tannenbaum, "Bob Geldof: An Interview," *Rolling Stone* (15 November 1990), 74–80; Neal Üllestad, "Rock and Rebellion: Subversive Effects of 'Live Aid' and 'Sun City,'" *Popular Music* 6, no. 1 (1987): 67–76; Bob Geldof, with Paul Vallely, *Is That It?* (New York: Weidenfeld and Nicholson, 1986); Lawrence Grossberg, *We Gotta Get Out of This Place: Popular Conservatism and Postmodern Culture* (New York: Routledge, 1991); and Michael Jarrett, "Concerning the Progress of Rock and Roll," *South Atlantic Quarterly* 90, no. 4 (1991): 803–18.

2. The Paterson Pageant, held in Madison Square Garden in 1912, was a benefit performance uniting Greenwich Village artists and actors with striking workers from the textile mills of nearby Paterson, New Jersey. Led by the anarcho-syndicalist

Industrial Workers of the World (IWW, or the Wobblies), the long strike was running out of money for the families of workers. The pageant took the form of a thousand workers, the majority of them women, reenacting key scenes of their strike on stage in the arena for a paying audience. If not the first example of a modern political benefit, it was certainly among the most imaginative and dramatic.

3. While I concentrate in this chapter on the anti-apartheid movement, of equal importance was the movement seeking to alter U.S. involvement in Central America. On this movement, see Christian Smith, *Resisting Reagan: The U.S. Central America Peace Movement* (Chicago: University of Chicago Press, 1996). The two movements are often linked together as "solidarity" movements, and had considerable overlap in membership.

4. In crude terms, the two sides of this debate are represented by the critical theorists of the Frankfurt school, and the cultural studies theorists of the Birmingham school. On the former, see David Held, *Introduction to Critical Theory: Horkheimer to Habermas* (Berkeley: University of California Press, 1980); and Andrew Arato and Eike Gebhart, eds., *The Essential Frankfurt School Reader* (New York: Urizen, 1978). On the latter, see Graeme Turner, *British Cultural Studies: An Introduction* (London: Unwin-Hyman, 1990); and David Morley and Kuan-Hsing Chen, eds., *Stuart Hall: Critical Dialogues in Cultural Studies* (New York: Routledge, 1996). Much of the best work these days avoids these dichotomous positions. For a brilliant work of theory that remains among the most useful attempts to combine these positions, see Fredric Jameson, "Reification and Utopia in Mass Culture," *Social Text* 1 (1979): 130–48. Jameson argues persuasively that even the most commercialized, reactionary texts of mass culture offer, despite themselves, utopian longings that, since they cannot be filled by current capitalist society, engender social discontent that has the potential to be turned in progressive directions. Some of the complex questions surrounding the issue of cultural imperialism are taken up in Andrew Goodwin and Joe Gore, "World Beat and the Cultural Imperialism Thesis," *Socialist Review* 20, no. 3 (1990): 63–80. For a general introduction to the topic, see John Tomlinson, *Cultural Imperialism: A Critical Introduction* (London: Pinter Publishers, 1991).

5. The name ironically captures the fact that these efforts were but a patch over the hemorrhaging wounds on the body of the African continent.

6. United Support of Artists for Africa, *We Are the World* (Columbia Records 40043, 1985).

7. Recent scientific evidence also suggests that the drought that drove the famine may also have been worsened by tiny particles called aerosols from the industrial world.

8. See Zoë Sofia (Sofoulis), "Exterminating Fetuses: Abortion, Disarmament, and the Sex-Semiotics of Extraterrestrialism," *Diacritics* 14 (1984): 47–59.

9. See Stuart Hall, *The Hard Road to Renewal: Thatcherism and the Crisis of the Left* (New York: Verso, 1988).

10. See Geldof and Vallely, *Is That It?* for a discussion of Geldof's political education.

11. See Tannenbaum, "Bob Geldof: An Interview."

12. Artists United against Apartheid, *Sun City* (Manhattan/Capitol Records EP ST53109, 1985).

13. The video is *The Making of "Sun City"* (Karl-Lorimar home video 012-VHS, 1986).

14. Speech read in *The Making of "Sun City."*

15. See Garofalo, "Understanding Mega-Events."

16. Quoted in Dave Marsh, *Sun City: The Making of a Record* (New York: Vintage-Penguin, 1985), 80.

17. On the postmodern nihilism of MTV, see E. Ann Kaplan, *Rocking around the Clock: Music Television, Postmodernism and Consumer Culture* (New York: Routledge, 1987).

18. Marsh, *Sun City: The Making of a Record.*

19. On connections to the local movements, see especially Garofalo, "If We Are the World, How Do We Change It?"

20. Neal Üllestad, "Rock and Rebellion."

21. On the U.S. anti-apartheid movement, see Tony Vellela, *New Voices: Student Activism in the '80s and '90s* (Boston: South End Press, 1988); Christine A. Kelly, *Tangled Up in Red White and Blue* (New York: Rowman and Littlefield, 2001); and Sarah A. Soule, "The Student Divestment Movement in the United States and Tactical Diffusion: The Shantytown Protest," *Social Forces* 75, no. 3 (1997): 855–83.

22. Garofalo, "Nelson Mandela, the Concert," 341.

23. Quoted in ibid., 266–67.

24. Quoted in ibid., 346.

25. See Robin Deneslow, *When the Music's Over,* 282.

26. Garofalo, "Nelson Mandela, the Concert," 346.

27. For an analysis of Amnesty International's rock concert tour as commodification of transnationalism, see Deena Weinstein, "The Amnesty International Tour: Transnationalism as Cultural Commodity," *Public Culture* 1, no. 2 (1989): 60–65.

28. On this development, see Naomi Klein, *No Logo* (New York: Picador, 1999).

29. See Weinstein, "The Amnesty International Tour."

30. Most critics see rock as a politically ambiguous force that most often serves domination, but that contains a self-mythologizing dimension which leaves it more open than most mass-mediated discourses to intervention from the left. These issues are much contested among critics of rock.

31. The relational, contextual rather than stable nature of these two discourses is suggested by the fact that many of the same personnel played on both *We Are the World* and *Sun City,* while their musical codings were unmistakably different. In addition to the works cited in note 4 above, see Michael Jarrett, "Concerning the Progress of Rock and Roll," *South Atlantic Quarterly* 90, no. 4 (1991): 803–18, for a discussion of the logic of the rock/pop dynamic.

32. See Weinstein, "Amnesty International Tour." This general position is perhaps most identified with French cultural theorist Jean Baudrillard, who sees no possibilities for resistance left in a fully self-imploding system of simulated cultural representations with no connection to history or material reality. This partial truth pays far too much attention to what is on computer screens, and far too little to the production line workers in the global South whose material conditions enable those screens to exist.

33. Fredric Jameson, "Notes on Globalization as a Philosophical Issue," in Jameson and Masao Miysoshi, eds., *The Cultures of Globalization* (Durham, NC: Duke University Press, 1998), 54–77, especially 56–57.

34. This analysis builds on the work of Andreas Rauh, "Grunge, from Local Scene to Global Phenomenon," master's thesis, Washington State University, 2003.

7. ACTing UP against AIDS

1. Douglas Crimp and Adam Ralston, *AIDS DemoGraphics* (Seattle: Bay Press, 1990), 13.

2. Cindy Patton, *Inventing AIDS* (New York: Routledge, 1990), 161.

3. Paula Treichler, "AIDS, Homophobia, and Biomedical Discourse: An Epidemic of Signification," in Douglas Crimp, ed., *AIDS: Cultural Analysis, Cultural Activism* (Cambridge, MA: MIT Press, 1991), 31–70, especially 31–32.

4. Ibid., 70.

5. Joshua Gamson, "Silence, Death, and the Invisible Enemy: AIDS Activism and Social Movement Newness," in Michael Burawoy et al., eds., *Ethnography Unbound* (Berkeley: University of California Press, 1991), 35–57.

6. On the connection between antiqueer and anticommunist hysteria, see, for example, David Savran, *Communists, Cowboys, and Queers: The Politics of Masculinity in the Work of Arthur Miller and Tennessee Williams* (Minneapolis: University of Minnesota Press, 1992).

7. Crimp and Ralston, *AIDS DemoGraphics*, 20.

8. Cited in Gamson, "Silence, Death," 47.

9. Crimp and Ralston, *AIDS DemoGraphics*, 29.

10. Cited in Urvashi Vaid, *Virtual Equality: The Mainstreaming of Gay and Lesbian Liberation* (New York: Anchor, 1996), 95–96.

11. Gamson, "Silence, Death," 48.

12. Ibid., 49.

13. Crimp and Ralston, *AIDS DemoGraphics*, 55.

14. While many in ACT UP were critical of the quilt for its alleged passivity, it has proven a brilliantly effective and affective device for increasing awareness of the epidemic and personalizing the crisis for those outside its reach, and for assisting the mourning of many within the crisis. For an astute analysis of the NAMES Project and the AIDS Quilt, see Marita Sturken, *Tangled Memories: The Vietnam War, the AIDS Epidemic, and the Politics of Remembering* (Berkeley: University of California Press, 1997).

15. Gamson, "Silence, Death," 35–57, 39.

16. Quoted in ibid., 39.

17. Patton, *Inventing AIDS*, 163n.16.

18. Crimp and Ralston, *AIDS DemoGraphics*, 19–20.

19. Among those noting that global capitalism has taken on a "networked" form is Manuel Castells, *The Information Age*, 3 vols. (Oxford: Blackwell, 1999). Noël Sturgeon makes this point more directly in relation to movements in her essay, "Theorizing Movements: Direct Action and Direct Theory," in Marcy Darnovsky, Barbara Epstein, and Richard Flacks, eds., *Cultural Politics and Social Movements* (Philadelphia: Temple University Press, 1995), 35–51.

20. See Vaid, *Virtual Equality*, 102, for a more complicated view of these interactions.

21. Handbook by Lesbian Avenger, available on-line at http://www.lesbian.org/chicago-avengers/avengerhandbook.html.

22. The term *cycles of protest* is most closely identified with social scientist Sidney Tarrow. Several of the elements in Tarrow's definition of cycles seem to fit ACT UP's influence: "a rapid diffusion of collective action from more mobilized to less

mobilized sectors; a quickened pace of innovation in new forms of contention; new or transformed collective action forms; a combination of organized and unorganized participation; and sequences of intensified interaction between challengers and authorities." See Tarrow, "Cycles of Protest," in Steven M. Buechler and F. Cylke Jr., eds., *Social Movements* (Mountain View, CA: Mayfield Publishing, 1997), 441–56, especially 441.

23. Vaid, *Virtual Equality,* 94.

24. Sarah Schulman, *Stagestruck: Theater, AIDS, and the Marketing of Gay America* (Durham, NC: Duke University Press, 1998), 104. On the phenomenon of marketing AIDS, see also Alana Kumbier, "Resignifying AIDS," master's thesis, Ohio State University, Columbus, 2000.

25. Fauci's comments refer specifically to Larry Kramer, the subject of the article, but more properly reflect the influence of countless ACT UP activists. See Michael Specter, "Public Nuisance," *New Yorker* (13 May 2002).

26. William Gamson, "Constructing Social Protest," in Buechler and Cylke, eds., *Social Movements,* 228–44, especially 228.

27. This romantic fatalism is analyzed in Sturken, *Tangled Memories,* 165–67.

8. Environmental Justice Ecocriticism

1. Ron Eyerman and Andrew Jamison, *Social Movements: A Cognitive Approach* (University Park: Pennsylvania State University, 1991).

2. The literature on environmental racism and environmental justice is extensive. Among the works most useful in an ecocritical context are the following: Robert D. Bullard, ed., *Confronting Environmental Racism: Voices from the Grassroots* (Boston: South End Press, 1993); Robert D. Bullard, *Unequal Protection: Environmental Justice and Communities of Color* (San Francisco: Sierra Club Press, 1994); Robert D. Bullard, *Dumping in Dixie: Race, Class, and Environmental Equity* (Boulder, CO: Westview Press, 1990); Al Gedicks, *The New Resource Wars: Native and Environmental Struggles against Multinational Corporations* (Boston: South End Press, 1993); Annie L. Booth and Harvey M. Jacobs, "Ties That Bind: Native American Beliefs as a Foundation for Environmental Consciousness," *Environmental Ethics* 12, no. 1 (1990): 27–43; Laura Pulido, *Environmentalism and Economic Justice: Two Chicano Struggles in the Southwest* (Tucson: University of Arizona Press, 1996); Devon Peña, *Chicano Culture, Ecology, Politics: Subversive Kin* (Tucson: University of Arizona Press, 1999); Devon Peña, *The Terror of the Machine: Technology, Work, Gender, and Ecology of the U.S.–Mexico Border* (Austin: University of Texas Press, 1997); Giovanna Di Chiro, "Nature as Community: The Convergence of Environment and Social Justice," in Michael Goldman, ed., *Privatizing Nature: Political Struggles for the Global Common* (New Brunswick, N.J.: Rutgers University Press, 1998), 120–43; and Daniel Faber, ed., *The Struggle for Ecological Democracy: Environmental Justice Movements in the United States* (Guilford, CT: Guilford Press, 1998). Robert Gottlieb's excellent history of the environmental movement, *Forcing the Spring: The Transformation of the American Environmental Movement* (Washington, DC: Island Press, 1995), brilliantly shows how a history of workplace safety issues can and should be seen as an environmental issue that can link the labor and environmental movements, and offers a striking image of how a more democratic environmentalism can bridge the racial, class, and urban/rural divides that have limited progress.

3. I am indebted throughout this section to Gottlieb, *Forcing the Spring*, and to Marcy Darnovsky, "Stories Less Told: Histories of U.S. Environmentalism," *Socialist Review* 92, no. 4 (1992): 11–54.

4. A version of this essay was first presented to the on-line conference "Cultures and Environments" in 1997. A later version appeared in Joni Adamson, Mei Mei Evans, and Rachel Stein, eds., *The Environmental Justice Reader: Politics, Poetics, and Pedagogy* (Tucson: University of Arizona Press, 2002).

5. Cheryll Burgess Glotfelty and Harold Fromm, eds., *The Ecocriticism Reader: Landmarks in Literary Ecology* (Athens: University of Georgia Press, 1996).

6. Ibid., xxvi.

7. Ibid., xxv.

8. Lawrence Buell, *Writing for an Endangered World* (Cambridge, MA: Belknap Press/Harvard University Press, 2001).

9. Glotfelty and Fromm, eds., *Ecocriticism Reader*, 182–202.

10. Buell also rereads DeLillo in light of this issue of toxicity in *Writing for an Endangered World*, but largely misses an opportunity to raise the racial implications of the image.

11. See, for example, Noël Sturgeon, *Ecofeminist Natures* (New York: Routledge, 1998). This book examines the effects of racial stereotyping and other racial dynamics in undermining the effectiveness of ecofeminism and other radical environmental efforts.

12. For an example of this latter approach, see Giovanna Di Chiro, "Local Actions, Global Visions: Remaking Environmental Expertise," *Frontiers: A Journal of Women's Studies* 8, no. 2 (Fall 1997): 203–31.

13. See, for example, Londa Schiebinger, *Nature's Body: Gender in the Making of Modern Science* (Boston: Beacon Press, 1995); and Donna Haraway, *Primate Visions: Gender, Race, and Nature in the World of Modern Science* (New York: Routledge, 1990); Donna Haraway, *Simians, Cyborgs, and Women* (New York: Routledge, 1991); and Donna Haraway, *Modest Witness@Second Millennium* (New York: Routledge, 1996).

14. One rich example of this kind of analysis can be found in Timothy Luke, *Ecocritique: Contesting the Politics of Nature, Economy, and Culture* (Minneapolis: University of Minnesota Press, 1997).

15. For examples of environmental justice art other than literature, see John O'Neil, "For Generations Yet to Come: Junebug Productions, Environmental Justice Practice," in Richard Hofrichter, ed., *Reclaiming the Environmental Debate* (Cambridge, Mass.: MIT Press, 2000), 301–12; and Giovanna Di Chiro's essay/interview in Adamson et al., eds., *Environmental Justice Reader*.

16. Patrick Murphy, *Farther Afield in the Study of Nature-Oriented Literature* (Charlottesville: University of Virginia Press, 2000).

17. June Jordan, "Poem about My Rights," in Florence Howe, ed., *No More Masks! An Anthology of Twentieth Century American Women Poets* (New York: Harper, 1993).

18. Adrienne Rich, "Trying to Talk with a Man," in *Diving into the Wreck: Poems, 1971–1972* (New York: W. W. Norton, 1973).

19. For a rich environmental justice reading of this western landscape, see Valerie Kuletz, *The Tainted Desert* (New York: Routledge, 1998).

20. For examples of this kind of criticism, see Kristin Hunt, "Paradise Lost: The Destructive Forces of Double Consciousness and Boundaries in Toni Morrison's

Paradise," in John Talmadge and Henry Harrington, eds., *Reading under the Sign of Nature: New Essays in Ecocriticism* (Salt Lake City: University of Utah Press, 2000); and Penny Hall, "Nature and Culture in Three Slave Narratives," paper presented at the "Culture and Environment" on-line conference, Washington State University, June 1997.

21. See Joni Adamson, *American Indian Literature, Environmental Justice, and Ecocriticism: The Middle Place* (Tucson: University of Arizona Press, 2001).

22. Perhaps the best, sustained example of environmental justice ecocriticism to date is Joni Adamson's *American Indian Literature, Environmental Justice, and Ecocriticism*, which combines excellent close readings with accessible theoretical insights and a personally grounded narrative connecting theory, movements, and experience. I have no desire to police the boundaries of environmental justice ecocriticism, but among the works that I think contribute to this evolving critical practice are the following: Kamala Platt, "Ecocritical Chicana Literature: Ana Castillo's 'Virtual Realism,'" in Greta Gaard and Patrick D. Murphy, eds., *Ecofeminist Literary Criticism* (Urbana: University of Illinois Press, 1998); Kamala Platt, "Chicana Strategies of Success and Survival: Cultural Poetics of Environmental Justice from the Mothers of East Los Angeles," *Frontiers: A Journal of Women's Studies* 18, no. 2 (1997): 48–72; Kuletz, *Tainted Desert*; Joni Adamson, "Toward an Ecology of Justice: Transformative Ecological Theory and Practice," in Michael P. Branch et al., eds., *Reading the Earth: New Directions in the Study of Literature and Environment* (Moscow: University of Idaho Press, 1998); Krista Comer, *Landscapes of the New West: Gender and Geography in Contemporary Women's Writing* (Chapel Hill: University of North Carolina Press, 1999); Michael Bennett and David W. Teague, eds., *The Nature of Cities: Ecocriticism and Urban Environments* (Tucson: University of Arizona Press, 1999), especially the interview with Andrew Ross, and the article by Kathleen Wallace; Glynis Carr, ed., *New Essays in Ecofeminist Literary Criticism* (Lewisburg, PA: Bucknell University Press, 2000). In the last-named volume, see especially the essays by Julie Sze on Karen Yamashita, Benay Blend on Chicana writers, Charlotte Walker on Alice Walker, and Greta Gaard on Linda Hogan and Alice Walker.

23. Mary Wood, "Spiders and Mice: Mary Antin, Immigrant 'Outsider' Identity, and Ecofeminism," paper delivered at the Pacific Northwest American Studies Association meeting, 10–12 April 1997. A perhaps related example of this kind of work is Robert Sullivan's *Meadowlands: Wilderness Adventures at the Edge of a City* (New York: Anchor, 1999), a delightful mock-heroic, Thoreau-like "adventure" in the industrial wasteland of New Jersey's historical wetlands. Sullivan misses some opportunities to sharpen his political critique, but the book is a welcome antidote to certain kinds of self-important wilderness personal discovery tomes. For a somewhat more serious set of literary forays into urban wilderness, see Terrell Dixon, ed., *City Wilds: Essays and Stories about Urban Nature* (Athens: University of Georgia Press, 2002).

24. See Di Chiro, "Bearing Witness or Taking Action? Toxic Tourism and Environmental Justice," in Hofrichter, ed. *Reclaiming the Environmental Debate*, 275–300.

25. See Pulido, *Environmentalism and Economic Justice*; Peña, *Chicano Culture, Ecology, Politics: Subversive Kin*; and Peña, *Terror of the Machine*.

26. The *locus classicus* for discussions of the capitalist "production of nature" is Neil Smith, *Uneven Development: Nature, Capital and the Production of Space* (Oxford: Blackwell, 1984). Smith and others have developed this concept in different ways.

For a survey of some of this work, see Noel Castree, "Marxism and the Production of Nature," *Capital and Class* 72 (2000): 5–36.

27. Theoretical issues at the interface of cultural studies and ecocriticism can be viewed, for example, in the following works: William Cronon, ed., *Uncommon Ground: Toward Reinventing Nature* (New York: W. W. Norton, 1995); Jane Bennett and William Chaloupka, eds., *In the Nature of Things: Language, Politics, and the Environment* (Minneapolis: University of Minnesota Press, 1993); Timothy Luke, *Ecocritique: Contesting the Politics of Nature, Economy, and Culture* (Minneapolis: University of Minnesota Press, 1997); Andrew Ross, *Strange Weather: Culture, Science, and Technology in the Age of Limits* (London: Verso, 1991); and Andrew Ross, *The Chicago Gangster Theory of Life: Nature's Debt to Society* (London: Verso, 1995).

28. Bennett and Teague, eds., *The Nature of Cities*, contributes to the field by underscoring that "nature" does not stop at the edge of the city, and by exploring a variety of ways in which urban environments, race, and class intersect.

29. See, for example, Richard Peet and Michael Watts, eds., *Liberation Ecologies: Environment, Development, Social Movements* (New York: Routledge, 1996); Bron Raymond Taylor, ed., *Ecological Resistance Movements: The Global Emergence of Radical and Popular Environmentalism* (Albany: State University of New York Press, 1995); and David Harvey, *Justice, Nature, and the Geography of Difference* (Oxford: Blackwell, 1999). Ramachanda Guha offered the classic early analysis of the limits of mainstream U.S. environmentalism from a Third World perspective in his essay "Radical American Environmentalism and Wilderness Preservation: A Third World Critique," *Environmental Ethics* 11, no. 1 (1989): 71–84.

30. Mazel in Glotfelty and Burgess, eds., *Ecocriticism Reader*, 37–146.

31. Mazel expands this notion and offers other provocative, theoretically informed readings in his book *American Literary Environmentalism* (Athens: University of Georgia Press, 2000).

32. See Chela Sandoval, *Methodology of the Oppressed* (Minneapolis: University of Minnesota Press, 2000).

9. Will the Revolution Be Cybercast?

1. Quoted in Jeremy Brecher et al., *Globalization from Below: The Power of Solidarity* (Boston: South End Press, 2000), x. To my mind this book offers one of the best practical analyses of the antiglobalization movement from a U.S. context.

2. For an argument that the current form of globalization represents a new kind of transnational "empire" different from and superseding traditional imperialism, see Michael Hardt and Antonio Negri, *Empire* (Cambridge, MA: Harvard University Press, 2000). My own view is that Hardt and Negri exaggerate the newness of the system, but they offer useful attempts to rethink categories.

3. The phrase "globalization from below," along with its opposite, "globalization from above," is credited to Richard Falk, and first appeared in print in Jeremy Brecher et al., eds., *Global Vision* (Boston: South End Press, 1993). This category includes both radical democratic and democratic socialist alternatives to the current system.

4. One key version of this process, elaborated by Third World theorist Samir Amin, entails the notion of "delinking" from the global system toward alternative,

nation-based and regional economic, political, and cultural structures. There is also an environmentalist version stressing bioregions, and an anarchist one stressing self-organization of society without government.

5. Brecher, *Globalization from Below,* 39.

6. Mike Prokosch, and Laura Raymond, eds., *The Global Activist's Manual: Local Ways to Change the World* (New York: Thunder's Mouth Press, 2002), 1.

7. Janet Thomas, *Battle of Seattle: The Story behind and beyond the WTO Demonstrations* (Golden, CO: Fulcrum, 2000), 77.

8. For an analysis of the mainstream media's treatment of Seattle, see Seth Ackerman, "Prattle in Seattle," available on-line at http://www.fair.org/extra/0001/wto-prattle.html (accessed 3/15/05). Also reprinted in Kevin Danaher and Roger Burbach, eds., *Globalize This!* (Monroe, ME: Common Courage Press, 2000).

9. Joseph Stiglitz, *Globalization and Its Discontents* (New York: W. W. Norton: 2002), 5.

10. One of the key activists on behalf of traditional and indigenous farmers, and against genetically engineered crops, is Vandana Shiva. Among her many works, see especially *Biopiracy* (Boston: South End Press, 1997).

11. See Brecher, *Globalization from Below,* 27.

12. For a survey of these developments, see Valentine M. Moghadam, "Transnational Feminist Networks: Collective Action in an Era of Globalization," in Pierre Hamel et al., eds., *Globalization and Social Movements* (London: Palgrave, 2001), 111–39.

13. Kim Moody, cited in Brecher, *Globalization from Below,* 129.

14. Ibid., 56, 141.

15. Solnit quoted in Benjamin Shepard and Ronald Hayduk, *From ACT UP to WTO* (New York: Verso, 2002), 247.

16. Ibid., 247.

17. Ibid., 248.

18. Naomi Klein, *No Logo* (New York: Picador, 1999). A "global" phenomenon, the book has been translated into sixteen languages.

19. Shepard and Hayduk, *From ACT UP to WTO,* 248.

20. An account of the turtle action can be found in Thomas, *Battle of Seattle,* 16–28.

21. "Shutdown the WTO," DAN Handbook, available on-line at http://depts .washington.edu/wtohist/ (accessed 3/15/05).

22. Paul Hawken, "N30: Skeleton Woman in Seattle," available on-line at http://www.mapcruzin.com/globalwatch/paul_hawken.htm. Also reprinted in Danaher and Burbach, eds., *Globalize This!*

23. Alexander Cockburn and Jeffrey St. Clair, *Five Days That Shook the World: Seattle and Beyond* (New York: Verso, 2000), 15–16.

24. Cockburn and St. Clair, *Five Days That Shook the World,* 23.

25. Cockburn, available on-line at http://www.counterpunch.org/seattlediary.html (accessed 3/15/05). A slightly rewritten version appears in Cockburn and St. Clair, *Five Days That Shook the World,* 24–25.

26. Cockburn and St. Clair, *Five Days That Shook the World,* 25.

27. Staude's story is told in Thomas, *Battle of Seattle,* 84–88.

28. Hawken, "N30: Skeleton Woman."

29. The local Seattle press carried stories about anthrax and other "terrorist threats" in the weeks preceding the protests, inducing paranoia in both the police and some protesters. See Thomas, *Battle of Seattle*, 129–30.

30. Cockburn and St. Clair, *Five Days That Shook the World*, 27–28.

31. Hawken, "N30: Skeleton Woman."

32. Ibid.

33. Ibid.

34. Tico Almeida, interview, WTO History Project, available on-line at http://depts.washington.edu/wtohist/Interviews/Almeida.htm.

35. Cockburn and St. Clair, *Five Days That Shook the World*, 47.

36. Costantini, available on-line at http://www.speakeasy.org/~peterc/wto/wtoint.htm (accessed 3/15/05).

37. Almeida, interview, WTO History Project.

38. Cockburn and St. Clair, *Five Days That Shook the World*, 113.

39. Hawken, "N30: Skeleton Woman."

40. Naomi Klein, "The Vision Thing," *Nation* (10 July 2000), available on-line at http://thenation.com/doc.mhtml?i=20000710&s=klein (accessed 3/15/05).

41. Ibid.

42. See Manuel Castells, *The Information Age*, 3 vols. (Oxford: Blackwell, 1999).

43. Lisa Lowe, *Immigrant Acts* (Durham, NC: Duke University Press, 1996), 171.

44. See the People's Global Action website: http://www.nadir.org/nadir/initiativ/agp/free/seattle/n30/n30calls.htm (accessed 3/15/05).

45. Various perspectives on the developing use of the Internet in transnational grassroots organizing can be found in the following: G. Lins Ribiero, "Cybercultural Politics: Political Activism in a Transnational World," in Sonia Alvarez et al., eds., *Culture of Politics, Politics of Culture* (Boulder, CO: Westview Press, 1998), 325–52; Harry Cleaver, "The Zapatista Effect: The Internet and the Rise of Alternative Political Fabric," *Journal of International Affairs* 51, no. 2: 621–40; and "Social Justice Movements and the Internet," special issue, *Peace Review* 13, no. 3 (September 2001).

46. See Paul de Armond, "Netwar in the Emerald City: WTO Protest Strategy and Tactics," available on-line at http://nwcitizen.com/publicgood/reports/wto/ (accessed 3/15/05).

47. Linda Setchell, "Democratizing Media," in *The Global Activist's Manual* (New York: Thunder's Mouth Press, 2002), 187–88.

48. Jeff Perlstein, interview with the WTO History Project, available on-line at http://depts.washington.edu/wtohist/interview_index.htm (accessed 3/15/05).

49. Ana Noguera, in Shepard and Hayduk, *From ACT UP to WTO*, 296.

50. Eddie Yuen et al., eds., *Battle of Seattle: The New Challenge to Capitalist Globalization* (New York: Soft Skull Press, 2001), 379–80.

51. See Danaher and Burbach, eds., *Globalize This!* 48–52.

52. Stiglitz, *Globalization and Its Discontents*, 9.

53. Martinez's article, "Where Was the Color in Seattle?" has been reprinted in several collections, including Danaher and Burbach, eds., *Globalize This!* and is also available on-line at http://www.arc.org/C_Lines/CLArchive/story3_1_02.html (accessed 3/15/05).

54. Chris Dixon, "Finding Hope after Seattle," available on-line at http://zmag.org/dixonseattle.htm (accessed 3/15/05).

55. For a list of such protests and an argument for their greater importance, see http://www.globalissues.org/TradeRelated/FreeTrade/Protests.asp (accessed 3/15/05).

56. Yutaka Dirks, "Doing Things Differently This Time: The Kananaskis G8 Meeting and Movement Building," available on-line at http://www.zmag.org/content/VisionStrategy/durks_kananaskis.cfm (accessed 3/15/05). For more on the Alberta actions, see http://www.alberta.indymedia.org (accessed 3/15/05).

57. Porto Alegre was chosen in large part because of its progressive government. The city is part of a growing political movement in Brazil that is systematically delegating power back down to people at the municipal level rather than hoarding it at the national and international levels. Brazil's Worker's Party has been the prime architect of this decentralization process.

58. The World Social Forum charter can be found online at http://www.forumsocialmundial.org.br/.

59. L. A. Kauffman, "All Has Changed," *Free Radical* 19 (17 September 2001), available on-line at http://www.alternet.org/story/11523/ (accessed 3/15/05)

60. The least unreliable source for the always-contested numbers of participants (police always underestimate, protesters always overestimate) is http://www.zmag.org/GlobalWatch/DiverseDemos.html (accessed 3/15/05).

61. Jesus Ramirez Cuevas, *La Jornada,* translated on Znet as "How Barcelona Defeated Violence," available on-line at www.zmag.org/content/VisionStrategy/ramirez_barcelona.cfm (accessed 3/15/05).

62. Yuen, *Battle of Seattle,* 329, 331.

10. Reflections on the Cultural Study of Social Movements

1. For those unfamiliar with the various schools of social movement theorizing alluded to here, a good introduction is provided by the collection of classic essays edited by Steven M. Buechler and F. Kurt Cylke, *Social Movements: Perspectives and Issues* (Mountain View, CA: Mayfield Publishers, 1997).

2. Two edited volumes suggest the emerging trajectory of "culture" within mainstream sociological analysis of movements. The first, *Frontiers of Social Movement Theory,* edited by Aldon Morris and Carol Mueller (New Haven, CT: Yale University Press, 1992), includes a mixed group of essays, several of which, along with Morris's concluding remarks, suggest increasing interest in cultural issues like identity and movement intellectual frames. A mere three years later, Hank Johnston and Bert Klandermans co-edited *Social Movements and Culture* (Minneapolis: University of Minnesota Press, 1995), a work whose title clearly indicates that cultural analysis was sufficiently central to deserve a volume of its own. That same year, a book co-edited by Marcy Darnovsky, Barbara Epstein, and Richard Flacks, *Cultural Politics and Social Movements* (Philadelphia: Temple University Press, 1995), presented an interdisciplinary collection of essays that similarly sought to focus on cultural dimensions of movements.

3. Verta Taylor and Nancy Whittier, "Analytical Approaches to Social Movement Culture," in Johnston and Klandermans, eds., *Social Movements and Culture,* 163–87, especially 163–64.

4. See Amy Swidler, "Cultural Power in Social Movements," in Johnston and Klandermans, eds., *Social Movements and Culture,* 25–40.

5. Swidler takes up this issue, ibid.

6. Cindy Patton, "Tremble Hetero Swine," in Michael Warner, ed., *Fear of a Queer Planet* (Minneapolis: University of Minnesota Press, 1993), 167.

7. Michael Denning, *The Cultural Front: The Laboring of American Culture in the Twentieth Century* (New York: Verso, 1996), 64.

8. A good place to enter the rich theoretical and methodological universe of Pierre Bourdieu is his essay collection *The Field of Cultural Production* (New York: Columbia University Press, 1993).

9. Steven Buechler, *Social Movements in Advanced Capitalism* (Oxford: Oxford University Press, 2000), 164–65.

10. Jeremy Brecher, Tim Costello, and Brendan Smith, *Globalization from Below* (Boston: South End Press, 2000 [2d ed., 2002]), xii.

11. Doug McAdam, "Culture in Social Movements," in Buechler and Cylke, eds., *Social Movements: Perspectives and Issues,* 473–86.

12. Ibid., 481.

13. Swidler, "Cultural Power and Social Movements," 33.

14. Steven Buechler develops this notion of "movement community" most fully in *Women's Movements in the United States* (New Brunswick, NJ: Rutgers University Press, 1990).

15. Rick Fantasia, *Cultures of Solidarity: Consciousness, Action and Contemporary American Workers* (Berkeley: University of California Press, 1988). He defines the concept of "cultures of solidarity" as an emergent structure less elaborated than a subculture, but more than random in its resistance to dominant cultural values.

16. John Lofland, "Charting Degrees of Movement Culture," in Johnston and Klandersmans, eds., *Social Movements and Culture,* 188–216.

17. Naomi Klein discusses both the power and the limits of "culture jamming" as a social change strategy in *No Logo* (New York: Picador, 1999), especially 279–309.

18. On this anecdote, see ibid., 302.

19. Raymond Williams develops the notion of "formations" in *Marxism and Literature* (Oxford: Oxford University Press, 1977) and *The Sociology of Culture* (New York: Schocken, 1981). Denning makes brilliant use of the concept in *The Cultural Front.*

20. See Denning, *The Cultural Front,* xix–xx.

21. A good, comprehensive introduction to many of the key texts in the history of subcultural studies is provided in Sarah Thorton and Ken Gelder, eds., *The Subcultures Reader* (New York: Routledge, 1997). The classic cultural studies text analyzing the disruptive semiotic potential of subcultures is Dick Hebdige, *Subculture: The Meaning of Style* (London: Methuen, 1979). In later work Hebdige moved closer to the position I articulate here in arguing that subversive qualities of subcultures become significant challenges to the dominant culture primarily when connected to those politicized subcultures I call movement cultures. See, for example, Dick Hebdige, *Hiding in the Light* (New York: Routledge, 1988).

22. Verta Taylor, "Social Movement Continuity: The Women's Movement in Abeyance," *American Sociological Review* 54 (1989): 761–75.

23. See Williams, *Marxism and Literature,* and *Sociology of Culture.*

24. Winnie Breines, *Community and Organization in the New Left, 1962–1968: The Great Refusal* (New Brunswick, NJ: Rutgers University Press, 1989).

25. Noël Sturgeon, "Theorizing Movements: Direct Action and Direct Theory," in Darnovsky et al., eds., *Cultural Politics and Social Movements*, 35–51.

26. Alberto Melucci's ideas can be found in compact form in "The Symbolic Challenge in Contemporary Movements," *Social Research* 52 (1985): 781–816, and in more elaborated form in his book, *Challenging Codes* (Cambridge, UK: Cambridge University Press, 1996).

27. T. V. Reed, *Fifteen Jugglers, Five Believers: Literary Politics and the Poetics of Social Movements* (Berkeley: University of California Press, 1992).

28. Among the most useful works on collective identity in movement terms are the following: Verta Taylor and Nancy Whittier, "Collective Identity in Social Movement Communities," in Buechler and Cylke, eds., *Social Movements;* Rick Fantasia, *Cultures of Solidarity* (Berkeley: University of California Press, 1988); David A. Snow et al., "Frame Alignment, Micromobilization and Movement Participation," *American Sociological Review* 51 (1986): 464–81; Debra Friedman and Doug McAdam, "Collective Identity and Activism," in Aldon Morris and Carol McClurg Mueller, eds., *Frontiers of Social Movement Theory* (New Haven, CT: Yale University Press, 1992); Aldon Morris, "Political Consciousness and Collective Action," in Morris and Mueller, eds., *Frontiers of Social Movement Theory;* Alberto Melucci, *Nomads of the Present* (Philadelphia: Temple University Press, 1989); and Melucci, *Challenging Codes.*

29. See Tarrow, "A Movement Society?" in Buechler and Cylke, eds., *Social Movements.*

30. James C. Scott, *Domination and the Arts of Resistance* (New Haven, CT: Yale University Press, 1990).

31. The term *structures of feeling* was developed by Raymond Williams in *Marxism and Literature.* He uses it to name something different from, but related to, worldview or ideology, and argues that these structures need to be examined in relation to institutions, cultural formations, and other forces that serve to organize subjectivity.

32. Melucci, *Challenging Codes,* 182.

33. I take the term *material-discursive* from feminist cultural theorist Donna Haraway who uses it throughout her crucially important body of work. Often mischaracterized as concerned only with "discourse," Haraway has always been a materialist as well, one who argues brilliantly against the politically disastrous effects of these and related dichotomies. A good place to enter Haraway's intellectual universe is via her essay collection, *Simians, Cyborgs, and Women* (New York: Routledge, 1991).

Index

Abu-Jamal, Mumia, 321n.28
academic disciplines: black studies, 302; Chicano studies, 109, 112, 128; environmental studies, 218–19; gay, lesbian, and queer studies, 187; women's studies, 99–101, 312
ACT NOW (AIDS Coalition to Network, Organize and Win), 205
"actorvists," 136, 144
ACT UP (AIDS Coalition to Unleash Power), 179–217, 252, 292–93, 301, 334n.22; actions, 188, 190–201, 205–6; expanding issues, 205–8; and queer culture, 186–89; spin-off groups, 194, 210–13; women's committee, 199–202, 207, 210–11
Acuña, Rudolfo, 113
Adamson, Joni, 236, 337n.22
Adbusters, 301
advertising industry: and ACT UP, 182
aesthetic, black. See black aesthetic movement
aesthetic, Chicano, 106–7
aesthetic ideologies, 302–3
aestheticization: in ecocriticism, 233
affinity groups: in ACT UP, 185, 189; in Direct Action Network, 260–61, 263
AFL-CIO, 253–54, 258
Africa: and AIDS epidemic, 216–17, 252; famine relief projects, 158–65

African Americans, 1–39, 47, 221, 309; and AIDS epidemic, 207–8. See also black power movement; civil rights movement
"Afro" hairstyle, 42–43, 68
agents provocateurs, 61, 63–64, 148
"agit-pop," 156
agribusiness, 162, 250
AIDS (acquired immune deficiency syndrome), 180
AIDS chic, 214–15
AIDS epidemic, 183–86, 215–17. See also ACT UP
AIDS Quilt, 205, 334n.14
AIDS "victims": use of term, 197–98
Alaniz-Healy, Wayne, 115
Alarcón, Norma, 121
Albany, Georgia, 22–23, 33
Albright, Madeleine, 263
Alcatraz Island: Native American takeover of, 132
alcoholism: Native Americans and, 149
Alexie, Sherman, 330n.3
Alicia, Juana: Las Lechugueras mural, 122
Allen, Pam, 89
Alliance for Sustainable Jobs and the Environment, 260
Almeida, Tico, 265, 268
alternative media. See independent media

ambiguity, strategic, 114, 190
American Civil Liberties Union
    (ACLU), 269
American Indian Movement (AIM), 58,
    129–55; film portrayals of, 137–55;
    male-centeredness, 147–48;
    occupation of BIA office, 134, 136;
    women in, 145–55
Amin, Samir, 338n.4
Amnesty International, 252, 269
anarchist groups: in Battle of Seattle, 266
ANC Mothers Anonymous, 82
anger, mobilizing, 203
anti-apartheid movement, U.S., 172, 246
anti-apartheid projects, 158, 165–74
anticolonial struggles, 9–10, 113
anti–corporate globalization movement,
    240–85, 305–6; internal tensions in,
    278–81; issue areas, 249–54. See also
    Battle of Seattle
Antin, Mary, 237
antinuclear movement, 185, 224, 246, 307
antiracism organizations, 132–33. See
    also American Indian Movement;
    Black Panther Party for Self-Defense
anti-Semitism: in work of Amiri
    Baraka, 48
antisweatshop movement, 246, 254
antiwar protests, 284–85, 307; and
    Chicano movement, 118–20
anti-WTO banners: in Battle of Seattle,
    251, 255–56
Anzaldúa, Gloria, 93–94, 121
appropriation. See cultural
    appropriation
appropriation art, 191
Apted, Michael, 131, 142
Aquash, Annie Mae, 155
archaeological desecration, 150
Arendt, Hannah, 152, 303
arrest strategy: and race, 279
art: and social movements, 302–3. See
    also community mural movement;
    graphic images
Art and Revolution, 254–55
Artists United against Apartheid, 165–66
art world: ACT UP and, 182, 190–91
Asian Americans, 58, 221

Asian Sisters, 82
Association for the Study of Literature
    and Environment (ASLE), 219
Audubon Society, 223
auto-ethnography, 94
AZT (anti-AIDS drug), 193
Aztec culture, 118
Aztlán: quest for, 110, 113, 116, 123

baby boom, 84
Baca, Judith Francisca, 121, 123–26
backlash: antifeminist, 101–2; against
    Chicano movement, 128
Bad Heart Bull, Wesley, 150
Baker, Arthur, 168
Baker, Ella, xix, 2, 4, 13, 21, 177
Baldwin, James, 10
"Ballad of Emmett Till" (Dylan), 25
"Ballad of the Sit-ins" (Carawan),
    16, 22
Bambara, Toni Cade. See Cade
    [Bambara], Toni
Band Aid, 157, 159
Banks, Dennis, 131
Baraka, Amiri (Leroi Jones), 45–49
Barcelona, 282–83
Bari, Judi, 253
barrios, 104, 106, 116–17
Barshevsky, Charlene, 263
baseball game: as site of ACT UP
    action, 201–2
Bass, Ellen, 97–98
Battle of Seattle, 240–85; assessments of,
    268–70; cultural resistance actions,
    254–58; cybercasting of, 274–78; edu-
    cation programs, 248–54; impact of,
    283–84; violence and conflict in,
    258–68
Baudrillard, Jean, 295–96, 333n.32
Bayne, Lawrence, 150
Beal, Frances M., 82
"beautification" projects: for barrios
    and ghettoes, 124
Bedard, Irene, 148
Beijing, 252
Belafonte, Harry, 160
Bellecourt, Clyde, 131
Bello, Walden, 248

benefit rock, 156–78. *See also* Live Aid;
Sun City (Artists United against
Apartheid)
Benetton advertisement: ACT UP
and, 201
Benford, Robert, 323n.2
Benjamin, Medea, 248
Benjamin, Walter, 303
Bennett, Lerone, Jr., 67
Bernal, Antonio: mural in Del Rey,
California (1968), 107–11
Bevel, James, 20
BIA. *See under* U.S. government
Bible: as source of liberation stories, 11
biocentrism, 226–27
biopiracy, 250
Birmingham school, 332n.4
birth control pill, 85
black aesthetic movement, 42–44, 47–
48, 52–53, 302, 308
black artists: and Live Aid, 159; in *Sun
City* project, 166
Black Arts Repertory Theatre and
School (BARTS), 47–48
Black Bloc, 263, 266
black church, 5, 11–12, 48. *See also* civil
rights movement
black colleges, 12
black community: and black power
movement, 54–55, 68
black history, 18
Black House, 50
Black Mountain poets, 97
Black Panther Party for Self-Defense,
40–74; decline of, 63–65; "Executive
Mandate #1," 41; formation of, 44–45;
ideology of, 57–59; image of, 110–11;
organization of, 57, 64; repression of,
59–63; survival programs, 53, 59, 66–
68; Ten-Point Program, 52, 59, 67–68,
72–74; use of drama, 50–51, 53; use of
rhetoric, 55–57; and violence, 55–56,
59–63; and weapon use, 53–54
black power: use of term, 38–39, 44
black power movement, 34, 36, 41–44,
110, 113–14, 306, 308. *See also* Black
Panther Party for Self-Defense
black rage, 320n.5

blacks. *See* African Americans
black theology, 42
Blair, Izell, 20
Blake, William, 222
"blaxpoitation" films, 68
Block, Sam, 28
blood symbolism: ACT UP and, 195–96
blowouts, 109, 112
blue jeans, 301
Boal, Iain A., 277
body, human: "put on line," 28–29
Bono, 178
Boston: and ACT UP, 182
Botello, David Rivas, 115
Bourdieu, Pierre, xvii, 291, 303
Bové, Jose, 248, 250
Boyd, Andrew, 257
"bra burners," 77
Brando, Marlon, 131–32
Bread and Roses, 88
Breines, Wini, 307
Brooks, Gwendolyn, 96
Brown, Elaine, 36, 64–65
Brown, James, 43
Brown Berets, 58, 112
Buechler, Steven, 81, 291, 298, 314
Buell, Lawrence, 230
Bullins, Ed, 49–50
Bulter, Octavia, 236
Burns, Stewart, 317n.3
Burroughs Wellcome, 193–95
bus boycott (Montgomery, Alabama),
16–19
Bush, George H. W., 178
Bush, George W., 178, 216, 284

Cade [Bambara], Toni, 42, 87, 92, 101, 236
California: and Chicano movement,
109, 112; gold rush era, 108; state
legislature, 40–41
California Save the Redwoods League,
223
"call and response": in black church, 48
camp: ACT UP and, 188–89
"cannery women" strikers, 104
Carawan, Guy, 19, 22, 33
Carmichael, Stokely, 38–39, 42, 44
carnalismo, 114

Carrillo, Graciela, 122
Carson, Rachel, 224–26
Carter, Joseph, 20
Castells, Manuel, 270, 334n.19
Castillo, Ana, 236
Catholic Church: as target of ACT
UP, 182
Catholic faith: Chicanos and, 109–10,
115–16, 122
cell phones: and Battle of Seattle, 273–74
Center for Campus Organizing, 254
Centro Cultural de la Raza, San
Diego, 116
Cervantes, Lorna Dee, 92
Cervantes, Yreina: La Ofrenda mural,
121–22
CGT, 282
chain stores: as focus of sit-ins, 20
Charles, Ray, 21, 23
Chávez, César, 105, 107, 109–10
CHER (Commie Homos Engaged in
Revolution), 189
Chessman, Andrea, 91
Chiapas, Mexico, 246
Chicago, 61–62, 182
Chicago Eight, 60–61
ChicanismA, 120–23
chicanismo, 111
Chicano: use of term, 105, 120
Chicano aesthetic, 106–7
Chicano moratorium, 118–20
Chicano movement, 103–28, 304; changes
in, 127–28; and male-centeredness,
120–23; portrayal of history, 107–11. See
also community mural movement
Chicano Park, San Diego, 115–17
Chicanos/Latinos, 103–5, 207–8, 221
Chomsky, Noam, 248
Chow, Rey, 95, 271
Christianity, 11. See also black church
Chrystos, 92
Church Commission, 321n.28
church music: and freedom songs, 15–19
CISPES (Committee in Solidarity with
the People of El Salvador), 246
Citizens Clearinghouse for Toxic
Waste, 221
Citizenship Schools, 38

city-reservation split: among Native
Americans, 133
Citywide Murals project (Los Angeles),
124–26
civil disobedience, 10, 16, 77; ACT UP
and, 191–96; and black power movement, 53; in civil rights movement,
29. See also nonviolence
civil rights movement, xv, 1–39, 110, 123,
290, 299, 306, 318n.5; Jubilee 2000
and, 249–50; preconditions for, 7–10;
roots of, 10–13; women in, 85–87. See
also black power movement
Clark, Mark, 62, 321n.28
class: and environmental issues, 221,
224, 228, 233–34, 236
Cleaver, Eldridge, 50, 64–65
Clinton, Bill, 216
clothing, African-style, 68
coalition building: Black Panther Party
and, 66
Cobbs, Price, 320n.5
Cockburn, Alexander, 261–62, 264, 266,
268–69
Cody, "Iron Eyes," 134
cognitive frames, 310
cognitive praxis, 79, 218
COINTELPRO (Counter Intelligence
Program), 61, 321n.28
Cold War, 9
collective identity formation, 308–9
Collier, Samuel, 20
colonialism, internal, 58, 113
Combahee River Collective, 82–83, 88
commitment, 28–29
commodification, 176, 232, 295
common sense, 69
communal production: in muralism,
123–26
communication outside the movement,
30–32
communism, 189; collapse of, 244
community: use of term, 126–27
community mural movement, 105–7,
123–27
community organizing, 22
conquistadors, Spanish, 103
consciousness, 309–11

consciousness-raising (CR), 76–78, 87–90, 324n.19, 325n.24; and poetry, 78–80, 94–95
conservationism, 222
consumer advocacy: and anti–corporate globalization movement, 252
contraceptives: use of, 85
"copyleft," 276
CORE (Congress of Racial Equality), 10, 26
Corona, Bert, 104–5
corporate scandals, 284
corporate sponsorship, 174
corporations, 182, 243. *See also* anti–corporate globalization movement
corridos (Mexican political ballads), 108
Cosmopolitan magazine: as target of ACT UP, 199–200
Costantini, Peter, 267–68
Costner, Kevin, 137
"cowboys and Indians" formula, 135–37, 142, 145, 147–48, 151
CR groups, 87–90
criminal justice system, 124, 132–33
criminal trials: of AIM members, 147; of Black Panther Party members, 60–63
Crimp, Douglas, 180, 185, 188–89, 209
critical pedagogy, 319n.15
cross-dressing: ACT UP and, 188–89
Crow Dog, Leonard, 151
Crow Dog, Mary, 146–55
Crusade for Justice, 112
Cruz, Manuel: *Homeboy* mural, Romana Gardens Housing Project, East Los Angeles (1974), 117–18
Cuban Revolution, 113
cultural appropriation, 214–15, 297, 300–301
cultural centers, Chicano, 116–17
cultural domain: in social movement theory, 292–95, 314–15
cultural elements (residual, emergent, and dominant), 306–7
cultural fields, xvii, 291, 303
cultural formations, 301–3, 306–7, 342n.19; in black power movement, 42–44, 67–71; in feminist poetry movement, 95–99

cultural front formation, 302
cultural imperialism, 157, 332n.4
cultural poetics, 94
cultural politics, 79, 179–80, 183–86, 289–91, 302–3
cultural studies, xvii, 237–38, 290–91, 304
cultural theory: and ACT UP, 183–86
culture, 79–80, 289–95; "American," 111
culture in movements, 296, 299–301
culture jamming, 301, 342n.17
cultures of solidarity, 298, 342n.15
Custer, South Dakota, 133, 150
cybercasting: and Battle of Seattle, 274–78
cycles of protest, 213, 334n.22

Dances with Wolves, 137, 145
Davis, Angela, 42, 51, 65
debt elimination: as anti–corporate globalization issue, 249–50
debt relief campaign, 246
decentralization of ACT UP, 208–10
Deep Dish TV, 274
deep ecology movement, 226–27
defusion of movement culture, 312–14
Deitering, Cynthia, 232
De Lauretis, Teresa, 325n.24
DeLillo, Don, 236; *White Noise*, 231–32
Deloria, Vine, Jr., 132
Del Rey, California, 107
Demme, Jonathan, 166
democracy: economic vs. political, 245
Democratic national convention (Chicago, 1968), 60–61
democratic societies: and subcultures, 305
Denning, Michael, 289, 302, 342n.19
desegregation, 8–9, 38
destruction of property, 266, 269, 283
Devall, Bill, 226
Di Chiro, Giovanna, 237
Dickinson, Emily, 97
"die-in," 195
differences, erasing, 160–62
diffusion of movement culture into mainstream culture, 297, 299–301, 312–14
DiFranco, Ani, 102

direct action, 247
Direct Action Network (DAN), 247,
254–55, 258–68; "DAN Handbook for
N30," 255
direct action tourists, 279
direct action tradition, xviii–xix
direct theory, 307
Dirks, Yutaka, 279–80
Dishong, Michelle, 135
distribution of profits from benefit
rock, 165, 168
diversity: of anti–corporate globalization movement, 242; in environmental justice movement, 221; in
gay activism, 206–8
Dixon, Chris, 279
Doctors without Borders, 252
"Do They Know It's Christmas?" 159
"double jeopardy": and women's
movement, 82, 89
dramatic action, xiv–xv, 320n.2; ACT
UP and, 180, 183, 187–88, 193, 208–10;
AIM and, 135–37, 155; black power
movement and, 42, 45–51, 53, 59–63,
67–69; Chicano movement and, 107.
See also feminist poetry; "festive
resistance"
drug approval process: ACT UP and,
192–96
Dylan, Bob, 25

Earth Day (1970), 226
Earth First! 224, 251
Earth Summit (Rio de Janeiro, 1992),
246
East Los Angeles, California, 112,
117–20
East Los Streetscapers: La Familia
mural, 115
ecocriticism, 218–20, 222; critique of,
228–33; schools of, 224–27, 237–38
Ecocriticism Reader (ed. Glotfelty and
Fromm), 229–33
ecofeminism, 94, 221–22, 227, 233, 253
ecological ecocriticism, 225–26
ecology: use of term, 225
economic change: and civil rights movement, 7–8

economic development: as anti–
corporate globalization issue, 249–50
economic domain: in social movement
theory, 292–95, 314–15
economic growth, 70
economic violence, 120
ecotourism, 237
education: in Battle of Seattle, 248–54
El Congreso de Pueblo de Habla
Español, 104
Electronic Disturbance Theater, 273
Electronic Hippies Collective, 272–73
el movimiento. See Chicano movement
El Salvador, 122, 246–47
El Teatro Campesino, 107, 112
El Teatro Campesino cultural center,
Del Rey, California, 107
emancipation, 11–12
Enron, 284
Environmental Defense Fund, 223
environmental feminisms, 94
environmental issues: and anti–
corporate globalization movement, 251
environmental justice ecocriticism,
218–39; and history of environmentalism, 223–24; trends in, 233–39
environmental justice movement,
220–22
environmental movement: and ecocriticism, 219–20; histories of, 222–
24. See also ecocriticism; environmental justice ecocriticism
equal rights: and women's movement,
84–85
Erdoes, Richard, 146–47
essentialism: AIM and, 154; in black
power movement, 48, 66; in Chicano
movement, 114; in feminism, 90,
325n.24, 326n.25
Estrada Courts housing project, East
Los Angeles, 118–20
ethnicity: changing concepts of, 271;
and social movements, 304
ethnic studies: and environmental
issues, 239
ethnocentrism: in ecocriticism, 228; in
Live Aid project, 159–61

Eyerman, Ron, 79
Eyre, Chris, 330n.3

"face" of the opposition, 202–4
"factory girls," 222
Fairness and Accuracy in Reporting, 274
Falk, Richard, 338n.3
family: in Chicano culture, 115
famine: images of, 162–63
famine relief projects, 157–65
Fanon, Frantz, 47, 61, 68–69
Fantasia, Rick, 298, 342n.15
Farmer, James, 26, 31
farm workers, Chicano: image of, 115–16, 122
farm workers movement, 109
fatalism, romantic: in gay community, 216
Fauci, Anthony, 215–16
fear as tool of oppression, 25–27
Featherstone, Lisa, 283
Federal Bureau of Investigation (FBI), 59, 61, 321n.28; and AIM, 134–35, 140, 142–45, 148
Fellowship of Reconciliation, 10
"feminine mystique," 84
feminism, 58, 75–78, 85–87, 94, 115. See also ChicanismA; feminist poetry; women's movement
feminist anthologies, 89, 92–94, 97–99
feminist bookstores, 100
feminist ideas, 75–76, 78
feminist music, 102
feminist periodicals, 100
feminist poetry, 76–80, 90–99, 102
feminist presses, 100
feminist theory, 78, 83, 89, 92–94
fence-sitters in civil rights movement, 31–32
Ferree, Myra Marx, 81
"festive resistance," 256–57
field of power, 291, 303
Fierro de Bright, Josephina, 104
Fifty Years Is Enough, 246–47
filmmaking: Native Americans and, 130, 154, 330n.3
films, 129–30; Dances with Wolves, 137, 145; Incident at Oglala, 142; Lakota

Woman: Siege at Wounded Knee, 130, 145–55; Mississippi Burning, 145; Powwow Highway, 130, 137–42; Smoke Signals, 330n.3; Spirit of Crazy Horse, 149; Thunderheart, 130, 142–45
fire department (Seattle): and Battle of Seattle, 262
First National People of Color Environmental Leadership Summit (1991), 221
fishing rights: Native Americans and, 132
"fish-ins": in Pacific Northwest, 132
folk culture: and diffusion, 313
folk song revival, 23
Fonda, Jane, 131, 145
Foucault, Michel, 184–85, 295
Fox network, 174
frame analysis, 323n.2
Frankfurt school, 332n.4
freedom: meanings of, 34–37
freedom rides, 22, 26
Freedom Schools, 38
Freedom Singers, 23
freedom song movement, 22–23
freedom songs, 2, 8, 13–19; and collective identity, 32–34; and empowerment, 23–27, 31; and ideology, 37–38; and jail context, 35–36; and outside audience, 30–32; strategic role of, 27–30
Freedom Summer (1964), 23, 145, 301
"free logging" agreement: WTO and, 251
Free Radio Berkeley, 274
Free Southern Theater, 47
Free Speech TV, 274
free trade, 244–45
Freire, Paulo, 319n.15
Friedan, Betty, 83
Friedman, Thomas, 248
Friends of the Earth, 223
Friends of the Earth International, 247
Fromm, Harold, 229
functions of culture in movements, 299–300
Furies, 88

Gage, Patrick, 204
Galería de La Raza, San Francisco, 123

Gamson, Joshua, 186
Gamson, William, 202, 216
Gandhi, Mahatma, 10
gangsterism of Black Panther Party, 64–65
gang violence: and Chicano movement, 117–18
Garrison, Ednie, 80
Gauley Tunnel tragedy, 237
gay bookstores, 187
gay community: and AIDS, 181–83. See also ACT UP
gay/lesbian activism, xxii, 4, 83, 186–87
gay liberation movement, 58, 65, 182, 305. See also queer culture
gay/straight dichotomy, 186
G8 summit meeting (Kananaskis, Alberta, Canada, June 2002), 279–80
Geldof, Bob, 158–59, 163–65
gender. See feminism; queer culture
gendered language, 88–89
general strikes, 253
generational conflict, 32
Genet, Jean, 58, 68
Genoa, Italy, 282
gestures of black power movement, 43, 52–53
Gibbs, Lois, 221
GI Forum, 104
Ginsburg, Allen, 96
Giovanni, Nikki, 92
Gitlin, Todd, 324n.15
Giuliano, Carlo, 282
Global Exchange, 248–49
globalization, 157, 176, 217, 240–45. See also anti-corporate globalization movement
globalization from below, 244–45, 271, 338n.3
global justice movement, 280–81, 283–85
Glotfelty, Cheryll Burgess, 229
GMHC (Gay Men's Health Crisis), 181–82
Gober, Berth, 23
Gonzales, Rudolfo "Corky," 112
gospel songs, 15
Gould, Robert E., 199
graffiti, 118

Grahn, Judy, 92
Gramsci, Antonio, xxiii, 69
Grandmaster Flash and the Furious Five, 70
Gran Fury collective, 190, 198–201, 214
Grant, Madison, 223
graphic images, 180, 190–91, 197–200, 202–4, 209
grassroots activism, 3–4, 169–72, 219, 246, 279
Great Society program, 119–20
Great Wall of Los Angeles, 124–26
Greene, Graham, 142
Greenpeace, 224, 251
Greens, 224
Greensboro, North Carolina, 20
Greenwich Village, New York City, 23
Greenwood, Mississippi, 24–25
Grewal, Inderpal, 95
GRID (gay-related immune deficiency), 180
Grier, William, 320n.5
Griffin, Susan, 92, 94
Gronk: Black and White Moratorium Mural, Estrada Courts housing project, East Los Angeles (1973), 118–20
Grover, Jan, 185
grunge subculture, 177
Guevara, Che, 113
Gunn Allen, Paula, 230

Habermas, Jürgen, 295
hacktivists: and Battle of Seattle, 274–78
Hall, Stuart, 163–64
Hamer, Fannie Lou, 37
Hampton, Fred, 62, 65, 321n.28
Haraway, Donna, 343n.33
Harjo, Joy, 92, 236
Harris, Ruth, 23
Harrison, George, 137
Hartford, Bruce, 25–26
Hawken, Paul, 261, 263–64, 269
Hayden, Casey, 86
health education: ACT UP and, 193
Hebdige, Dick, 342n.21
hegemony, 42
Herman, George, 55–56

Herrón, Willie: *Black and White Moratorium Mural,* Estrada Courts housing project, East Los Angeles (1973), 118–20; *Wall That Cracked Open,* mural, City Terrace, East Los Angeles (1972), 118
Hess, Beth, 81
hidden transcripts, 310–11
high culture: and diffusion, 313
Highlander Folk School, Tennessee, 1, 7, 16, 19, 22, 33
Hijas de Cuauhtemoc, 82
Hilliard, David, 55–56
hip-hop culture, 70–71, 102, 261
hippie subculture, 305–7
Hispano land grant movement, 109–10
historians, Chicano, 109
history: portrayed in murals, 124–26
history, sense of: in Chicano movement, 108–9
HIV (human immunodeficiency virus), 185. *See also* AIDS
Hoffman, Abbie, 61
Hoffman, Julius, 61
Hoffman-LaRoche, Inc., 204
Hogan, Linda, 236
holidays, 43
Hollingsworth, Tony, 173
Hollywood: and AIM, 130–31, 135–37
homophobia, 4, 48, 65, 71, 180, 185, 199, 207–8
homosexuality. *See* gay community; gay/lesbian activism; lesbians
Hoover, J. Edgar, 59
Horton, Zilphia, 33
housewives: in postwar America, 83–84
Howe, Florence, 97–98
Huerta, Dolores, 107, 109, 121–22
Hughes, Langston, xv
human rights issues: and anti–corporate globalization movement, 251–52
humor: and ACT UP, 188–89
hymns, Christian, 15, 17–19

identity: black, 34, 66, 68, 308–9; collective, 32–34; ethnic, 126; gay, 185; individual, 32–33; Mexican

American, 104–5; queer, 185–86. *See also* essentialism
identity formation, 185–86
identity politics, 66, 126, 185–86, 308–9
ideology, 294, 309–11; of ACT UP, 208–10; of Black Panther Party, 57–59; expressed in poetry, 92–94; of Reaganism, 163–64; of rock music, 174–75; and social movements, 36–37
"I'll Be Alright," 33
image-system of Chicano murals, 106–7
"I'm on My Way to Freedom Land," 32
imprisonment: of AIM members, 153; of Black Panther Party members, 60, 321n.28; of civil rights workers, 35–36
Incident at Oglala, 142
independent media, 274–78
indigenismo, 108, 114–16, 118
Indigenous Environmental Network, 248
indigenous people: as issue in anti–corporate globalization movement, 250–51
Industrial Workers of the World (IWW, Wobblies), 332n.2
Indymedia collective, 274–78
infiltration of radical groups, 61
innovation in cultural production, 297
"instant historicizing," 15–16
institution building: feminism and, 99–101
institutions, parallel, 100
instrumentalism, 300
insurance industry: ACT UP and, 196
integration: in federal government bureaucracy, 9; of public schools, 19. *See also* desegregation
intellectual formations, 218–19
intercommunalism, 66
Interdisciplinary Studies of Literature and Environment (ISLE), 219
International Forum on Globalization, 248
internationalism of Black Panther Party, 66
International Monetary Fund (IMF), 162, 243, 249, 283
Internet, 241, 270–74

intravenous drug users, 183, 207
Iraq: U.S. war on, 284–85
I Wor Keun (Red Guard), 58

Jackson, Michael, 160
jail as context for freedom songs, 35–36
Jameson, Fredric, 176, 295, 332n.4
Jamison, Andrew, 79
ji Jaga, Geronimo (Elmer Pratt), 321n.28
Joan, Polly, 91
Johnson, Lyndon, 119–20
Jones, Leroi. *See* Baraka, Amiri
Jordan, June, 92, 96, 318n.5; "A Poem
    about My Rights," 234–35
Joseph, Stephen, 203
Jubilee 2000, 246–47, 249

Kahlo, Frida, 122–23
Kaplan, Caren, 95
Karenga, Ron, 42, 45
Karve, Chitra, 173
Kaufman, L. A., 281–82
"Keep Your Eyes on the Prize," 30
Kegley, Don, 258
Kennedy, Florynce, 87
Kennedy, John F., 84
King, Katie, 81, 89, 92–93
King, Martin Luther, Jr., xxiii, 2–3, 5, 10,
    17–19, 46, 110, 319n.12
King, Mary, 86
Kingsolver, Barbara, 236
Kingston, Maxine Hong, 302
kiss-ins, same-sex, 200–201
Klein, Naomi, 245–46, 248, 257–58, 270,
    342n.17
Klepfitz, Irena, 92
Koch, Ed, 203
Kramer, Larry, 182
Ku Klux Klan, 6

La Adelita, 108, 121–22
labor force: feminization of, 253
labor movement, 7, 82, 104, 253–54, 258–
    59; popular front, 104, 106, 109–10
labor songs, 23, 31, 33
labor unions, 7
LaDuke, Winona, 236
Lafayette, Bernard, 20

Lakota Woman: Siege at Wounded Knee,
    130, 145–55
land mines: campaign to ban use of, 246
language: of black power movement, 43,
    55–57; and women's movement, 88
La Raza Unida Party, 111–12
Last Poets, 43
"lavender menace," 83
League of Conservation Voters, 223
legislation, federal: civil rights acts
    (1964, 1965), 38, 85; Equal Pay Act
    (1963), 85; Patriot Act, 282, 321n.28;
    Termination Act (1953), 133
LeGuin, Ursula, 236
Lesbian Avengers, 187, 212–13
lesbian liberation movement, 182
lesbians, 82–83, 94, 199–200, 210–11. *See
    also* gay/lesbian activism
"Let the Record Show" exhibition,
    190–91
Lewis, John, 36
Lewis and Clark College, Portland,
    Oregon, 263
liberation musicology, 13–14
liberation theology, 13–14
literary history: and women's move-
    ment, 96–101
Little Rock, Arkansas, 19
Little Willie John, 20–21
Live Aid, 157–65
local level: importance of, 3–4, 279
Lofland, John, 298
longshoremen's union, 258
López, Alma, 127
Lorde, Audre, 78, 92–94, 100, 236,
    318n.5
Los Angeles, 44, 105, 182; Citywide
    Murals project, 124–26
Los Angeles Times, 119
Lowe, Lisa, 271
Lowell, Amy, 97
Lowell, Robert, 97
Lowndes County, Alabama, 44
Lubiano, Wahneema, 69
LULAC (League of United Latin
    American Citizens), 104
Lumpens, The, 43
lynching: of blacks, 8, 24–25

MacKinnon, Catherine, 324n.19
Making of "Sun City" (video), 169–70
Malcolm X, 42, 45–46, 52, 61, 110
Mandela, Nelson, 158, 172–74
Mani, Lata, 95
Market Dynamics/ABC poll, 54
Marley, Bob, 304
Martinez, Elizabeth "Betita," 105, 278
mass culture: and subcultures, 176–77
mass meetings, local, 34
material-discursive processes, 309–11, 343n.33
Mauss, Marcel, 288
MAYO (Mexican American Youth Organization), 111
Mazel, David, 238
McAdam, Doug, 296–97, 318n.10
McCain, Franklin, 20
McDew, Chuck, 35–36
McNeil, Joseph, 20
Means, Russell, 136, 151
MEChA (El Movimiento Estudiantil Chicano de Aztlán), 112
media, 31, 157–58, 179–80, 187, 241–42, 309; and ACT UP, 182–83, 189–90, 196–200; and AIM, 135–36, 151–52, 155; and black power movement, 41–42, 51, 53. *See also* films; Indymedia collective
Media Island International, 274
medical research: ACT UP and, 191–96, 211
Melucci, Alberto, 305, 307
Méndez, Consuelo, 122
men's movement, 137
Merritt, Judy, 154
Mexican Americans, 103–5. *See also* Chicanos/Latinos
Mexican-American War, 103
middle class, African American: and bus boycott, 17–19
military-corporate culture: parody of, 255–56
Minneapolis, Minnesota, 131, 133
minority: use of term, 114
Mirikitani, Janice, 92
misogyny, 48, 65, 155
Mississippi, 24–26

Mississippi Burning, 145
MK-46 pepper spray (Def-Tech), 264
mob action, 29
mobilizing, xix, 13, 177, 280. *See also* organizing
modernization, 162, 251
Moffett, Donald, 203
Mohanty, Chandra, 95
Montgomery, Alabama, 16–19
Montoya, José: mural of crucified farm-worker, Chicano Park, San Diego, 115–17
Moore, Amzie, 32
Moore, Michael, 263
Moraga, Cherríe, 92–93, 121
Morgan, Robin, 92
Morris, Aldon, 290
Morrison, Toni, 58, 101, 302–3
Moses, Bob, 32
"Mother Nature," 233
Mount Rushmore, South Dakota, 133, 150
movement communities, 81, 85, 298
movement cultural imperialism, 284
movement cultures, xv–xvi, xvii, 14, 37–38, 294, 296, 298–99, 301–7
movements. *See* social movements
movements in culture, 296–98
movement societies, 309
Moves Camp, Richard, 154
movimiento, el. See Chicano movement
MTV network, 160, 171
Muir, John, 222
Mujeres Muralistas: *Latinoamérica* mural, 122
multiculturalism, 38, 124–27
Multilateral Agreement on Investment (MAI), 246
multiracial coalitions in the work-place, 104
muralism, 111, 115–20. *See also* community mural movement
muralists, Mexican, 106, 111
mural programs, government-sponsored, 106

murals, Chicano: Bernal mural, Del
Rey, California (1968), 107–11; *Black
and White Moratorium Mural*
(Herrón and Gronk), Estrada Courts
housing project, East Los Angeles
(1973), 118–20; Che Guevara image,
113–14; in Chicano Park, San Diego,
115–17; crucified farmworker mural
(Montoya and Rebel Chicano Art
Front), 115–17; *Homeboy* (Cruz),
Romana Gardens Housing Project,
East Los Angeles (1974), 117–18;
Homenaje a Frida Kahlo (Ríos), San
Francisco, 123; *La Familia* (East Los
Streetscapers), 115; *La Ofrenda*
(Cervantes), 121–22; *Las Lechugueras*
(Alicia), 122; *Latinoamérica* (Mujeres
Muralistas), 122; *Wall That Cracked
Open* (Herrón), City Terrace, East
Los Angeles (1972), 118
muralthon (1977–78), 117
Murieta, Joaquín, 108
Murphy, Patrick, 234
Museum of Modern Art (MOMA),
New York, 191, 197–98
music: in Battle of Seattle, 261; as captivity narrative, 34–36; and collective
identity, 32–34; as communication,
30–32; *corridos* (Mexican political
ballads), 108; feminist, 102; and movement culture, 37–38; as movement
"history," 14–19; punk, 221, 306; rap,
70–71, 302; rave, 261; rhythm and
blues, 20–21; rock, 174–75; soul, 36,
306; as source of pleasure, 36–37;
spirituals, 15, 18, 23, 33, 306; as strategy and tactic, 27–30, 48. *See also*
benefit rock; freedom songs
musical apartheid: use of term, 168–69

NAACP (National Association for the
Advancement of Colored People), 3,
9, 12–13, 16
Nader, Ralph, 248, 301
Naess, Arne, 226
naming: and ACT UP, 189, 197–98. *See
also* self-naming
Nashville, Tennessee, 20–22

Nashville Quartet, 20–22
National Black Feminist Organiza-
tion, 82
National Council of American Indians
(NCAI), 132
National Indian Youth Countil
(NIYC), 132
National Institutes of Health, Office of
AIDS Research, 211
nationalism: black, 44–45, 49, 59, 69–71,
304; Chicano, 111–12, 128
National Organization for Women, 81
national park system, 222
National Welfare Rights Organiza-
tion, 82
Nation of Islam, 71
Native American groups: Anishinabé,
131, 133; Oglala, 134–35; Ponca, 132
Native Americans, 133, 221; contemporary daily life of, 137–42; and film
industry, 130, 154, 330n.3; Vietnam
veterans, 140, 153. *See also* American
Indian Movement
Natural Resources Defense Council, 223
nature: representations of, 236. *See also*
ecocriticism; environmental
movement
nature writing: alternate traditions of,
234–37
Neblett, Chuck, 23
Neely, Barbara, 236
neoliberalism, 241, 243–44, 252, 284
neo-punk subculture, 305
network of networks, 270–74
New Age, 137, 305
new left, 85–87, 307, 324n.15
New Museum of Contemporary Art,
Soho, New York, 190
Newton, Huey, 41–42, 44, 49–52, 54, 57–
60, 63–66, 101
New York City, 182–83
New York Crimes, 196–99
New York Radical Women, 88
New York Times, 135, 196–99, 248
NGOs (nongovernmental organiza-
tions), 247. *See also names of
organizations*
Nike Corporation, 301

Nixon, E. D., 16–17
Nixon, Nicholas, 197–98
Nixon, Richard, 223
Nkrumah, Kwame, 52
"noble savage," 137
Noguera, Ana, 277
nonviolence, 5–7, 29–30, 319n.12
North American Free Trade Agreement (NAFTA), 246
Nossiter, Bernard, 55–56
nostalgia: in American culture, 147
not-in-my-backyard attitude, 224
NOW (National Organization for Women), 81
nuclear family, 84

Oakland, California, 44, 64
O'Connor, Cardinal James, 203
"Onward Christian Soldiers," 17–18
"open source" software, 276
opposition, "face" of, 202–4
organizing, xix, 13, 22, 177, 280. See also mobilizing
Orozco, José Clemente, 106
Ortiz, Simon, 236
outside audience for freedom songs, 30–32
"Over My Head I See Trouble in the Air," 33

Paper Tiger Television, 274
Pappas, Ike, 55–56
paradox of diffusion and defusion, 313
paranoia: Black Panther Party and, 64
Paris (rapper), 71
Parker, Pat, 92
Parks, Rosa, 16
parody, 26–27, 255–56, 301
Paterson Pageant (Madison Square Garden, 1912), 331n.2
Patton, Cindy, 183, 185, 208, 289
Payne, Charles, 23–28, 32, 34, 123
PBS network, 171
Peace and Freedom Party, 58
Peltier, Leonard, 142, 147
Peña, Devon, 237
People's Global Action (PGA), 247, 260, 272

Pérez, Irene, 122
performativity in black community, 52
Perlstein, Jeff, 275
Perry, Hart, 166
pharmaceutical corporations: ACT UP and, 192–96, 214–15
Piercy, Marge, 92
Pinchot, Gifford, 222
Pinkos, 189
pink triangle: as ACT UP symbol, 190, 215
Plath, Sylvia, 97
playfulness of ACT UP, 187–88
Plymouth Rock, Massachusetts, 133
poetry as performance, 96–97, 100, 102
poets: beat, 96; Black Mountain school, 97; confessional, 97; feminist (see feminist poetry); "protest," 96; Romantic, 222, 225
police brutality, 119
police department (Seattle): and Battle of Seattle, 262–68
police observation plans, 53, 133
political-cultural, the, 290–95
political culture, 289–90
political domain: in social movement theory, 292–95, 314–15
political process model, 318n.10
politics, 289–95; of articulation, 127; Black Panther Party and, 63–64; of representation, 127; of shaming, 193
pop songs, 36
popular culture, 157–58, 313; and black power movement, 42–43, 52–53. See also cultural formations
population shifts: and civil rights movement, 7–8
Porto Alegre, Brazil, 280–82, 341n.57
postcolonial theory: and environmental issues, 238
postmodernism, 179–80, 183–86, 190–91, 208–10, 295–96
poverty, 70, 104, 119–20, 149; feminization of, 89, 253
poverty programs, governmental, 51
Powwow Highway, 130, 137–42
POZ magazine, 215
precursors: search for, 97

preservationism, 222–23, 225
preservationist ecocriticism, 225
Presidential Committee on the Status
    of Women (1961), 84
prisoner rights movement, 65
prison-industrial complex, 252
professionals: as supporters of ACT UP,
    183, 188
progressivism, xiv
prostitutes: ACT UP and, 183
Public Citizen, 247–48, 252
Public Enemy, 71
public happiness, 152
public health issues: in anti–corporate
    globalization movement, 252
public/private spheres, 77–79, 87–91
public space, reclaiming: ACT UP and,
    200–202; Chicano movement and,
    115–17
publishing industry: and women's
    movement, 89, 92–94, 97–99
Pulido, Laura, 237
punk subculture, 261, 306
puritanism of the left, 169
push-pull strategy: ACT UP and, 210

Quakers: and civil rights movement, 10
Queen Latifah, 102
queer culture, 186–89
Queer Nation, 187, 189, 211–12
Quintana, Alvina, 121

race: and ACT UP, 207–8; and anti–
    corporate globalization movement,
    279; and environmental issues, 220–
    21, 224, 228–30, 233–34, 236; and
    women's movement, 82, 325n.24
"racial uplift" ideology, 18
racism, 4–6, 86, 104, 119–20, 168, 185,
    199, 207–8; internalized, 6, 47, 105.
    See also essentialism
radical chic, 60, 321n.24
Radicalesbians, 88
Radio for Peace International, 274
Rainforest Action Network, 251
Ralston, Adam, 180, 188–89, 209
Ramona Gardens Housing Project,
    East Los Angeles, 117–18

Randolph, A. Philip, 8
"rap groups," 87–90
rap music, 70–71, 302
Rastafarians, 159, 304
rational actor model, 308
rave music, 261
raza, Chicano, 110
"reading formations," 171
Reagan, Ronald, 40, 51, 70, 163–64, 180,
    203–4
Reaganism, 163–64
Reagon, Bernice Johnson, 14, 22–23, 29,
    33, 250, 317n.1
Reagon, Cordell, 23, 26
Rebel Chicano Art Front: mural of
    crucified farmworker, Chicano Park,
    San Diego, 115–17
Reclaim the Streets (RTS), 256–57
reconciliation narrative: and AIM, 141
recruitment into social movements, 305
Redford, Robert, 131, 142
redomestication of American women,
    83–84, 126
red power movement. See American
    Indian Movement
red ribbons: as symbol of "AIDS
    chic," 214
Redstockings, 88
religious right: and AIDS epidemic,
    180, 198
relocation: Native Americans and, 133
repression: of AIM, 147; of Black
    Panther Party, 59–63; of Chicano
    movement, 120; post–September 11,
    2001, 281–84
reproductive rights, 85, 89
"Republican drag": ACT UP and,
    188–89
resocialization, 79
resource mobilization theory, 290
revolutionism: of Black Panther Party,
    64; in Chicano movement, 113
rhetoric of Black Panther Party, 55–57
Rich, Adrienne, 92, 94, 96, 100; "Trying
    to Talk with a Man," 235–36
Richie, Lionel, 160
Richmond, David, 20
Ricks, Willie, 38–39

right to vote: women's movement and, 80
Ríos, Mike: *Homenaje a Frida Kahlo* mural, San Francisco, 123
Riot Grrrlz, 102, 177
riots, racial: of 1960s, 44
"risk behaviors": use of term, 198
"risk groups": use of term, 198
Rivera, Diego, 106, 123
Robinson, Jo Ann, 17
Robinson, Ruby Doris Smith, 86
rock and roll activism, 156–58, 333n.30
Roddick, Anita, 264
Rodríguez, Patricia, 122
Rome, 282
Roosevelt, Eleanor, 84
Roosevelt, Theodore, 222
Rose, Wendy, 92
Rosie the Riveter, 126
Rubin, Jerry, 61
Rukeyser, Muriel, 96–97, 99; *Book of the Dead*, 236–37
Rustin, Bayard, 4

Salazar, Rubén, 119–20
Sanchez, Sonia, 92
Sanders, Scott Russell, 230–31
San Diego, California, 115–17
Sandoval, Chela, 81, 121, 238
San Francisco: and ACT UP, 182
Sanger, Kerran, 29
Santa Barbara, California, 112
"savage wilderness," 233
Schell, Paul, 266
Schellenberg, August, 151
school system, California, 112–13
Schulman, Sarah, 214–15
SCLC (Southern Christian Leadership Conference), 3–4, 19, 21
Scott, James C., 310
Scott, Joan, 325n.24
Scott-Heron, Gil, 41, 43, 274
SDS (Students for a Democratic Society), 58, 85–87; Economic Research and Action Projects (ERAP), 85–86
Seale, Bobby, 41, 44, 50–52, 54, 60–61, 64, 68
Seale, Malik Nkrumah Stagolee, 52

Seals, David, 139, 142, 154
sea turtle brigade, 258
Seeger, Pete, 33
segregation, de facto: in American North, 53–54
segregation system: in American South, 6, 38, 46
Seidman, Steven, 317n.4
self-hatred, internalized: among blacks, 47
self-naming: in ACT UP, 189; by African Americans, 309
self-representation, 154
self-understanding: in social movements, 294
Sessions, George, 226
sexism, 48, 71, 80, 86, 185
Sexton, Anne, 97
sexual harassment, 89
Shakur, Afeni, 71
Shakur, Tupac, 71
shantytown demonstrations, 172
Shea Stadium, New York, 201–2
Shepard, Sam, 144
Shepperd, A. J., 203–4
Shiva, Vandana, 248, 339n.10
Sierra Club, 223
silence about homosexuality, 200–201
Silence = Death Project, 182, 189–90, 203, 214
Silko, Leslie Marmon, 139, 230, 236
Singh, Nikhil Pal, 56, 63
singing, 18, 26–29, 36–37. *See also* music
Siquieros, David Alfaro, 106
sit-in movement, 10, 19–22
slavery, 11
slogans, 190; "black is beautiful," 52–53; "the personal is political," 77; "We Are Not a Minority," 113–14; "We're here, we're queer, get used to it," 189
Smith, Andrea "Andy," 137
Smith, Paul Chaat, 131–32, 135, 155
Smoke Signals, 330n.3
SNCC (Student Non-violent Coordinating Committee), 3–4, 21–23, 26, 33, 47, 86–88
Snow, David, 323n.2

Social and Public Art Resource Center (SPARC), Venice, California, 328n.6
social cultural studies, xvii, 317n.4
social differences: and women's movement, 80–81
social domain: in social movement theory, 292–95, 314–15
social justice: and queer movement, 206–8
social movement industries (SMIs), 271
social movement organizations (SMOs), 271, 298
social movements, xvi; and cultural politics, 179–80, 183–86; defining and recognizing, xiii–xiv; and ideology, 36–37; as messages, codes, and direct theory, 307–8; as models for ecological activism, 223–24
social movement sectors (SMSs), 271
social movement theory, 78–80, 286–315
social norms: challenged by ACT UP, 186
social texts: movements as, 307–8
sociology, xvi, 287–89, 304
Sofia, Zoë, 163
solidarity, 111, 113, 298
Solnit, David, 254–55
song lyrics: remaking of, 15–16, 31
songwriting, 15–16
"soul," 43
soul food, 42, 49
South Africa: and anti-apartheid projects, 165–74
"southern justice," 24
Soviet Union: demise of, 244
Speak Truth to Power Tour, 71
Spirit of Crazy Horse, 149
spirituality: and civil rights movement, 5; Native American, 151
Spivak, Gayatri, 95
Stagolee, 52, 68
Staley, Peter, 194
Stamper, Norm, 267
"star book" form: and Sun City project, 170
Staude, Sarah Joy, 263
Stein, Gertrude, 97
Steinem, Gloria, 293
Stiglitz, Joseph, 278

Stonewall Bar, Greenwich Village, 305
Stop the Violence movement, 71
street style, black, 52–53
street theater, 49, 59, 172
Stripes, James, 136
structural adjustment programs (SAPs), 243–44, 253
structures of feeling, 343n.31
student movement, 10, 19–22, 112, 305. See also SNCC
students, 172, 254; Chicano, 109
Students for a Democratic Society. See SDS
Studio X, 274
Sturgeon, Noël, 307, 334n.19
subcultures, 176–77, 301, 303–7, 342n.21; musical, 168–69
subjectivity, 309–11
suburbs, 84, 238
Sugar Hill Gang, 70
Sun City, South Africa, 165–69
Sun City (Artists United against Apartheid), 158, 165–69, 333n.31
survival programs: of Black Panther Party, 53, 59, 66–68
survival strategies: in Chicano movement, 115–20
sustainable development, 228, 251
Sweet Honey in the Rock, 250. See also Reagon, Bernice Johnson
Swidler, Amy, 288–89, 297
symbolic challenge of social movements, 307–8

TAG (Treatment Action Group), 194, 211
Tarrow, Sidney, 309, 334n.22
Taylor, Verta, 288, 305
teach-ins: at Battle of Seattle, 248–54
television, 320n.2
terrorism, white, 23–27, 38
terrorist attacks of September 11, 2001, 281–84
textual analysis: role of, xvii
Thatcher, Margaret, 163–64
Thatcherism, 163–64
theater. See dramatic action
theatrum mundi, 320n.2
therapy: consciousness-raising as, 89

Thin Elk, Ted, 144
Third World, 160–62, 243–44, 249. *See also* Africa
Third World Network, 249
Thoreau, Henry David, 222, 225
"Thunderheart," 145
Thunderheart (film), 130, 142–45
Tijerina, Reies López, 109–11
Till, Emmett: murder of, 24–25
Tilly, Charles, xiv
Time magazine, 54, 136
Title IX ruling on women in athletics, 85
totalitarian societies: and subcultures, 305
"toxic tourism," 237
trade rights: and human rights, 252
tradition, sense of, 15
traffic in women, 253
"Trail of Broken Treaties" car caravan, 134
transcendence, 27, 33
Treaty of Guadalupe Hidalgo, 103
Treichler, Paula, 184
Trinh T. Minh-ha, 95
Trudell, John, 135–36, 144
Turner, Kathleen (cultural critic), 135
Turner, Nat, 11
Turner, Ted, 137, 145, 154

UFW (United Farm Workers), 107, 109
un-American activities, 189
"Uncle Tom," 46
underground railroad, 11
unemployment, 149
Union Carbide, 237
United Nations, 167, 247
United Slaves, 63
U.S. Constitution: Equal Rights Amendment (proposed), 85; Nineteenth Amendment, 80
U.S. government, 168, 180–82, 284–85; Bureau of Indian Affairs (BIA), 133–34, 136; Food and Drug Administration (FDA), 193–96
U.S. Supreme Court: *Brown v. Board of Education*, 9; *Roe v. Wade*, 85
United Students against Sweatshops (USAS), 254

urban ecocriticism, 237–38
"urban insurrections" of 1960s, 44
"urban jungle," 233

Vaid, Urvashi, 213
Valdez, Luis, 107, 112
Van Deburg, William, 43, 57, 67
"vanishing Indian," 154
Van Zandt, "Little Steven," 166–68, 170
Varela, Maria, 105
victim-savior dichotomy, 161
Vietnam veterans, Native American, 140, 153
Villa, Pancho, 108
violence: AIM and, 148; in Battle of Seattle, 258–69; Black Panther Party and, 55–56, 59–63
Virgen de Guadeloupe, 109
virtual sit-in, 272–73
Visual AIDS, 214
Vizenor, Gerald, 236

Walker, Alice, 92, 100, 236
"Walk Together Children," 18
Wallach, Lori, 248
Ware, Cellestine, 88
Warhol, Andy, 136
WARN (Women of All Red Nations), 148
Warrior, Clyde, 132
Warrior, Robert, 131–32, 135, 155
"warriors": AIM as, 144, 147–48
Washington Post, 241
water supply: sale of, 251
Watney, Simon, 185
wave metaphor: for women's movement, 80, 101–2
WEAL (Women's Equity Action League), 81
weapons: AIM and, 148; Black Panther Party and, 53–54; Chicano movement and, 122
"We Are the World," 159–60, 333n.31
"We Are the World/USA for Africa," 157
Weber, Max, 288
Web sites, "shadow," 273
welfare rights, 89
welfare state: collapse of, 244

"We Shall Overcome," 1–2, 7, 29, 32–33, 299
WHAM (Women's Health Action and Mobilization), 210–11
"Which Side Are You On?" 23, 31
White, Ben, 258
White, Ryan, 198
White Citizen's Council, 6, 24–25
"whiteface": used by black actors, 48
white flight, 84, 126, 224
Whitehead, Kim, 95–96
white privilege, 279
Whittier, Nancy, 288, 325n.21
Williams, Mance, 47, 49–50
Williams, Raymond, 95, 292, 303, 306, 342n.19, 343n.31
Wilson, Mary, 131
Wilson, Richard "Dickie," 134–35, 140
WITCH, 88
"Woke Up This Morning with My Mind Set on Freedom," 36
Wolfe, Tom, 60
women: African American, 4, 17, 94; Asian/Pacific American, 94; of color, 80, 82; native, 94; working-class, 80, 82
women in social movements, 86–87; in ACT UP, 199–202, 207, 210–11; in AIM, 145–55; in Black Panther Party, 65; and Chicano/a movement, 120–23; in civil rights movement, 85–87; and environmental justice movement, 221–22; in new left movement, 85–87. See also feminism; gay/lesbian activism
Women of All Red Nations (WARN), 82
women-only groups, 87
women poets: and feminist poetry movement, 96. See also names of poets
women's caucuses within organizations, 86
women's health movement, 193
"women's libbers," 85
women's liberation, 85, 87–90, 92

women's movement, 75–102, 219, 305, 312–13; expressed in poetry, 90–95; roots and strands, 80–87
Women's Political Council, 17
women's rights: and anti–corporate globalization movement, 252–53
women's world congresses, 252–53
Wonder, Stevie, 160
Wong, Nellie, 92
Wood, Mary, 237
Wordsworth, William, 222
World Bank, 162, 243, 246, 249, 283
WorldCom, 284
World Social Forum (WSF), 280–82
World Trade Organization (WTO), 240, 243, 249, 251, 278. See also anti–corporate globalization movement; Battle of Seattle
World War I, 113
World War II, 8, 83
Wounded Knee, South Dakota: AIM standoff at, 134–36, 144–55
WPAC (Women's Political Action Caucus), 81
writing groups in women's movement, 100

X, Malcolm. See Malcolm X

Yaeger, Patricia, 324n.19
Yamashita, Karen, 236
"You Better Leave My Kitten Alone," 20–21
Young, Stacey, 327n.40
Young Lords (Puerto Rican), 58
youth: and community muralism, 124–26; and cultural resistance, 257–58
youth culture, 107
Youth International Party (Yippies), 61

"zap actions," 77, 83, 193
Zapata, Emiliano, 108
Zapatistas, 246
Zellner, Bob, 35–36

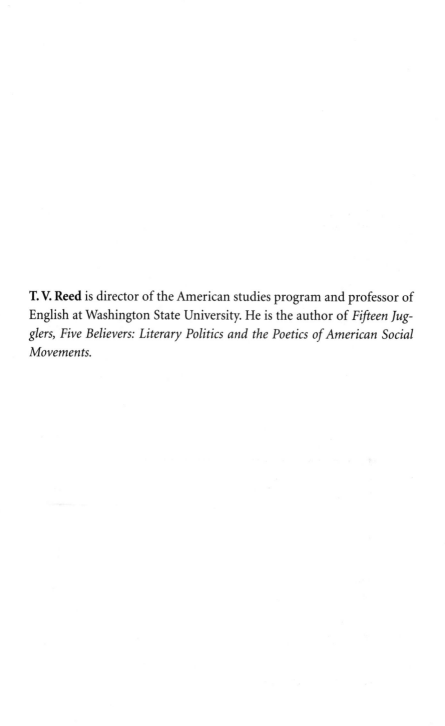

T. V. Reed is director of the American studies program and professor of English at Washington State University. He is the author of *Fifteen Jugglers, Five Believers: Literary Politics and the Poetics of American Social Movements.*